THE GAY REPUBLIC

The Gay Republic
Sexuality, Citizenship and Subversion in France

ENDA McCAFFREY
Nottingham Trent University, UK

LONDON AND NEW YORK

First published 2005 by Ashgate Publishing

Reissued 2018 by Routledge
2 Park Square, Milton Park, Abingdon, Oxon OX14 4RN
711 Third Avenue, New York, NY 10017, USA

Routledge is an imprint of the Taylor & Francis Group, an informa business

First issued in paperback 2018

© Enda McCaffrey 2005

Enda McCaffrey has asserted his right under the Copyright, Designs and Patents Act, 1988, to be identified as the author of this work.

All rights reserved. No part of this book may be reprinted or reproduced or utilised in any form or by any electronic, mechanical, or other means, now known or hereafter invented, including photocopying and recording, or in any information storage or retrieval system, without permission in writing from the publishers.

A Library of Congress record exists under LC control number: 2005021161

Notice:
Product or corporate names may be trademarks or registered trademarks, and are used only for identification and explanation without intent to infringe.

Publisher's Note
The publisher has gone to great lengths to ensure the quality of this reprint but points out that some imperfections in the original copies may be apparent.

Disclaimer
The publisher has made every effort to trace copyright holders and welcomes correspondence from those they have been unable to contact.

ISBN 13: 978-0-815-39779-3 (hbk)
ISBN 13: 978-1-138-62100-8 (pbk)
ISBN 13: 978-1-351-14656-2 (ebk)

Contents

Acknowledgements	*vii*
Introduction	1

PART ONE: THEORETICAL CONSIDERATIONS

1	Universalism in the Republic: A Political, Religious and Conceptual Divide	15
	What is the Republic?	16
	The Church and the Right	19
	The Political and Intellectual Left	28
	Universal Equality: 'L'oeuf fécondé' in the Republic	33
	Conclusions	41
2	'La Différence des sexes': Difference or Distinction?	45
	'La Différence des sexes': From the Physiological to the Sexual	48
	The Anthropological Question: From Nature to Culture	55
	The Crisis in Psychoanalysis: From Symbolic Order to Symbolic Orders	64
	Conclusions: The Queer Escape?	70
3	From 'Crisis' of Law to a New 'Esprit des Lois'	75
	'Personne juridique' and 'Sujet du désir'	82
	A Sociological Comparison	87
	Legitimacy in the 'fait social'	90
	The Law, Homosexuality and the PaCS	93
	Conclusions	96
4	Lesbian and Gay Identity and the Politics of Subversion	101
	Strategies of Sameness and Difference in the Modern and Postmodern State	108
	Queer Strategies of Gay Identity: Theory and Practice	113
	ACT-Up Paris: AIDS, Communities, Political Manifestos	120
	Positive Discrimination: Pros and Cons	127
	Conclusions	130

vi   *The Gay Republic*

PART TWO: PRACTICAL CONCERNS

5   Adoption and Filiation: The New PaCS Pact   137
     Adoption: Two Case Studies and Their Implications   142
     The Maternal/Paternal Axis and the Child's Rights of Origin   150
     'Filiation', 'Désaffiliation' and 'Pluriparentalité'   157
     Conclusions   164

6   Between Marriage and Concubinage: The Dilemma of the Lesbian
     and Gay Couple   167
     Concubinage: Definitions and Drafting Legislation   173
     Concubinage, PaCS and the Couple   179
     'La Différence des sexes', 'Mixité', 'Vie privée'/ 'Vie publique' 181
     Marriage: 'Unicité' and 'Égalité'   189
     Conclusions   193

7   Homophobia: Mimesis, Legislation and 'Outing'   195
     Some Defining Markers   204
     Homophobia: The Silent/Verbal Dialectic   206
     Homophobia and Anti-Discrimination Legislation   209
     Homophobia and the Threat to New Ideologies   212
     Homophobia and the Practice of 'Outing'   216
     Conclusions   222

Conclusion   225

Bibliography   *231*
Index   *241*

Acknowledgements

This book would not have been possible without the help and collaboration of many people inside and outside the academic community. First and foremost, I would like to express my gratitude to my family for their unqualified love and enduring support. I also owe a considerable debt of gratitude to colleagues in Modern Languages, and particularly the French section, at Nottingham Trent University. Under the research leadership of Professor Jean-Pierre Boulé, who was and remains a constant source of encouragement, I enjoyed the benefit of a sabbatical and teaching relief over recent years in order to complete this manuscript. The good will, support, patience and humour of colleagues have been invaluable in this respect. I would also like to thank Murray Pratt, Jean-Pierre, Gregory Woods and Liz Morrish who read chapters of the manuscript and offered constructive advice. In France, I would like to extend my appreciation to the Association Française de Sociologie (Réseau no. 28: Recherches en sciences sociales sur la sexualité) for giving me the opportunity to air and discuss my research. Finally, I would like to thank Jane Haddon who agreed to help with the formatting of this manuscript, and has done a commendable job.

Introduction

When I started to research the subject of lesbian and gay citizenship, people asked me why France and why a book about lesbians and gays in France. The simplicity, but accuracy, of the question set in train a range of preconceptions and presumptions. For example, it was presumed that my agenda for this book would be to describe gay lifestyle in France, explore the gay 'scene' and show how the French might 'do' gay differently to other nations. While acknowledging the contemporary relevance of these observations, I felt that they did not really address my particular interests. I was more interested in citizenship, definitions of citizenship and in particular how lesbians and gays defined themselves as citizens within social, political and philosophical paradigms. It was clear that my perceptions didn't sit easily with public perceptions. In an attempt to steer readers towards my line of thinking, I replied tentatively that France was different, that it was a republic, and that it had a special notion of how citizenship was constructed. I remember making reference to an interview I had read at the time in which Professor Theodor Zeldin characterised the French nation as follows: 'Sa force, c'est d'inviter les gens à développer des idées universelles plutôt que nationales.'[1] I made further attempts to compare France with other nations, such as Britain. I argued that Britain does not have a written constitution and that its citizens are subjects of the crown. Without a written constitution, British subjects, I opined, belonged to a liberal Anglo-Saxon tradition in which there was more room for individual expression and difference. *La Déclaration des droits de l'homme*, on the other hand, set out a code of behaviour for French citizens that sought to balance the needs for individualism and social responsibility. I even suggested that one of the great advantages of the French *Déclaration* was that, as a code, it could also function as a template for world citizenship.

What appealed then in discussions and subsequently was what I was later to understand as the uniqueness of the French context. France was born out of a sense of self-interest and general interest. France was concerned with national ideas (as Zeldin defined them) and universal ideas. France saw itself as a representation of national citizenship and as a model for a perfectibility of citizenship that could be exported globally.[2] It was clear that France's uniqueness was in fact its integral duality. As a nation, it seemed capable of harnessing the local and the global, the

---

[1] Theodor Zeldin, 'Regards d'étrangers sur la France', Entretiens avec Hector Bianciotti et Theodore Zeldin (propos recueillis par Stéphane Louhaur), *Label France*, no. 39, avril 2000.

[2] Theodor Zeldin continues to expound on this idea in this interview when he states: 'La France croit en la Perfectibilité de l'Homme.'

2   *The Gay Republic*

ideal and the real, the theoretical and the practical. The concept of universalism was perceived to be sufficiently malleable to respond simultaneously to the aspirations and idealism of humankind, as well as the immediate concerns of citizens. From a political angle, this duality could also be characterised as a debate between republicanism and democracy, the former being seen to uphold the traditional values of universalism and the indivisibility of the republic, while the latter had a more performative function as a regulator of individual behaviour in the socio-temporal space.

My initial surprise at the immensity (some would say arrogance) of the French republican model has been tempered over time by research into questions about its continuing relevance, effectiveness and, specifically, the balance it seeks to achieve between idealism and reality, what Pierre-André Taguieff has defined as 'concevoir l'idéal et d'ajouter le réel.'[3] Over the course of the twentieth century, France has modified its constitution (notably in 1946 and 1958) in response to war and socio-cultural change. *La Déclaration* has accompanied these constitutional modifications (in the form of a 'préambule') bearing witness, in the face of change, to the ideals and foundations of the republic, and introducing its own subtle changes along the way. However, as time has evolved and French society has changed even more radically, there is a growing *décalage* between the essence and spirit of *La Déclaration* and its contemporary relevance. Carrying the legacy of the past into the present and future has its drawbacks and benefits. On the one hand, over reliance on the past can be a handicap. On the other hand, a valued legacy can serve as a touchstone for the future. However, in very simple terms, there are options open to republicans if the need to resolve this 'crisis' is as acute as it seems; do without a *déclaration*, rewrite it, draft a new one or update the old one. In the absence of any consensus on a way forward, there is currently a stalemate in France which has resulted in a compromise between a respect for the idealism of the past and a concern for the practicalities of the present. Hence, the underlying principle of universalism has taken on a more localised significance in that, rather than referring to the enlightenment and the universalist tradition, the term has accrued a more focused (albeit national) significance in its reference to the context of French citizenship *per se*. Today, universalism is more intricately connected to a unique definition of republican citizenship in which public (universal) space is distinct from private space. The sociologist Sami Naïr characterises this duality as

> un contrat d'appartenance au 'nous' français. C'est un contrat politique. Il suppose l'adhésion à des valeurs communes et à la liberté la plus sûre dans le domaine de la vie privée. En effet, la citoyenneté républicaine implique que si l'espace public est régi par l'égalité en droits et en devoirs, l'espace privé est fondé sur la liberté laïque, c'est-à-dire sur la possibilité donnée à chacun de voir respectés ses croyances particulières, ses

---

[3] Pierre-André Taguieff, *La République menacée* (Paris: Les Editions Textuel, 1996), p. 65.

Introduction 3

attachements culturels, son identité personnelle. La laïcité est la meilleure garantie, en ce sens, contre l'intolérance privée ou collective.[4]

In contemporary France, public space is equated with equality of laws, whereas private space is equated with freedom of expression. The implication in this model of citizenship is that never the twain should meet. In other words, rights to freedom of expression (no less worthy than rights to equality) are confined to the private space, but are not applicable in the public space. There is a clear dichotomy in the conception of republican citizenship between the rights (universal) shared by all citizens in the public space (what we could also call the universal space), and the rights of freedom of expression that are enjoyed and only tolerated in the private space. From the republican perspective, this model of citizenship equalises all individuals before the law as abstract persons endowed with the same values and rights. It does not discriminate nor differentiate between individuals in terms of gender, difference or ethnicity. This is universalism in perfection. However, in the pursuit of a perfectly equal model of citizenship, it could be argued that this model sidelines the social, cultural and sexual specificities of identity construction as a basis on which to reconsider equality of rights.

Bearing in mind this difference in perceptions of citizenship, one could with some justification question the validity of concepts such as 'gay citizenship' or a 'gay republic.' Conservative republicans would clearly point to the absurdity of the idea of basing citizenship on a sexual orientation. But is the concept of 'gay citizenship' the paradox that it seems? We see today that definitions of citizenship are changing in the wake of asylum seekers, global terrorism and increasing immigration from the African continent and from eastern European countries. Citizenship is clearly high on national agendas, and nations are now becoming more prescriptive in their citizenship pre-requisites.[5] On the one hand, the demand for rigour and tighter controls is the result of our heightened socio-political climate, the threat of war and illegal immigration. But rigour and control may also be seen as the consequence of a greater sensitivity to individual circumstances, and further evidence of the wider parameters within which citizenship may need to be addressed.

---

[4] Sami Naïr, 'Les défis de l'immigration', Entretien avec Sami Naïr (propos recueillis par Anne Rapin et Stéphane Louhaur), *Label France*, no. 38, janvier 2000.

[5] In Britain, citizenship is being continually redefined in the light of EU enlargement and immigration. A Nationality, Immigration and Asylum Act was passed in 2002. Identity cards are set to be introduced by 2006. Citizenship ceremonies have been introduced for new UK citizens where they pledge allegiance to a set of common British values. In France, a law that bans the wearing of the muslim hajib (headscarf) and the display of other religious symbols in schools was passed in 2004. In Eire, the constitution has been amended in respect of Irish citizenship in order to prevent the growing trend of pregnant mothers from outside the EU arriving in Ireland solely to give birth, and then claiming Irish citizenship for their children and wider family members.

4   *The Gay Republic*

This is not to say that it would be fair or accurate to advocate a definition of citizenship on the basis of sexuality, religious affiliation or ethnic origin. What I would suggest, however, is that sexual orientation (in effect, the principle of diversity), while never the foundation on which citizenship should be established, is nevertheless beginning to inform and influence issues and sensitivities around constructions of citizenship. And, specifically in France, debates on sexual orientation, parity and the PaCS are bringing to the surface anomalies, inconsistencies and contradictions in the concept of universal equality, itself the cornerstone of citizenship in France. In short, any perception of a paradox in the title of this book may well be overshadowed by the potential for more profound anomalies and paradoxes at the heart of French republican citizenship. One of the main aims, therefore, of this book is to question the relevance of republican universal equality in its articulation of the concept of citizenship. In other words, has republican citizenship, with the accommodation of difference within the binary of public and private space, still an effective role to play in addressing the needs and concerns of citizens in contemporary France? Furthermore, has republican citizenship struck the right balance between privileging the perfectibility of humankind and responding to more immediate claims for individual rights? In short, has the pursuit of perfectibility, or universalism, come at the expense of the individual or the immediacy of the 'fait social' as the true benchmarks of citizenship?

*

> On pourrait plutôt décrire les transformations contemporaines comme le passage d'une sexualité construite par des contrôles et des disciplines externes aux individus à une sexualité reposant sur des disciplines internes. Il ne s'agirait pas d'une libération, mais d'une intériorisation et d'un approfondissement des exigences sociales. Les changements doivent sans doute être moins considérés comme une émancipation que comme une *individualisation*. Avec l'intériorisation des contrôles, l'individu doit établir lui-même ses normes et sa propre cohérence intime, tout en continuant à être jugé socialement.[6]

Michel Bozon's characterisation of contemporary sexuality is founded on notions of internal discipline, the interiorisation of social demands, and critically, a process of individualisation. Individualisation, however, within a republican context is a double-edged sword because it allows one to establish one's own norms but then these norms are subject to a form of social judgment (control). There are three ways of reading Bozon's articulation of sexuality. The first would be to suggest that he exposes the myth of an individual/social separateness. This could be problematic for the private/public binary of traditional republican citizenship. The second reading would be that sexuality, as he claims, is not a

---

[6]   Michel Bozon, 'Révolution sexuelle ou individualisation de la sexualité', Entretien avec Michel Bozon, *Mouvements*, 20 (2002): 15.

Introduction 5

freedom or an emancipation, but more a *process* in which the individual's sexuality evolves naturally in conjunction with a sense of social responsibility, what other commentators have defined as a process of 'mixité.' The third reading, which brings the first two together, reflects how Bozon sees sexuality in the current French republic. On one level, Bozon appears to cede individual sexuality to the supremacy of the social as final arbiter. In this sense, Bozon endorses citizenship with a republican imprimatur, whereby the public or social space carries the ultimate sanction in relation to individual or private space. This reading is potentially problematic in that such an articulation of gay sexuality may reproduce structures of dominance and could be seen to be complicit with heteronormativity.[7] However, what is interesting in Bozon's hypothesis is the way in which he seeks to extend the limits of private space, giving it more coherence and self-regulation and, as a consequence, tipping the balance of citizenship away from republican control towards individual self-discipline. It would appear that Bozon sees a way forward for a sexual dimension to citizenship, with the attendant subversive potential therein. However, it is clear that he is working within a republican framework that is a guarantor of public interest over private particularism.

Important questions are raised by Bozon's analysis. For example, is sexuality (or private space) subservient to social judgment (public space)? Is sexuality, in the French context, consigned to a cul-de-sac of reiteration, self-reflexivity and political posturing? In other words, can lesbians and gays share the same equality of rights enjoyed by other sexual citizens within the public space? As long as the republican model of citizenship is conceived as it is, then it would appear that alternative sexualities (as an expression of private space) will always come off second best in respect of being able to challenge for equality of rights within a heterosexualised public space. But let us explore this further. The expression of sexual difference, for instance, has been confined to the abstract principle of collective universal equality where all individuals are the same regardless of their sexual difference. To this degree, equality of citizenship is guaranteed to all. However, adherence to the abstraction of this principle is conditional on the recognition of some of its tenets, in particular the biological difference of the sexes as the only legitimate construction of sexual identity, and the French republican system of symbolic representation in which only the heterosexual male is universalised. Given these conditions, it is not hard to see how the concept of 'sexual' citizenship in France seems fair if you happen to be born in France, male and heterosexual, but unfair if you are lesbian, gay or a heterosexual female. The challenge for lesbians and gays in the reform of 'sexual' citizenship is twofold. Firstly, equality of citizenship can be sought internally via a reform of the principle of universalism that is perceived to have failed to treat all citizens equally except if

---

[7] 'Complicity'/'aping'/'reproduction' are words deployed widely in the debate on gay citizenship in France. One of the central aims of this book in this context is to steer a course through this debate with the help of insights from Didier Eribon, Pierre Bourdieu and Paul Yonnet among others.

6 *The Gay Republic*

they conform to certain rules. Secondly, the real challenge for a revaluation of the concept of citizenship takes effect once lesbians and gays seek to define themselves at variance with the principle of universalism and demand social and legal recognition *on their own terms.*

In November 1999, the French socialist government passed legislation that would have a direct bearing on the institutionalisation and legalisation of lesbian and gay couples. The PaCS (*Pacte civil de solidarité*), as it was known, was a legally binding contract between two people, regardless of sex, which enabled them to avail of certain rights previously exclusive to married couples. On the same day that this legislation was passed, the law on 'concubinage' was reformed, legalising the formerly free and open-ended 'status' of *union libre* and, in the same breath, legalising lesbian and gay 'concubins.' For the first time in French history, two alternatives to the institution of marriage were enshrined in French law. Today, same sex couples in France are legally recognised, putting them on a par with their American, Danish, Scandinavian and now British counterparts, and heterosexual couples have a real choice between marriage and *union libre*, without having to suffer the stigma often associated with 'living together.'

The timing of these two pieces of legislation is not insignificant. From the early 1990s, the French government had been engaged in a long and extensive consultation process with lesbian and gay groups, family associations, academic and social institutions, and of course with groups across the political spectrum. That both legislations should be passed on the same day seemed wholly logical and appropriate. What was not factored in to this logic was the way both legislations would be received. On the whole, the PaCS legislation stole the headlines, with *union libre* seemingly downgraded to the status of a footnote. On the one hand, it is remarkable that the law on *union libre* (which effects significantly more people across the hexagon than the PaCS does) should have commanded so little attention and since fallen into 'désuétude', given the widely recognised perception that one is better off (legally and financially, gay or straight) 'pacsé' than 'living together.' On the other hand, as this book will seek to demonstrate in part, it should not come as a surprise that an interest in what was and continues to be perceived as gay legislation should not only eclipse a seemingly more mundane change in the law on *union libre*, but itself go on to act as a benchmark for the rest of society.

Put another way, how can it be that a relatively minor piece of legislation (affecting approximately a tenth of the French population) should generate so much concern and controversy when an equally important piece of legislation (affecting a significantly greater number) goes largely unnoticed and unchallenged? Is the wider public more interested in lesbian and gay issues than we give it credit for? Or is this interest a sign of concern about what impact the PaCS might have on established notions of the couple? It is, in part, this degree of interest that prompted me to give the matter more serious reflection. And what I have discovered in the course of researching this book is that the PaCS, first and foremost, addresses the situation of lesbians and gays in France. It represents, by and large, a series of modest gains for them and points towards further recognition,

Introduction

integration and acceptability. But the PaCS is not just about lesbians and gays. The legislation itself embraces homosexual *and heterosexual* couples and their mutual circumstances. It represents a legal attempt to respond to the specific circumstances of the new post-millenium couple, defined by its proximity in legal commitment to that of marital status but significantly distinct from marriage in order to appeal to other alternative and unconventional unions. To this degree, I would suggest that the reason for the wider and more concerned debate around the PaCS has to do with what this legislation reveals about the state of the French republic today, with the equal interests of all its citizens at heart.

The sociologist, Eric Fassin, one of the leading commentators on the PaCS, appears to reinforce my hypothesis that the legislation has significant wider implications. However, rather than seeing the legislation as contributing *indirectly* to a wider social debate, Fassin links the PaCS historically to the context of homosexuality in the nineteenth century in which the latter was perceived, not as a pretext for a revaluation of the social order, but as a 'point de départ.' In his preface to the book *Le Sens de l'altérité* by social anthropologist Rommel Mendès-Leite, Fassin confirms my observation that interest in the PaCS is partially inspired by an interest in society in the circumstances of lesbians and gays, and particularly in how these concerns are reflected within the republican tradition. This interest, he claims, is quite distinct from any positive or genuine evaluation of gay issues *per se*. Fassin's central argument is that the homosexuality debate over the course of the twentieth century has generated its own social and political momentum. Homosexuality, for Fassin, is no longer considered just another 'issue' for discussion within the wider socio-cultural panoply. Rather, homosexuality and what it has to say about society is now the prism (or the '*the* issue') through which society can begin to look seriously at its social, sexual, political, cultural, legal codes and values. He writes:

> ce n'est plus tant la société qui se penche, avec un mélange d'inquiétude et de compassion, sur les homosexuels – groupe méconnu, qui gagnerait à être connu. A partir de l'homosexualité, c'est désormais un ensemble de questions fondamentales qui se trouve posé à la société dans son entier: le PaCS aura ainsi provoqué une réflexion plus générale sur les règles de la procréation et les lois de la parenté, sur la structure du couple et l'organisation de la famille. Tout comme au dix-neuvième siècle, l'homosexualité se trouve donc au centre d'une vaste interrogation sur l'ordre social, sexuel et sexué.[8]

Fassin's case for the rehabilitation of homosexuality as a catalyst for reflection on the state of the republic is explored further in his co-edited volume *Au-delà du PaCS. L'expertise familiale à l'épreuve de l'homosexualité*. As the title of this volume implies, and in bringing together some of the leading figures in the debates rising out of the PaCS, Fassin argues that the PaCS has political, scientific and

---

[8] Preface to Rommel Mendès-Leite, *Le Sens de l'altérité. Penser les (homo)sexualités* (Paris: L'Harmattan, 2000), p. 17.

The Gay Republic

cultural implications that stretch far beyond the exclusive interests of lesbians and gays: 'Ce livre n'est pas consacré à l'homosexualité. De la même manière, le PaCS n'est pas un projet réservé aux homosexuels. L'enjeu n'est donc pas seulement le sort de quelques-uns; c'est l'évolution de la société dans son entier.'[9]

I have highlighted the approach of Eric Fassin because his approach is inclusive and, from a methodological perspective, quite innovative. In effect, what Fassin does is subvert the traditional republican notion of universalism (in which general interest subsumes individual interest) by putting the case for sexual diversity (lesbian and gay interest) at the service of the rest of society. However, I think it is important to raise two points of caution in respect of Fassin's methodology. Firstly, by claiming that advances in lesbian and gay rights are significant because of their knock-on effects to the rest of society is problematic in that it fuels the aforementioned danger of complicity with heteronormativity, and recasts gays and queers as adjuncts in the service of universalism. Secondly, in defence of Fassin, I am of the opinion that his altruism is not only genuine but strategically useful as a tool of subversion. As we will see in the course of this book, this type of internal subversion from within the republic will become more widespread and effective as a means of redressing the balance of power between individual and society in the republic. Fassin's approach is also distinct from the more exclusive preoccupations of other writers. Many of the debates before and after the PaCS have been conducted in article form in specialised journals of sociology, social science and anthropology, in particular *L'Esprit, Les Temps modernes, Le Débat, Mouvements, L'Homme*, and the general press including the lesbian and gay press. Debates on the impact of the PaCS legislation have clustered around very exclusive themes, such as 'homoparentalité' (Dubreuil, 1998, Gross, 2000, Nadaud, 2002, Cadoret, 2002), the couple and family (Singly, 1996, Théry, 1998, Zucker-Rouvillois, 2001) or the legal technicalities of the legislation (Bach-Ignasse, 2000, Iacub, 2002). However, Fassin's edited collection represents the first attempt to provide a wider perspective on the social, political and legal impact of the legislation.

My book seeks to takes Fassin's social approach further by engaging in a systematic fashion with the implications of the PaCS on two critical levels. Firstly, on a conceptual level, I want to show how cherished principles of universal equality, 'l'intérêt général', 'la vie 'privée', 'la différence des sexes', for long the foundation stones of the French republic, are being questioned directly by the PaCS and its implications. In this context, I want to explore and develop at a socio-political level Fassin's double-edged strategy that homosexuality can simultaneously serve and subvert the republic and its concept of citizenship. The first part of this book, entitled *Theoretical Considerations*, will cover some of the key scientific, legal and anthropological issues in play. Secondly, on a practical level, I want to demonstrate how the PaCS is having a direct impact on how the French live as individuals (heterosexual and homosexual), in couples, in

---

[9] Eric Fassin and Daniel Borrillo, *Au-delà du PaCS. L'expertise familiale à l'épreuve de l'homosexualité* (Paris: PUF, 1999), p. 4.

Introduction

singlehood, in families, and as citizens in social and legal contexts. The second part of the book therefore, entitled *Practical Concerns*, will address how theoretical concepts are challenged and radicalised by individuals in their everyday lives.

The PaCS legislation has brought important issues to the attention of the French public and also international commentators. In its legalisation of the lesbian and gay couple, the PaCS asks trenchant questions about the relevance of the traditional family, the function of adoption and the wider implications for parenting, kinship and filiation. It questions the definition of the couple, marriage, and increasingly new forms of procreation. It raises concerns about equality between men and women, heterosexuals and homosexuals, lesbians and straight women, gays and straight men. The PaCS also makes us look again at the role of biological difference in the construction of sexuality. It promotes the construction of a lesbian and gay 'identity' in a universal republic, and the means by which this 'identity' can survive through a politics of subversion. The PaCS highlights the extent of homophobia in contemporary France, from its silent and verbal forms to its institutional and ideological manifestations. In the absence of anti-homophobia legislation until as recently as 2004, the PaCS alerts us to the dangerous practices of violence, defamation and 'outing.' Critically, the PaCS also reveals a crisis in the law, at the levels of partiality, representation, terminology and legitimacy.

These issues (which will be covered in chapters to follow) will be discussed within the conceptual framework of republicanism and democracy. This framework will enable us to position the PaCS debate within an appropriately political and social context, specific to France. The PaCS will therefore be a vehicle by which one can measure the relevance of some of the respective concepts and ideas associated with republicanism and democracy. In particular, I will set up oppositions between abstract and practical, universal and specific, essentialism and constructionism, scientific and universal, legal and arbitrational. The function of this oppositional structure is threefold. It is designed to outline the respective merits and weaknesses of the republican and democratic traditions. Secondly, it facilitates a clearer indication of the tensions at the heart of the concept of citizenship in France and highlights the conflicting ways in which the interests of the citizen are widely served or not. Most significantly, however, this structure points to the site of the 'social' as the defining space of citizenship; the 'social' is described as the place where the real legitimacy of these respective traditions and their conceptual underpinnings will be tried and tested.

The concept of the social is an abstraction on the one hand in that it denotes a construct of complex socio-cultural and political interactions. This abstraction is reinforced in the perception that the social is also external to the individual in imposing its norms and demands. As the sociologist Michel Bozon suggests in the quotation opening this section, this articulation of the social, particularly in the context of sexual behaviour, has undergone a transformation in the latter half of the twentieth century. Bozon claims that the sexual revolution of the 1960s was constructed on a hypothesis of sexual *liberation* that had its source in 'des contrôles et des disciplines externes aux individus.' Since then, sexuality, he asserts, has become a more individualised process, the consequence of which has been the 'intériorisation' and 'approfondissement des exigences sociales.' It would seem that Bozon is making the case for proximity between the social and the individual, indeed for a greater integration of the social within the individual. As he suggests, the sexual individual today is obliged to create his own norms and 'cohérence intime', which is not to imply that one can dispel the social (he repeats that the individual continues to be judged socially) but rather that the individual has assumed a level of internalised social responsibility in relation to the expression of sexuality. This places the individual in a unique position to articulate a sexuality that responds to the joint demands of the individual and the social, rather than adopt norms imposed from without. This idea of social responsibility will be a key element of sexual citizenship.

I have used the example of Bozon to illustrate the central direction of this book. In the same way that Bozon defines the sexual citizen and articulates a new language of sexual citizenship inside the republican model, so this book seeks to map out a range of similarly subversive strategies for lesbians and gays in France today. In so doing, the social will become the battle ground for the hearts and minds of sexual citizens. The PaCS legislation (and in particular lesbian and gay sexuality) has opened up the social to a range of appropriations. On the level of sexuality, the distinction between biological sexual difference and gender is articulated at the point of the social, the latter being used by advocates of gendered identity to reinforce the notion of sexuality as *socially* constructed rather than biologically determined. In this same debate on sexuality, the social is seen to be the place where sexuality is politicised to the extent that the biological argument of male/female sexual difference is challenged by the socially and politically contested terms of heterosexuality and homosexuality. To this extent, the struggle for territorial control of the social is also evident in the debate on citizenship, where the republic's hold on the abstraction of the social is contested by democracy's attempt to occupy and personalise the social at the level of the individual, and specifically with the political backing of *les droits de l'homme*. The social as a site of empirical trial is also manifested in the scientific/theoretical clash with sociology and democracy. The role of science, as an 'expertise' and with its focus on absolutes, universals, and axiomatic definitions, is counterbalanced by the variability of the social and the latter's inadaptability to the template of scientific mimesis.

As such, the social can be perceived as a place of subversion of dominant scientific, political and sexual orders. Leo Bersani, Pierre Bourdieu, Didier Eribon, Marcel Gauchet, Claude Lefort, Evelyne Pisier, Murray Pratt, Irène Théry, Paul Yonnet, all of whose ideas will underpin my analyses of lesbian and gay 'identity', point to the potential for solidarity within the social (the capacity of the lesbian and gay movement to embrace the wider social movement) as a way of strengthening the lesbian and gay power base. This in turn enables lesbians and gays to question and usurp the institutions that produce marginalisation of certain groups, and the institutionalised discourse of 'stigmatisé'/'stigmatisant' that is a by-product of a

Introduction 11

structure of domination. Implicit in this tactic of subversion is a critique of the law, and its loss of legitimacy as an objective, impartial and representative arbiter. Again, the barometer of the social will be seen to come to the rescue of the principle of legitimacy by privileging the 'fait social' (where law moulds its legitimacy) over 'règle' (law as an inherited, totemic absolute).

The republican and democratic underpinnings of the principle of legitimacy will be seen to be played out within the legal system itself in its classification of the individual; the 'personne juridique', defined as the abstract model of the ideal republican citizen, will be challenged by the construction of a 'sujet du désir' who is autonomous and self-regulating. All these contexts, legal, subversive, sexual, scientific and political are part of two wider struggles. The first is the struggle for lesbian and gay equality in France as a fundamental pre-requisite for citizenship. The PaCS represents a significant step towards an acknowledgment of this struggle. But this book also seeks to surpass this exclusive lesbian and gay agenda in order to view the PaCS as an optic through which to assess the 'social' state of the republic. The second struggle is of an ideological nature, embodied in the divide between republicanism and democracy for control of the social sphere. This book looks to explore the liberating and tyrannical dimensions of these struggles. Ultimately, what we discover is that these struggles reach some resolution when their conceptual and theoretical underpinnings are put to the test in what Eric Fassin has called 'la grammaire des usages sociaux.'[10]

*

In the first part of this introduction, I asked the question whether the concept of republican citizenship had struck the right balance between perfectibility of humankind and recognition of individual rights. It is not easy to give a clear answer to this question, because the duality of French republican citizenship is its uniqueness. On the one hand, it is not easy to tinker with republican tradition, and the values of perfection and idealism associated with it. On the other hand, it is incumbent on any objective observer to point out the realities of socio-political debate today, where equality is no longer necessarily an eternal invariable, but rather a right to be negotiated. To this degree, I am an advocate of change and evolution in the concept of republican citizenship and this book reflects this trajectory. It offers a number of strategies by which individual expressions of difference (particularly lesbian and gay) can be put to the service of a different, modern and representative universalism.

My justification for this position is based on a methodology grounded in social theory. This will take us in two main directions. The first is theoretical. The term sexual citizenship is problematic because traditionally neither sex nor sexuality can be defined as a universal right. To remove sexuality from the domain of private

---

[10] Eric Fassin, 'Usages de la science et science des usages', *L'Homme*, 154-155 (2000): 407.

space and bestow on it citizenship status is to break the private/public condition of republican citizenship. Resistance to this breakage comes from the traditional citizenship model, shored up, on the one hand, by essentialist, anthropological and psychoanalytic preconceptions of behaviour, and, on the other hand, by political, religious and sociological defences. In contrast, a different series of oppositions, emerging out of a negotiable and variable *social* space, will be seen to collide with axiomatic definitions of citizenship. Theoretically, therefore, social space, defined through notions of diversity, pluralism, practicality, subversion, immanence and legitimacy, will be seen to challenge the hierarchy of universalism, act as an arbiter of real legitimacy and proffer the possibility of a credible sexual inflection to citizenship.

The second direction is practical. If sexual citizenship can exist in theory, then the second part of this book looks at how it operates in the social space. By examining situations of adoption, filiation, familial ties, parenting and marriage, I will demonstrate how theoretical notions of diversity, individualism and legitimacy (on which sexual citizenship was theorised) must themselves be inflected with social values such as responsibility, common value, altruism, 'mixité', pragmatism, choice, and a language of negotiation. Similarly, the socio-political dimension to the social space (epitomised in the republican and democratic camps) will bring out its own set of demands on the sexual citizen. These will be examined in two main ways. Firstly, I will use the political backdrop of contemporary France (and particularly the PaCS legislation) to locate the struggle of lesbians and gays for recognition and for full equality of rights in the republic. Secondly, and critically, the defence and promotion of sexual citizenship will be taken up by the democratisation of private space as a platform upon which to build strategies to subvert republican citizenship from the inside.

PART ONE
THEORETICAL
CONSIDERATIONS

Chapter 1

Universalism in the Republic: A Political, Religious and Conceptual Divide

Before we can conceive the idea of a lesbian, gay or sexual citizenship in France, we need to understand not only how the republic formulates its unique concept of citizenship, but also the motivations and concerns that have given rise to questions over how the republic defines citizenship in France today. At the heart of this debate is the role of the republic itself, what it stands for and the perceived 'crisis' of its relevance to contemporary France. Defenders of a traditional image of the republic invoke its heroic foundations and transcendent aspirations. They point to the much-vaunted principle of universalism as a model of perfectibility and adaptability to social change and diversity. They feel threatened by what is perceived to be a growing democratisation of the republic in which money, image and globalisation are being seen to undermine the eternal and mystical relationship between the indivisibility of the state and the subject. Critics of this image of the republic point to the intransigence and anti-modernisation tendencies of traditionalists. They see in this a refusal to embrace the consequences of social change, and a reluctance to move away from notions of citizenship rooted in the rights of state and subject towards the origin of rights as defined in *les droits de l'homme*.

This politicisation of citizenship has been heightened by recent legislation in France in which the rights of lesbians and gays have been enshrined in law. The PaCS legislation will be deployed as a yardstick to measure the relevance of the republic and its definition of citizenship, as well as the means by which we can evaluate the responses of political and religious institutions to a highly controversial piece of legislation. In the second part of this chapter, I will examine the reaction of the Catholic church and the political right to the PaCS, with particular emphasis on perceptions of collusion and collaboration between church and state, duplicity of message and fears for the traditional family and marriage. By contrast, the political and intellectual left will be seen to respond favorably to social evolution by inviting a closer proximity between social change and legal representation. Specifically, I will look at how the left has welcomed the PaCS legislation by couching its acceptance in terms of human rights, the democratisation of citizenship, and the deconstruction of citizenship pre-requisites

16 *The Gay Republic*

of the sovereign heterosexual male and the private/public binary. In the final part of the chapter, I analyse one of the fundamental principles of republican citizenship, namely universalism. One of my aims is to expose some of the flaws, inadequacies and presumptions underpinning it.

What is the Republic?

The perception of a crisis in the relevance of a 'republican' France has given rise in recent years to a body of critical literature that has come to the defence of the republic against new changes in world and European politics. Pierre-André Taguieff has highlighted the dangers of the developments in globalisation and immigration for the republic in his work *La République menacée*. Régis Debray has underlined the consensual and mediatic influences that have contributed to this crisis in his work *Que vive la République*. Blandine Kriegel, in *Philosophie de la République*, has charted the political philosophy of the republic, from its origins in Antiquity to today, and pointed out the changing shape of the republic particularly from the sovereignty of the subject to the humanity of the individual. What is characteristic in the historical and ideological representations of the republic by these writers is its transcendent qualities. For Taguieff, the republic is a sacrifice, an ideal, a sublime, a heroic aspiration. For Debray, it is a throne and an altar, threatened respectively by money and image. For Kriegel, the republic is sovereign and superhuman. The link between the subject and the state in the republic is an indivisible link, which translates in the republican tradition into a relationship in which the individual as a unique and subjective identity is subsumed by the subject in his total and unique identification with the state. This combination of transcendent qualities and self-abnegation have served to define French republicanism over recent centuries. And yet, today, there is the perception that these qualities are too removed from the experience of daily life. In other words, there is a sense that republican idealism is in a crisis over its capacity to make itself relevant to people's lives. Part of this crisis, as Taguieff suggests, has to do with a misunderstanding of the nature of the republic, and the relationship between idealism and reality. Taguieff disputes the idea that there is a gulf between idealism and reality. He prefers to describe the relationship as one of 'concevoir l'idéal et d'ajouter le reel.'[1] But in this comment, Taguieff admits to the nature of the challenge facing the republic today. The virtue of tolerance that underpins the idealism of the republic needs to be modified in the light of the socio-cultural demands and affective nuances of democratic politics.

Can we assume therefore that the broad brush that is French republicanism is failing its citizens, and that a new model is needed to address the different demands of globalisation, and ethnic and sexual diversity? Defenders of the idealism of the republic seem resistant to any fundamental upheaval. Taguieff, for example, is scathing of proposed changes to republican idealism. His argument is that the

---

[1] Taguieff, La République menacée, p. 65.

Universalism in the Republic 17

social component within existing republicanism is sufficiently *inclusive* to accommodate new cultural dynamics. He contests the perception that multiculturalism has redefined tolerance of difference (for him a republican value) in terms of respect for minorities as victims. Instead, Taguieff believes that tolerance of difference/minorities is the natural function of civil, republican society. In short, Taguieff questions the need for specific democratic representation when civil society, he claims, can accommodate diversity within the principle of universal equality. Régis Debray is more aggressive in his condemnation of what he sees as the cultural replacement of the social. He claims that any consensual politics is the way to a dead society and the totalitarianism of public and media opinion.[2] Debray believes that the republic must retain its dialectical quality of being both *laïque* and mystical. It is this type of paradox that Debray believes gives the republic its *real* and eternal values. The question to ask, however, is how do these defenders of an eternal republic justify their resistance to change in the face of wider social, political and democratic transformations? We will address this question in the course of this chapter, suffice to say at the moment that there is the perception that the republic does not need to change, that its historical legacy is still intact, and that there is a sense of immunity to evolution and progress. Taguieff, for example, is dismissive of democratic egalitarianism. He describes it as confusing, dangerous and a form of constitutional patriotism. He characterises the replacement of the individual by a 'community', to which the latter is assigned by virtue of his difference or separateness, as utopian and misguided. In short, Taguieff condemns democratic egalitarianism as part of an imaginary postmodernism that pays lip service to reality in all its biocultural diversity. In the same vein, and with what appears an even greater degree of intransigence, Debray justifies his argument for the defence of the republic on the grounds that there is a conspiracy of realism and consumerism that wants to undermine the historical and ideological 'truths' of the republic. Debray questions the legitimacy of egalitarian politics by saying that it is an artificial construction in which the media has paraded consensus as ideal and natural.[3]

Given these arguments in favour of the republic, it is no surprise that communitarianism is a dirty word among conservative republicans. Taguieff says of communitarianism: '[Il]implique le culturalisme, qui enferme les individus dans des groupes d'appartenances fermés sur eux-mêmes, et débouche sur une société de ségrégation et une société multiconflictuelle.'[4] Communitarianism creates cliques of separate indentification which are perceived to be contrary to the model of integrative universalism. Taguieff defines integrative universalism as a *compromise* between universalism and a respect for identities and cultural specificities. However, what Taguieff does not address in this definition is the critical idea that compromise comes with the precondition that universalism is the

---

[2] Régis Debray, *Que vive la République* (Paris: Editions Odile Jacob), p. 95.
[3] Debray, *Que vive la République*, p. 95
[4] Taguieff, La République menacée, p. 65.

18   *The Gay Republic*

dominant player in this compromise, and that specificity is confined to the discrete and private space of 'la vie privée.' Universalism, therefore, becomes the public expression of equality regardless of difference, with cultural, ethnic and sexual specificity a private interest. Once again, Taguieff's defence of this position is grounded in the notion that cultural or sexual diversity is 'accommodated' by civil society, by inclusive universal equality and by national identity. He describes national identity as a broad church which is not exclusive of other 'forces.' Taguieff states: 'Une idenitité nationale constituée peut se payer le luxe de tolérer des forces qui menacent l'homogénéité culturelle qu'elle suppose.'[5] Taguieff's belief in the idealism and absoluteness of the republic borders on condescension, particularly in his characterisation of the republic as being able to afford to 'tolerate' any cultural and sexual diversity that might threaten it. The arrogance and presumption of Taguieff's position is matched by his seeming reluctance to consider the possibility that the republic may need to update itself and make itself more relevant in a postmodern age.

The origins of Taguieff's thinking reside in the idea that modernity itself is a transient phase and that, as Debray claims, the more the republic tries to modernise itself, the more it will need to return to its original values. In other words, for Taguieff and Debray, modernity, by definition, will always be subject to temporal necessity and itself become outdated and archaic. The 'true' value of the republic, according to Debray, is that its spiritual and eternal values will live longer and ultimately triumph over the modern and postmodern demands made upon it.[6] And underpinning this spiritual transcendence is the untouchable principle of integrative universalism. Taguieff admits that universal equality can be exploited, and he is careful not to promote it as a form of dominant ideology. But, as a principle, he defends it because it represents the spirit of the republican mentality. He states that the principle of universalism is founded on the idea that 'il ne se réduit pas à ses mises en oeuvre contingents.'[7] In other words, universalism is a principle that prioritises the general over the specific. This principle, for Taguieff, gives universalism its validity. It is a principle that does not deny the expression of difference (within certain confines) but nor does it see the need to shift its priority away from the defence of the interests of the majority of citizens.

By contrast, Blandine Kriegel has stated that the republic in postmodernity has to come to terms with the move away from the tyranny of the subject as the foundation of the political order and guarantor of the nation/state contract, towards a new 'généalogie' of natural and individual rights. This, for Kriegel, is what democratic citizenship in the postmoden age demands. Kriegel has also responded to the stagnation within the republican defence of universal equality by highlighting the politicisation of citizenship in democratic representation. She claims that there is a need to rethink freedom and to redefine a philosophy of

---

[5]   Taguieff, La République menacée, p. 78.
[6]   Debray, *Que vive la République*, p. 117.
[7]   Taguieff, La République menacée, p. 82.

Universalism in the Republic

citizenship that is no longer rooted in the rights of state or subject but is firmly embedded in the individual and *les droits de l'homme*. Kriegel says:

> La généalogie de la Modernité est à refaire. Construire la citoyenneté de la république démocratique actuelle nous impose de repenser la liberté et de trouver une philosophie de la citoyenneté enracinée dans les droits de l'homme. Ceci implique de cesser de penser le citoyen comme un sujet pour se le représenter comme un individu par la liberté dont la république a été clivée, la philosophie de la liberté a été écartelée.[8]

In contrast to Taguieff and Debray, Kreigel suggests that the politicisation of citizenship has not enjoyed a harmonious passage in the evolution of the republic, and that in fact it poses real problems for the republic in respect of what she calls 'représentation', 'qualification', 'limitation' and 'inscription.' The nature of the terminology points to the complexity of the debate on citizenship in France today. In the face of, on the one hand, a resolute defence of the republic and the principle of universalism and, on the other hand, a political and democratic approach to change, two questions emerge which will underpin the course of this chapter. The first is how the republic, in its political right and left representations, has responded to the PaCS legislation and whether the diversity that the latter promotes has found a natural home in the nation state or in a form of communitarianism? Secondly, can the principle of universalism (defined as the sum of its parts) remain in its current form, or is there a need to change and democratise it?

The Church and the Right

The family and marriage have occupied a privileged space in the life of the French. After the Second World War, France was the only European country to have 'une politique familiale' which the government used to encourage couples to have large families. For example, the government introduced very generous family allowances, including bonuses for the birth of a new child, accommodation subsidies and reductions on transport for large families. Behind this policy, however, was the unambiguous message that in order to avail of these 'allocations' it was necessary to get married and procreate. And if one lived, for instance, in a rural community, the way to get on in life was to get married, set up the 'entreprise familiale' in which all members of the family and future offspring would work. The family, therefore, represented a traditional, state-approved, economic and viable entity.

Of course, in the later decades of the twentieth century, chinks have appeared in the armour of this relatively stable notion of the family. In recent times, the number of marriages has steadily declined[9] and the birth rate has also dropped,[10] although

---

[8] Blandine Kriegel, *Philosophie de la république* (Paris: Plon, 1998), p. 317.

[9] The number of marriages in France has continued to drop over the nineties and into the new millennium. By 2003, the number of marriages in France was 275 963, the lowest ever on record. It is anticipated that by 2005 this figure will have reduced further. For more on

20 *The Gay Republic*

the number of children born outside of marriage has increased.[11] In accordance, the decline in marriage has been accompanied by a rise in cohabitation,[12] and the divorce rate has also risen.[13] Statistics point to a growing disaffection for marriage as no longer the most essential union in life, and also indicate that attitudes to unmarried couples living together and rearing children have softened. In short, the notion of social and political control over the behaviour of citizens (as exemplified by state-approved marriage and various benefits) appears to have weakened. The decline of the traditional family has been accompanied by new social and global transformations such as urbanisation, the 'société de consommation', and the usurpation of the 'entreprise familiale' by the 'grandes enterprises.' These changes have deflected attention away from the centrality of the family and from marriage as the 'acte fondateur du couple', towards the creation of new ways of living founded more closely on individual preference and a growing respect for individualism, equality of rights and *les droits de l'homme*. The sociologist François de Singly has characterised these developments as the emergence of 'le mouvement d'individualisation' accompanied by the phenomenon of 'la famille recomposée.'[14]

In the course of the debate on the PaCS, the Catholic church and the political right were for the most part united against the new law, but for different reasons. Historically, the position of the church within the republic is well established. After the separation of church and state at the turn of the twentieth century, Catholics in France rallied to the defence of the republic, and the adherence of the Catholic church to traditional republican values has been particularly noticeable in debates surrounding the PaCS. However, there is the official church position on the PaCS and an unofficial one. Officially, the Catholic church has been strongly opposed to the PaCS on the basis that it devalues the importance of the traditional family. This

---

this and related demographic changes, consult Claude Laudet and Richard Cox, *Le Peuple de France aujourd'hui* (Manchester University Press, 1995), and the INED website (www.ined.fr/population).

[10] Birth rates have also dropped but not dramatically. In 2004, there were 764 700 births recorded in France, compared to 761 464 in 2003.

[11] The percentage of births recorded outside marriage was 42.5% in 2004, the highest ever on record. See the above website.

[12] In 1994, 'concubins' represented 14% of people living as couples, tantamount to 4.2 million people. This picture has changed significantly over the last decade. The number of family 'ménages' (married couples with children) was recorded at 17 844 369 in 1999, and the number of single parent households at 3 054 873. Most noticeable, however, has been the increase in cohabitees with children, recorded in 1999 at 14 789 496. Consult the INED website, and see also Laurence Folléa, 'L'union libre, ces millions encore négligés par le droit', *Le Monde*, 30 mai 1998, p. 10.

[13] Divorce rates have climbed over the last decades, from 44 700 in 1972 to 119 189 in 1995 and 125 175 in 2003.

[14] François de Singly, 'Le renforcement du mariage est dû à l'existence d'autres formes de la vie commune', *Le Monde*, 2 mars 1999, p. 12.

line has been reinforced by Christian groups such as the *Association pour la fondation de service politique* (AFSP), Catholic journals such as *Golias* and *Liberté politique*, and a host of high profile priests and bishops. The late Pope John Paul II commented that 'rendre équivalentes au marriage, et en les légalisant, d'autres formes de relations entre des personnes est une décision grave qui ne peut que porter préjudice à l'institution conjugale et familiale.'[15] The official Catholic church has couched its rejection in terms of an opposition between the evils of modernity and the natural purity of family values. The PaCS, therefore, has been seen to represent a decline in moral values. According to Monsignor Louis-Marie Billé, it has contributed to 'la tyrannie des moeurs' which in turn has led to 'une fragilisation de la société, [à] une confusion de repères essentiels.'[16] Another member of the French clergy, Père de Vial, who is well known to the political right and a close ally of the anti-PaCS advocate Christine Boutin, has commented that 'qu'il y ait des aménagements juridiques en faveur des homosexuels, pourquoi pas, mais pas sous forme d'une loi. La loi doit-elle accompagner des catégories particulières ou doit-elle veiller au bien commun?'[17] In both these comments, the socio-political reservations of the Catholic church concerning the PaCS are expressed in the form of a reverence for republican values. Mgr Billé invokes implicitly the highly controversial issue of 'la différence des sexes' (in his reference to 'repères essentiels') as the dominant heterosexual order, and thus lays claim to the principle of universal equality for all citizens on this basis, eschewing any construction of sexual citizenship outside of this binary. Similarly, Père de Vial's 'republicanism' is more explicit in his condemnation of laws (the PaCS) that legislate for specific interests rather than the general interest.

In addition to its critique of the socio-cultural implications of the PaCS, the Catholic church in France has also invoked philosophical positions to undermine homosexuality. For example, the views of Thibauld Collin, editorial advisor to the philosophical journal *Liberté politique*, have been appropriated by the church to convey the notion that 'derrière les bons sentiments affichés [dans le projet de loi sur le PaCS], il y a la ferme volonté de changer la société et son fondement anthropologique dans la lignée de la révolution homosexuelle post-1968.'[18] Combined with perceptions that homosexuality is a rejection of alterity ('la différence des sexes') and of procreation, and that the recognition of any union other than that of marriage is to undermine the familial and conjugal institutions, the Catholic church has presented an image, at least in public, that is firmly

---

[15] Quoted in *Le Monde*, 'PaCS: Jean Paul II est intervenu en condamnant toute forme de reconnaissance d'"unions"', 26 octobre 1998, p. 28.

[16] Quoted by Henri Tincq, 'L'Eglise de France accentue sa pression contre le pacte civil de solidarité', *Le Monde*, 3 novembre 1998, p. 17.

[17] Quoted by Clarisse Fabre, 'L'influence discrète de l'aumônier des parlementaires', *Le Monde*, 12 octobre 1998, p. 6.

[18] Nicolas Weill, 'Une "société de pensée" proche des traditionalistes au service d'une mission politique', *Le Monde*, 13 octobre 1999, p. 7.

opposed to the PaCS legislation. Emerging from these interventions by the church is the role that it sees itself playing in the socio-political debates of the day. At its plenary conference in Lourdes in November 1998, the bishops of France addressed specifically the PaCS legislation and defended their right to comment on social issues and their moral impact. On the PaCS, they reinforced their opposition to the legislation on the grounds that it undermined marriage and sent out confusing signals to the younger generation. In terms of its wider role in society, the bishops defended the church's right to comment on political and legal issues by saying that, while recognising the *laïque* tradition in France, it was acting in its role as servant to *laïcité* and that the legitimacy of its moral discourse had a right to be heard.

At what point, however, does the church's perception of its role as guardian of the moral fabric of society risk conflation with the political right, conservative republicanism and even the far right of *lepensisme*? When this point was raised at the Bishops' conference in 1998, Mgr Billé replied: 'J'espère qu'en parlant comme nous avons choisi de le faire nous servons *la démocratie, la laïcité, la citoyenneté*' [my italics]. This is a reserved and diplomatic defence of its position given the continued privilege of the Catholic church in French *laïque* society. However, given its claim to be a servant to democracy, it may be worth pursuing the church further on this and explore how objective and critical the church is on some specific and controversial issues. We have already seen the nature of its opposition to the PaCS legislation. Further investigation, however, reveals a more duplicitous strategy. The Catholic church has opposed the creation of any hierarchy of the couple (represented not only by the PaCS but also by the legalisation of concubinage) that might threaten conjugal and familial institutions. The church is particularly concerned about the messages, both social and moral, that such legislations would import. From the Catholic church's perspective, there is a clear danger that legitimation of the homosexual relationship would also give legitimacy to homosexuality as a moral discourse which could compete with heterosexuality. Part of the strategic thinking of the church therefore has been to play a double role in its pronouncements on lesbian and gay issues. The church does not want to marginalise lesbians and gays. This would be unChristian and discriminatory. Instead, it has tried to placate homosexuals by underlining its respect for them in their search for social integration and rejection of discrimination: 'l'orientation particulière de la personne homosexuelle n'est pas une faute morale. L'inclination n'est pas un péché';[19] and 'il faut savoir qu'on n'ira jamais assez loin dans le respect des personnes homosexuelles, dans la recherche de leur intégration sociale, dans le refus des discriminations.'[20] However, Roselyne Bachelot, the liberal Gaullist *député*, has claimed that this strategy of the church is 'subtilement

---

[19] La documentation catholique (no. 2115): 'L'homosexualité; qu'en dit l'Eglise?' [online] www.portsnicolas.org.

[20] Quoted by Henri Tincq, 'L'Eglise de France accentue sa pression contre le pacte civil de solidarité', *Le Monde*, 3 novembre 1998, p. 10.

stigmatisant.'[21] Her argument is that lesbians and gays are welcome within the church because they are perceived not to be responsible for their sexuality. Their 'orientation' (or 'inclination') is excusable because the church sees it as having been foisted on them. The church believes that homosexuality (a 'sin' in itself) has hijacked lesbians and gays against their will. In other words, for the church, lesbians and gays are not abnormal. They are redeemable and open to salvation. It is homosexuality that is the curse. In short, for Bachelot, the position of the Catholic church on homosexuals and homosexuality is duplicitous.

The Catholic church, however, is adamant that there can be no equality between homosexuality and heterosexuality and that no law should ever contemplate such an equivalence. Mgr Billé reinforces this point: 'il n'est pas possible de faire comme si hétérosexualité et homosexualité étaient équivalentes et comme si cela était sans importance pour la vie d'une société.'[22] Clearly, the church has looked beyond the PaCS as a temporary and legislative issue to its long-term implications for social and moral codes. It is also significant that it appears to view the PaCS less as an opportunity to help integrate lesbians and gays (a laudable aim, it claims), and more as a threat to the heterosexual binary of 'la différence des sexes.' In spite of these reservations, I think it is possible to argue that the PaCS represents an acceptable compromise in the eyes of the church, if viewed as legislation that *legalises* lesbians and gays as separate and distinct couples (which is what it does), but does not *legalise* equality or equivalence with heterosexuals and heterosexuality (which is what it does not do). Within a republican context of safeguards and contractual citizenship, there is no reason why this level of legal recognition for lesbians and gays should not be acknowledged particularly in the light of the church's 'respect' for homosexual persons. Critically, the church's defence of its socio-political role as a servant to democracy is questionable in this regard. It defends privately homosexuals 'dans la recherche de leur intégration sociale', but this defence is not backed up at any political or legal level. It defends (theoretically, theologically?) the social integration of lesbians and gays, but it won't commit to it on a point of principle. The church, in effect, shows the duplicity of its stance by invoking democracy (and

---

[21] Roselyne Bachelot, *Le Pacs entre haine et amour* (Paris: Plon, 1999), p. 154. The ambiguity of this strategy has been highlighted by other critics, notably Andrew Sullivan. In his work *Virtually Normal: An Argument About Homosexuality* (London: Picador, 1999), he charts the history of church attitudes to homosexuality. He identifies the difference in thinking between gay acts as intrinsically abnormal and the need for the church to acknowledge and recognise homosexuals as people (love the sinner not the sin). Sullivan's central argument, however, is that the church's position is untenable; to be gay, for Sullivan, is a structural condition which one cannot give up. The act is part of the condition. He argues that homosexuality is about love, just as heterosexuality is, and suggests that homosexuality should be perceived as a complementary otherness to heterosexuality, a type of foil for the latter. In short, his argument about homosexuality is an argument in favour of the variety of human nature.

[22] Tincq, 'L'Eglise de France accentue sa pression contre le pacte civil de solidarité', p. 10.

24 *The Gay Republic*

the words 'démocratie', 'citoyenneté' and 'égalitariste') to defend its own role, interests and participation in society, while at the same time denying these rights to lesbians and gays.

There are, however, voices of tolerance within the church towards the plight of lesbians and gays, although it should be said that these voices are confined to individuals and their private philosophical writings. One such voice belongs to the priest Père Xavier Thévenot who is a theologian on morality and a specialist within the Catholic church on homosexuality. In an article entitled 'Les homosexualités masculines et leur nouvelle visibilité' published in the Jesuit journal *Etudes*, Thévenot takes a different line to the church's official rejection of the PaCS and homosexuality on the grounds of the protection of 'la différence des sexes.' Thévenot claims that this rejectionism on the basis of alterity (the necessity of heterosexuality) leaves young lesbians and gays with no one understanding or respecting their own separate alterity (otherness to heterosexuality). He claims therefore that lesbians and gays are subject to a 'double contrainte' which he encapsulates in the form of a paradoxical injunction on homosexuals: 'Reconnaissez davantage l'altérité, tel est votre devoir, car selon nous l'homosexualité est déni de la différence sexuelle; mais ne la reconnaissez pas, car vous ne devez pas vous comporter autrement que les hétérosexuels.'[23] The bind of homosexuality in the republic, as expressed by Thévenot, is defined in terms of a private/public binary. On the one hand, it is acceptable to rejoice privately in one's difference (as a matter of *raison d'être*), but, on the other hand, lesbians and gays are restricted in their public behaviour, forced, as Thévenot implies, to act like heterosexuals.

Thévenot goes on to make a case for homosexuality as a 'a-normative' form of sexuality. On this he constructs an argument in favour of a respect for 'une diversité des situations' of which homosexuality is one variation: 'en réalité, il y a des homosexualités ou, plus précisément encore, il y a des sujets dont les personnalités comportent, parmi d'autres dimensions, des traits homosexuels aux formes variés.'[24] Thévenot's characterisations of sexuality lend themselves more to psychoanalysis than they do to religious doctrine. Nevertheless, they reflect a different approach to the question of homosexuality, looking at it less from the perspective of heterosexual/homosexual alterity and more from the perspective of a complex and multi-faceted sexual phenomenon. On the basis of these deliberations, Thévenot distances himself from conservative republican discourse on homosexuality that rejects it on the basis of 'la différence de sexes' but is tolerant of it within integrative universalism as a function of 'la vie privée.' For Thévenot, homosexuality and its social recognition is part of a wider debate on sexuality. In this context, he states that sexuality, homosexual or heterosexual, 'ne peut jamais être enfermée dans la seule sphère privée, bien qu'elle touche, plus que toute autre

---

[23] Père Xavier Thévenot, 'Les homosexualités masculines et leur nouvelle visibilité', *Etudes*, avril (1999): 27.

[24] Thévenot, 'Les homosexualités masculines et leur nouvelle visibilité', p. 29.

réalité, à l'intimité des personnes.'[25] What is different therefore about the republican backdrop to Mgr Billé's and Père Thévenot's observations is that the latter situates the debate on sexual difference in the public domain. Implicitly, he removes the condition on privacy that underpins republican integrative universalism and opens the debate to the democratic scrutiny of individual rights.

Ideally, the role of the church in a *laïque* republic might be limited to 'neutral' pronouncements. Its role would be more that of a noble citizen speaking in the broad interests of democracy. However, in reality, the role of the church is more complex. On issues of political economy, for example, it tends to keep a certain distance. This distance is seemingly compromised on issues relating to moral order, where comments, like those of Mgr Billé, verge more towards recommendations for social, cultural and political consumption. The line between serving *laïcité* (as the church claims to want to do) and influencing it is very fine. In a republic, where *laïcité* might be perceived as a constraint on, if not a hindrance to, the influence of the church on state affairs, the opinions of the Catholic church still command respect, and (ironically) considerably more respect when those opinions tend to chime with traditional republican values. Hence, the perceptions of collaboration and collusion between the church and conservative republicans on points of common morality are never far from the surface of events. However, the views of Père Thévenot, although hardly condoned by church leaders and teachings, serve as a reminder that republican solidarity with the Catholic church also belies voices of democratic dissensus.

On the right, the collective reassessment of political identity after the PaCS legislation gave rise to serious reflection on whether the right's political strategy on the legislation was well advised. In the run-up to the PaCS, the right (characterised by the UDF, the RPR, the DF and the FN) had been unremitting in its opposition to the legislation. It was particularly united on the crucial issue of the sanctity of the family, with only degrees of difference distinguishing parties. The National Front views the family as the organic foundation of the nation, a belief that is couched in the language of a utopian yesteryear. As a threat to 'l'âge d'or de la famille', the PaCS was described by the FN leader Bruno Mégret as 'un mariage bis destiné à détruire la famille, mais aussi une porte ouverte à l'immigration par le biais de PaCS de complaisance.'[26] Other viewpoints from the moderate and central right were opposed to the law on the grounds of it being 'inadapté aux besoins de la famille.' In comparison with the FN, these views were less inflammatory in tone. The official position of the right was to question, on the one hand, the constitutionality of the new legislation given that its passage through parliament was plagued with delays, and was perceived not to have followed due process.[27]

---

[25] Thévenot, 'Les homosexualités masculines et leur nouvelle visibilité', p. 30.

[26] Quoted by Christiane Chombeau, 'M. Mégret se pose en défenseur de la famille traditionnelle', *Le Monde*, 13 avril 1999, p. 11.

[27] Clarisse Fabre, 'Le report du PaCS révèle les embarras parlementaires du gouvernement', *Le Monde*, 2 juillet 1999, p. 8.

On the other hand, the right's central critique of the PaCS focused on the content of the legislation. Concerns were raised as to the open-ended nature of the contract between two 'pacsés', the lack of definition on the notion of 'vie commune', and the rupture in the principle of equality (see later), where married couples and single people were seen to be disadvantaged in fiscal and inheritance matters in comparison with their 'pacsé' counterparts. Legal concerns were also raised in the area of compensatory arrangements in the case of the termination of a PaCS (a decision that could be taken simply by sending a letter to one's partner and then informing a judge) as well as the absence in the legislation of provision for children. While the left, under Lionel Jospin, sought to address the complex relationship between 'l'évolution des moeurs' and the need for new legislation to address the rights of lesbian and gay couples, the right defended the position that the republic was still flexible enough to accommodate *recognition of difference* within its own interpretation of the principle of universal equality. The right wanted to protect this principle and viewed any correction to it as an affront to the republic.

As with the Catholic church, part of the strategy of the political right was to placate lesbians and gays with the carrot of integration (and thus no need for separate legislation to regulate their specificity), but at the same time deny them legal status. We recall, for example, the duplicitous stance of the Catholic church in its compassion for the plight of lesbian and gay integration, but its refusal to recommend any legal accommodation, let alone an equivalence between homosexuality and heterosexuality. A similar stance was adopted by prominent politicians on the right, notably Nicolas Sarkozy, Secretary General of the RPR. In a speech to young members of the RPR, he said:

> Notre idée et notre vision de la famille devront s'ouvrir, se moderniser, s'actualiser. J'aime la famille. Je crois en la famille [...] car réussir sa famille c'est réuissir sa vie. Mais il nous faudra être plus à l'écoute et plus tolérants à l'endroit de ceux qui ont fait un autre choix, par exemple celui qui consiste à s'aimer en dehors du mariage et qui sont porteurs du même amour, de la même sincérité, de la même confiance en l'avenir. J'étais contre le PaCS et je le demeure. Mais je regrette que nous n'ayons pas pu nous faire davantage entendre ou comprendre d'une communauté homosexuelle qui a parfois pu être blessée par ce qu'elle a cru entendre. Nous devons être à l'écoute de toutes les différences parce qu'elles sont parfois synonymes de souffrances. [28]

Behind his conciliatory tone, Sarkozy's modern vision is still undermined by stereotypic misrepresentation (to be different is synonymous with suffering) and by prejudice in his fundamental opposition to the legality of the PaCS. While appearing to want to find solutions to the problems created by social evolution (including the financial difficulties of 'concubins' and the need for 'une attestation de vie commune' for lesbians and gays under the PaCS), the right remained officially opposed to the legal recognition of homosexuals (in the same way that

---

[28] Quoted in *Le Monde*, 30 août 1999, p. 5.

the Catholic church was), whom it perceived as a threat to marriage and the family. The seeming intransigence of the right on the issue of legal status for lesbian and gay couples was further reinforced in its refusal in parliamentary debates to address seriously the point of sexual specificity. From the standpoint of the right, sexual difference was not an issue for debate, neither in terms of specificity nor in terms of linguistic definition. Instead, sexual difference was referred to generically as 'la vie commune' of the couple, in other words a private matter. Sexuality (in word and identity) was a victim of both linguistic and political repression. In this respect, the political right echoed the sentiments not only of the official Catholic church but also of the republic: 'C'est la logique de la *sensibilité républicaine*, qui dans la culture française préfère toujours ce qui est universel à ce qui est spécifique.'[29]

It has only been after the PaCS that attitudes on the right have shown signs of change. Douste-Blazy, President of the UDF, expressed regret for the malicious tone of the debate leading up the passing of the legislation, but not for the vote itself. The level of argument during the course of the debate on the PaCS in the National Assembly descended into invective and homophobia on the right, which the latter only later conceded had damaged its image.[30] And yet this public admission – whether it be interpreted as political posturing or a damage limitation exercise – only belied deeper and more serious divisions within the right to which the PaCS gave rise. For instance, the appointment of Christine Boutin as spokesperson for the UDF during the PaCS debate, and in particular her outspoken homophobia, were questioned by young militant members of the party who considered her to be too removed from issues relating to contemporary life. Indeed, in the fallout after the PaCS legislation, the right perceived itself to be out of touch with contemporary life. The PaCS debate, it claimed, had exposed divisions within its ranks, bringing to light evidence of an internal ideological split between a defence of its republican 'emblèmes' and a search for a modern direction. In hindsight, these divisions provided an opportunity for the right to reassess its own identity, particularly in relation to issues about lifestyle and 'les sujets de société.' As Dominique Paillé, *député* (UDF) des Deux Sèvres, stated: 'Il y a, à droite, sur les sujets de société, des conservateurs et des progressistes.'[31] How permanent this conservative/progressive split is and how far it will develop is open to conjecture. However, it is clear that the PaCS revealed a crisis of identity within the right 'en matière de moeurs', from which two scenarios might emerge. The first points in the direction of a socio-cultural shift within the right and its republican guard, which may prove significant in terms of a rethink on issues relating to universal equality. The second points to the question of the willingness and capacity of the

---

[29] Irène Théry, 'Le contrat d'union sociale en question', *Esprit*, 236 (1997): 164.

[30] The following comments were made by a range of *députés* from the the political right: 'Il n'y a qu'à les stériliser!'; 'En guise d'innovation, le PaCS annonce le retour à la barbarie'; 'Les homos, je leur pisse à la raie' (quoted in *Le Monde*, 26 juin 1999, p. 10).

[31] Dominique Paillé in 'La droite partagée entre défense de ses "emblèmes" et quête de modernité', *Le Monde*, 12 octobre 1999, p. 8.

28 *The Gay Republic*

French political and legal machinery to adapt to social and cultural change.

In a recent article in *Le Monde*, the respective President and Secretary General of the *Collectif national pour le PaCS*, Jan-Paul Pouliquen and Denis Quinqueton, summed up the concerns of the political right in relation to the PaCS in two points. The first point described the right's reaction to the PaCS in the form of a question: 'N'est-il pas un peu dérisoire de baser une politique sur une sexualité?'[32] The second point highlighted the right's strategic use of the PaCS as a threat to social and sexual mores by playing on the fears of the elderly and an electorate characterised as conservative on moral issues. These two points underlined for Pouliquen and Quinqueton the level of 'mauvaise foi' that had consumed the right on this issue. In deriding sexuality as a legitimate political issue, and denying lesbians and gays the democratic oxygen to make balanced judgments for themselves about their sexuality, the right was confirming its own perceptions of itself as out of touch with contemporary society and culture. In addition, Pouliquen and Quinqueton criticised the right for resorting to pseudo legal arguments to convince itself of the fallacy of the PaCS legislation. For them, this degree of self-duplicity, in conjunction with the duplicitous nature of its political strategy, reinforced how badly the right had misjudged the entire issue. By contrast, Pouliquen and Quinqueton appear to rescue the republic from the monopoly and manipulation of the right and relocate it within the democratic rights of all citizens: 'Mais la république ne doit pas être celle des avocats et des notaires. Elle doit rester celle de tout le peuple.' The 'tout' is particularly apt in the context of the PaCS. For the co-authors, the PaCS debate complicated the nature of the moral order in contemporary France, and focused attention on the need to modernise the relationship between the *laïque* republican tradition and a new democratic moral order. In other words, they claimed that there was a need for a clear and balanced case to be made for a democratic revaluation of the republic along the lines of difference:

> Parce qu'à force de discuter d'une loi pour toutes et tous, nous avons amené nos concitoyens, nos voisins, nos collègues de travail, nos amis, à considérer – autrement qu'en caricature – les différentes parties de ce tout. Et l'idée que des personnes différentes peuvent cultiver leurs points communs et appartenir à une même société, en somme être des citoyennes et des citoyens, a avancé pendant ces années. La liberté de chacun, autant que la cohésion sociale, y ont gagné.[33]

The Political and Intellectual Left

> Le PaCS introduit une distinction entre la relation amoureuse, stable et durable, et la famille; il introduit l'idée que la relation amoureuse n'a pas obligatoirement pour finalité

---

[32] Jan-Paul Pouliquen and Denis Quinqueton, 'Le PaCS est-il républicain?', *Le Monde*, 15 octobre 1999, p. 19.

[33] Jan-Paul Pouliquen and Denis Quinqueton, 'Le PaCS est-il républicain?', p. 19.

la procréation, mais doit tout de même être considérée comme un lien commun parce qu'elle permet aux êtres, quel que soit le choix sexuel, de se construire et de s'épanouir.[34]

Where the ideology of the left appears to have stolen a march on the right in its implementation of the PaCS is through the harmonisation of legislation with social evolution, and in its capacity to re-invent the links between politics and *les droits de l'homme*. A misconception of *les droits de l'homme* is that it is a nostalgic invocation of individual freedom that belongs to a distant, revolutionary past and thus has little relevance to contemporary reality. On the contrary, the reality of the concept (as this book confirms throughout) is its continued relevance to citizenship today and its centrality at the heart of the defence and legitimation of the particular interests of individuals. To this degree, *les droits de l'homme* is a potentially dangerous concept from the perspective of a conservative republic that wants to prioritise general interest over particular interest. By recognising lesbians and gays and their status as couples in the PaCS, the left was responding in effect to the call of *les droits de l'homme* and to the democratisation of citizenship in which the republic was being recast as no longer the prerogative of the *sovereign male subject* but the entitlement of the individual. This *politicisation* of citizenship does not imply the negation of the republic nor of the state, but serves to shift the balance of power away from the state as a centralising force to the effective participation and full representation of the individual in the state. Similarly, this politicisation of citizenship unlocks universalism's hold over the discourse on difference from within the category of 'la vie privée', and frees up the public domain as a legitimate space of democratic representation. The philosopher Claude Lefort, who has reinvigorated the concept of *les droits de l'homme* as an agent of change, has suggested new ways of approaching the relationship between social interaction and the state. Lefort uses the notion of *les droits de l'homme* to propose an alternative social model based on the 'les droits de rapport' which are defined in terms of their public space:

> En mettant les hommes en relation, ils produisent, en effet, un espace de rencontres, d'échanges, de débats où se définissent les règles de la vie commune et où se construit la légitimité. Pour autant, L'Etat n'est pas nié; il est seulement remis à sa place comme instance de pouvoir ne détenant pas le principe de sa légitimité et comme simple partie d'un tout qui ne peut prétendre à devenir la totalité.[35]

With the state reduced in its republican function as Supreme Being, and rendered conditional on the public space as the site where it must earn its right to act, 'l'espace public' becomes the locus of legitimacy, structured on the principle of negotiation on issues relating to 'l'organisation des formes de vie': 'c'est par le

---

[34] *Sénateurs votez pour le PaCS* [online]: www.multimania.com/pacs.

[35] Claude Lefort, *L'Invention démocratique. Les limites de la domination totalitaire* (Paris: Livre de Poche, 1983), p. 79. See also Dominique Rousseau's article, 'Fonder la politique sur les droits de l'homme', *Le Monde*, 16 juillet 1999, p. 16.

30 *The Gay Republic*

débat et la mobilisation de l'espace public que l'égalité des sexualites a pu être prise en charge, que la femme comme composante de l'universel humain et non comme catégorie a pu être pensée.'[36] By shifting the focus away from an out-dated notion of the republican state as the bearer of universal wisdom to all its citizens, Lefort redresses the balance of power by relocating the agency and legitimacy of democratic change *within* the social, a move which the political left has embraced by seeing in 'l'évolution des moeurs' a social space in need of legitimate recognition.

We can use Lefort's insights as a way of explaining in part the right's problematic response to the implementation of the PaCS legislation. With the right's tendency to endorse the privatisation of sexuality (a republican discourse in which homosexuality is viewed as a 'problème d'ordre privé'), the implication is that sexuality is taken out of the domain of public legitimacy, self-determination and accountability. In its place is a pre-ordained order of (hetero)sexual citizenship which, in the guise of universal inclusion and participation, has the effect of excluding lesbians and gays from full representation, full legitimacy and full equality. The right's defence of this predetermined sexual citizenship is clearly distant from Lefort's organic interpretation of sexual and legislative agency in the social. Where the left has created clear water between itself and the right on the issue of the PaCS is in its embrace of socio-cultural change, its validation of the agency of the social and the acceptance within the law of 'un droit de cité' for gays and 'concubins.' And, while pro-PaCS advocates agree that full equality has not yet been achieved, they are of the opinion that legal status for lesbian and gay couples (as opposed to recognition) is one of the stages towards it. Furthermore, with homosexuality gaining in public tolerance (indeed being seen as of 1997 as 'une manière acceptable de vivre sa sexualité'[37]), it could be argued that the PaCS represents the political corroboration of the evolution of public opinion.

However, is responding to social change and public opinion the basis on which political and democratic decisions should be made? Régis Debray, we recall, slammed the tyranny of public opinion and reminded us of how modernity and social evolution are subject to temporality, while the republic fixes our attention on transcendent and eternal values. Debray's argument is a seductive one but it also raises some issues about how the left and right are perceived. One of these perceptions is that the left is synonymous with change and progress, and the right with the status quo. Also, there is the perception that because the political and intellectual left appears to have its finger on the pulse of social change, the natural corollary is that the consensus for socio-cultural change has to be reflected politically and legally. These are naïve assumptions about both left and right, and

---

[36] Quoted by Rousseau in, 'Fonder la politique sur les droits de l'homme', p. 16.

[37] *Le Nouvel Observateur* (3 juillet 1997) compared the results of two surveys carried out in 1981 and 1997. Among other revelations, it was noted that the percentage of those polled, who believed that homosexuality had become a more acceptable way of living, had increased from 29% in 1981 to 55% in 1997.

we need to be careful not to misrepresent either. However, as we have demonstrated, the political left and right are underpinned by principles and ideologies that tell us how they are responding to the inevitability of social change. I think it is important to scotch the impression that the left's embrace of social change and sexual difference (in the context of lesbian and gays) is a sop to political correctness and neo-liberalism. On the contrary, its advocacy is political (equality for all citizens is paramount) and ideological (*les droits de l'homme* inform its direction). Equally, Debray's defence of the republic is also political and ideological, but we may want to question to what extent his defence is shaped by a reverence for the eternal grandeur of the republic and universalism, at the expense of their practical relevance or relevance to the lives of modern French citizens?

The issues at stake here are relevance and compromise. Pierre-André Taguieff, like Debray, appeals to the ideal aspirations of the republic. But Taguieff, like Blandine Kriegel, recognises that structures need to change if the republic is to remain relevant to contemporary society. Taguieff, we recall, describes the republic as an ideal worth striving for. But he also acknowledges that this aspiration exposes human failing in the sense that as fallible human beings the pursuit of an ideal republic is by definition unattainable. This is the paradox of Taguieff's republican construction: 'Nous nous voulons des surhumains et nous nous savons des demi-humains.'[38] The implication of Taguieff's position is that idealism and aspiration on their own are not enough to bring about a workable republic. Naturally, Taguieff, as we have seen, falls back on his defence of universal equality (and the implication of an 'accommodating' civil society) as the means by which the republic compensates for human fallibility. But his reservations are telling. I think the critical issue here is the extent to which the human/temporal dimension in the republic (as opposed to established principles and norms) is allowed to influence change. We have seen how republican citizenship is carefully managed in respect of the public/private binary and other preconditions. The example of Lefort, however, gives a greater role for individual self-determination in the construction of new lines of human communication. It could be argued also that Lefort allows greater room for compromise between state and individual demands. And lest we forget, Taguieff's vision of the republic as a theoretical ('concevoir') and a practical ('ajouter') construction reflects the importance of reaching a common ground between the competing demands of republican idealism and democratic common sense. In short, therefore, the left, in its implemenation of the PaCS, is not pandering to modern individualism, common sense or some neo-liberal tendency. It is acknowledging that the republic in its current state is not having the effect that it was designed to have. Society has changed fundamentally and the model of universalism, idealistic and intellectually enlightened as it may be, is in need of modification. The PaCS, I would argue, has brought this message to our attention: 'Le PaCS intéresse *aussi la République et la société*, puisqu'il reconnaît le couple et installe une plus grande stabilité des

---

[38] Taguieff, La République menacée, p. 95.

relations'[39] (my italics).

The idea that the PaCS can bring stability to human relations flies in the face of the views of the Catholic church and conservative republicans. But as this quotation also implies, the PaCS has a wider and perhaps more important brief than the one of providing new legal status to lesbian, gay and heterosexual couples. The PaCS addresses the straitjacket of republican citizenship and its exclusive tendencies. The PaCS highlights the absence of compromise between intransigent republicanism and liberal democracy. The PaCS is responding to the socio-cultural fragmentation of the family and marriage. As earlier statistics have indicated, the family and marriage are no longer the central forces of unity and stability in society. New social, cultural and sexual transformations, which themselves have created new forms of (in)stability and (dis)unity, are questioning the privileged place of the family in French society. And underpinning much of this process of transformation is the new-found meaning in *les droits de l'homme*. The politicisation of *les droits de l'homme* has stimulated a wider intellectual debate and given a new momentum to the democratic charge. One of the facets of this debate (in the context of the family) has been the need to name an alternative symbolic order to that of the family. This is part of a process that has been ongoing in France since the 1960s. One of the powerful messages of the 1968 era was the way in which individuals were given the freedom to define themselves first and foremost through themselves, and not in terms of their familial links. Individuals were perceived to have rights other than the rights ascribed to them by the institution of the family. The aftermath of 1968 has produced a tension between these conflicting roles. While the traditional family provided a system where the individual was able to realise his identity via the support and love of those within the family, this system fell short in terms of its ability to satisfy the principles of autonomy and freedom. The philosopher Sabine Prokhoris (among whom we might include Pierre Bourdieu and Remi Lenoir) has exposed the mythical order of this ideal family. She refers to its 'totalitarisme familial' in the imposition of a 'nostalgie d'éden' on the child. She highlights the ways in which the family construct has indoctrinated the father, mother and child in what she describes as the prolongation of lifelong 'étiquettes' ('mère', 'père'). For Prokhoris, these terms have defined and restricted the full potential of the individual and denied him the possibility of 'pouvoir inventer des liens et de s'inventer soi-même à travers ces liens.'[40] As the sociologist François de Singly has suggested, there is an undeniable 'mouvement d'individualisation' in the human condition. This has not only contributed to a destabilisation of the family institution, but it has also transformed the conjugal relationship post 1975 (with divorce by mutual consent) and created a new space of multiple partners and divided emotional loyalties.

---

[39] Catherine Tasca, 'Un nouveau cadre, un nouveau regard: *Le Monde* pour ou contre le PaCS', *Le Monde*, 10 octobre 1998, p. 7.

[40] Sabine Prokhoris, 'Inventer de nouvelles formes de vie, cela ne veut pas dire qu'il n'y a pas d'ordre', *Le Monde*, 3 novembre 1998, p. 15.

In the current climate, the PaCS, concubinage, parity and the politicisation of the *les droits de l'homme* have rekindled this debate between the institution of the family and individualism. Singly recognises that the traditional family has evolved and will continue to evolve into a reconstituted form in order to accommodate the new affective and individualist logics of the day.[41] In identifying these two logics as the primary values operating in contemporary society – the emotional needs provided by the proximity of a family and the self-fulfilling concerns of the modern 'individu mobile' – Singly highlights the dilemmas of many thousands of individuals (childless or not, homosexual or heterosexual) who want to organise and legalise a common life with one another, based not necessarily on binding obligations and institutional demands but on a mutual respect for the freedom of the individual.

Universal Equality: 'L'oeuf fécondé' in the Republic

Where the debate on the left has been particularly controversial is on the notion of universal equality. Naomi Schor has defined universalism as being 'grounded in the belief that human nature, that is rational human nature, was a universal impervious to cultural and historical differences.'[42] She sets up neatly the dual nature of this concept, positing, on the one hand, its broad applicability to the human species, and on the other hand, highlighting its immunity to appropriation by culture, history or identity. In post-war France, where immigration was first welcomed and then problematised, universalism assumed the new garb of assimiliationism; everyone was assimilated equally under the republic, regardless of their differences. However, assimilation presented problems of a unique nature, particularly the degree to which difference was recognised. Sylviane Agacinski has claimed that equality has never been opposed to difference: 'le principe de l'égalité n'exclut donc pas la reconnaissance de la différence.'[43] Theoretically, therefore, recognition of difference has never been denied by universalists. Agacinski confirms this by claiming that recognition of difference does not mean to abandon the universal, but rather to 'rendre possible la reconnaissance du contenu concret et différencié de l'universel.'[44] For Agacinski, recognition of difference within universalism is a matter of interpetation. Difference appears to be accommodated within universalism but it is a question of defining the limits to the expression of difference. Indeed, as we will see later, her concrete and differentiated articulation of recognition is contingent on several in-built conditions (such as 'la vie privée'

---

[41] In this respect, compare the views of Jeffrey Weeks in *Invented Moralities: Sexual Values in an Age of Uncertainty* (Cambridge: Polity Press, 1995), and Ulrich Beck and Elisabeth Beck-Gernsheim in *The Normal Chaos of Love* (Cambridge: Polity Press, 1990).

[42] Naomi Schor, 'The Crisis of French Universalism', *Yale French Studies*, 100 (2001): 46.

[43] Sylviane Agacinski, *Politique des sexes* (Paris: Editions du Seuil, 1998), p. 185.

[44] Agacinski, *Politique des sexes*, p. 81.

34 *The Gay Republic*

and 'la différence des sexes').[45]

Nevertheless, Agacinski is responding to the crux of what universalism is about. From a republican perspective, the universal erases difference (not to the point of 'méreconnaissance' but to the point of 'indifférence', in which case sexuality becomes an affair of 'la vie privée'). It is a position which many democratic republicans support, including factions within the gay 'community', feminism and on the left of French politics. It is a position, many would claim, which respects *in the most objective way possible* the 'intérêt général' of all citizens without privileging any one particular group of individuals. The alternative position, more subjective in focus, seeks to approach universalism from the perspective of difference, and establish equality between differences, thus setting up equal but separate identities. What we have here, therefore, is one of the paradoxes of universalism; a claim to equality for all in the interest of the majority but a claim which simultaneously highlights the inequalities of some. 'The host nation's dilemma', as Naomi Schor has suggested in the context of immigration in France, and echoing Derrida's notion of *same duty*, 'is not only to welcome and integrate difference but also to recognise and accept its alterity.'[46] The drama of this paradox is also played out in the context of the PaCS.

The sociologist Irène Théry and Professor of Law Evelyne Pisier have both been critical in their assessments of the shortcomings of the PaCS legislation, perceiving it respectively as a 'minimum symbolique' and 'un projet en demi-

---

[45] Agacinski's views are defended by prominent jurists. Anne-Marie Le Pourhiet, Professor of Public Law and prominent critic in the area of positive discrimination, sees the republic threatened by what she calls the 'exigences tyranniques' of militant groups whose 'droit à la différence est, en premier lieu, beaucoup moins invoqué comme un droit-liberté, un "droit de", que comme un droit-créance, un "droit à."' Described as free-wheelers and creators of the law, militant groups, she claims, play on the culture of victimisation and are seen as corruptors of democracy. Most worryingly for Le Pourhiet, and in a comment reminiscent of Debray's disdain for the media, she states: 'Le plus grave est sans doute le passage quasi-direct de ces exigences tyranniques dans le droit français par capitulation de la démocratie représentative devant la démocratie dite "d'opinion" qui n'est en réalité que la négation de la démocratie tout court puisqu'elle assure la victoire despotique de l'exigence minoritaire sur la volonté majoritaire en évacuant toute médiation. A vouloir consacrer le droit de tout et à son contraire le droit finit par devenir illisible et incohérent et perdre sa force et son autorité' in 'Egalité et différence dans la France contemporaine", *Revue politique et parlemenatire*, 1017-18 (2002): 44-9. Nathalie Heinach also defends universalism on issues of parity, PaCS and the headscarf. For her, all these controversies centre on the idea of equality which she defines in two ways, either as an affirmation of difference or as a suspension of difference in the interests of a universal belonging to the human race. She defends herself against accusations of homophobia and discrimination by reinforcing her idea that public space (as opposed to private space) is a civic space (a space of values, consensus and republican values). See her article, 'Lorsque le sexe paraît: de quelques confusions dans des débats brûlants', *Le Débat*, 131 (2004): 170-78; also Cyrille Duvert, 'Le droit jetable', *Le Débat*, 131 (2004): 179-92.

[46] Schor, 'The Crisis of French Universalism', p. 53.

mesures.'[47] Théry views the PaCS as a missed opportunity to discuss the central issue of 'la spécificité du lien de couple', and the fundamental lack of recognition of the homosexual who is granted a status almost by dispensation. Théry, as we will see in the course of this book, is a central figure in the PaCS debate because she occupies a pivotal position as one who has articulated the concerns of homosexual 'identity' and the gay couple (calling for a separate 'contrat de vie de couple' for lesbian and gay couples), but who also stops short of full equality between homosexuality and heterosexuality. In this respect, she embodies the republican universalist position of recognition of difference, but not at the expense of the 'intérêt général.' Pisier, on the other hand, while agreeing with Théry, in so far as the PaCS is an incomplete piece of legislation, addresses the issue from historical and philosophical perspectives. Her views reflect a debate within the debate of universal equality. In other words, within the context of the political seesaw of right and left on the PaCS legislation, there has been an equally important and ongoing debate that goes to the heart of French society and culture, and which questions the role of the principle of universalism (and sexual equality in the name of the universality of the republic) in a modern pluralist society.

In her article 'Du PaCS et de l'ambiguïté d'une tolérance', Pisier believes that modernity has created a new context in which universalism needs to be rethought. Modernity, for Pisier, has created the legitimacy of a democratic debate on universalism which pits what she calls the 'Juste" against the 'Bien.' The latter is identified as the moral code of the pre-modern age when universalism as a principle was first conceived by Bodin, Hobbes and Rousseau. The logic of this universalism in the pre-modern age was founded on the creation of 'des exceptions prépolitiques au nom de différences énoncées comme naturelles.'[48] What Pisier means by differences perceived as natural and prepolitical is the creation of categories such as the inferiority of women, their domestication and the universal and symbolic dominance of men over women. This prepolitical amnesty has given rise, according to Pisier, to a host of 'injonctions' relating to 'la différence des sexes', the family and heterosexuality. Homosexuality, on the other hand, has been 'dénoncée comme étrangeté repoussante.' While she admits that justice in today's world has sought to expose the exclusionary nature of these prepolitical notions (perceived in their time to be good, honorable and universal in their wisdom), she remains sceptical that justification is enough to change laws and bring about equality.

To this degree, her argument reaches a crisis in terms of being able to deliver change. As a result, Pisier looks at ways how the 'Juste' can actually make a difference. In this, she targets universalism itself and democracy as the arbiter of change. In the first instance, she adheres to the existence of universalism as a legitimate model for the French republic. However, she claims that in order to

---

[47] Irène Théry, 'PaCS, sexualité et différence des sexes', *Esprit*, 257 (1999): 140.

[48] Evelyne Pisier, 'Du PaCS et de l'ambiguïté d'une tolérance', *La Revue des deux mondes*, novembre-décembre (1999): 157.

36 *The Gay Republic*

retain any democratic credibility, universalism must renegotiate the terms of equality along the lines of 'un universalisme au nom duquel la différence entre un homosexuel et un hétérosexuel ne justifie ni des statuts inégaux ni même le refus d'un égal accès aux droits.'[49] In the second instance, the role of democracy is also criticised but Pisier recognises that democracy has its limits and that, while it might be more on the side of the 'Juste', democracy must also accommodate what is good ('Bien'). In balancing the just and the good, democracy has the very delicate task of not being seen to legislate in favour of every difference imaginable. Democracy, she claims, is about finding *le juste milieu*. In this respect, Pisier acknowledges some of the good things that universalism has achieved in terms of fixing limits to 'la dynamique égalitaire de l'accès aux droits.' Similarly, she is sensitive to the necessary balance to be achieved between 'droits fondamentaux' and the role of the law to make sure that such rights 'ne contredisent pas son souci de protéger la dignité de l'ensemble des membres de la société.' Even for a radical like Pisier, the 'intérêt général' is seen to have a positive function. In her conclusion, Pisier sums up the concept of the universal as a betrayal. However, this betrayal is not a betrayal of principle, but more a betrayal by what she calls so-called 'universalistes' who, in conceiving and approving such a flawed and prejudicial universal model, showed their contempt for the true value of the universal.[50]

For Pisier, republican discourse on universalism has stifled democratic deliberation, forcing free expression of identity and belonging into a straitjacket. According to her, sexual equality between men and women under universalism was a misnomer until the constitution of 1946. The founding fathers of universalism excluded women from the frame of reference; women were concerned with issues 'de vie', men with issues 'du monde.'[51] Sexual difference between men and women was perceived as a biological issue. It was defined in terms of the biological 'différence des sexes', itself the foundation of marriage and the human

---

[49] Pisier, 'Du Pacs et de l'ambiguïté d'une tolérance', p. 158.

[50] Pisier's distinction between 'universel' and 'universalistes' highlights the idea that, as a principle, the universal works but that in its drafting and application there have been weaknessess. Apologists will make the case for a historical reflection of the universal. However, this is not a sentiment shared by other critics of universalism who see the principle itself as 'tronqué' and 'fétichiste.' In this regard, see Hugues Jallon and Phillipe Mounier, *Les Enragés de la république* (Editions de la Découverte, 1999), p. 119. Post-PaCS and parity, and even among some of universalism's robust defenders, a consensus is emerging that modifications to the principle are in order. Anne-Marie Le Pourhiet, a defender of the principle of universal equality, calls for an updated version: 'C'est précisément ce que je suggère aux juges français s'agissant du principe d'égalité: déterminer et appliquer effectivement des critères objectifs et rationnels concrets au lieu de se contenter de formules abstraites et incantatoires visant un vague objectif d'intérêt général ou d'imperceptibles différences de situation' in 'Deux conceptions du droit', *Le Débat*, 117 (2001): 178.

[51] For more on the history of the distinction of the sexes, see the article by Irène Théry, 'La côte d'Adam: retour sur le paradoxe démocratique', *Esprit*, 3-4 (2001): 10-22.

Universalism in the Republic 37

species. This was the binary that equalised all citizens within the republic and simultaneously excluded any one outside it. It is a binary which is also at the heart of a universalist response to the PaCS; sexualities and identities built on sexual orientation are perceived as variations on the theme of 'la différence des sexes' and thus discredited. It is also a binary around which certain academics like Irène Théry, Sylviane Agacinski and Elisabeth Roudinesco[52] have clustered (some would claim selfishly, and with varying degrees of acquiescence to the lesbian and gay agenda), to promote a new politicised feminism in the debate on parity. Anne Garréta reflects the hypocrisy of the *paritaires* in their blatant betrayal of sexual difference in favour of a normalising sexual, symbolic order:

> The theoretical re-engineering of *la différence des sexes as la Différence* itself, the founding, primordial, symbolic difference – which can only be recognised, for it was always already there, simply hidden from view – logically entails a casting out or a dissolution of all minor or minority differences. It is no coincidence that the intellectual guarantors of the *parité* doctrine could take a position against extending legal recognition to same-sex couples.[53]

What is alarming in the parity debate is the way in which 'la différence des sexes' has been appropriated by a post-feminist lobby, and naturalised as the norm. It would appear that *paritaires*, in seeking equality with men, have in fact invoked difference in the notion of 'la différence des sexes.' On the surface, this seems contradictory. Why invoke difference when you want equality? The reason, for *paritaires*, is because the concept of 'la différence des sexes' is the biological premise on which an argument for equality can be constructed. However, while this concept may serve the immediate purpose of arguing for equality, the very precondition of 'la différence des sexes' works against *paritaires* and their design for equality because this concept enshrines a *symbolic* difference between men and women, which no amount of negotiated equality can achieve. Marie-Jo Bonnet claims that universal equality is very much the preserve of the male subject; women and homosexuals are legally recognised in the republic but they are *symbolically* unrecognised.[54] In the context of the PaCS debate, the right has been

---

[52] In the current parity debate, Elisabeth Roudinesco seeks to distance herself from 'agenda' politics by confirming anatomical sexual difference between men and women as 'fact' and therefore impossible to efface. She goes on to highlight the dangers of conflating sexual difference with identity, and repositions the emancipation of women within 'une conception de l'inconscient qui refusait toute forme d'ancrage dans la psychologie des peuples, des ethnies ou des identités' in 'Une parité régressive', *Le Monde*, 11 février 1999, p. 12. This philosophical, feminist and deeply universalist position, however, seems to fly in the face of the practicalities of everyday life, like unequal pay and the myriad forms of discrimination that surface from the PaCS legislation.

[53] Anne F. Garréta, 'Re-enchanting the Republic: "PaCS", *Parité* and *Le Symbolique*', Yale French Studies, 100 (2001): 161-62.

[54] Marie-Jo Bonnet, 'Gay Mimesis and Misogyny: Two Aspects of the Same Refusal of the Other?', *Journal of Homosexuality*, 41 (2001): 265-80.

38 *The Gay Republic*

keen to invoke this natural and symbolic difference as the foundation of the couple, the family and society. 'La différence des sexes' is seen as that which dictates law and therefore includes and excludes. By contrast, democratic revisionism of 'la différence des sexes' seeks to challenge *politically* its biological, essentialist and natural foundations by arguing for a socially constructionist response to sexual orientation (see next chapter on 'la différence des sexes'). For the democratic lobby, equality is a political issue (not a biological one), and part of its strategy is to denounce what it sees as universalism's subservience to 'la différence des sexes' as a way of legitimating 'l'exclusion de l'homosexualité hors de l'enceinte sacrée du mariage et de la famille.'[55] As a further tactic of exclusion, this notion of 'la différence des sexes' is perceived to be grounded anthropologically, giving it the force of the law of nature and culture. Pisier has questioned the arbitrariness of a law based on this 'natural' difference, asking: 'Si l'altérité sexuelle est une loi de nature, que faire du "même" dans la paire? [...]. La revendication égalitaire défie la limite que la nature est censée imposer à l'universalisme des droits.' [56]

And yet, in spite of these significant reservations, the straitjacket of universalism remains in place. This leaves the democratic opposition in its own particular bind of how to approach change. Pisier pointed out earlier that one of the most effective ways to combat inequality was to tackle universalism from within, and from the perspectives of principle and democracy. This approach has incorporated a range of approaches to universalism, from abstract to radical, and a combination of both. Abstract universalism incorporates integrationists who see all difference as being dissolved within the equality of 'la vie privée.' They are, as Naomi Schor calls them, the 'unsexed, ungendered, unraced, unclassed' for whom being a citizen of the republic means to be 'a neutered subject devoid of all particularities.'[57] Radical universalism brings together lesbian and gay activists and militants (ACT-Up in particular) who will stop at nothing short of full equality of sexes and sexualities, including rights for lesbians and gays to marry and adopt children. Alternatively, we have seen that Pisier and Théry see the PaCS as a half-way between abstraction and radicalism. On the one hand, the PaCS can be interpreted as the recognition and integration of lesbians and gays within universalism, but this does not equate to full equality as defined by symbolic representation or legal equivalence. Where gender is nullified in the interests of 'l'intérêt général', one has to question how the abstraction that is universalism can ultimately serve equality of citizenship between homosexuals and heterosexuals? On the other hand, from a radical perspective, the PaCS can be viewed as an inadequate and demeaning legal settlement because anything short of full equality of citizenship is tantamount to discrimination.

---

[55] Daniel Borrillo, Eric Fassin and Marcela Iacub, 'Au-delà du PaCS: pour l'égalité des sexualités', *Le Monde*, 16 février 1999, p. 17.

[56] Evelyne Pisier, 'PaCS et parité: du même et de l'autre', *Le Monde*, 20 octobre 1998, p. 18.

[57] Schor, 'The Crisis of French Universalism', p. 62.

Universalism in the Republic

In its current form, universalism is of the abstract variety. As such, the net of abstract universalism can adapt to various levels of political and sexual pressure without compromise to its principle of universal equality and the proviso of 'la vie privée.' In effect, universalism as it is has managed to accommodate the PaCS legislation without any real loss of face. Marriage is protected, gay couples are legally recognised (with conditions in place), and access to the holy grail of 'droit familial' is largely the preserve of the married heterosexual couple. Evelyne Pisier has pointed out that the same accommodation has taken place with respect to universalism and parity. She claims that *paritaires* may have won the argument of ridding universalism of its masculine domination in the political arena through a strategy of deference to 'la différence des sexes.' But, in doing so, she claims that parity has folded in on itself, and facilitated an argument for the exclusion of all other particularisms beyond the pale of 'la différence des sexes.' For Pisier, parity has embraced a restrictive and exclusive universalism.[58] In response to the capacity of universalism to adapt, in chameleon fashion, to different circumstances, the sociologist Shmuel Trigano has called for a redefinition of universalism, away from its monolithic and exclusive dimensions towards a measured rethink of its relevance to individuals' lives. He states:

> Il ne s'agit pas de nier le principe d'unité du genre humain et du droit qu'il entraîne. Mais de le redéfinir [...]. L'expérience historique nous a montré qu'elle était monolithique et exclusive [...]. Cet universel rendait impossibles l'assomption de l'identité et la jouissance simultanée de l'égalité car il n'y a que des identités singulières qui peuvent jouir de l'égalité.[59]

Trigano is careful not to 'dumb down' universalism. Like Taguieff, he sees the value of universalism as a principle which has political and intellectual significance, and which does not reduce easily to the 'éléments qu'il rassemble.' But, at the same time, he admits that universalism requires redefinition in respect

---

[58] See Pisier's article 'Sexes et sexualités: bonne et mauvaises différences', *Les Temps modernes*, 609 (2000): 156-75. While Pisier has been critical of *paritaires*, other critics have defended the strategy of *paritaires* to proclaim their sexual difference by claiming that they had no choice but to act in the way they did. In their work *Les Enragés de la République* (Paris: Editions de la Découverte, 1999), Hugues Jallon and Pierre Mounier point out that parity is a necessary addition to the constitution and to universalism in that, as part of the human species, women are unconditionally and fundamentally equal. The 'human' argument is seen to protect *paritaires* from serving their own interests through a defence of 'la différence des sexes.' Parity, they claim, is an exceptional case and must be distinguished from other categories and specific communitarian interests. Furthermore, the co-writers claim that parity introduces a necessary sexual dimension to the concept of the universal and is a wake-up call to its male defenders: 'Elle [parité] invitait à ouvrir un véritable débat sur le sens des mots et expressions qu'ils utilisent: l'égalité, l'Universel, la citoyenneté. Elle invitait surtout à sortir du règne de l'incantation et à confronter les principes à la réalité qu'ils prétendent réguler', p. 122.

[59] Shmuel Trigano, 'Les droits de l'(autre) homme', *Le Monde*, 18 novembre 1998, p. 16.

40   *The Gay Republic*

of its capacity to represent the range of individual experience.

A variation on Trigano's flexible universalism is Pisier's concept of a revised universalism, founded on a revaluation of the concept of nature. Critical of 'la différence des sexes' as the natural order that underpins universalism, she asks why a universal law has to be derived from the alterity of 'la différence des sexes'?:

> La logique universaliste est conviée à plier devant une autre nature qui fait que l'homme et la femme différents et donc complémentaires pour assurer, par la procréation, la survie de l'espèce. Mais de ce fait, si incontestable soit-il pour le moment, pourquoi faut-il en tirer une loi?[60]

For Pisier, this law is tantamount to a law of heterosexuality, which, in her view, subjugates homosexuality in the name of 'la différence des sexes.' She goes on to suggest that it is the role of modernity to rethink the role of nature and invent an alternative based on 'les droits d'une multitude d'êtres différents partageant ensemble une commune humanité, quels que soient leurs races, leurs sexes et…leurs sexualités.'[61] Both Trigano and Pisier see the need to reinvent the idea of the universal. Trigano is less adventurous in the nature of the redefinition. He is content to integrate rather than overhaul, a position summarised in his equation: '(l'égalité des droits, l'unité du genre humain) *avec* la différence (les identités singulières)'[62] (my italics). Pisier, on the other hand, is more radical in her claim that universalism is fundamentally flawed because of its central axis of heterosexuality and the politics of male domination masquerading in the guise of *les droits de l'homme*. Also, their respective viewpoints diverge significantly on the emphasis each places on the role of 'la différence des sexes', and on the relationship between 'commune humanité'/'genre humain' and difference. Pisier appears to privilege difference at the centre of humanity whereas Trigano privileges the centrality of the human being from which difference can derive. This in itself is a significant distinction because it goes to the heart of the republican integrative approach (Trigano), as opposed to the democratic and differentialist approach (Pisier).

The cultural historian Paul Yonnet adds a further variation in the interpretation of universalism in the context of the PaCS. He begins by applauding those who scripted the legislation for the way in which they inscribed the ethos of the PaCS within a republican tradition: 'ils ont fait valoir que la tradition républicaine (c'est-à-dire révolutionnaire) française s'opposait à toute organisation communautaire, par nature discriminatoire.'[63] On the surface, Yonnet's comments reflect a defence of the republican tradition, with echoes of a strong anti-communitarianism. However, by valorising this 'tradition républicaine' (a radical move in itself, given the pride in the notion of a homosexual 'community'/identity), Yonnet claims that

---

[60] Pisier, 'PaCS et parité: du même et de l'autre', p. 18.
[61] Pisier, 'PaCS et parité: du même et de l'autre', p. 18.
[62] Trigano, 'Les droits de l'(autre) homme', p. 16.
[63] Paul Yonnet, 'PaCS: un mariage républicain', *Le Débat*, 112 (2000): 106.

Universalism in the Republic

the writers sought to identify with the republic first as individuals and, in so doing, were able to appropriate for their own 'communal' benefit, what he goes on to call 'le mécanisme spécifique dont la Révolution française a offert une variante radicale et volontariste.'[64] In other words, the PaCS strategists embraced the republican model on the basis that a Republic recognises, integrates and emancipates, within the French nation, *individuals* ('des personnes individuellement citoyennes') and not groups, communities, or nationalities. Yonnet views the strategy to position homosexuals within a integrative French republic '*de nature individualiste*' as being crucial to the justification and approval of the PaCS legislation. In describing the PaCS law as 'une révolution', Yonnet situates it within a republican tradition that is essentially 'anticommunautaire', but crucially he goes on to suggest that the legislation will then operate like 'une *matrice révolutionnaire* dont l'oeuf fécondé réside dans l'équivalence posée entre hétérosexualité et homosexualité.'[65]

Yonnet puts faith in the democratic/subversive force of the legislation to chart a revolutionary path *from within* the republic. It is an interpretation that is significant on two fronts. Firstly, it recognises the potential impact of the legislation to address the divisive issue of 'la différence des sexes', and prepare the ground for an equivalence between heterosexuality and homosexuality. Secondly, it is founded on a realistic assessment of the parameters of universalism and of how the republic works. By contrast, Pisier's call for a root and branch reform of universalism's perceived heterosexism has its own validity, but seems to lack any realistic plan of implementation. Trigano's approach reflects current integrationist practice, with difference added as an appendage to universal equality. The reality to be confronted by all these approaches is that the legislations on the PaCS and concubinage have been passed. They have their respective pros and cons and they *will* change people's lives. Only time will tell if the seeming invariable that is universalism will change as well.

Conclusions

The PaCS debate has thrown into sharp focus the republican/democratic opposition at the heart of French socio-cultural discourse. The Catholic church and political right have been seen to have upheld and sought to preserve the traditional values of the republic, particularly in areas relating to the family, moral order and the uniqueness of civil marriage, all three predicated on what we have seen to be an increasingly controversial subscription to 'la différence des sexes.' The latter is one of the touchstones of the republican discourse on universalism because it privileges the two sexes as the legal and public binary of sexual life and relegates sexualities to the annexes of legal 'recognition' and privacy. While not overtly hostile to homosexuality, the Catholic church and the political right have expressed tolerance

---

[64] Yonnet, 'PaCS: un mariage républicain', p. 106.

[65] Yonnet, 'PaCS: un mariage républicain', p. 108.

42 *The Gay Republic*

of it within the confines of sexuality as a matter of private concern, but not an issue for public debate, let alone legal equivalence. The democratic opposition (in its political and intellectual expressions) has succeeded through concubinage and the PaCS in politicising sexual equality as an inalienable right of citizenship. In raising the consciousness of citizenship (sexually and individually) as a function of *les droits de l'homme*, democratisation has questioned some of the principles of the republic, in particular the universal veto on sexuality. However, the changes and freedoms that have ensued have also given rise to concerns (the limitations of the PaCS[66] for example) and ideological splits about how the new legislation addresses (or fails to address) the issue of equality. Homosexual groups claim that the legislation does not go far enough on equality, and that it represents nothing more than a republican ruse to appease advocates of sexual difference. Intellectuals, notably Pisier, Théry and Trigano, have sought to investigate universalism with varying degrees of success.

For the time being, universalism remains set in stone. Exclusionary it may be by definition,[67] but the reality for lesbian and gay couples, who are the primary target of the PaCS legislation, is that they must live with it in the most fulfilling way possible. As we have seen, they have options. The integrative option gives legal recognition, with social and fiscal benefits. The radical option holds out for more substantial change and full equality. The abstract option theorises equality on the grounds of asexuality. All three compete to win the hearts and minds of citizens. Currently, the integrative option (even in the light of the PaCS) prevails. How long this will last is open to conjecture. Anne F. Garréta has suggested that the PaCS (while securing modest personal gains for lesbians and gays) has not really achieved very much in terms of altering the principle of universalism. With gay marriage, gay adoption and access to family rights all highly controversial and ongoing debates, 'the French "PaCS" appears as what, despite all its pretences at enlightened modernity, it harks back to: a good old-fashioned edict of toleration [...]. Like any edict of toleration, it can't bear to name, distinguish, or acknowledge what it tolerates.'[68] Whether integration or civil toleration, I would venture an optimistic note to her pessimism, in the words of Paul Yonnet. We recall that Yonnet approved the way in which the PaCS set about integrating lesbians and gays as individuals into the republic, allowing them subsequently to avail of 'le mécanisme spécifique dont la Révolution française a offert une variante radicale et volontariste.' Like a revolutionary cell (*'matrice révolutionnaire'*) working from within, the PaCS represents a challenge to the republic, the future make-up of which remains undetermined. Furthermore, the title of Yonnet's article

---

[66] It is worth mentioning that the PaCS can only cope with one-to-one relationships, while many people who have responded to social changes after the 1960s live in looser clusters – or even alternative 'families' – than a couple-based law allows.

[67] Naomi Schor raises the idea of the exclusionary dimension to universalism, particularly in relation to women, in her article 'The Crisis of French Universalism', pp. 42-64.

[68] Garréta, 'Re-enchanting the Republic: "PaCS", *Parité* and *Le Symbolique*', pp. 165-66.

'PaCS: un mariage républicain' is deliberately ambiguous. That the PaCS is equivalent to republican civil marriage is clearly not the case (at least not yet). However, what the PaCS does represent for Yonnet is a marriage *with* the republic. As such, the prospects for future development of this legislation are not only fruitful but significantly increased by virtue of being *legally* bethrothed.

Chapter 2

'La Différence des sexes': Difference or Distinction?

Continuing the theme of pre-requisites to republican citizenship in the context of sexuality, universalism raises the highly contentious issue of 'la différence des sexes.' Defined as essential biological difference on which procreation, humanity and society resides, 'la différence des sexes' carries a weight of historical and deterministic significance into the sexual debate, particularly in relation to lesbian and gay issues, and most critically in the areas of marriage, parenting, filiation and adoption. This chapter approaches 'la différence des sexes' from several perspectives. I research the historical representation of sexual difference from Renaissance (holistic and physiological) traditions, in which the 'sexual' dimension to difference was classified more in terms of *distinctions* of temperament and physiology between the 'sexes', to post-enlightenment Foucauldian theory which differentiated between the sexes in terms of specifying individuals in relation to sexual 'identities.' I proceed to analyse how the process of differentiation is naturalised and acculturated as norm and as symbolic order.

However, the PaCS legislation and the debates around it have also thrown into question the assumptions and pre-determinism of biological difference as the sole measure by which sex is defined. Opponents of the PaCS, mainly political, religious and some academic commentators, have been seen to appropriate scientific expertise and anthropological argument to reinforce their positions. In opposition to the anthropological, essentialist and symbolic codes that reify 'la différence des sexes', I examine the social, cultural and constructionist positions which question the borrowing from 'science' for political consumption, the normalising effects of biological determinism, and the controversial ways that representations of 'la différence des sexes' appear to bypass cultural, political and democratic screening. In the final section of the chapter, I look to the varied implications of this territorial debate. There is the sex versus sexuality conflict, which itself invites myriad complications between 'la difference des sexes' and constructions of *sexuality*, (particularly homo*sexuality*). There is also the politicisation of this difference by essentialists and constructionists but for different effect. There is the use of the political to reconfirm *a priori* absolutes, while there is the use of the political to negotiate *a posteriori* possibilities. Other 'queer' alternatives are also investigated. At the heart of all these debates is the centrality of the social space as a place where norms, whether inherited or realised, can be

46   *The Gay Republic*

transformed. And the implications of these debates for sexual citizenship are critical.

> Dieu crée d'abord Adam, soit l'homme indifférencié, prototype de l'espèce humaine. Puis, dans un deuxième temps, il extrait en quelque sorte de ce premier Adam un être différent. Voici face à face Adam et Eve, prototypes des deux sexes. Dans cette curieuse opération, Adam a changé d'identité, puisque d'indifférencié qu'il était il est devenu mâle, d'autre part il est apparu un être qui est à la fois membre de l'espèce humaine et différent du représentant majeur de cette espèce. Tout l'ensemble, Adam, ou dans notre langue l'homme, est deux choses à la fois; le représentant de l'espèce humaine et le prototype des individus mâles de cette espèce. A un premier niveau hommes et femmes sont identiques, à un second niveau la femme est l'opposé ou le contraire de l'homme. Ces deux relations prises ensembles caractérisent la relation hiérarchique, qui ne peut être mieux symbolisé que par l'englobement de la future Eve dans le corps du premier Adam. Cette relation hiérarchique est généralement celle entre un tout (ou un ensemble) et un élément de ce tout (ou de cet ensemble): l'élément fait partie de l'ensemble, lui est en ce sens consubstantiel ou identique, et en même temps s'en distingue ou s'oppose à lui. C'est ce que je désigne par l'expression: "englobement du contraire."[1]

This quotation from Louis Dumont could be read on several levels. It could be interpreted as confirmation that masculine superiority over women has its origins in the very story of the creation of the human species. On another and more contemporary level, it could be read as the beginning and the end of the principle of French universalism; Adam was created 'indifférencié', a protopype of the human species, without sex and without a sexual identity. With the creation of woman, he became a representative of the male species, and both identical (woman created from him) and opposite to woman. As with universalism, created by men, simultaneously representing all humankind but specifically excluding difference, categorisation and women (symbolically), its governing principle is the undifferenciated nature of all its citizens, equal all in kind regardless of difference. The singular built-in inequality in this story of creation is the hierarchical nature of this representation, with Adam symbolising the 'englobement' of Eve. Irène Théry, who has discussed Dumont's interpretation of the story of creation, asks us not to be misled into reading too much into the male superiority thesis. Rather, as she claims, 'il ne dit rien de la façon dont, au sein d'une société donnée, la distinction des sexes se trouve *concrètement* hiérarchisée. Elle ne l'est en effet qu'*indirectement*, dans la mesure où les statuts associés à l'un et l'autre sexe sont eux-mêmes hiérarchisés en valeur.'[2]

The paradox, which she refers to in the title of her article (and which is at the centre of this chapter), is the relationship between nature and culture and the opposing sets of beliefs that cluster around each of these notions in the determination of the meaning of 'la différence des sexes.' Théry encapsulates this

---

[1]   Louis Dumont, *Homo hierarchicus* (Paris: Gallimard, coll. "Tel", 1979), p. 397.

[2]   Irène Théry, 'La côte d'Adam: retour sur le paradoxe démocratique', *Esprit*, 3-4 (2001): 16.

'La Différence des sexes': Difference or Distinction? 47

paradox in her interpretation of the Dumont story of creation, by highlighting the concept of 'la différence des sexes' as having a natural origin in the creation of male and female, and a cultural/social value attributed to each by social reality. What is interesting, however, in respect of this paradox, is the way Théry appears to confirm the natural signification (the natural/physical difference between male and female is incontrovertible, '*concrètement* hiérarchisé'[3]), and devalue the cultural signification, suggesting that social constructionist notions of difference[4] and positions of hierarchy between the sexes are not only applied arbitrarily but modifiable. Théry's interpretation serves to highlight the essentialist and constructionist positions in the debate on 'la différence des sexes.' It also prepares the ground for the nature of this debate, the centre ground of which will be heavily contested.

In the parity and PaCS legislations, the notion of 'la différence des sexes' has been central to the political debate. By confirming the duality of the human species (a notion acknowledged under republican universalism but unspecified, and for women a harbinger of multiple forms of discrete discrimination), *paritaires* announced a new era of equality where la 'différence des sexes' (from their perspective an exclusionary formulation that privileged male universalism) became 'la différence *entre* les sexes', and as a consequence of which the paradigm of universalism changed: 'On remet l'universel sur ses *deux* pieds.'[5] On the one hand, the concept of 'la différence des sexes' was seen as a triumph for women in both political and constitutional terms. On the other hand, the fallout from the parity debate produced a backlash, with *paritaires* being criticised for exploiting 'la différence des sexes' for personal reasons and at the expense of other marginalised groups.[6] They were accused of betraying the universality of the republic and making the universal 'sexué' (which goes against the anti-communitarian ethos).[7] They were accused of personalising political debate and deflecting attention away from the real value of the debate itself.[8] Furthermore, they were criticised for making women a category, and for serving a self-centred political agenda that sought to rid universalism of its masculine domination.[9] In the context of the PaCS debate, 'la différence des sexes' has been particularly divisive, splitting right and

---

[3] This natural difference between the sexes (an anatomical male/female difference without the political baggage of arguments of superiority, inferiority or heterosexism) is vital to the theory of 'la différence des sexes' espoused by Théry, Agacinski and certain *paritaires*.

[4] Constructionist approaches to concepts of identity (largely an American import) focus on the ways in which sexual identity is produced socially and culturally as gender, in opposition to fixed forms of natural, biological difference.

[5] Evelyne Pisier, 'Sexes et Sexualités: bonnes et mauvaises différences', p. 161.

[6] Eric Fassin and Michel Fehr, 'Parité et PaCS: anatomie politique d'un rapport' in Eric Fassin and Daniel Borrillo (eds), *Au-delà du PaCS. L'entreprise familiale à l'épreuve de l'homosexualité* (Paris: PUF, 1999), pp. 13-44.

[7] Hugues Jallon and Pierre Mounier, *Les Enragés de la république*, pp. 115-22.

[8] Elisabeth Roudinesco, 'Une parité régressive', *Le Monde*, 11 février 1999, p. 12.

[9] Pisier, 'Sexes et sexualités: bonnes et mauvaises différences', pp. 156-75.

48 *The Gay Republic*

left, church and state, republicans and democrats, traditionalists and libertarians. 'La différence des sexes' has become the dividing line between inclusion and exclusion, between the norms of marriage, parentage, filiation, and heterosexuality, and the political and social consequences of sexual difference.

In short, 'la différence des sexes' has become a reference point for different socio-political positions. This chapter will focus on three of these positions. Firstly, 'la différence des sexes' has became synonomous with a symbolic order of alterity that structures the future of the species (the essentialist position). It is a position founded on biological difference and on the concept of 'finitude' (the idea that in both sexes the sexual function is defined solely in respect of procreation[10]). In contrast, there is a body of opinion that claims that 'la différence des sexes' is not founded on biological difference but on socio-cultural distinction,[11] in other words that distinctions between the sexes are produced and instituted by social and cultural structures that determine sexual identity. As such, 'la différence des sexes', conceptualised in terms of gender, becomes a more fluid and culturally inflected concept than straight biological difference. Often referred to as 'sexe social', this constructionist position posits a space where sexual identities coexist *in distinction* from each other, but distant from the exclusionary binarism of difference. Cécile Barraud, who has elaborated on this opposition, also points to a third position to be discussed in this chapter. Barraud focuses on the difference between gender constructions in 'sexe social', an interactive space where the potential for identity overlapping is significant. While Barraud's central thesis is to show how culturally and socially constructed inequalities between the sexes become legitimised as 'natural' in western societies, the tone and suggestion of her argument approximate in part the ideas of current queer theory. Both look beyond the biological interpretation of 'la différence des sexes' to a post-identity construction of sexuality (in Barraud's case more a relational construction), free of the unitary and exclusive assumptions of identity politics. In short, this third position seeks to locate a space for a discussion of sexuality beyond the essentialist divide, and somewhere between constructionism and queerness.

'La Différence des sexes': From the Physiological to the Sexual

The term 'la différence des sexes' became familiar to many French feminists in the 1970s under the abridged form of 'la Différence', the latter term more appropriate to the wider concerns of feminists in the militant struggle for equality and freedom from oppression. Indeed, the addition of 'des sexes' seemed wholly unsatisfactory

---

[10] Irène Théry defines 'la différence des sexes' as 'reconnaître la finitude de chaque sexe qui a besoin de l'autre pour que l'humanité vive et se reproduise' in 'Homosexualité, mariage et famille', *Le Monde*, 5 novembre 1997, p. 21.

[11] Cécile Barraud highlights the opposition between 'distinction' and 'différence' in her article 'La distinction de sexe dans les sociétés; un point de vue relationnel', *Esprit*, 3-4 (2001): 105-29.

to many feminists because in their view there did not seem to be any clear dichotomy of the human species along biological lines. In fact, as Liliane Kandel points out, any such biological assumptions were contradicted by social reality and anthropology: 'Les chercheurs féministes [...] s'attacheront à montrer à leur tour que les notions de "sexe" et de "différence des sexes" sont, pour les scientifiques eux-mêmes, floues, imprécises, confuses – souvent contradictories.'[12] If this was the consensus among feminists for whom the concept of 'Différence' had greater significance in the 1970s, then what is the origin of the term 'la différence des sexes'? Sylvie Steinberg has traced the idea of difference between the sexes back to the turning point of the Revolution. She argues that in the Renaissance period, differences between men and women were defined physiologically: womens' organs being represented as the 'organes retournés et rentrés de l'homme.'[13] On this, a whole 'grammaire' of 'apparences sexuées' was established based on differences of physiognomy, whereby men and women could be distinguished in terms of complexion, heat, and cold. A series of oppositions 'parfait/imparfait', 'chaud/froid', 'sec/humide', 'extérieur/intérieur' was deployed to differentiate the sexes. Within these oppositions there was no sexual dimension nor hierarchical distinction. Rather, the sexes were perceived in terms of complementarity.[14] Steinberg goes on to suggest that a rupture occurred at the end of the eighteenth century with the sexualisation of the body by enlightment scholars:

> désormais, toutes les caractéristiques physiques et morales des hommes et des femmes découlent en droite ligne de leurs sexes, c'est-à-dire de leur conformation biologique et de leur rôle dans la reproduction [...]. Les savants des Lumières tirent deux conclusions. La première est que les comportements de "genre" (sexe social et culture) qu'ils identifient dérivent directement du sexe [...]. La seconde conclusion est que le corps féminin n'est formé que pour servir à la maternité.[15]

This absence of the sexualisation of the body prior to the enlightenment is mirrored in the holistic societies described by Irène Théry. She sets up a similar opposition to Steinberg in the binary of physical nature and 'esprit humain' which divided the pre-modern from the modern representation of the sexual body. Where Théry offers an alternative vision to Steinberg's is in her substitution of the modern period with the cosmology of a holistic society where 'la dynamique de la différenciation sexuée' is radically different. Whereas in Steinberg's representation of the modern period, where science and enlightenment have affected the gendered

---

[12] Liliane Kandel, 'Sur la différence des sexes, et celle des féminismes', *Les Temps modernes*, 609 (2000): 295.

[13] Sylvie Steinberg, 'L'inégalité entre les sexes et l'égalité entre les hommes: le tournant des Lumières', *Esprit*, 3-4 (2001): 28.

[14] 'L'homme et la femme sont donc dans un rapport de complémentarité hiérarchique et leurs caractéristiques morales et physiques sont accidentelles', (Steinberg, 'L'inégalité entre les sexes et l'égalité entre les hommes: le tournant des Lumières', p. 34).

[15] Steinberg, 'L'inégalité entre les sexes et l'égalité entre les hommes', p. 31.

50 *The Gay Republic*

body, the holistic society does not perceive of the body as distinct from the physical nature of the universe. As such

> les corps y sont moins "donnés" que "construits" en référence à l'univers chargé de significations et de sacré dont participent les humains [...]. Distinction éminemment sociale et culturelle, le genre est si fortement construit par les institutions de la vie sociale, si éminemment référé au sacré. Qu'il peut même dans certains cas transcender le sexe biologique.[16]

Théry uses the holistic society as a model for contemporary western civilisation. The holistic model confirms biological difference, but does not institutionalise 'directement un statut de femme ou d'homme.' The implication is that it is only via the mediation of institutions that differences or distinctions between the masculine and feminine are established. The holistic model, for Théry, demonstrates that 'la distinction des sexes' does not exist in itself, but 'comme une dimension consubstantielle à chacun des statuts qui assurent à la société sa cohésion de totalité, en assignant à chacun sa place comme une partie de ce tout.'[17]

Let us take breath from these representations and draw some conclusions. For Steinberg, enlightenment's sexualistaion of the body has been responsible for a radical rupture with the less divisive physiological model of 'la différence des sexes.' By contrast, Théry has sought to oppose western modernity (and its divisive 'différence') with a holistic modernity (and its distinctive 'genres'). Under the subtitle, 'Sexe et genre: le dualisme des modernes', she states that 'la différence des sexes' in the western modern model is a 'donné', in other words a difference that one assumes exists and has always existed. By contrast, the holistic model presents a distinction between the sexes that is socially and culturally constructed. Significantly, 'la distinction des sexes est différente de toutes les autres, au sens où elle "n'exprime aucun ordre *a priori*."'[18] The western model, on the other hand, is represented as imposing a binarism of biological difference that appears to negate any interaction of the two sexes. The holistic model signifies a more accommodating distinction of the sexes, where both (in their separate and related forms) are intimately linked with their physical, social and cultural environments:

> Il n'existe rien dans la société qui ne soit référé au masculin et au féminin: rituels, statuts, fonctions, tâches, espaces, objets, gestes, vêtements ou parures, chargés de signification, valorisent dans la distinction de sexe la valeur accordée à ce qui lie en distinguant. Séparés mais liés, on comprend que le masculin et le féminin puissent alors aussi s'échanger, comme dans les rituels d'inversion qui subvertissent l'ordre du monde comme pour mieux en affirmer la valeur.[19]

---

[16] Irène Théry, 'La côte d'Adam', p. 16.
[17] Théry, 'La côte d'Adam', p. 17.
[18] Théry, 'La côte d'Adam', p. 17.
[19] Théry, 'La côte d'Adam', p. 17.

'La Différence des sexes': Difference or Distinction? 51

The representation of 'la différence des sexes' in modern societies is a heavily contested and highly sexualised debate between biological difference and constructionist distinction. The turning point of the enlightenment is, however, a crucial development. Pre-enlightenment models of 'la différence des sexes' did not divide the sexes; the latter were perceived as a continuum based on cosmological principles.[20] Biological knowledge of the genitalia was construed as organic, a necessity of nature from which derived the reproduction of the species. As such, the 'sexual' dimension of the body was restricted to procreative matters: 'Si la nature a divisé l'homme et la femme, c'est pour que l'un ait la vertu pour engendrer [...], l'autre, la puissance passive "pour faire la fonction de la cause matérielle."'[21] Any physical or moral characteristics to each sex remained the property of physiology and cosmology. However, sexual initiation of the body was accompanied by a series of interventions, both physical and spiritual. The Nature/Spirit axis proved critical in this development. Nature, as Steinberg points out, 'n'a pas le dessein de donner à l'un ou l'autre sexe la force ou la faiblesse, la hardiesse ou la timidité.'[22] While nature's logic was not to differentiate between the sexes, the spirit ('l'âme') was seen to give birth to a division of the species.[23] Male organs were deemed to be bigger than female organs, more prevalent, as well as 'destined' for reproduction. Physiological notions of temperament, virtue, passivity and activity assumed gradations of sexual and moral hierarchy. And such transformations in human thought were seen to be in response to the superior will of God. Enlightenment confirmed the differences between men and women,

---

[20] Steve Garlick highlights the relationship between constructions of sex and gender before and after the eighteenth century. The eighteenth century was a key period for the emergence of the modern gender regime. See in this respect Thomas Laqueur's work *Making Sex: Body and Gender from the Greeks to Freud* (Cambridge MA, Harvard University Press). Garlick states: 'Prior to the enlightenment, what we today call sex and gender, were explicitly bound together in a 'one-sex model' in which it was gender rather than sex that was primary or real. Since the eighteenth century, however, it is the stable, ahistorical sexed body, as posited by biology, that has been understood as the epistemic foundation for the social order. Laqueur claims that "sometime in the eighteenth century, sex, as we know it, was invented. The reasons for this invention are tied up with the decline of the traditional religious legitimation of gender differences and the need for a new, and scientific basis ('the two-sex model') to replace it" in 'What is a Man? Heterosexuality and the Technology of Masculinity', *Men and Masculinities*, 6 (2003): 163.

[21] Steinberg, 'L'inégalité entre les sexes et l'égalité entre les hommes', p. 32.

[22] Steinberg, 'L'inégalité entre les sexes et l'égalité entre les hommes', p. 34.

[23] Garlick has characterised this idea of spirituality or the soul in terms of confronting and rationalising human mortality, death being perceived up to the eighteenth century with greater 'familiarity', and 'acceptance.' Death becomes a means of restoring one's sense of sexual identity by rationalising death away and thereby regaining control of one's life. Garlick says: 'it is the death of the other that is feared more than the death of the self', p. 167.

52   *The Gay Republic*

promoting difference as an accidental consequence of nature to the status of a divinely influenced plan.

Enlightenment initiated a modern symbolic order of biological difference between the sexes. This symbolic order was a natural and sacred reference point; natural, because it rooted difference in the masculine/feminine dichotomy, sacred because this difference was approved ethically and spiritually by the church as the source and future of the human species. However, knowledge of a difference brought with it the dynamic of a power relationship between the sexes in which the roles and function of each sex became inscribed in cultural traditions. From the Foucauldian perspective, the deployment of sexuality in the eighteenth century became the means of *specifying* individuals. Sex made it possible to group together in artificial, anatomical units biological functions, conducts and sensations. In short, sex and sexuality became synonymous with identity.[24] Foucault, however, sought to problematise the power relations that were constructed as a result of these units by deconstructing the naturalisation of these artificial units. In this way, he was able to disrupt the power/knowledge matrix that solidified their 'truth.' In similar mode but different context, Marcela Iacub, who has exposed the artificiality of the procreative order in the context of contemporary lesbian and gay parenting, analyses how western societies are founded on the premise of filiation, which itself is constructed on an equivalence between 'compétences biologiques' and 'compétences parentales.'[25] This equivalence brings social status and legal control of offspring. What Iacub sets up in opposition is the new role for the biological in the social. This will be discussed in more detail later but it may be useful to sound a cautionary note at this point. There is little doubt that the symbolic order of 'la différence des sexes' (in its essentialist format) has a powerful role to play in human consciousness and the future of the species.[26] The question that arises is that of its function (prescriptive and dictatorial, or flexible and tolerant) in a pluralistic society where the constructionist argument is seen to be challenging the hegemony of 'la différence des sexes', and where *distinction* of sexes is undercutting *difference* of sexes.

Given the transformations in western societies today where homosexuality, lesbianism and transgendered identities are now acceptable and common lifestyles, there is still a highly respected academic elite who still subscribe to the essentialist position of 'la différence des sexes' and who claim that recent debates have

---

[24]   For Garlick, this was tantamount to the 'heterosexualisation of modern society' (p. 164).

[25]   Marcela Iacub, 'Homoparentalité et ordre procréative', in Eric Fassin and Daniel Borrillo (eds), *Au-delà du PaCS*, p. 203.

[26]   The necessity of biological difference for the future of the human species is a given. However, as we will see in the course of this chapter, critics qualify their acknoweledgement of this 'fait' in the light of political affiliation, sexual preference and developments in scientific and medical technology.

'La Différence des sexes': Difference or Distinction?

rekindled a support for its binary ideology.[27] The allusion to the parity debate, where 'la différence des sexes' was the pivotal issue in serving to promote equality for women, has fomented this essentialism, although the cost, as we have suggested earlier, may be a high one. The politicisation of 'la différence des sexes' has featured prominently in recent articles from *Esprit* and *Les Temps modernes*, picking up on a growing confusion over the interpretation of 'la différence des sexes.' We discussed in the previous chapter the conceptual framework in which Irène Théry and Sylviane Agacinski have formulated 'la différence des sexes.' For Théry, it is linked to the concept of the 'sexué' (the masculine and the feminine), while for Agacinski it is formulated in terms of different 'sujets de désir' and the necessary interdependence of the sexes. Both these essentialist arguments have been criticised for promoting an inherent heterosexism. Critics have stated that to invoke 'la différence des sexes' is tantamount to exclusion of lesbians and gays from the family and marriage.[28] Naomi Schor reinforces this invocation in her critique of Agacinski's endorsement of inequalities 'de fait et de condition.'[29]

In response, both Théry and Agacinski have been careful to dissociate 'la différence des sexes' from heterosexuality and heterosexism. For Théry, there is no sexual or prejudicial dimension to the symbolic order of 'la différence des sexes', which she claims is male/female biological difference and nothing more. Her argument is essentialist even in its language: 'des personnes qui n'assument pas leur finitude' suffer from 'régression biologique.' Indeed, she refutes Eric Fassin's critique of heterosexism by accusing him of assimilating 'la différence des sexes' with the male/female *couple*, and the couple *with* heterosexuality (which she claims suits the communitarian argument of opposition to heterosexuality). Evelyne Pisier appears not to contest the issue at the biological level *per se* (difference between the sexes is natural). What she disputes is the way the term is used by some groups to subjugate others. In particular, she links its abuse to those who privilege a dominant heterosexuality, with its strong moral, theological roots, and the discrimination suffered by homosexuals via inequalities between the two.[30] There are several key ideas at work in these exchanges. The first is the

---

[27] See Kandel, 'Sur la différence des sexes, et celle des féminismes', pp. 283-306, and Patrice Maniglier, 'L'humanisme interminable de Claude Lévi-Strauss', *Les Temps modernes*, 609 (2000): 216-41.

[28] Daniel Borrillo, Eric Fassin and Marcela Iacub, 'Au-delà du PaCS: pour l'égalité des sexualités', *Le Monde*, 16 février 1999, p. 17.

[29] Agacinski's concept of equality is one that is legally constituted but in which there are inconsistencies of treatment. Agacinski recognises this in respect of equality. Equality for Agacinski is equality of civil and political rights and does not mean that two people are equal by virtue of nature or as a condition of sex. For Agacinski, however, there exists the possibility of equality between the sexes outside the law. This argument for equality is a social utopia. It is an argument distinct from her essentialist position of biological difference between men and women.

[30] In this regard, see Pisier's articles 'Sexes et sexualités: bonnes et mauvaises différences', pp. 156-75, and 'PaCS et Parité: du même et de l'autre', p. 18.

54 *The Gay Republic*

continuation of the role of the symbolic 'différence des sexes' in the socio-political climate of France today. The second is the way in which the symbolic has been actualised from benign role (simple masculine/feminine difference) to live function, the aim of which is to promote difference (in the case of *paritaires*) and establish the norm of heterosexuality. The third dimension to this politicisation is the challenge mounted by communitarians, militants and critics who are opposed to a process in which they believe the symbolic, by dint of its very symbolism and sacredness, becomes legitimised as natural.[31] What is significant in these exchanges is the variable nature of the term 'la différence des sexes' and the political, sexual and cultural assumptions that are deduced from the use of it.

The protean nature of the term has garnered the support of feminists and historicists who, for similar reasons, see in its variability a challenge to the hegemony of its symbolism. In the 1970s, the term was described as 'une rupture radicale' and the 'fondement d'une révolution théorique.'[32] In her analysis of the period, Kandel highlights the views of key feminist thinkers, notably Françoise Collin:

> La différence des sexes n'est plus perçue comme relevant de l'immuable mais se voit saisie par l'histoire. Ainsi un champ nouveau est-il ouvert à la réflexion, un champ d'incertitudes et le cas échéant de conflits puisque ne sont livrées avec évidence que des incarnations historiques, locales, voire singulières de la différence des sexes, marquées par les conditions d'inégalité qui ont présidé à leur cristallisation.[33]

For Collin and the constructionist lobby, to couch the term of 'la différence des sexes' within a specifically historical context, and thus exposed to socio-political conflict, throws into sharp relief the essentialist interpretation of biological difference. The anomaly that we are presented with in this historical positioning is the recent parity debate where 'la différence des sexes' has been invoked by *paritaires* in its purely biological sense, flying in the face of decades of feminist struggle which was characterised not by selfish self-interest but by 'toutes les autres formes d'injustice, d'oppression, et d'exploitation.'[34] And yet, for selfish or altruistic reasons, Eric Fassin, one of the vociferous critics of the *paritaires*, has sought to re-engage feminists with their historical roots. In his conclusion to a synthesis of the different feminist reactions to the PaCS and parity debates,[35] he proposes an historical interpretation to 'la différence des sexes', which runs contrary to Agacinski's and Théry's definition of the term as the anthropological foundation of sexual culture. In his own way, Fassin aims to achieve two things.

---

[31] The passage of 'la différence des sexes' from natural to cultural legitimisation will be discussed in a later section of this chapter.

[32] Kandel, 'Sur la différence des sexes, et celles des féminismes', p. 298.

[33] Quoted by Kandel, 'Sur la différence des sexes, et celles des féminismes', p. 299.

[34] Kandel, 'Sur la différence des sexes, et celles des féminismes', p. 299.

[35] Eric Fassin and Michel Mehr, 'Parité et PaCS: anatomie politique d'un rapport', pp. 13-14.

First, he relocates the biological invariant of 'la différence des sexes' to what he calls a Bourdieu style of 'habitus', a lived-in context where the female condition experiences and expresses history and its oppressiveness: 'Dans cette logique théorique, la parité ne repose pas sur une donnée biologique universelle, mais sur une histoire partagée, individuelle autant que collective: la différence des sexes ne peut être pensée indépendamment d'une histoire, qui est celle des rapports de pouvoir entre hommes et femmes.'[36] The second aim, linked to the first, encourages *paritaires* in particular to think of parity 'pragmatiquement', in other words not as a biological or philosophical principle but as an arm against all forms of discrimination. For Fassin, with the dual forces of history and pragmatism 'on fait l'économie d'un "ordre symbolique" qui n'a que faire de la discrimination et de la domination, la différence masquant l'inégalité.'

Fassin's argument has much merit and appeals to grass roots feminists and supporters of the PaCS. It is also in tune with some of the founding mothers of parity.[37] But Fassin's agenda is far removed from any rehabilitation of feminism. Despite the valid perception that the PaCS and parity legislations share the common aim of a fairer representation of women, lesbians and gays within the universality of the republic, there remains a different and deeper common denominator shared and underpinned by both legislations, which is the inherent postulation of an anthropological foundation to 'la différence des sexes', with a pronounced heterosexual bias. However, by situating 'la différence des sexes' within what he would see as the flexible and negotiable parameters of history and pragmatism, Fassin deflects attention away from anthropological presumption.

The Anthropological Question: From Nature to Culture

As a science, anthropology reflects on the development of the human species from two privileged but often conflictual standpoints. On the one hand, it is bound to establish 'absolutes' on which to construct patterns of human behaviour. On the other hand, absolutism is often challenged by cultural traditions that hold in check the former's claim to authority and expertise. As such, anthropology is not an exact science, nor is it defined by any one dominant trend. Indeed, the dual nature of the science reminds us of the variability of the scientific approach and its conclusions. The reasons why anthropology features in this discussion of 'la différence des sexes' is twofold. Firstly, anthropology forms part of a wider debate about the role of science in politics, and particularly whether the expertise of science can provide new solutions to political problems, which could be characterised as problems with a human dimension. The second reason is the value that science, and particularly anthropology, can bring to an understanding of 'la différence des sexes.'

---

[36] Fassin and Mehr, 'Parité et PaCS: anatomie politique d'un rapport', p. 35.
[37] Eric Fassin and Michel Mehr invoke Françoise Gaspard (one of the main founders of parity) and Janine Mossuz-Lavau in support of their pragmatic approach to parity (pp. 35-6).

On the first issue, there is considerable disagreement. Eric Fassin has written extensively on this and his critique of what he calls 'l'illusion anthropologique' is founded on two ideas. He claims that anthropology privileges an essentialist interpretation of 'la différence des sexes', and that anthropology, despite its claims to scientific expertise and the primacy of 'la définition universaliste',[38] is itself subject to historicity. In the different context of family politics (although not entirely unrelated given the preconditions of certain norms of filiation assumed by an essentialist position on 'la différence des sexes'), the American sociologist Joan Wallach Sccott reinforces Fassin's claim that human relationships (in the context of childbearing and childrearing for gay parenting) are 'the product of history – the result of highly contested social policy decisions – not a requirement of nature or of its alter ego in the current debate on the "the symbolic."'[39] The historicist argument, therefore, is that natural, biological (and anthropological interpretations of 'la différence des sexes' that support this essentialist position) are underwritten by history and are thus subject to re-interpretation.

Historicism, however, does not have it its own way in terms of what role science can play in political debate. While many sociologists with a strong historicist inflection (in particular Fassin) will undermine dogmatic anthropology because it avoids democratic debate,[40] others have a less prescriptive approach and are willing to concede a role for anthropology and the symbolic in politics. One of the main proponents of this latter idea is Patrice Maniglier. In a debate that has engaged a number of leading academic luminaries,[41] Maniglier, while very aware of the risks of parachuting in anthropology as a panacea for political controversy, reserves the right to ask the question whether the symbolic (by which he means anthropology's preservation of biological difference) can be improved on to offer new possibilities to political debate. By retaining the premise of the symbolic, he proceeds to open up two pathways by which the symbolic can effect socio-political structures. The first is the normative but controversial pathway by which biological difference is coded (or made sacred, in psychoanalytical debate); in other words, how it is integrated in a symbolic system (the family structure for example) and becomes a cultural product. The alternative route is to follow the first pathway as far as the coded stage of its trajectory, but then attach other coded *symbolics* to the previous, which in turn form not one symbolic system but a plural system that is subsequently culturalised. An example of this alternative route is the function of 'la différence des sexes' in a family with gay parents. Maniglier states:

---

[38] Fassin, 'Usages de la science et science des usages', p. 401.

[39] Joan Wallach Scott, 'Feminist Family Politics', *French Politics, Culture and Society*, 17 (1999): 27.

[40] Fassin, 'La voix de l'expertise et les silences de la science dans le débat démocratique', *Au-delà du PaCS*, pp. 89-110, and see his article 'Usages de la science et science des usages.'

[41] The debate about the role of science in politics has engaged Michel Tort, Patrice Maniglier, Liliane Kandel, Eric Fassin, Françoise Héritier and Maurice Godelier.

'La Différence des sexes': Difference or Distinction? 57

> on ne voit pas pourquoi on ne pourrait plus signifier l'acte reproducteur alors même que les deux parents sont de même sexe, ce couple, ou même un groupe tout entier, pouvant très bien donner un sens affectif extrêmement fort à la naissance d'un enfant. Et l'anthropologie se trouverait confrontée au fait que la parenté ne constituerait plus comme tel un système de signes; les événements biologiques seraient donc interpretés, mais relativement à d'autres systèmes symboliques mettant en jeu d'autres instances, tout aussi composées d'oppositions distinctives et constituant également des systèmes.[42]

The thrust of Maniglier's argument is that the symbolic still has a role to play in political debate, but that it cannot be a dictatorial role. In other words, he proposes a coexistence of symbolisms, the plural character of which acts as a cohesive system rather than a divisive one.

Several points emerge from Maniglier's proposals. His interpretation of 'la différence des sexes' approximates the theory of distinction rather than difference. While his aim is to make anthropology serve politics in order to find *universals* for improving humanity and political exchange, he recognises the impossibility of this task given his acknowledgement that the idea of 'la différence des sexes' (as flexible a notion as he has tried to make it) is not a static and fixed idea but a process that is always in the making. For Maniglier, 'la différence des sexes' is always present in its biological dimension but it is also always in deferral because of the absence of concrete representation. This real/ethereal characterisation leaves the concept of 'la différence des sexes' open-ended, in fact in danger of being abused by both essentialists and constructionists. Nevertheless, and most interestingly, Maniglier's theory that the principle of the symbolic has a theoretical validity feeds into other debates on the subject. Liliane Kandel has criticised the biological dichotomy of 'la différence de sexes' because she sees it as being contradicted by social realities. However, the recent politicisation of the issue has led her to ask a question about whether for example the parity debate represents a new departure in the debate of 'la différence des sexes.'[43]

Support for Maniglier's systemic approach and less dogmatic interpretation of anthropology comes from Eric Fassin. Up to now we have seen the historical dimension to Fassin's interpretation of parity and 'la différence des sexes.' In fact, Fassin is a sociologist which, on the one hand, confirms his historical contextualisation of these isiuses, but his academic discipline also reflects wider concerns about the role of science in political policy-making, in particular the

---

[42] Maniglier, 'L'humanisme interminable de Claude Lévi-Strauss', pp. 226-27.

[43] The implication throughout this chapter has been that the parity debate has not advanced the issue of 'la différence des sexes', but rather represents a regressive step in its adherence to biologism. Kandel seems to suggest at the end of her article that the parity debate and its exclusive focus on biological difference is far removed from the philosophical import of historical feminism: 'Il est certain que le "différend" de F. Collin, le philosophème "différence des sexes" de G. Fraisse, la "valence différentielle des sexes" de F. Héritier n'ont que de très lointains rapports avec la "différence des sexes" brandie, telle la Bible de Christine Boutin, par les adversaires du PaCS – ou même par le plus ordinaire des machos', in 'Sur la différence des sexes et celle des féminismes', p. 301.

The Gay Republic

battle for hegemony within the social sciences on an issue such as 'la différence des sexes', and in particular the tension that exists between Fassin's sociology and the binary anthropology of Françoise Héritier. The crux of Fassin's analysis of 'la différence des sexes' is democracy; democracy situates debate in a context of deliberation, equality and the avoidance of discrimination. In short, Fassin believes in democracy at both the socio-political level and the individual level. Indeed, the greater the harmony between the two the better. What he refutes are forms of resistance to change, in particular the reification of symbolic notions (such as 'la différence des sexes') that become legitimised, not through any democratic process, but via a process of codage, symbolic naturalisation, scientific 'expertise' and an infantry of ethics, morality and religion. To this degree, he contests the mythical status that anthropology has acquired in society:

> C'est en ce sens qu'on peut parler d'une transcendance anthropologique: de même que la religion pouvait jadis se placer au-delà du politique, de même aujourd'hui, dans une société "démocratique et laïque", certains voudraient poser l'anthropologie en deçà du politique. La différence des sexes aurait ainsi un fondement, non pas suprapolitique, mais infrapolitique – non pas théologique, mais anthropologique.[44]

Specifically, Fassin disputes the way in which certain anthropologists (and politicians who then invoke certain anthropological concepts) oppose 'homoparentalité' and gay couples who wish to adopt children, on the basis of an essentialist position on 'la différence des sexes' and who insist on the importance of keeping the line of filiation 'straight.'[45] Fassin argues that the use of anthropology in this way is an abuse of science because it is used as a means to avoid democratic discussion. He is particularly scathing of what he sees as the hypocrisy of Irène Théry (sociologist) and Pierre Legendre (anthropologist) who, duplicitously for Fassin, defend the recognition of homosexuality but also promote an exclusivity in their underwriting of a symbolic order and a biological definition of 'la différence des sexes.' Fassin goes on to deconstruct the pretensions he sees within anthropology. He highlights society's fixation with 'le savoir *a priori*', which appears to carry with it the benefit of knowledge of the past. He exposes what he sees as its pretensions to impose structures and norms on society and politics, and fix universal limits (in turn legitimised) to what is possible and what is

---

[44] Fassin, 'La voix de l'expertise et les silences de la science dans le débat démocratique', *Au-delà du PaCS*, p. 96.

[45] See in this context Cyrille Duvert's article 'Le droit jetable: A propos des débats sur l'homoparentalité', *Le Débat*, 131 (2004): 179-92. The thrust of Duvert's argument is that if the law does not permit marriage or adoption for lesbian and gay couples on the basis of natural law (essentialism or biologism), then it makes sense to advance the argument from a different *political* level. Duvert suggests that there needs to be a new balance between the symbolic argument that opposes legislation and the 'artificialiste' argument that supports it, while at the same time underlining the fact that the law should not be used as a tool of social engineering. In short, Duvert claims that the symbolic can be altered, not brutally but gently.

'La Différence des sexes': Difference or Distinction?   59

impossible, to what is thinkable and unthinkable. In his celebrated article 'Usages de la science et science des usages', Fassin claims that when scientific 'expertise' becomes confused with nature and culture and then replaces democratic argument, it represents an abuse of science. He targets specifically the use of axiomatic definitions (for example the notion that 'la différence des sexes' is the singular universal of sexuality) that are appropriated by the political élite and deployed in arguments that militate against careful and expert reflection. He is most critical of one of the standard bearers of this dogmatic anthropology, Françoise Héritier, who also had a significant role to play in parliamentary debates on the PaCS.[46] For Héritier, 'la différence des sexes' (in its most essentialist form) is at the heart of all thought. For her, biological difference between the sexes forms, informs and impacts on all aspects of human existence.[47] Quoting Héritier, Fassin writes:

> Penser, c'est d'abord classer, classer, c'est d'abord discriminer. Et la discrimination fondamentale est basée sur la différence des sexes. C'est un fait irréductible: on ne peut pas décréter que ces différences-là n'existent pas, ce sont des butoirs indépassables de la pensée, comme l'opposition du jour et de la nuit [...]. Nos modes de pensée et notre organisation sociale sont donc fondés sur l'observation principale de la différence des sexes. Et l'on ne peut pas raisonnablement soutenir que cette différence se déplace au coeur du couple homosexuel.[48]

Fassin dismisses this universalist tendency in anthropology (and by extension Héritier). He dismisses its pretension to normativity and exposes the role of science as being a servant to rules. The crux of Fassin's article, however, is to make a vital distinction between strands within anthropology that verge towards setting universalist definitions and the social, historical 'caractères' who (dis)embody these definitions. In other words, Fassin disapproves of the abuses of science in determining pre-requisites and universals. But for Fassin, the real problem is not with the definitions or classifications *per se*, or the universalisation of certain 'givens', such as 'la différence des sexes', 'parenté' or marriage. Fassin admits that axiomatic dogmatism is a dangerous notion in the migration of science to politics, but he remains convinced that it is the field of reception of the axiom that makes

---

[46] Françoise Héritier is a perfect example for Fassin of the dangers of importing scientific knowledge into politics. As Professor of Anthropology at the Collège de France, she was invited to the national Assembly during the PaCS deliberations to provide her 'expert' scientific advice on gay parenting. Her forthright views against this development and her essentialist interpretation of 'la différence des sexes' were perceived as widely respected scientific responses that contributed to the discussion of the PaCS legislation. For Fassin, the Assembly's supplication of Héritier was an example of politicians' absurd and discriminatory reverence for scientific dogmatism which only serves to undermine democracy.

[47] Compare this interpretation of biological *difference* that underpins western thought with Théry's interpretation of *distinction* that underpins cultural production in holistic societies.

[48] Fassin, 'La voix de l'expertise et les silences de la science dans le débat démocratique', *Au-delà du PaCS*, p. 106.

60   *The Gay Republic*

the crucial difference. What is fundamentally subversive for Fassin, in this context, is how the axioms react within the infinitely variable space of the social, in what Fassin calls 'la place des acteurs', 'des pratiques', 'le monde social', 'la grammaire des usages sociaux.' In short, Fassin sees the place of the social as the place where the true legitimacy of science is ultimately contested.

The question we might ask here is whether Fassin himself is being too dogmatic in rejecting any form of symbolic order? Why is Maniglier's proposal of a coexistence of symbolisms so unappealing to Fassin? I think Fassin's ideas, despite his rigorous opposition to dogmatic anthropology, may approximate Maniglier's position within an empirically based anthropology, and perhaps within the perspective of sociology. The first point to make here is that Fassin does acknowledge the symbolic order of heterosexuality. It is a given which he concedes to anthropology, albeit with an element of irony: 'A l'anthropologie, il s'agit en réalité de faire dire, simplement, mais avec autorité, qu'il y a des hommes et des femmes – l'ordre de l'hétérosexualité reposant sur l'ordre de la différence des sexes.'[49] In his contrast of Françoise Héritier's dogmatic and normative anthropology and the rationalism of that of Claude Lévi-Strauss, Fassin makes a case for a structural anthropology built on the interaction between cultural traditions, between what he calls 'la pensée savante' and 'la pensée sauvage.' The point that Fassin is keen to make in respect of this cultural anthropology is that, in the context of filiation (and equally applicable to 'la différence des sexes'), the history of civilisation is such that there is nothing new to know about sexuality and sexual difference.[50] Fassin's version of a comparative/cultural anthropology reinstates relative 'norms' as opposed to universally dogmatic ones.[51]

It is in this light that Fassin's role for sociology as benefactor to democratic politics may have some validity. In the current debates on parity and the PaCS,

---

[49] Fassin, 'La voix de l'expertise et les silences de la science dans le débat démocratique', p. 96.

[50] The allusion here may be to sexual practices (homosexual parenting) in the African continent and Antiquity where, for example, pedagogic pederasty was elevated to an institution. For more on these issues see respectively Anne Cadoret's article 'La filiation des anthropologues face à l'homoparentalité' in Eric Fassin and Daniel Borrillo (eds), *Au-delà du PaCS*, pp. 209-28 (particularly her synopsis of anthropological studies carried out on tribes in Africa and Burkina Faso), and Morris B. Kaplan's chapter 'Historicizing Sexuality: Forms of Desire and Construction of Identities' in *Sexual Justice. Democratic Citizenship and the Politics of Desire* (New York: Routledge, 1999), pp. 47-8 (the sections on Greek love and the hermeneutics of sexuality).

[51] Cécile Barraud explores a similar thesis. She claims that social anthropology is weighed down by 'un présupposé d'inégalité' which obliges it to interpret 'la différence des sexes' in terms of male domination which is linked to western ideology. She balances this out with reference to cultural relativism which allows her to posit her own alternative: 'une anthropologie comparative cherchant à comprendre la dimension sociale de l'homme en considérant la variante occidentale comme un cas particulier' in 'La distinction de sexe dans les sociétés: un point de vue relationnel', pp. 115-16.

'La Différence des sexes': Difference or Distinction? 61

anthropology may carry more scientific clout than sociology (the evidence of the *a priori* argument seems to have it over the speculation of the *a posteriori* argument[52]), but for Fassin the latter is more in tune to democratic structures and is closer in time to the voice of citizenship. Also, sociology for Fassin reflects a holistic approach to the implications of 'la différence des sexes', contextualising any particularly western or biological determination within 'le fait *global* de la société'[53] [my italics]. Sociology, for Fassin, is not about the past nor about what precedes the present. Sociology is in harmony with the evolution of society: 'elle enregistre des transformations [...]. Elle revendique d'accompagner les mouvements des moeurs, non de les précéder.'[54] In short, sociology, for Fassin, is more representative of distinctive and socially constituted sexual identities than the claims made by anthropology.

The role of science (and specifically anthropology) in politics remains disputed along three lines: biological determinism, the validity of this determinism in democratic politics, and the alternative pragmatic historicism offered by the social sciences (and particularly sociology). All three bring with them an element of controversy, but the second of these has provoked much discussion in academic journals. The issue with the validity of the role of biological determinism in politics has to do with its function. The nature of this function has been characterised as the passage from nature to culture, in other words the means by which society acculturates and legitimises biological determinism. Several factors are at work in this process. They cluster around the sequence of nature, culture and politics (specifically the law). The essentialist position seems straightforward; the natural male/female dichotomy is the foundation of life, and as such has an automatic cultural and legal acceptability. This process in turn establishes a (hetero)sexual norm. The questions that need to be asked here are the following: How does the idea of the sexual foundation of life acquire a cultural currency to the extent that politics and law make social models and laws from it? How arbitrary a process is this, and is the legitimisation of the process absolutely necessary?

Defenders of the process point to preservation of the species on which natural structures of the family, parenting and filiation are built. Cynics point to preservation with exclusion, others to innate heterosexism and self-preservation. Others have focused attention on the logic of the symbolic nature of 'la différence de sexes' and the weakness within the nature, culture, law sequence. Anne F.

---

[52] For Fassin, anthropology enjoys the benefit of bringing expertise from the past to current debates, while sociology appears blighted by commenting on realities 'qui sont encore invisibles.'

[53] Louis Dumont, *Essias sur l'individualisme* (Paris: Le Seuil, coll. "Esprit", 1983), pp. 11-12. Dumont's notion of considering societies as empirical 'touts' and not in abstract isolation, mirrors Fassin's democratic sociology.

[54] Fassin, 'La voix de l'expertise et les silences de la science dans le débat démocratique' p. 102.

62 *The Gay Republic*

Garréta's thesis has linked the 'différence des sexes' to a symbolic order, which she claims is sacred and thus 'off-limits' to democratic debate. The logic of the symbolic is therefore one inspired by force of will, religious sacredness and by a transcendental quality that is resistant to the body politic. She states: 'The normative power of democracy is incomplete: the political and legal orders cannot sustain themselves without grounding in a realm prior to them, an order – the Symbolic itself – that transcends the institution of laws achieved through political deliberation. The prepolitical conditions of the subject's construction precede and trump the determination of the citizen.'[55] Garréta's argument of the symbolic reveals an important aspect of the process whereby the natural (in a symbolic form) appears to bypass the stages of acculturation and politicisation, imposing its logic on society. It is an argument that is founded on two notions that defy resistance to it. The first is the idea that the natural precedes the political, and the second is that the sacredness of this natural is at the heart of the rational.

We can see from Garréta's thesis how the symbolic as norm can be enshrined as cultural and political artefact. It is not the only way that norms can be established. Closely linked to this invisible infiltration of the symbolic into the cultural arena, is the way in which the human body can be represented as a puppet of both nature and culture, and thus at the whim of either discourse. It is a theory put forward by Maurice Godelier in which the body is described as possessing a social and unconscious dimension. It is the latter, characterised in the form of a ventriloquist's doll, which can mimic the discourse of biological determinism or socio-sexual engineering. This game of representation has a serious and twofold purpose. Firstly, it highlights how the body, regardless of its sex or sexual identity, speaks a discourse that does not come from it but from those who pull its strings (nature or culture, or nature's naturalisation of culture). The powerlessness of the body to control itself shows the ease with which, for example, biological determinism can reproduce itself in the social sphere and gain cultural validity. Secondly, in Godelier's representation of the body, the latter is disinvested of any human or sexual reality. It becomes instead a vehicle for conflictual and competing discourses. Godelier's conclusions are significant. He claims that sexuality is itself a servant to social realities. It does not belong within the body but speaks in it and through it. Sexuality, he goes to suggest, is an imaginary, fantastic construct, a creation that is removed from bodily experience, in short a creation of society. He states:

> Bref, les sexes, les corps, fonctionnent partout et toujours comme des poupées ventriloques que l'on ne peut jamais faire taire et qui tiennent, à des interlocuteurs qu'elles ne voient pas [...]. Et c'est précisément dans la mesure où la sexualité doit servir à exprimer et à legitimer des réalités qui n'ont rien à voir avec elle qu'elle devient

---

[55] Garréta, 'Re-enchanting the Republic: "PaCS", *Parité* and *Le Symbolique*', pp. 162-63.

'La Différence des sexes': Difference or Distinction? 63

source de fantasme et d'univers imaginaire. Mais ce n'est pas la sexualité, ici, qui fanstame dans la société; c'est la société qui fantasme dans la sexualité.[56]

We can take two significant ideas from Godelier's theory. As with the logic of the symbolic and its unimpeded passage to acculturation, Godelier's theory of the body as a vessel that mimics unconsciously external discourse indicates how easy the passage can be for a naturalist discourse to dominate the social reality. The second idea is Godelier's implication of the death of the sexual body. We recall in an earlier section of this chapter how the sexualisation of the body by the enlightenment marked a radical change from the physiological neutrality of male/female in Renaissance times. Godelier appears to suggest that today the sexualisation of the body has been substituted by disembodied sexual discourses that compete with each other within the social sphere.

Garréta and Godelier demonstrate the ease with which nature is naturalised as culture, and subsequently normalised. However, outside the realms of the symbolic and the body as 'machine ventriloque', the process is decidedly more problematic. Within the sequence we alluded to above (nature, culture, law), the critical point at which normalisation occurs is stage two, the cultural stage; the latter either confirms the naturalisation of 'la différence des sexes' or it resists its naturalisation. In the context of the PaCS debate where 'la distinction des sexes' (as opposed to 'la différence des sexes' in the parity debate) characterises the social and sexual climate of our contemporary age, we can see instances of socio-cultural resistance to natural 'givens.' In the area of filiation (see later chapter on adoption and filiation), Marcela Iacub and Anne Cadoret debate the natural 'creator' versus cultural 'inventor' dualism around the issue of 'parenté', particularly in the light of homosexual couples wanting to adopt and form families.[57] Cadoret throws into question the symbolic order of 'la différence des sexes' by suggesting that sex can no longer be limited to a purely biological/coital/sexual essentialism because of new medical technologies and the growing intervention of artificial insemination and anonymous donors. Resistance to the natural also comes from sociological/social, anthropological and social constructionist quarters. Western ideology's fixation with biological difference (and its differences of male/female, superiority/inferiority) has been questioned by comparative studies of sexual practice.[58] Similarly, constructionists privilege a

---

[56] Maurice Godelier, 'La sexualité est toujours autre chose qu'elle-même', *Esprit*, 3-4 (2001): 101.

[57] See their respective chapters in Eric Fassin and Daniel Borrillo (eds), *Au-delà du PaCS*. In contrast to Cadoret's critique of the genealogical model of filiation, Catherine Labrusse-Riou highlights the dangers of medical technology in disrupting filial lineage in 'La filiation en mal d'institution', *Esprit*, 12 (1996): 91-110. See also my later chapters on adoption and filiation.

[58] See in particular Cécile Barraud's article 'La distinction de sexe dans les sociétés: un point de vue relationnel', and Marie-Elisabeth Handman's chapter 'Sexualité et famille: approche anthropologique' in *Au-delà du PaCS*. The latter's anthropological approach is

cultural construction of gender, in which all relations between individuals are fashioned by gender, over biology. For Barraud and Marie-Elisabeth Handman, the deconstruction of the natural by the social is a process of empowerment in which individuals are seen to activate their new identities. For Barraud, 'La notion de "sexe social" [...] se comprend par rapport aux sujets agissants (*social agents*), à leur identité, à leur perception des différences, en fonction des symboles et des significations que les divers systèmes culturels leur attribuent.'[59] As Barraud goes on to say, the concept of agent is central to the sociology of symbols and meanings in that it is the agent who invests sense and meaning to new symbols. In contrast to the passive status of the individual who inherits a biological difference which nature has given him (or the disembodied mouthpiece in Godelier's case), the social agent participates in the construction of the organisation of social, sexual and political life.[60]

Social agency counteracts the function of the symbolic by a process of modification and the institutionalisation of alternative symbols. But, as we have demonstrated in the course of this chapter, an idea such as the symbolic 'différence des sexes' (which can precede the political, transcend the social and political, and impose its logic on the social consciousness) does not disappear totally from view. The role and function of science in political discourse have contributed to the longevity of the symbolic, particularly when the expertise of scientific research is harnessed to the symbolic, as in the case of anthropology and biological essentialism. It is vital, therefore, that debates take place within science about its external applications, and that observers of scientific applications to social and political discourses highlight its many uses and misuses. We have identified anthropology as a science from which politicians have borrowed to reinforce their own political views on 'la différence des sexes.' A crisis over 'la différence des sexes' is also deepening within the field of psychoanalysis.

The Crisis in Psychoanalysis: From Symbolic Order to Symbolic Orders

In her article 'Malaise dans la psychanalyse', Caroline Eliacheff claims that psychoanalysis has been in crisis ever since the explosion in sexual mores with the advent of May 1968.[61] In particular, she highlights for discussion feminism and homosexuality. In the case of the former, she suggests that, until feminism came to

---

grounded in a comparative analysis of western models of 'sexe biologique' and non-western models (American Indian and Sudanese) of 'sexe social.'

[59] Barraud, 'La distinction de sexe dans les sociétés: un point de vue relationnel', p. 112. Handman also states: 'il importe peu que la nature vous ait fait homme ou femme; ce qui importe, c'est le rôle que vous êtes amené à jouer, que ce soit ou non l'expression de votre volonté', in 'Sexualité et famille; approche anthropologique', p. 252.

[60] See my discussion of Claude Lefort in Chapter 1 and his use of social space as the agency of legitimacy for sexual citizenship.

[61] Caroline Eliacheff, 'Malaise dans la psychanalyse', *Esprit*, 3-4 (2001): 62-76.

'La Différence des sexes': Difference or Distinction? 65

make its impact on the French theoretical consciousness, psychoanalysis was still largely defined within the phallocentrism of Freud. Notions of equality between the sexes, let alone the existence of a distinct female libido (outside the human libido which was of male origin according to Freud), were exterior to psychoanalysis. Similarly, in the case of homosexuality, which Freudian psychoanalysis had difficulty categorising within the Oedipus[62] (although Freud did not consider it deviant behaviour as his Letter to an American Mother will testify), homosexuality was seen to defy 'la différence des sexes' (the equivalent to parricide by Lacan in its symbolic destruction of the law of the Father). As a consequence, psychoanalysis at the end of the twentieth century has been confronted by two problems. The first is described succinctly by Eliacheff as a rethink of Freud's phallocentrism: 'La revendication de l'égalité entre les sexes (entre les hommes et les femmes) a entraîné une remise en question radicale du "phallocentrisme" de Freud.' The second is a rethink of the Lacanian symbolic : 'La revendication de l'égalité entre les sexualités (les hétérosexuels et les homosexuels) entraîne aujourd'hui une remise en question du "symbolique" lacanien.'[63] Both point to the way in which these 'revendications' have divided psychoanalysis into traditional and progressive camps.

At the heart of both divisions is how psychoanalysis addresses 'la différence des sexes.' The traditionalists (Tony Anatrella, Christian Flavigny, Jean-Pierre Winter) subscribe to the centrality of a naturalist, biological, Freudian definition of 'la différence des sexes' and link it to all forms of social engineering. The dominant value attributed to paternity in the Freudian system (which corresponds to male domination) 'vectorise donc l'histoire freudienne des rapports entre les sexes.'[64] Upon this biological link, traditionalists have constructed biological and cultural arguments against 'homoparentalité' based on the risks for children, on a child's need for a mother and a father and on the breakdown in 'la transmission de la vie' that can accompany unconventional families.[65] One of the leading firebrands of the traditionalist camp is priest and psychoanalyst Tony Anatrella. His condemnation of the PaCS is founded on a characterisation of contemporary society in which individuals are free to invent their own laws, what he calls the notion of 'chacun sa loi.' He claims that the symbolic 'différence des sexes' (as an objective norm) has been replaced by individualism, subjectivism and the irrational: 'Cette fin de siècle voit peu à peu l'individualisme régnant faire éclater

---

[62] And some current psychoanalytic thought has expressed reservations about the legal status of homosexual couples, particularly in respect of rearing children. See in more detail Eliacheff's article mentioned above, and Michel Tort's article, 'Quelques conséquences de la différence "psychanalytique" des sexes', *Les Temps modernes*, 609 (2000): 176-215.
[63] Eliacheff, 'Malaise dans la psychanalyse', p. 68.
[64] Tort, 'De la différence "psychanalytique" des sexes', p. 194.
[65] As we will see in subsequent chapters, there is a strong body of opinion that supports adoption by lesbian and gay couples and gay families, as well as a change in the law to legislate for this.

66   *The Gay Republic*

les distinctions nécessaries entre le psychologique et le social.'[66] Most pointedly, he has enraged many lesbians and gays and perhaps even his Freudian heritage by claiming that homosexuality 'reste le symptôme d'un problème psychique et d'un en-deçà de la différence des sexes.'[67]

There is a danger here in demonising traditionalists, and misrepresenting what to them are very real concerns, particularly the collapse of the traditional family and the threats posed by filial disarticulation. But, as we have seen, it is impossible not to evaluate these concerns within traditional and progressive contexts, and how these contexts are seen to produce values and norms. Opposition from traditionalists to socio-political progress has led not only to a reluctance to acknowledge and recognise legally social and sexual evolution, but this resistance is grounded in a historical reification of biological difference and the association of social and sexual norms to be derived from it. Biological difference, in effect, has been the spearhead of division between traditionalists and progressives in the field of psychoanalysis. The former's interpretation of Freud can be selective, omitting, as it does, the inherent pleasure principle (and its access to subjective erotic discovery), and the patriarchal control that biological essentialism exercises over women. Also, as we saw in the debate about science and politics, there are dangers with the normative approach to promoting socio-political harmony; the charges of exclusiveness and the creation of a false symbolism based on a fictional heritage are real and potentially discriminatory. Equally problematic, however, is the fear that appears to be rife within traditional psychoanalysis about confronting new realities that might undermine some of its cherished and established principles. Clearly, the crisis in traditional psychoanalysis is as much to do with the unknown as it is to do with freeing itself from the past. But the consequences of not moving forward are too severe to contemplate, with charges of regressiveness and loss of academic and intellectual standing very damaging.[68]

The progressive camp (Gérard Pommier, Sabine Prokhoris, Michel Tort and to a lesser degree Elisabeth Roudinesco) has picked up on this crisis within psychoanalysis by focusing on, what it sees as, the creation of the Freudian/Lacanian myths, the role of psychoanalysis in the political arena and on the heated debate about its prescriptive/normalising function. Sabine Prokhoris exposes the 'double mouvement' (of power and historicity) at the centre of the Lacanian theory of 'L'Ordre Symbolique (de la Différence des sexes)', a movement that she claims has been affected by a sideral and ambiguous use of capital letters which serve to confer an unwarranted authority on the symbolic and

---

[66] Tony Anatrella, 'A propos d'une folie', *Le Monde*, 26 juin 1999, p. 17.

[67] Anatrella, 'A propos d'une folie', p. 17.

[68] Caroline Eliacheff quotes the work of Rebecca Majster who has commented that psychoanalysis today exercises both an attraction and repulsion among diverse social groups.

'La Différence des sexes': Difference or Distinction? 67

thus on psychoanalysis.[69] Michel Tort exposes the founding myth of power relations established by Freud's 'la différence des sexes', harbinger, as we said earlier, of a host of inequalities between the sexes. As with Freud, Tort sees Lacan as having constructed a Symbolic Order from nature, and particularly the privileged status of the father. Building on Freud's paternal principle, and from a desire to resurrect the 'imago paternelle' which Lacan believed had suffered a 'névrose contemporaine', Lacan elevated the figure of the father (including its heavenly symbolism in the figure of the Lord and its *eternal* representation in the terrestrial symbolism of the phallus) to the status of an Order/'Loi du Père' ('Loi-de-la-différence-des-sexes'[70]) that underpinned all human experience. The problem with this construction for certain contemporary psychoanalysts was the concept of order to which it alluded. For Prokhoris, it was a fabricated order, founded on the 'pure artifice' of capitalisation which psychoanalysis had cultivated over time:

> l'appel à la psychanalyse a fonctionné essentiellement sous la forme du rappel à l'ordre, et rien moins qu'à l'ordre Symbolique. Avec une impressionante majuscule. Ont suivi, en cortège, d'autres majuscules: la Référence, à l'ordre de la différence des sexes, elle-même articlulée à la Loi (symbolique encore) de la Castration (symbolique toujours) du Phallus, Signifiant-Maître du désir.[71]

For Tort, it was a fictional order invented so as to present the symbolic as natural. If, as Prokhoris and Tort would have us believe, psychoanalysis had fallen prey to these symbolic orders, then it comes as no surprise that it is open to the charge of creating and justifying spurious norms and prescriptions.

In a scathing and now celebrated article appropriately entitled 'Homophobies psychanalytiques',[72] Michel Tort accused elements within the pyschoanalytic profession of bending to socio-political lobbying in the PaCS debate (in fact of siding with the ideas of the anti-PaCS advocate Tony Anatrella), of dereliction of duty in respect of maintaining objectivity with patients, and of reproducing unconsciously the Freudian/Lacanian vulgate which, he claims, had lead to narcissism and a corrupt form of social psychoanalysis. In short, he accuses the profession of the crime of homophobia (ironic given the fear and incomprehension of homosexuality in psychoanalysis[73]). However, where Tort is particularly critical

---

[69] Sabine Prokhoris, 'L'adoration des majuscules', in Eric Fassin and Daniel Borrillo (eds), *Au-delà du PaCS*, pp. 145-59.

[70] This is Michel Tort's unique formulation; the hyphens serve to convey the idea of linkage between 'la Loi du Père' and 'la différence des sexes' (p. 214). Sabine Prokhoris has a similar formulation ('la différencedessexes'); written as one word, she interprets the idea as symbolic of the unbreakable link between male and female. It should be borne in mind that both formulations form part of wider arguments in which the biological determinism of 'la différence des sexes' is undermined.

[71] Prokhoris, 'L'adoration des majuscules', pp. 151-52.

[72] Tort, 'Homophobies psychanalytiques', *Le Monde*, 15 octobre 1999, p. 18.

[73] Michel Tort claims that many psychoanalysts have been corrupted by Anatrella's very public role and statements in the PaCS debate. He claims that they have bought into

68   *The Gay Republic*

of his profession is in its predilection towards prescription. He derides a tendency that appears to measure social and human behaviour against normative constructions that are, for him, the inheritance of Freud and Lacan. As with the anthropological question and the ways in which its norms were invoked in socio-political debate, Tort is concerned that psychoanalysis (given its 'Symbolic' roots) is following a similar route, and thus promoting a culture of normalcy and exclusion. For Tort, whose progressive theories we will come to discuss shortly, psychoanalysis and normativity are incompatible. But in the light of this incompatibility, he remains optimistic of a way forward for psychoanalysis: 'Les véritables contributions psychanalytiques donnent toujours le sentiment que le sujet a été entendu, que la figure de la norme s'est transformée, assouplie [...]. Il s'agit de tenir à distance l'objet d'analyse et d'exorciser les sujets.'[74]

Tort's claim that psychoanalysis is incompatible with norms is a provocative statement. On the one hand, it situates him within a radical tendency that has rejected psychoanalytic conformism,[75] but on the other hand, it stokes the fires of mainstream traditionalists and, let us not forget, a sizeable number of patients for whom psychoanalysis is not simply a theoretical discipline but a practical one, and where norms can be key pointers to personal development. Several points emerge here. In defence of Tort, his concern for the patient is paramount. He wants to rehabilitate pyschoanalysis as both theory and practice. And, his concept of normativity is not as prescriptive as it may appear. In a clever example to illustrate the interconnectedness of these issues he states:

> La vie psychique des sujets dont le choix sexuel est un partenaire du même sexe constitue un secteur parmi d'autres du champ de la psychanalyse comme pratique et comme théorie. Il n'y a *a priori* aucune raison pour que les sujets homosexuels soient épargnés par les aléas de la vie psychique, y compris les difficultés liées à leur choix sexuel. C'est en quoi ils ne diffèrent en rien des hétérosexuels.[76]

Tort brings homosexuality in from the margins, puts it on an equal footing with heterosexuality, and perceives its psychoanalytic relevance in practical and theoretical terms. His reservations about psychoanalysis and norms has to do with the *a priori* tag that affixes itself to norms and often cannot be removed. As he implied in an earlier quotation, best psychoanalytic practice occurs when 'la figure

---

Anatrella's rhetoric of the denunciation of pathological homosexuality, its denial of alterity, its deviant and archaic behaviour, and the dangers it poses to children. For Tort, these rejections are tantamount to a ruse which deflects attention away from any serious reflection on the homosexual condition.

[74]   Tort, 'Homophobies psychanalytiques', p. 18.

[75]   Gilles Deleuze et Félix Guattari, *L'Anti-Oedipe* (Paris: Minuit, 1972).

[76]   Tort, 'Homophobies psychanalytiques', p. 18.

'La Différence des sexes': Difference or Distinction? 69

de la norme s'est transformée, assouplie.' For Tort, norms have a relevance when they are subject to change, not subjugating change.[77]

The subjugating norm, in Tort's vocabulary, is linked to a deference to image construction. Norms form part of 'la mécanique d'images globales' and of a 'orthopédie visuelle' in which individuals are seen to belong and have a place. In effect, norms can be seen to be linked to the *a priori* symbolic order. The question we asked of anthropology in respect of the role of biological essentialism in the political sphere resurfaces here, only in this case it concerns the role of the symbolic in the psychoanalytic domain. We recall that Eric Fassin, despite his critique of the use of anthropology in politics, conceded the existence of a symbolic function for 'la différence des sexes' but with significant reservations. Similarly, Michel Tort and others[78] acknowledge the evidence and relevance of the symbolic in psychoanalysis but contest strongly the creation of a Symbolic Order with its Freudian/Lacanian connotations, and its historical embeddedness in the human psyche. The thrust of Tort's progressive approach to psychoanalysis is to open up new relational structures outside the Oedipus structure, question the legitimacy of the paternal figure as a universal, and look to new ways of approaching male/female relations which are not subject to what he sees as the destructive structures of the past. In the same way that Patrice Maniglier set up a plurality of systems that challenged the hegemony of any one particular system in the debate on anthropology, Michel Tort proclaims the death of the Symbolic Order and the rise of *symbolics*, underpinned by a strong humanism:

> L'Ordre Symbolique n'existe donc pas. Ce qui existe sous ce nom est un objet virtuel singulier. Il existe des symbolisations qui s'exercent dans les espaces sociaux, des empilages, des connexions entre des réseaux de symbolisation, par exemple lorsqu'une culture entreprend d'imposer son régime de symbolisation à une autre, en l'interdisant, en la détruisant, etc. Nul besion de fabriquer, à partir de cette pluralité historique, un Ordre, un Lieu, un Dieu, pendant qu'on y est. L'Ordre symbolique, avec les représentations mystérieuses de la différence des sexes qui lui correspondent dans le Dernier Testament, c'est cette fiction de "Référence" anhistorique qu'a inventée l'ordre positif du jour qui règle les rapports de sexes, les parentés. Cette fiction a l'avantage de présenter le symbolique comme "naturel" en faisant des arrangements plutôt instables des humains la nature même du symbolique. Or, il suffit de rêver un instant aux ingrédients baroques, fabuleux dont le fameux "ordre symbolique" a été composé, il y a cent ans, deux cents ans, mille ans, pour sourire gaiement des prétentions d'universalité éternelle. On retrouve dans le symbolique ce qu'on y a mis. Reste donc la vraie question: qu'y mettrons-nous?[79]

---

[77] Sabine Prokhoris shows how norms can be a source of suffering and physical distress. See her book *Le Sexe prescrit. La différence sexuelle en question* (Paris: Aubier, 2000).

[78] Maniglier recognises the role and function of the symbolic but challenges its tyranny.

[79] Tort, 'Quelques conséquences de la différence "psychanalytique" des sexes', pp. 214-15.

70 *The Gay Republic*

Conclusions: The Queer Escape?

Norms accrue currency over time and history. They become naturalised and legitimised through the glue of law and order. But we have seen that this glue can come unstuck, and reveal cracks within the law and order process. Evelyne Pisier and Elisabeth Roudinesco have questioned the legitimacy of creating *a law* of 'la différence des sexes' in the parity debate.[80] Norms of heterosexuality linked to natural filiation have also been shown to be inadequate in responding to social change. The passage from nature to cultural acceptability also involves the process of legitimation and ordering, whether via law or the creation of elaborate psychoanalytic narratives. However, internal crises within the latter, for instance, have revealed the breakdown within concepts of order and the symbolic; the grand Freudian and Lacanian narratives are unravelling, producing discrete narratives that challenge traditional notions of paternity.[81] Michel Tort's triumph of symbolisations over the Symbolic are indicative of a change from a prescriptive order to a multiplicity of orders. And yet, is this proliferation of orders and symbolisations the only way forward?

The nature of the argument thus far on 'la différence des sexes' has been to divide the issue between the essentialist and constructionist camps. The latter, mainly an American import, has gained considerable currency in France. To perceive sex as sexuality and subsequent splitting into multiple sexualities (gender/'sexe social') has become not only a fashionable way to construct sexual identity but also the democratic way. But what is essentially an American model has not grafted easily on to the French psyche, where multiculturalism is in continual conflict with republican universalism. However, the uniqueness of the French context highlights a central concern with the constructionist argument about identity, which is whether identity is constructed purely and separately, or whether any separateness must de differentiated within the content of universal identity (Sylviane Agacinski's position). It may seem that whatever way one turns on this issue, the notion of sexual identity is shackled, either within the communitarian approach which can become snared in its own isolationism, or within the net of universal republicanism. At this juncture, a queer alternative may be worth considering. Building on notions that sex and sexuality do not define identity, and that sexuality is not an expression of sex, queer theorists have moved away from any identification between gender and 'la différence des sexes.' Gender is described as

---

[80] Addressing 'la différence des sexes', Pisier asks: 'Mais de ce fait brut, si incontestable soit-il pour le moment, pourquoi faut-il en tirer une loi?' in 'PaCS et Parité: du même et de l'autre', *Le Monde*, 20 octobre 1998, p. 18.

[81] The psychoanalyst Gérard Pommier, for example, has expounded the idea that homosexuality could function today as the ideal paternal and help resolve in part the paternal complex. See his article 'Pour l'amour du Père et du phallus: l'homosexualité en première ligne', *La Clinique lacanienne*, 4, Erès (1998): 1-19.

'La Différence des sexes': Difference or Distinction? 71

un ensemble varié d'effets qui produit des comportements et des relations sociales dans les corps et qu'alimentent les discours institutionalisés, les pratiques critiques, epistémologiques et quotidiennes aussi bien que le cinéma [...]. Les discours qui alimentent la vérité du sexe positionnent le sexe comme la cause des pulsions ou du désir alors qu'il est un effet de ces discours. Les discours sur les genres les positionnent comme étant causés par le sexe (dit biologique), comme si sexe et genre entretenaient un rapport expressif ou descriptif (le genre masculin exprimerait naturellement le sexe biologique masculin), alors que l'identité de genre est le résultat d'un effet de répétition régulée des codes de performance de genre.[82]

From this description of gender construction, Marie-Hélène Bourcier situates gender within a constructionist/social framework, but appears to go beyond the 'comfort zone' of social construction to suggest that gender *identity* is itself subject to 'performance' and repetition of codes.[83] Hence the rejection of the term identity by queer theorists, from both a sexual and gender perspective; queerness is opposed to forms of regulation and reification via sex and gender. In this respect, queer theory distinguishes itself from both essentialism and constructionism. It denounces normative assumptions between sex and gender. It is also opposed to the politics of sexual identity (gay, lesbian, communitarianism), and 'unifying', 'stable', 'coherent' constructions of identity (whether feminism or heterosexuality). In short, queer signifies a resistance to the production of sexual identities and normative genders.

But does queerness represent a valid alternative to the binary ideology of 'la différence des sexes'? In France, the PaCS and parity debates have shaped the binary nature of this ideology. Parity has shown that France still remains attached to the biological difference of the sexes as that which determines sexuality. Conversely, the idea of 'sexe social' (gender) is still trying to embed itself in the social consciousness. Queer, for the French, is an American import and the *dada* of subversive collectives like Le Zoo, Queer Factory and Gloss. Theoretically, its construction of sexuality as a resignifiable post-identity has attracted some French theorists (mainly of a post-structuralist orientation). Others, notably Marie-Elisabeth Handman, have denounced its flippancy and fundamental reliance on biological difference: 'Si cette théorie semble permettre de s'affranchir du dimorphisme sexuel, en réalité elle permet seulement de s'affranchir des rôles de genre, puisque se comporter tantôt comme un homme et tantôt comme une femme revient à reconnatre qu'il existe bien fondamentalement deux sexes biologiques.'[84] It would appear, therefore, that queer theory's opposition to hegemonic order and identity construction belies some tensions in respect of a prescriptiveness about sexuality. Similarly, its location of sexuality in the eternal slippage between sexes points to a sexual identity as a materialism of the body, alienated from social, cultural or historical contexts.

---

[82] Marie-Hélène Bourcier, '*Queer* Move/ments', *Mouvements*, 20 (2002): 39.

[83] Author of the work *Queer Zone* (Paris: Balland, 2001).

[84] Marie-Elisabeth Handman, 'Sexualité et famille: approche anthropologique', p. 254.

In North America, queer has enjoyed greater exposure given a wider multicultural consensus. However, the jury is still out on its impact. Queer commands considerable attention as an intellectual pursuit among American academics. But as a modality with socio-political influence, it is limited. What can be stated clearly is that the essentialist/constructionist debate (currently gripping France in the context of 'la différence des sexes') has been overtaken in the US by the issue of what constitutes identity. In America, the essentialist argument has been long defeated in theoretical terms, while in France it has been redeployed to help change the constitution in the parity stakes. In America, the constructionist position is where the debate has been redefined. But how exactly? Gendered identity found fertile ground through the 1970s and 1980s in America, but recently this ground has become less secure. Steven Seidman has chartered the nature of this debate, from the rehabilitation of identity and its link to sex as a core identity in the 1980s, to the limits of identity politics[85] in the 1990s (a pertinent reminder perhaps to communitarians in France). Significantly, he has dismissed the queer notion of a post-structuralist, decentered logic 'which dissolves any notion of a substantial unity in identity constructions, leaving only rhetorics of identities, performances, and the free play of difference and possibility.'[86] Seidman urges a return to 'an analysis that embeds the self in institutional and cultural practices.'[87] He favours a politics of resistance that is guided by a transformative and social vision, the values of which would receive their moral warrant from local traditions and social ideals, not foundational appeals. In short, Seidman rejects the theories and systems approach, preferring 'social sketches' that frame narratives rather than theories that analyse.

It is a vision defended, albeit in different formats, by other important commentators, notably Leo Bersani and Murray Pratt. For Bersani, gay identity has been 'degayed.'[88] In other words, gayness has lost its social transgression and aptitude for contesting oppressive structures. Bersani claims that gay identity has become synonymous with shoring up existing dominant structures, so concerned is the gay lobby with proceeding towards normalisation. The dangers of this, for Bersani, are multiple. But principally, complicity with 'heteroized' society leads to a gay identity defined by categories fashioned by heterosexuality. In order to

---

[85] Steven Seidman writes: 'In framing identity as a social positioning we need to avoid assuming that all individuals who share a social location by virtue of their gender or sexual orientation share a common or identical history or social experience. The notion that a hetero/homosexual social positioning creates two antithetical unitary collectivities, the former positioned as one of privilege while the latter is positioned as an oppressed and resisting subject, lacks coherence' in 'Identity and Politics in a "Postmodern" Gay Culture: Some Conceptual Notes' in Michael Warner (ed.), *Fear of a Queer Planet. Queer Politics and Social Theory* (University of Minnesota Press, 1993), p. 136.

[86] Seidman, 'Identity and Politics in a "Postmodern" Gay Culture: Some Conceptual Notes', p. 135.

[87] Seidman, 'Identity and Politics in a "Postmodern" Gay Culture...', p. 137.

[88] Leo Bersani, *Homos* (Cambridge: Harvard University Press, 1995), p. 152.

'La Différence des sexes': Difference or Distinction?

articulate a genuine gay identity, Bersani claims that lesbians and gays need to move away from the heterosexual/homosexual opposition (including the whole concept of 'la différence des sexes') and the notion of 'relationality' with heterosexual society, and derive their own specificity from a desire of sameness. This subversive argument, which alienates Bersani from Seidman and Judith Butler (whom he accuses of collaboration with society and avoiding the specificity of gayness) finds resonance in the 'strategic practicality' that characterises Murray Pratt's treatment of queer receptions in contemporary France.[89] In a dense and original argument which responds to the implications of Bersani, Seidman and French activists, Pratt questions whether any political homosexual rights activism is possible in today's atomised and global gay market. Like Bersani and Hocquenghem (whose fears of normalisation and the sexual repression of desire are highlighted in order to reinforce the importance of avoiding the traps of heteronormativity), Pratt exposes the parody, resignification and ultimately collaborative instincts of queer. In its place, he advances 'a recycling and rethinking of activism which the dominant culture cannot cope with' in the form of a marriage of practice and theory, in which French activists unite real social benefits with a critique of heteronormative structures.

Queer may transcend the essentialist/constructionist divide on one level but on another it is also subject to criticisms of being concerned more with the surface of sexuality than its depth. It is seen to rely on dominant heteronormative constructions of identity and avoid social and political responsibility. As Pratt says, queer is so removed from the 'sense-making world.'[90] But, how does Pratt's post-queer 'strategic practicality' chime with Seidman's 'social sketches'? The contexts are clearly different, one French, the other American. But Seidman's vision has some relevance to a French context. Firstly, it converges in part with the French perspective in respect of identity politics. His vision implies limits on identity politics for lesbians and gays in France, for whom sexual identity as political strategy has been crucial in their struggles for recognition and against heterosexual domination. Indeed, it could be said that Seidman's vision plays into the hands of traditional republican values and in particular French universalism. Seidman exposes some of the myths of a common gay identity for which the only traditional route of expression has been communitarian activism. In this respect, he gravitates more towards Frédéric Martel's position of a 'droit à l'indifférence', where individuals no longer need to announce their difference but can bask in the anonymity of post-different indifference.[91] Seidman's shift from theories to

---

[89] Murray Pratt, 'Post-Queer and Beyond the PaCS: Contextualising French Responses to the Civil Solidarity Pact' in Kate Chedgzoy, Emma Francis and Murray Pratt (eds), *In a Queer Place. Sexuality and Belonging in British and European Contexts* (Ashgate, 2002).

[90] Pratt, 'Post-Queer and Beyond the PaCS: Contextualising French Responses to the Civil Solidarity Pact', p. 193.

[91] My intention in this conclusion is not to set up as an ideal the notion of 'indifférence' or 'banalisation' of homosexuality. Martel seems convinced that normalisation of gay identity

74   *The Gay Republic*

practices, from analysis to narratives, from natural to cultural definitions of sexuality are, as he claims, 'guided by a transformative and social vision.' Seidman locates sexuality (whether it be in terms of difference or distinction) in social and historical conditions. He engages substantially with the *politics of sexual identity* (not its *faux ami* identity politics) and breathes new life into the social as the space where norms can be effectively transformed. He concludes: 'In a postmodern culture, anticipation of the "end of domination" or self-realization pass into local struggles for participatory democracy, distributive social justice, lifestyle choice, or reconfiguring knowledges. I prefer a pragmatic approach to social criticism.'[92]

By contrast, Pratt, like Bersani, is far more suspicious of the social centre as a site for gayness to not only express itself unconditionally, but also to avoid collusion with heteronormative institutions and structures. For Pratt, there needs to be a more subversive element to gay identity, other than the pragmatism offered by Seidman. Bersani locates this subversion in the essentiality of gayness (not the biological essentialism of 'la différence des sexes' but a radical essentialism of sameness that excludes relationality and sociability). Pratt, on the other hand, locates it in a post-queer state of active and strategic resistance. In conclusion, it is evident that there are two simultaneous and competing debates preoccupying commentators on gay identity in France today. The first is a theoretical debate between biological essentialism and constructionism. The second debate goes beyond this theoretical binary to address in both practical and subversive ways how best to preserve the 'essence', autonomy and reactionary integrity of gayness.

---

within society (a form of indifferent blending into sameness) is the *apogée* of lesbian and gay acceptability. Seidman has also recently eulogised the normalisation and routinisation of homosexuality in the United States. Seidman's intepretation of normalisation, however, is implicitly more political and radical than that of Martel's.

[92]   Seidman, 'Identity and Politics in a "Postmodern" Gay Culture…', p. 137.

Chapter 3

From 'Crisis' of Law to a New 'Esprit des Lois'

In establishing the theoretical parameters of sexual citizenship, it is clear that a dichotomy is forming in our perceptions. On the one hand, sexual citizenship is being construed in terms of political and integrative universalism underpinned by certain anthropological, essentialist and psychoanalytic pre-conditions. In addition, French republican society is perceived as an invariable and symbolic space in which sexual citizenship is controlled within the confines of 'la vie privée.' These non-negotiable pre-conditions are upheld and reinforced by the political right, conservative republicans, the Catholic Church and a select group of sociologists and academics. On the other hand, there is strong perception that what we have thus far identified as the social, with its diversity, pluralism and quotidian practicality, is giving increasing and legitimate rise to the renegotiation of sexual citizenship. As a consequence, the social is emerging as a site where axiomatic norms of sexuality (culled from the discourses of biological, symbolic and natural pre-determination) are themselves being subject to transformation.

Control of the social is therefore the battleground on which the struggle for sexual citizenship is being fought. From a socio-political perspective, Claude Lefort has opened up the social as a space where the 'organisation des formes vie' in its formulation of new 'droits de rapport' is producing new templates of sexual legitimacy. Sociologist Eric Fassin has privileged the social as the true testing ground for the collapse of axiomatic absolutes generated by scientific expertise and anthropology. Steven Seidman, as we have seen, elevates the personal narratives produced out of social and historical contexts above institutional and cultural norms in his own personal and pragmatic approach to sexual citizenship. Murray Pratt and Leo Bersani are more suspicious of the social as a space controlled by heteronormativity and thus free to nullify attempts at democratic sexualisation. Before we try to bring these differing viewpoints together, we need to address one important aspect of the social which underpins many of the above. The social is a highly contested *legal* space where the very legitimacy of the law and its consequences for sexual citizenship are being challenged at a profoundly sociological level. This chapter will highlight a crisis in French law at the heart of which is its relationship with the social.

The founding fathers of the French legal system, Montesquieu and Rousseau, based their philosophies on the centrality of equality of citizenship as the principle differentiating democracy, monarchy and autocracy. Montesquieu, in his *De l'Esprit des lois*, wrote: 'L'amour de la république, dans une démocratie, est celui de la démocratie; l'amour de la démocratie est celui de l'égalité. L'amour de la démocratie est encore celui de la frugalité.'[1] Love of frugality limited the desire to possess things beyond one's needs, and Montesquieu was keen to attach frugality to the concept of equality because he recognised that wealth gave a power to the citizen that he could not use for himself and which would run counter to equality. In the same way that Rousseau's theory of the general will involved the total submission of the minority to the whole, Montesquieu recognised that the preserve of equality against the particularities of individual differences was going to involve some measure of compromise. To this degree, Montesquieu believed in the idea of a census that would reduce difference and iron out inequalities in the interest of equality. He wrote:

> Quoique dans la démocratie l'égalité réelle soit l'âme de l'Etat, cependant elle est si difficile à établir, qu'une exactitude extrême à cet égard ne conviendrait pas toujours. Il suffit que l'on établisse un cens qui réduise ou fixe les différences à un certain point; après quoi, c'est à des lois particulières à égaliser, pour ainsi dire, les inégalités [...]. Dans certains cas, l'égalité entre les citoyens peut être ôtée dans la démocratie pour l'utilité de la démocratie.[2]

In Book XII, Montesquieu went on to highlight the paradox of equality in a democracy when he entertained the notion that it is possible in a democracy for the constitution to be free and the citizen not, and vice versa: 'Il pourra arriver que la constitution sera libre, et que le citoyen ne le sera point; le citoyen pourra être libre, et la constitution ne l'être pas. Dans ces cas, la constitution sera libre de droit, et non de fait; le citoyen sera libre de fait, et non de droit.'[3] At a first reading, Montesquieu's admission of the potential for inequality between citizen and constitution indicates that the idea of perfect harmony between individual freedom and constitution is potentially illusory. It also suggests, however, that the room for inequality is quite real. However, at closer inspection, this statement reveals a telling truth about Montesquieu's representation of the constitution in that while it may not be free *in fact* (in contrast with the citizen), it will always be free *by right*. In other words, Montesquieu suggests that the constitution may be faulty in its misrepresentation of individual liberties. His suggestion, therefore, that the constitution is not free in contrast to the citizen's freedom is only a ruse. In truth, Montesquieu underlines the infallibility of the constitution which, while not free in fact, is always free by right. In his conclusion to the first chapter, he writes: 'Il n'y a que la disposition des lois, et même des lois fondamentales, qui forme la liberté dans son rapport avec la constitution. Mais, dans le rapport avec le citoyen, des moeurs, des manières, des exemples reçus, peuvent la faire naître, et de certaines

---

[1] Montesquieu, *De l'Esprit des lois*. Livre V, Chapitre III (Paris: Garniers Frères, 1748), p. 41.

[2] Montesquieu, *De l'Esprit des lois*, Livre V, Chapitre V, p. 45.

[3] Montesquieu, *De l'Esprit des lois*, Livre XII, Chapitre Premier, p. 171.

From 'Crisis' of Law to a New 'Esprit des Lois'   77

lois civiles la favoriser.'[4] Once more, Montesquieu achieves a tense balance between constitutional rigour and individual predilection. On the one hand, he confirms that it is laws which form liberty in their relation to the constitution. On the other hand, he offers a chink of hope for the citizen for whom customs and particularities might *give rise* to freedom. In truth, however, Montesquieu and Rousseau follow the same line of the submission of the individual to the whole, of the submission of mores and manners to the disposition of laws. Mores and manners can help the creation of liberty but they do not carry the same *gravitas* of laws that form freedom.

Alain-Gérard Slama compares two models of citizenship based on Rousseau and Locke. In Rousseau's concept of general will, public opinion is not a sum of private choices but a 'relatively autonomous product derived from the will of far-sighted actor-citizens [...]. In contrast, Locke's theory sees general opinion as a sum of points of view expressed in the short term by self-seeking individuals.'[5] With political systems interpreting these concepts differently, we can see Locke's theory being deployed primarily in the USA where the power of the majority is limited in order to protect minorities, to the extent that differentialist claims are part of the democratic process. By contrast, in France under the legacy of Rousseau, the submission of the minority to the whole translates into a 'formal and not real' respect for minorities. As visionaries of the modern legal and political systems, Montesquieu and Rousseau bequeathed a unique but problematic legacy. Slama contextualises this troubled legacy in the inexorable collapse of republicanism and its cherished ideals of common will, *jus soli*, assimilation and the consummate bond between people and state. François Furet has termed this collapse famously as the 'end of French exceptionalism'[6] in the advent of global politics, all of which have dented the republican idea of a society of equals based on human will. For Slama, France in the modern era has struggled to respond to changing economic and social contexts. Critically, and as a consequence of this lack of response, 'a new division of political ideas – Real democracy versus Republicanism – has opened up and is now more important than the classical struggle between Right and Left. This division plays itself out in the realms of law and of representation, and is also manifested in the decomposition of the nation into a multitude of conflicting identities.'[7]

Slama's identification of two new juridical cultures (he borrows the concept from Laurent Cohen-Tanugi[8]), one assimilatory, the other arbitrational, points to

---

[4] Montesquieu, Livre XII, Chapitre Premier, p. 171.

[5] Alain-Gérard Slama, 'Democratic Dysfunctions and Republican Obsolescence: The Demise of French Exceptionalism', in Gerald Flynn (ed.), *Remaking the Hexagon: The New France in the New Europe* (Westview Press, 1995), pp. 55-6.

[6] François Furet, Jacques Julliard, Pierre Rosanvallon, *La République du centre* (Paris: Calmann-Lévy, 1988), pp. 29-31.

[7] Slama, 'Democratic Dysfunctions and Republican Obsolescence...', pp. 54-5.

[8] Laurent Cohen-Tanugi, *La Métamorphose de la démocratie* (Paris: Odile Jacob, 1989),

78   *The Gay Republic*

the nature and measure of the split that the political division has produced at a legal level in France. The assimilatory culture is founded on Montesquieu's notion of seeing the law as emanating from the common will as expressed by the legislature: 'This is linked to the Jacobin conception of the superiority of the majority to the minority, and the public interest to the private.'[9] The second culture, based on Madison's ideas, applies the law according to the principles of natural rights: 'rather than being an agent of the general will as expressed in law, he [the judge] is an arbiter between the rights of the individual and the general will.'[10] Slama claims that the 'crisis of law' in France is that French law is becoming less sovereign and more influenced by the Madison model. This is particularly the case with the pre-eminence of European law, and the effects of the Maastricht treaty. It would seem, at least on one level, that the departure from the assimilatory culture would bring with it some positive gains for the individual in the struggle for ethnic, political and sexual difference. The growth of differentialism (from the consequences of the PaCS to the celebrity of José Bové) has produced a new set of assumptions of what it means to be French in a newly invigorated democratic republic. Differentialism also makes one reflect on the assumptions Montesquieu made on the infallibility of the constitution, and the necessity to reduce all difference in the interests of equality and love for democracy. What is also noticeable, particularly in Montesquieu, was the need to instil removal from the democratic fold were the citizen to either desire too much or, being too free, become too arrogant and have designs on being more powerful than other citizens. Throughout *De L'Esprit des lois*, Montesquieu admits not only the potential for difference but the need for it to be constrained. In fact, a strong case could be made that, in the need to constrain difference, Montesquieu belies the continued presence of inequality not only in society but in law.[11]

The 'benefits' of the recent culture of differentialism have also however brought with them a whole new juridical tradition, with a new set of problems. Slama has highlighted the increased profile of judges and experts as arbiters in the decision-making process. The 'principle of negotiation', according to Slama, has become the new basis of legitimacy that has replaced the dying concept of the national interest. Judges and experts with specialised knowledge are seen to bring a renewed balance and credibility to the legal process. However, in areas such as genetics, filiation and medical progress, the law has entered a minefield of ethical

---

pp. 29-31.

[9]   Slama, 'Democratic Dysfunctions and Republican Obsolescence...', p. 57.

[10]   Slama, 'Democratic Dysfunctions and Republican Obsolescence...', p. 57.

[11]   Marcela Iacub has questioned the value of the law as an impartial entity. In particular, she has criticised the law for establishing what she sees as divisive categories (the distinction of men/women over individuals) with unequal measures of power. Her premise is that the law is not about equality but about promoting inequality and an uncontroversial 'efficacité générale.' See her article 'Reproduction et division juridique des sexes', *Les Temps modernes*, 609 (2000): 242-62.

From 'Crisis' of Law to a New 'Esprit des Lois' 79

dilemmas. Slama, for example, highlights the confused role of the law in its intervention in the private lives of individuals. On the one hand, the law sees itself as having a responsibility to intervene on issues such as medically assisted procreation in order to prevent abuses. On the other hand, it assumes an authority of the doctor in trying to fix ethical limits. More controversially, the law sets limits on who can and cannot have access to PMA ('procréation médicale assistée'). The denial of access of lesbian and gay couples to PMA is one of the more recent and publicly debated issues. In short, the law can be caught between a rock and a hard place; in the new culture of arbitration, the law is summoned to bring cases of private and ethical interest into the social debate, and then bound to pronounce justice on them.

This attempt by the law to rationalise individual behaviour, by intervening in people's private lives supposedly for their own good, is also explored by Ariane Poulantzas in her article 'Du PaCS à la famille homoparentale: quel avenir pour la parenté?' The medical advancements of PMA and IAD ('insémination artificielle avec donneur') have opened up legal loopholes as regards the status of children born genetically with anonymous donors, and the status of the father. In a tightly knit argument, Poulantzas opposes juridic obligation with 'real' obligation, stressing the importance of being able to 'définir ce qui fonde le statut de parent, juridiquement bien sûr, mais aussi réellement.'[12] In the case of genetically born children, the 'conjoint' is the only recognised father of the child, not the donor. The law is seen to hide the real origin of the father in the interests of the child and his/her immediate upbringing. The 'wisdom' of this jurisprudence is questioned by critics, notably Geneviève Delaisi de Parseval, who sees the need for greater transparency and knowledge of the biological father for the long term benefit of the child. In a separate but related issue, Poulantzas questions the 'wisdom' of the legal introduction of the controversial legislation known as 'accouchement sous X' where the anonymity of the mother is guaranteed after birth. Parseval interprets this legislation as the denial of pregnancy and maternity to women; for her, such women have not been pregnant in the eyes of the law.[13] The counter (or real)

---

[12] Ariane Poulantzas, 'Du PaCS à la famille homoparentale: Quel avenir pour la parenté?', in Nicolas Demorand and Hugues Jallon (eds), *L'Année des débats 2000-2001* (Paris: Editions de la Découverte, 2000), pp. 143-49.

[13] According to Marcela Iacub, pregnancy has now become the new legal space in which inequalities between men and women are debated. In her article 'Reproduction et division juridique des sexes', she states her central aim: 'Nous tenterons d'analyser le processus par lequel le droit français a reconduit, à travers le nouvel ordre de la reproduction, les inégalités entre les hommes et les femmes, en essayant de montrer la place centrale qui a été octroyée à la grossesse. Nous allons examiner, dans un premier temps, comment celle-ci est devenue source de pouvoirs inégaux et complémentaires entre les hommes et les femmes en ce qui concerne la venue au monde des enfants [...], comment cette puissance de faire naître s'articule avec les règles qui établissent la filiation maternelle et instituent la grossesse comme lieu de non-disponibilité, de fixité et de contrainte pour les femmes.' (p. 245). See also Geneviève Delaisi de Parseval, 'La construction de la parentalité dans les couples de

80 *The Gay Republic*

argument is that the law is responding to the immediate situation, in this instance that of the upbringing of the child by adoptive parents for whom knowledge of the birth mother is not of immediate concern. In both these controversial legislations, the law is seen to mask certain realities in order to legitimate other realities. In doing so, one set of valid realities is delegitimised, with unforeseen and potentially damaging consequences.

The challenge posed for the law by this new culture of arbitration has been compounded by what sociologists have called the tyranny of the 'je.' Current debates in sociology on the individual are divided between the benefits afforded by the autonomy of the individual as the foundation for a new democracy of the 'quotidien', and the dangers of what is seen as the tyranny of intimacy in which investment in the public and social is abandoned, where narcissism is on the increase and where the illusion of individual omnipotence is the new dominating structure.[14] I raise this sociological analogy at this point for two reasons. Firstly, it demonstrates the nature of the challenge facing the legal system in contemporary France and beyond where the traditional forces and institutions of the law (what Philippe Corcuff has called the 'tyrannies traditionnelles du *nous*'[15]) are now being undermined by the new tyrannies of the 'je.' Individuals and minorities are now encouraged to resort to the law for resolution to conflicts. In the context of France, one is witnessing the replacement of one centralised system (assimilation) by another decentralised system (arbitration). The latter has clearly brought dividends as we have seen but, as others have pointed out, it brings with it its own set of tyrannies and fallacies of power. Slama has referred to this process as one 'which presumes to advance toleration and/or rationality' but 'runs the risk of destabilizing the very freedom that they suppose to protect.'[16]

The second reason for the sociological analogy is that current sociological debate on individualism in France mirrors the course of a current technical and legal debate on the role of the individual in society, which will form a substantial part of this chapter. In short, the sociological debate couches the individual in an opposition between autonomy and socialisation. In a later section of this chapter, I will return to the multiple variations within this opposition, suffice to say for the moment that the crux of the debate centres on the social origin and dependency of

---

même sexe', in Eric Fassin and Daniel Borrillo (eds), *Au-delà du PaCS.*

[14] A recent issue of the journal *Le Débat* brought together a series of articles by leading sociologists Jean-Claude Kaufmann, Marcel Gauchet and Philippe Corcuff under the theme of 'Une sociologie de l'individu est-elle possible?', *Le Débat*, 119 (2002). Corcuff's article, which is a response to the leading article by Kaufmann in which he has welcomed the individualisation of society, highlights the dangers of individualisation. With detailed reference to American sociologists Christopher Lasch and Richard Sennett, Corcuff claims that individualisation brings with it its own tyrannical and individualist norms that can be counterproductive to social reality.

[15] Philippe Corcuff, 'L'individualisme contemporain en question', *Le Débat*, 119 (2002): 120.

[16] Slama, 'Democratic Dysfunctions and Republican Obsolescence...', p. 63.

all individual thought and action. The essence of the legal debate opposes two concepts of the individual. The first, from a legal perspective, defines the individual as an abstract person but rooted in social normativity. The second defines the individual as a physical person, rooted in his own subjectivity which is outside any legal jurisdiction; the autonomy of this 'sujet' is debated in direct opposition to the prescribed 'personne juridique.' While the aim of this chapter is not to compare legal and sociological perspectives, it is clear that current academic and legal debates in France in these areas are converging on the same problematic, which is the degree to which the individual is socialised and cogniscient of the responsibilities therein, or whether the individual can defend both ideologically and legally his autonomy in the face of existential, social, sexual and legal demands.

By focusing on a technically legal debate, I want to avoid some obvious traps which I feel could have derailed me. The morality of the law in respect of sexual matters is not a matter for consideration in this chapter, nor do I intend to provide a legal guide to the legislation that led to the implementation of the PaCS legislation.[17] The PaCS is not directly discussed in this chapter but the consequences of the technical legal debate have a clear impact on lesbian and gay identity in respect of the construction of a sexual identity within and outside the law. In theory, my point of departure is the juncture/crisis that Alain-Gérard Slama identified between the assimilatory and arbitration juridic cultures. In exploring the latter, as I have done partially up to now, I want to turn more directly to the French legal system itself and examine how it is dealing internally with this crisis. The value of this approach will not be assessed in terms of trying to determine why the law takes the decisions that it does. Rather my approach is designed to show how branches of the law theorise individual thoughts and actions. Therein, I want to reflect two wider concerns that chime with the overall direction of this book. Firstly, the technical nature of the legal debate in France today reflects the current political divide between what Slama referred to as republicanism and real democracy; juridic distinctions highlight some key theoretical concepts which themselves appear to have significant political origins. Secondly, and interconnected with the first, is the idea that the crisis in French law today is a crisis of legitimacy in which the law has seen itself become detached from its social and representative roots.

'Personne juridique' and 'Sujet du désir'

In a recent edition of the journal *Esprit*, the anthropologist Stéphane Breton wrote two long and technically challenging articles under the theme 'Le Droit, le Sujet et la Norme.' The first of his articles was entitled 'De la nécessaire clarification du

---

[17] For a step by step guide to how the PaCS came into being as a piece of legislation, see Hugues Montouh, 'L'Esprit d'une loi: controverses sur le Pacte civil de solidarité', *Les Temps modernes*, 603 (1999): 189-204.

82   *The Gay Republic*

langage juridique', and the second was called 'Norme juridique et normativité sociale.' These articles were written in response to a body of legal opinion, espoused primarily by the legal historian Yan Thomas who created a legal controversy by claiming that the individual, defined legally as a 'personne de droit purement abstraite', could be reinterpreted as incorporating another legal definition, that of the 'sujet du désir.' The individual, according to Thomas, would be divided into two categories. For Thomas, this distinction would serve to rebalance the established formal, abstract, and universal legal template for the individual, and force the law to consider private and subjective constructions of the individual centred on autonomy, self-determination and notions of body and sexual singularity. Stéphane Breton analyses both positions and makes some telling observations.

Before discussing Breton's analysis, it may be worth making two preliminary remarks. The first is that the divisions themselves appear to reflect a political division between republican universalism and democratic differentialism. The direction of my analysis reflects this division, although this is not made explicit by the legal arguments themselves. The second point is that Breton himself appears to favour the 'republican' legal analysis. I propose not to approach this as partisanship because given the nature of my analysis, and the context of differentialism of which I have spoken considerably up to this point, his comments are constructive and make a positive contribution to the concept of differentialism. Breton's analysis of division between the 'personne de droit purement abstraite' (or 'personne juridique' as I shall refer to it from now on) and 'sujet du désir' is discussed on three main issues. The first division is existential and reflects how each category is defined in general terms. The 'personne juridique' is defined as an abstraction, an artefact, furthermore as an institution. As an institution, it is constructed on normative social foundations. It is also not defined in terms of its corporeal attributes, described instead as a 'point géometrique sans propriétés physiques.'[18] The key notion to take from this initial portrait is that the 'personne juridique' is defined in close relation to society, legal norms and universal abstraction (which is not a contradiction to the sociality of the 'personne'). Rather, the 'personne juridique' is seen to derive a certain unity from these social, legal and abstract associations, which in turn give meaning to its existence. In Breton's terms, this characterisation of the person is called 'être selon le droit.' By contrast, 'être selon le corps' is what encapsulates the category of 'sujet du désir.' Thomas contrasts the abstraction of the juridic person, who exists for Thomas as a bodiless form, with the 'sujet', described as the author of life and the sovereign of its own existence. Thomas borrows the Kantian idea of 'le sujet corporel comme la chose en soi' to define the total autonomy of this 'sujet.' For Breton, in his evaluation of the two categories, the distinguishing feature between the two is the role of the social in both categories. For the 'personne juridique' it is central. In the case of

---

[18] Stéphane Breton, 'De la nécessaire clarification du langage juridique', *Esprit*, 285 (2002): 31.

the 'sujet', the social appears to be less prevalent, although Thomas argues strongly that the social should not be contrived erroneously as the monopoly of the 'personne jurdique.' He argues that for the 'sujet' the social must be defined in different terms to that of the 'personne juridique.'

The second division is the way in which the body and sexuality are represented by the 'personne juridique' and the 'sujet du désir.' In the case of the 'personne juridique', the body is perceived as a corporeal subject that is socially constructed. The body is 'un objet construit, un objet social, de part traversé par la normativité.'[19] Sexuality, in turn, is defined as 'un acte sexuel', a technique of the body, an object of teaching and exercise. The aim of sexuality is the link that is achieved between the physical body and the social body. The laws of society, in particular those that instil normativity, serve to institutionalise the body; as such, sexual relations are not seen to be subjective, as is the case with the 'sujet.' What is key to the expression of sexuality for the 'personne juridique' is the social 'usage' to which the body is put. While the 'personne juridique' may reify this relation of sexuality-usage-'être social', the 'sujet du désir' reifies the singularity of the body as the new 'esprit de loi' which is seen to resist alienation in normativity and the finality of social existence. Following on from its existential position as sovereign subject, the body for the 'sujet du désir' is perceived by Thomas as the agent of sexuality. In contrast to the 'personne juridique', where sexuality is defined in its social usage, sexuality for the 'sujet du désir' is defined as subjective, singular and private; it is seen to be able to exist through its own individual expression. Described by Breton as a sanctuary, the body 'vaut par lui', in contrast to the juridic mantra that the body 'ne va pas de soi.'

The law is the third significant division between the two constructions. For the 'personne juriduiqe', the law must govern society. The law is described as being born out of common life and social interaction. The law is seen to represent the indispensable need within society for regulation, hence its elevation to reference point and place of absolute intelligibility. The law is also described as inheriting the title of totem, a symbolic guarantor of absolute meaning, which has the effect of overriding all factual and subjective discourse. From the perspective of the 'sujet', individuals decide laws, not inherited or symbolic systems. For the 'sujet', the totemic or sanctified status of law is perceived to be fallible, particularly if it pre-exists all individual facts and developments that might contradict and weaken it. In short, Breton summarises the conceptual legal difference between the 'personne juridique' and the 'sujet du désir' as one in which French law is currently more comfortable in dealing with individuals as 'entités comparables' and less comfortable in dealing with them as 'des êtres irréductiblement singuliers.'

Several points emerge from these juridic divisions of the individual. The first point is the position of Stéphane Breton. His position may on the surface appear convoluted, but in truth it not only shapes the nature, depth and intensity of the

---

[19] Breton, 'De la nécessaire clarification du langage juridique', p. 39.

argument, but also feeds into a political division, which I want to explore further. My representation of the divisions above underplays the intense and intellectual context between two juridic contexts. The debate between Yan Thomas and Stéphane Breton sees Breton, the author, for subjective or academic reasons, take on the role of devil's advocate and proceed to unpick Thomas' legal argument. I will show some examples of this with the aim of revealing the political underpinnings of this hypothesis and to underscore the centrality of the key differentiating structure between 'personne juridique' and 'sujet du désir', namely the fight for control of the social. The tug-of-war between Thomas and Breton is at its most intense in the combined areas of body/sexuality and the law. I demonstrated earlier one of the key differences between social usage of the body from the juridic perspective, and the private use of the body from the standpoint of the 'sujet.' This simplification belies a prolonged exchange which sees Breton criticise the presumption of the 'sujet' as the author of existence, denounce individual presumption as a mythology, and lambast the tactics of defenders of the 'sujet' to supposedly free the body by withdrawing it from social normativity and retreat into the subjectivity of desire. Breton states:

> Le corps est construit, donc un objet de normes: il n'est ni autonome ni naturel. Il est élaboré dans le rapport social. Il ne saurait donc être le sanctuaire du sujet naturel puisqu'il est partie socialement disponible et socialement aliénable. Les aspects qui le composent – les substances, par exemple – sont socialisés. Il ne paraît donc pas possible de constituer le corps comme une chose privée. Le corps n'est pas une chose en soi, opaque et ineffable, c'est au contraire un usage, lequel prend une forme socialement et institutionnellement. Il n'y a rien dans le corps, même son absolue contingence, dans la mesure où nous nous percevons en tant que corps et où nous nous représentons notre corps, qui puisse l'être selon un langage commun, compréhensible par tous. La sexualité elle-même relève de 'l'ordre du représenté et du séparé.'[20]

Breton's tirade does not stop here. He proceeds to undermine the presumption of western notions of sexuality, which appear to legitimise the subject as autonomous and self-sufficient, and promote the construction of the 'sujet de faire cause commune avec son corps.' On the point of law, Breton invokes wilfully the renowned anthropologist Pierre Legendre and the latter's totemic and religious sanctification of the law, and also the linguistic theories of Wittgenstein. In an instructive analogy with language and meaning, Breton demonstrates how the law can be compared usefully to the construction of language in which the latter is built on the organisation and classification of facts, which in turn give language its intrinsically normative effect. Meaning is thence only possible on the basis of common rules of understanding. In the same way, the law presupposes an implicit pact of understanding between subjects in the social arena. One of the consequences of Wittgenstein theory, which rings true with Breton, is that there is no possibility of a private language; once entered into language, the social subject renounces part of his subjectivity. He becomes social and relational, conditional on

---

[20] Breton, 'De la nécessaire clarification du langage juridique', p. 44.

the public grammar of desire and respect. The intensity of Breton's argument can also be measured in the way he which he dissects the defence of Thomas' 'sujet du désir.' He debates the way in which the 'sujet' constructs the position of a protected sanctuary, questioning the origin of such notions of autonomy, which he believes to be institutionalised if not invented. On the highly controversial issue of norms, Thomas sees the law to be a fiction in cases where it creates controversial legislation that appears to run contrary to individual and social experience (the cases of IAD and PMA that I referred to earlier are cases in point). While Thomas contests the idea of 'faits' adapting to established norms, Breton sees in this adaptation a triumph for normativity and the domination of a legal conceptual order. It is a crucial difference between Thomas and Breton and is analysed further under the difference attributed respectively to the words 'fiction' and 'règle.' Thomas sees the law as 'artificialiste'; it is a 'fiction juridique' which prioritises norm over fact. Breton states :

> La règle est un attracteur conceptuel qui structure entièrement le champ puisque la fiction ne l'annule pas et se contente de modifier le point de son imputation. La fiction ne touche pas la norme en tant que telle, seulement son objet [...]. On ne peut prétendre que modifier la qualification des faits pour les appliquer à une norme restée constante change la nature de celle-ci. Un tel pragmatisme manifeste au contraire une extraordinaire rigidité normative.[21]

According to Breton, the primacy of 'règle' (norm) remains intact in the face of whatever fictions social 'faits' might invent. It is a position Breton summarises in the phrase: 'Les faits peuvent varier, la structure qui les comprend ne change pas.'[22]

Thomas' argument in favour of the primacy of 'faits' over 'règle' is based on the need for the law to recognise that the objects of laws (people, contexts) differ and change over time to the ways in which the law was traditionally or originally designed to be perceived. It is an argument based on a need for the law to respond to and accommodate social and individual change. The problem, as identified by Thomas and reinforced by Breton, is that norms limit the extent of change and subordinate change to the level of 'qualification.' Normative rigidity, of which Breton charges Thomas, could also be redirected back to Breton in his obedience to the fact that norms remain intact, above the law so to speak. The key and distinctive feature of this element of the debate has to do with the role that is assigned to the origin of the law. Under Breton's concept of the 'personne juridique', the law has a mythology. At a glance, this may appear to devalue origin but, for Breton, this mythology is elevated, as is the sanctity of the law, to a position of total and absolute reference. It could even be argued that this elevation takes place regardless of the law, or because of what the law is and has represented from its Greek and Roman foundations. Breton openly admits to this

---

[21] Breton, 'De la nécessaire clarification du langage juridique', p. 49.
[22] Breton, 'De la nécessaire clarification du langage juridique', p. 49.

mythologisation of the law and defends his use of the term to root his belief that people desire laws and normativity, and that people wilfully draw up laws and want to obey them for the simple reason that they want to make action intelligible. Laws, for Breton, give sense to things and to social experience. In contrast, Thomas contests the origins of this mythologisation and sanctity, claiming that these are perceptions external (and not internal) to the law and therefore do not justify its status. With the mystical quality of the law superseding any social and institutional weight, Thomas argues that this is one of the reasons why the law enjoys the degree of autonomy that it does, and why norms acquire their uncontested status.

As such, Thomas wants to see more limits and controls placed on the institutions that promote this mythologisation. More crucially, and more controversially as I shall argue later, Thomas defends the position of the 'sujet du désir' as 'hors du droit.' His defence is based on the notion of the autonomy of the individual who is socially constituted outside of law and who operates according to his own private 'law.' While Breton sets up the construct of a social, abstract and public individual defined by the law, Thomas claims that beneath this public subject there is a private and autonomous subject that the law cannot reach and over whom laws of normativity have no control. Appropriating Breton's analogy with language, Thomas proposes that under public language is a private language 'affranchi de toute norme d'entendement commun.'[23] As with the body, Breton responds with a defence of the social usage of language, and that language serves no purpose if it is uncommunicable. Thomas' thesis is 'qu'il a de la signification possible avant la règle d'usages des signes et que cette signification déjà présente, mais en un lieu occulte, reste simplement à découvrir [...]. Or, l'idée d'un sens sous-jacent préexistant à la norme: on a affaire dans les deux cas à une ontologie préservée de toute actualisation, logée mystérieusement dans un autre monde.'[24]

Thomas' idea of a linguistic pre-existence to norms (and which we assume can be applied to the condition of the 'sujet du desir') has its positive and negative aspects. Theoretically, the 'sujet' is free, both ontologically and linguistically; norms, both ontological and linguistic, would compromise this freedom. How this freedom would be actualised and where it would be actualised remains undetermined. The references to 'à découvrir' and 'un autre monde' serve to romanticise, if not mythologise, this freedom. Breton's argument, which carries more practical concerns, is that the 'sujet' cannot position himself beyond, or opt out of, normative language to express or find himself in an ultra language which seems more authentic. For Breton, this authenticity is itself conditional, predetermined, institutionalised. The same principle, he states, applies to the law: one cannot position oneself outside of the law because it is only in the law that things have sense. Nor is it possible, he claims, to customise law to suit one's

---

[23] Yan Thomas quoted in Stéphane Breton, 'Norme juridique et normativité sociale', *Esprit*, 285 (2002): 71.
[24] Breton, 'Norme juridique et normativité sociale', p. 72.

private desires because the law is founded on commonality not subjectivity.

In one of his concluding remarks on his analogy between law and language, Breton states that his insistence on the normative in language is not to show the source of production of what he calls 'l'Interdit', but rather that his aim is to demonstrate that it is in the social dimension of signs that normativity is to be found. Language, he states, is a 'mise en commun par la règle', just like law. What is significant in this statement and throughout the exchanges between Thomas and Breton is the intellectual struggle for control over the social. The social is the nucleus to both arguments but it is the position that it occupies and how the individual relates to it that is the source of debate. In the construction of the 'personne juridique', the unity of the person rests on its social foundation. The 'personne juridique' is defined as anchored existentially, bodily and legally in the social. The social is the pre-existent order, the source of life, and most importantly the source and goal of any individual agency. The way Breton represents the 'sujet du désir' is as an autonomous agent who is the inventor of an unnatural and asocial individualism. For Breton, the construction of law on the 'sujet du désir' is tantamount to founding law on 'rien', rejecting Thomas' hypothesis that there is a regulatory principle that can be found in subjectivity as opposed to social experience. For Breton, if the social is invalidated then there can be no legitimacy of subject. Thomas' position locates the individual at the centre of the social; the social is not denied or rejected. Rather, Thomas privileges the autonomy and individuality of human nature with the capacity to decide laws. In short, whereas for Breton the social is the pre-requisite for individual agency, for Thomas autonomy and individuality are pre-requisites to the social.

A Sociological Comparison

These are fine but important distinctions because they highlight two of the key elements of the debate, namely the status of the relationship between the social and the individual, and the nature, limits and conditions of individual autonomy within the social. Breton has downgraded constantly the primacy of the individual over the social; for him, there can be no individualism without society. For Thomas, society is an external imposition on the individual and thus unacceptable. Breton and Thomas agree to disagree on this point. But Breton, in one of his concluding remarks, points obliquely to the fact that the law cannot ultimately resolve this distinction, that resolution lies somewhere outside the law and within the social. He states: 'Le droit dans sa positivité ne constitue qu'une normativité seconde, réflexive, par rapport à l'échafaudage de relations instituées que l'on appelle une société.'[25] In other words, Breton points to sociological factors to shed light on this area. Current sociological debate has returned to this area with a recent issue of the journal *Le Débat* asking the question 'Une sociologie de l'individu est-elle possible?.' The consensus among its contributors (Jean-Claude Kaufmann,

---

[25] Breton, 'De la nécessaire clairification du langage juridique', p. 50.

88   *The Gay Republic*

Philippe Corcuff and Marcel Gauchet) is that the individual is social, that interiorisation has a social origin, and that the individual cannot exist alone as 'une entité substantielle.' Jean-Claude Kaufmann states:

> L'individu n'est rien sans son corps, il n'est rien sans action. Sans les profondeurs implicites qui cristallisent une infinité d'évidences, un patrimoine de schèmes infraconscients, fondateur de son identité. Ce patrimoine n'est ni dans le corps biologique, ni dans les pensées. Il est dans l'environnement le plus proche et le plus intime, au plus près de soi, dans l'espace (continuellement travaillé) de la familiarité.[26]

However, within this consensus, there are subtle differences that qualify this view. Kaufmann, in a synthesis of his recent book *Ego. Pour une sociologie de l'individu*, borrows Bourdieu's term of the *habitus*[27] as the space where individuals are socialised and their actions classified. But Kaufmann introduces the notion of *habitudes* as an offshoot of the *habitus*. In trying to determine from where the individual emerges, Kaufmann claims that there is a divergence between the *habitus* and *habitudes*, with the *habitus* fragmenting and giving rise to *habitudes*. *Habitudes* form part of the history of individualisation in which the individual frees himself from the hegemonic centrality of the *habitus* and begins to structure his own modality of living. Kaufmman is careful to point out that it is not the individual who has produced the divergence from *habitus* to *habitudes* but rather divergence is at the origin of the historical process of individuation which has brought about a schism between *habitus* and *habitudes*: 'l'habitus perd sa centralité et se diffracte dans de multiples sous-univers spécifiés.'[28] The key point to remember in Kaufmann's analysis of the individual and the social is that even when the central structure of the social *habitus* is seen to implode as a result of individuation, the new process of individuation is a remodelled, individualised version of the original social structure. He sums this up in the formula: 'Structures

---

[26] Jean-Claude Kaufmann, 'L'expression de soi', *Le Débat*, 119 (2002): 119.

[27] Pierre Bourdieu defines the *habitus* as a principle and a system of classification. He also descirbes it as a structuring structure which organises practices and the perception of practices, and also a structured structure. For the benefits of our discussion, it is the role of the individual within this *habitus* which is of significance. On this particular point, Bourdieu states: 'Les individus ne se déplacent pas au hasard dans l'espace social d'une part parce que les forces qui confèrent sa structure à cet espace s'imposent à eux (à travers, par exemple, les mécanismes objectifs d'élimination et d'orientation), d'autre part parce qu'ils opposent aux forces du champ leur inertie propre, c'est-à-dire leurs propriétés, qui peuvent exister à l'état incorporé, sous forme de dispositions, ou à l'état objectivé, dans des biens, des titres, etc. [...]. Il s'ensuit que la position et la trajectoire individuelle ne sont pas indépendantes statistiquement, toutes les positions d'arrivée n'étant pas également probables pour tous les points de départ: cela implique qu'il existe une corrélation très forte entre les positions sociales et les dispositions des agents qui les occupent ou, ce qui revient au même, les trajectoires qui ont conduit à les occuper et que, par conséquent, *la trajectoire modale* fait partie intégrante du système des facteurs constitutifs de la classe' in *La Distinction* (Paris: Les Editions de Minuit, 1979), pp. 122-23.

[28] Kaufmann, 'L'expression de soi', p. 121.

From 'Crisis' of Law to a New 'Esprit des Lois' 89

socialement structurées structurant l'individu, elles deviennent alors également des structures individuellement restructurées structurant l'individu et le social.'[29]

Marcel Gauchet is equally scathing of the 'idéologie égocéphalocentrique' that promotes self-sufficiency and independence of the individual. He supports Kaufmann's view that the ideology of individualisation has been given a fair wind in the course of the twentieth century. He agrees that it has superseded the holistic model of the past and refashioned collective practices and institutions. But crucially, and in this he strengthens his connection with Kaufmann, he believes that societies and changes *within them* have individualised individuals, and it is not autonomous individuals who have brought about change from within themselves:

> Ce n'est pas seulement qu'une 'idéologie individualiste', forgée de longue main, en rupture avec 'l'idéologie holiste' des sociétés anciennes, en est venue à s'emparer des esprits et à remodeler les pratiques collectives et les institutions, à partir de là. C'est que le mécanisme social lui-même s'est transformé par le dedans, d'une manière qui le fait passer désormais, pour une part substantielle et croissante, par de 'individus individualisés', si l'on dire [...]. L'intronisation de l'individu est d'abord un fait social; elle relève d'un changement fondamental dans les rouages et les canaux de l'action collective.[30]

Gauchet proceeds to qualify Kaufmann's theory of divergence between *habitus* and *habitudes* by seeing more of a collusion between *habitus* and *habitudes* in the production of the greater socialisation of the individual. While the notion of *habitudes* for Kaufmman appears to elevate the sovereignty of the individual, for Gauchet the notion of *habitudes* ties down the individual as an agent of social change which reinforces the idea of society changing because of the role that the individual has in it. However, for Gauchet, this socialisation of the individual is only half the story. At this point, Gauchet suggests the need for this socialisation to be legalised. Gauchet recognises the benefits that individualisation have brought to the social process in the fields of cognition and representation. Individualisation, he claims, has brought about a sea change in the way societies treat individuals and their rights, pointing to the *Déclaration des droits de l'homme* as the concretisation in law of what he classes as the importance of 'fait social.' The 'fait social' is the locus for Gauchet of legitimacy; it is the ground where the law moulds its legitimacy. Legitimacy, for Gauchet, is founded on 'immanence' to the social facts, and not on norms that either precede or transcend the individual. Gauchet concludes his case by suggesting that the socialisation of the individual has its prolongation and eventual completion in the law. In this way, the law is seen to look to the inside of the collective and social mechanism which produces the individual for its legitimacy. Similarly, the law must consider how society thinks and looks at itself and how it justifies its order and the means by which the social dynamic of individualisation penetrates that order. In short, the law must look to

---

[29] Kaufmann, 'L'expression de soi', p. 121.

[30] Marcel Gauchet, 'Les deux sources du processus d'individualisation', *Le Débat*, 119 (2002): 134-35.

90 *The Gay Republic*

Legitimacy in the 'fait social'

Gauchet's recommendations are particularly apt in the light of our legal discussion, and they provide serious food for thought about the relevance of laws to social realities, which I shall address shortly. However, in the context of the juridic debate between Breton and Thomas on the relation between the individual and the social, both Kaufmann and Gauchet are agreed that the autonomy of a rational and independent individual who is self-sustaining and self-fulfilling is a fiction. Autonomy of the individual, from their perspectives, is a creation of social institutions which have adapted to fashion responsible and self-reliant individuals. This sociological perspective appears to fit neatly with Breton's legal argument that society is the source of all individual agency. But Gauchet raises a potentially divisive issue when he suggests that the legitimacy of the socialisation of the individual is conditional on the capacity of the law to reflect social situations. Breton, we recall, discussed this issue in conjunction with a debate on norms, and argued that norms predate and transcend social realities as founding stones of the law. Breton has also been critical of the culture of autonomy of subject which, he claims, has contributed to the creation of *les droits de l'homme*. What on the surface appears to be a sociological and legal pact may now come undone because of questions over the legitimacy of the law to reflect adequately the 'fait social.' By contrast, Thomas' creation of a split identity between 'personne juridique' and 'sujet du désir' may not have strong sociological grounding, but what it does appear to have is a legal basis for a defence of individual rights.

The comparative value of the sociological and legal debates has highlighted the importance of the social as a structure from which the individual derives a meaningful existence and a legitimacy on which to found citizenship. However, Marcel Gauchet problematises this structure by questioning the source of this legitimacy for citizens, whether it be 'd'origine transcendante [...] dans un ordre qui les précède et les dépasse' (in which case he states there is no individual) or whether legitimacy 'est immanente dans sa source, et elle ne peut sortir que des atomes individuels, elle ne peut procéder que d'un rassemblement à partir d'une dispersion primordiale.'[31] For Gauchet, this legitimacy, with its source in individuals, 'a vocation à devenir un fait social.' He claims that the importance of the individual in the social structure is vital because he acts as a conduit from source to social legitimacy. As such, the importance of the individual in the legal and sociological equation is vital. Thus far, the legal and sociological debates have been split between the primordiality of the social over the individual and vice versa. Gauchet emphasises the intrinsic, conditional link that must be preserved for the survival of both. But most crucially for the nature of the remainder of this chapter, Gauchet hones in on what is ultimately significant and what represents the

---

[31] Gauchet, 'Les deux sources du processus d'individuation', p. 136.

From 'Crisis' of Law to a New 'Esprit des Lois' 91

true test for the crisis in French law, which is that legitimacy of the law is conditional on its representation as a 'fait social' and not as an abstraction either of the person or the body. Gauchet is scornful of those (sociologists and jurists) who try to misrepresent the historical process of individualisation by seeing it primarily as a revolution of ideas rather than a revolution of the individual and the social:

> On ne peut pas décrire l'individualisation de nos sociétes en faisant abstraction de cette révolution dans la légitimité et de sa lente infiltration dans les rapports sociaux. Elle n'a pas que la consistance impalpable d'idées et de valeurs encloses dans la tête des acteurs. Elle a son répondant et son prolongement directs dans l'opérateur efficace qu'est le droit, dont il faut cesser de mésestimer la capacité intrinsèque de modeler, d'informer et de transformer les liens de société.[32]

Gauchet's contribution opens up our discussion in two new but connected directions. Implicit in his concept of legitimacy is a critique of the abstraction of the republican mindset which, I would argue, underpins the legal differences between Breton's 'personne juridique' and Thomas' 'sujet du désir.' At the same time, Gauchet appears to lean towards a more democratic mindset that is reflexive and self-questioning:

> Il faut chercher, en effet, à l'intérieur du mécanisme collectif ce qui produit de l'individu, ce qui lui confère un rôle éminent et toujours plus large dans le processus social [...]. Il faut aussi prendre au sérieux la manière dont la société se pense elle-même dans ce qui justifie son ordre et les voies par lequelles cette représentation contraignante pénètre son ordre.[33]

As alluded to earlier by Alain-Gérard Slama, there is a clear political division shadowing this technical and legal debate and which reflects the growing republican/democratic opposition running through many aspects of contemporary French life. The nature of the legal debate, as espoused by Breton and Thomas, reflects broadly the political contours of contemporary French society. Breton's 'personne juridique' is the modern day face of republican man; an abstract, geometric form, devoid of physical and sexual attributes. Self-effacing in his loyalty to social and universal equality, he is the epitome of general will over private will, of public interest over private interest. Republican man is content to be part of a republic in which 'le peuple en corps a la souveraineté.'[34] Republican man exists for the common cause. He has no need to negotiate his place in law as it is already decided for him in his interest by preset norms. In comparison, democratic woman is obliged by her autonomy to negotiate her existence, her body (and sexuality) and her rights. Not symbolised, enshrined or fully represented in republican law, she is required to arbitrate over the conditions of her acceptance within the social. Democratic woman must constantly redefine her inclusion in the social (parity being an apt example) because, unlike republican man for whom

---

[32] Gauchet, 'Les deux sources du processus d'individuation', p. 136.
[33] Gauchet, 'Les deux sources du processus d'individuation', p. 136.
[34] Montesquieu, *De l'Esprit des lois*. Livre II, Chapitre II, p. 10.

equality is universal and whose citizenship is eternally guaranteed, she can take nothing for granted. Misrepresentation and the threat of a masculinised universal hover precariously over democratic woman, so real is the danger of her singularity being subsumed by the universal will.

The simplistic nature of the above political portraits do not reflect the complexity of the legal distinctions analysed by Breton and Thomas. My argument is that, in broad terms, their legal positions bear the hallmarks of a political divide. But the political waters become muddied under closer examination. If Breton's defence of the 'personne juridique' has a republican imprint, then why does he dispute the validity of the juridic distinction between 'personne juridique' and 'sujet du désir'? Is there the suggestion that Breton, in contesting the validity of this distinction, is calling for a *rapprochement* between the two, some sort of legal compromise? This is clearly one interpretation. However, a different interpretation reveals an altogether different agenda in which *rapprochement* is abandoned in favour of *méreconnaissance*. Throughout his argument, Breton questions the autonomy of the 'sujet.' He questions the legal premise on which the 'personne juridique' is split into a 'sujet':

> Je ne conteste donc nullement la définition classique de la personne de droit, mais celle d'un sujet sous-jacent qu'on entend désormais déduire de ce contraste. Si l'on peut éventuellement affirmer que la personne juridique est l'abstraction d'un sujet (mais de quel sujet? tout est là), rien ne nous contraint à déduire les qualités supposés d'un prétendu sujet naturel.[35]

Breton's reluctance to recognise the status of the 'sujet' is grounded legally in the juridic hierarchy of person over body. As such, the legal capacity of the person is not derived from his body or subjective desires (which are beyond the law) but from 'une identité permanente, univoque et stable.' For Breton, this permanence is a key feature of the law because to construct laws on things that are 'mouvant ou divisé' is to invoke chance and caprice. Hence the unity of the person as an unchangeable, unequivocal and total entity is central to the construction of the 'personne juridique.' This unity also explains his deconstruction of what he sees as arbitrary divisions between body and person, desire and abstraction. Breton's legal justification for the obfuscation of the 'sujet', based on the uniformity and universal equality of the person, is clearly underpinned by a republicanism in which both French law and republican ideals appear reconciled in the theorisation of the *person* at the expense of individuality.

Thomas' argument for the resurrection of the 'sujet' is similarly open to the same charges of political collusion, although of a different hue. Sociologically, we have seen how the total autonomy of the subject from both a social context and from the juridic construction of normativity are difficult to uphold. Although, it should be repeated that Thomas has always claimed that the social is as much on the side of the 'sujet' as it is on the side of the 'personne juridique', the difference

---

[35] Breton, 'De la nécessaire clarification du langage juridique', p. 35.

for Thomas being that not only does autonomy and individuals predate the social but, as a consequence, the 'sujet' is seen to have a greater say in the construction of the social. It could be argued that it is this difference between 'sujet' as agent of social change and the position of the 'personne juridique' in which society is the source of individual agency, which has generated the split culture of differentialism and republicanism in contemporary French society. The promotion of the 'sujet' as an *individual* with rights of and to difference (expressed in body and desire) is now challenging for juridic status within the hegemonic structure of the 'personne' as universal abstraction. But, in constructing this 'sujet' around fashionable notions of the body and desire, is Thomas not guilty of splitting the 'personne juridique' when, as Breton claimed, there is no legal basis on which to do so? Breton, we recall, questioned the legal and ontological origin of the 'sujet logé dans un corps.' In fact, could Thomas not be accused of pandering to the communitarian lobbies, which have their own political agenda of separation from the republican mould? These are legitimate concerns, which carry the same danger signs as those we flagged up with Breton and republicanism. The critical difference is that Breton has been defending a construction of the law based on a set of principles which, as Gauchet observed, are losing their legitimacy in the face of the 'fait social.' Thus political reasons that may be shoring up what may seem an increasingly ineffective construction of the law need to be examined. Thomas' legal argument, still modish in its terminology and not without its conceptual shortcomings, is nevertheless tapping into a rich vein of social disaffection.

The Law, Homosexuality and the PaCS

In French law, homosexuality is a juridic category. Hugues Montouh states: 'L'homosexualité constitue précisément une catégorie juridique, au sens où le droit l'a intégrée à son lexique et lui a attaché des conséquences juridiques.'[36] The problem with this category is that it is one founded on discrimination. This, for Montouh, is the paradox of homosexuality in the law. As minorities, lesbians and gays are the victims of the universality of the law and of its homogenising and egalitarian effects. As we have argued in the course of this chapter, juridic principles appear to reflect republican values where individuals are only recognised in their abstract nudity rather than in their everyday clothes. In exposing the paradox of the law, Montouh goes on to argue that the struggle for homosexuals over recent decades has been twofold. Firstly, they have fought against discrimination within the law and for the right to be no longer persecuted. Secondly, they have campaigned for their full and legal recognition within the law by advocating a 'politique de la différence.'

Of course, the decriminalisation of homosexuality in 1982 and the recent PaCS legislation have gone some ways in addressing Montouh's concerns. And while

---

[36] Hugues Montouh, 'L'esprit d'une loi: controverse sur le pacte civil de solidarité', *Les Temps modernes*, 603 (1999): 191.

94 *The Gay Republic*

these legislations in themselves are landmarks in the homosexual landscape, they do not reveal the full picture of how the law continues to misrepresent lesbians and gays. Daniel Borrillo has written widely on this subject.[37] In one of his articles, Borrillo explores in more depth than Montouh the nature of the juridic construction of the homosexual. He writes:

> Ce personnage, défini par pas sa singularité, est caractérisé par des traits qu'on lui attribue et auxquels il ne peut pas échapper. C'est cette singularité essentielle qui viendrait justifier le traitement discriminatoire effectué par le droit. En dehors du droit commun, l'homosexuel ne participe pas des caractéristiques communes à l'ensemble des personnes hétérosexuelles 'normales.' Dans le fantasme des juristes, l'homosexuel apparaît pluôt comme un homme, dangereux pour les enfants, narcissique car incapable de reconnaître et d'aimer l'autre; il est infidèle, riche et, de par sa nature subversive, dangereux pour l'ordre social. Ces hommes riches et dangereux sont également organisés en de puissants lobbies ayant pour but la destruction des fondements anthropologiques de la culture occidentale.[38]

For Borrillo, this representation of the homosexual is part of what he calls the 'doctrine des juristes.' He claims that jurists have engaged in a sinister and concerted campaign of misrepresentation of homosexuality. Borrillo exposes the tactics of this campaign from the perpetuation of a homosexual sub-citizenship, as outlined above, to the construction of a fallacious homosexual exceptionalism that is radically different to the heterosexual norm. For Borrillo, a lawyer himself, it is a tactic which avoids dealing with lesbian and gay identity by dismissing it emotionally, derogatorily and euphemistically.[39] It is a campaign also designed to make it seem that the problems of lesbians and gays are of their own making in the sense that their singularity is self-inflicted and runs contrary to social existence and sexual propagation. The cumulative effect of this campaign is to deny homosexuals basic rights, to deny them personal dignity, and to dehumanise homosexuals by denying him a public face. On a technical front, Borrillo summarises the current juridic doctrine on homosexuality as a matter of private concern which is outside the remit of legal influence. The reality of the PaCS legislation, however, is that homosexual unions are now very much part of the legal framework, although Borrillo points out that, with the law now recognising homosexual couples, the doctrine of jurists has changed direction and is now targeted on exposing the

---

[37] See in particular his edited collection *Homosexualités et droit* (Paris: PUF, 1998).

[38] Daniel Borrillo, 'Fantasmes des juristes vs Ratio juris: la doxa des privatistes sur l'union entre personnes de même sexe' in Eric Fassin and Daniel Borrillo (eds.), Au-delà du PaCS, pp. 161-92.

[39] Both Borrillo and Montouh point to this pattern within the legal system to euphemise homosexuality and homosexuals as part of a strategy of denigration and discrimination. Mountouh writes: 'Les juristes français, quant à eux, préfèrent euphémiser et parler de catégorie, qui caractérise tout fait ou ensemble de fait, tout acte ou ensemble d'actes auxquels la loi ou toute autre règle de droit attache des conséquences juridiques' in 'L'esprit d'une loi: controverse sur le pacte civil de solidarité', p. 191.

From 'Crisis' of Law to a New 'Esprit des Lois' 95

inadequacies of the legislation itself: 'Toutes les branches du droit ont été mobilisées pour signaler les imperfections et démontrer les incongruités d'une loi "médiocre", "partisane" qui suscite la "perplexité" et engendre le "doute" et "l'incertitude."'[40]

Besides the exploitation of traditional juridic practice, Borrillo's article sheds further light on the legal and sociological distinctions we have examined thus far. Firstly, he proposes a new legal departure in the representation of the homosexual, which calls for a redefinition of the 'sujet.' Unlike Montouh, and the majority of lesbian and gay groups who have campaigned for gay rights on the slogan of 'la politique de la différence', Borrillo calls for a redefinition of the legal citizen in terms of the 'indifférenciation du sujet de droit.'[41] Borrillo's argument is that legal recognition of the homosexual couple is not simply the award of 'droits subjectifs d'un groupe spécifique.' Borrillo claims that anonymity of subject (gay, straight, ethnic) is the pre-requisite of any egalitarian legal undertaking. In principle, this description appears to differ considerably from the conception of the 'sujet', defined by Yan Thomas in terms of the body. Borrillo appears to strip the subject of a specific identity, but he then situates the subject within a legal model of recognition. Thomas' conception is the reverse; the subject is removed from formal legal representation (free to articulate his own) but ascribed a body with a clear singularity and difference. The difference between the two concepts may also be linked to the political goals of each. Borrillo's concept of the 'sujet' is partially hitched to the struggle for equality not only of lesbians and gays but all minorities, hence the occlusion of the subject as a specific identity in order to encompass all other identities. Thomas' concept is clearly established in opposition to the legality of the 'personne juridique' and thus the association of the 'sujet' with its own defining space of the body is a necessary corollary to the legalised 'rationality' of the 'personne.'

A second issue that Borrillo addresses at the end of his article and which is linked directly to Gauchet's sociology of the individual is the way the 'doctrine des juristes' has translated into a denial of the social and historical impact of the PaCS legislation. In directing his focus on some of the technical dysfunctions of the PaCS legislation, Borrillo criticises the legal establishment for failing to see beyond the permanence of its own legal structures and for refusing to acknowledge the role that 'fait social' plays in the formulation of the law. He writes:

> La doctrine [des juristes] s'adonne à des commentaires techniques qui ne prennent nullement compte de l'épaisseur historique et du contexte politique au sein duquel la loi fût adoptée. En évacuant la dimension historique dans leurs analyses, les juristes mettent de côté un élément indispensable pour la compréhension du problème. En effet, ils omettent soigneusement d'indiquer que le PaCS a été créé pour résoudre l'impasse

---

[40] Borrillo, *'Fantasmes des juristes vs* Ratio juris...*'*, p. 185.
[41] Borrillo, *'Fantasmes des juristes vs* Ratio juris...*'*, pp. 163-4.

juridique dans laquelle se trouvaient les couples homosexuels après le refus de reconnaissance de la qualité de concubins par la Cour de cassation.[42]

Borrillo is scathing of what he describes as the self-denial of the law in its refusal to accept responsibility for its role in denying equal rights to lesbian and gay couples. The significance of this self-denial, and the denial of a social and historical dimension to the issue of lesbian and gay identity, are problematic from the sociological perspective. For Gauchet, it is not only symptomatic of the distance between traditional juridic structures and social interaction, but it is also indicative of the extent to which the legitimacy of the law is being seen to be determined more by its own self-perpetuation and axiomatic norms, and less by the source of legitimacy in the individual in society.

Conclusions

What Borrillo's analysis shows is that in respect of both 'sujet' as a legal concept, and the law as the agency of legitimacy, neither can afford to detach themselves from their socio-cultural contexts. The way the legal debate has been conducted takes us back to Slama's initial characterisation of a crisis in the French legal system. But more than a crisis with political overtones, the crisis has deepened into a crisis of legal terminology, of representation and of legitimacy. The Breton/Thomas wrangle over the respective status of 'personne juridique' and 'sujet du désir' is primarily a legal distinction with obvious and potentially serious social implications. The individual is defined either as 'être selon le droit', with its institutional, social and normative conditions, or 'être selon le corps' with its set of social and autonomous obligations. In short, the legal debate seems guilty of laying down its own set of preconditions to the social debate in terms of a power struggle between person and subject, between public and private, between norms and 'faits' and over who has a monopoly of the social (the individual in the social, or the social in the individual). However, as distinctions that either reflect accurately the socio-cultural landscape or which could be applied to this landscape, they are fraught with difficulties. In the context of lesbian and gay sexuality, the legal distinction of 'personne juridique' and 'sujet du désir' has clear merit in opening up the debate on sexuality and providing a potentially legitimate space in the 'sujet' for the articulation of a lesbian and gay identity. But, the legal model, based on a 'in/out' dichotomy, seems problematic and unrepresentative. The legal debate appears to have created, in the interest of rationality, polarised categories of individual and behaviour which do not reflect the intricacies of social reality.

The reality of the PaCS is that lesbians and gays want their autonomy as subjects (free to privatise the law and their sexuality) but also want to be recognised as legal citizens within the wider understanding of the law. Lesbians and gays want to negotiate the sociability (or asociability as Bersani would put it)

---

[42] Borrillo, '*Fantasmes des juristes vs* Ratio juris...', p. 187.

From 'Crisis' of Law to a New 'Esprit des Lois'   97

and private legality of their sexuality, not on terms of the conventional and legal principle of heterosexual alterity, but on terms of gay sexuality as having its unique sexual and social relevance.[43] However, the problem posed by lesbian and gay sexuality, from a legal perspective, is that lesbians and gays want to be simultaneously inside traditional juridic law so as to be recognised, and outside it so as to be free to create their own laws. In this context, Breton's defence of the rationalising principle and absolute intelligibility of the law seems a forlorn hope. The complexity of the social tapestry (at least in the lesbian and gay context) highlights the need to revisit some cherished legal principles. The first is the presumption of legal terminology in the definition of the individual, in particular the efficacy of terms such as 'personne juridique' (and its abstract associations) and the 'souveraineté' of the subject. The law has been seen to have problematised the individual by creating hierarchies of the self, which presume a debatable legitimacy. Secondly, if the law is to be effective (representative and legitimate), it must take its cue from the interaction of individuals with socio-cultural change.

The crisis in French law is one in which the law has appeared to eschew its responsibility to legitimacy. As Marcel Gauchet pointed out, the role of the individual in society has evolved significantly. The rise of individualism has not only reined in the dominance of the holistic model of past societies, but it has superseded this model not in an ideological fashion but as a social reality. For sociology, as represented by both Kaufmann and Gauchet, society has changed from within in such a way that *socially individualised individuals* are now emerging out of the social. Gauchet, in particular, has highlighted the significance of the notion of *habitudes* being forged out of the decline of the *habitus*. But it is the new role of the individual as a consequence of this transformation which is of special interest to him. He states:

> L'individu émerge et s'impose comme un opérateur de cohérence. Il est amené à fonctionner comme un pivot d'intégration pour son propre compte, mais aussi pour la société. A son niveau singulier, il est en charge de construire la société comme une totalité, par la manière dont il associe et tisse ensemble les différents ordres dans lesquels il est pris. C'est ce qui en fait, à sa minuscule échelle, un authentique et puissant auteur du changement.[44]

Gauchet's description of the genesis of the individual from within the 'fonctionnement social' is, however, incomplete without its legal legitimacy: 'Il est indispensable d'élargir la perspective et de reconnaître au droit sa fonction effectuante et son épaisseur de fait social.'[45] In other words, this transformation of the individual from within the social and the new profile of the individual as a 'auteur du changement' is incomplete without its legal recognition. Such legal

---

[43] As we have seen, this uniqueness can be channelled in different ways. Bersani locates it within gay desire, Seidman in a cultural transformation of the social, and Pratt in a post-queer strategic consciousness.

[44] Gauchet, 'Les sources du processus d'individualisation', p. 135.

[45] Gauchet, 'Les sources du processus d'individualisation', p. 136.

98 *The Gay Republic*

recognition is an indication for Gauchet of a new representative politics and an acknowledgement of the function of the empowered individual. He states: 'Il faut y [l'individualisme] revenir, d'abord, en donnant à cette idéologie sa véritable portée de mode de représentation de la communauté humaine. Il faut y revenir, ensuite, en observant qu'elle possède un puissant outil de traduction au sein du tissu social avec la logique du droit des individus.'[46] For Gauchet, the logic of the rights of individuals is founded on their capacity to represent themselves and justify their organisation. From this comes legitimacy. Gauchet goes further on this point by claiming that legitimacy has its primordial (a word he uses on several occasions) source in individuals (in fact individual atoms), but that legitimacy can only proceed as a process of 'rassemblement.' In other words, legitimacy is a two way process: 'elle ne peut pas sortir que des atomes individuels, elle ne peut procéder que d'un rassemblement à partir d'une dispersion primordiale. Il ne s'agit, encore une fois, que d'un fait de représentation, que d'une organisation du pensable.'[47]

Gauchet's establishment of a primordial and representative link to legitimacy reinforces the inseparability between the individual and the social, and the constructive role of the individual in the formation of the social. It is my contention in this chapter that the crisis in French law is a crisis of legitimacy. Alain-Gérard Slama has characterised the crisis as a crisis of juridic traditions between Montesquieu and Madison, between assimilation and arbitration. He has also explained that recent European laws and directives are now playing their part 'in the silent revolution that is inverting the French juridical tradition.'[48] Slama also expresses concern about the decline of traditional legal structures as institutions of state, particularly when what he describes replacing them is a culture of experts and judges who owe their 'legitimacy' more to their professional competence and social prestige, and less to the rule of law. He questions the legitimacy of the culture of expertise presiding over the law, its credibility and the credibility of the legal process. Concerns within sociology also point to the rise of a dangerous strain of *über* individualism characterised by pathological narcissism.[49] Distinct from the benign social variant, this strain of individualism nevertheless raises concerns about the dangers of individualism if left to detach itself from its social roots.

Given these crises, there is all the more reason to return to source. The crisis in French law is as much within the system as it is outside. The crisis is one of its own legal legitimacy in which it has failed to adjust to the primordial and representative chain of legitimacy, and stifled the creative 'fonction effectuante' of the individual. Traditionally, French law has sourced its legitimacy in the application of the universality and abstraction of the individual. As we are seeing in the course of this book, both these principles are increasingly open to the charges of misrepresentation and fiction. Current sociology is rediscovering the

---

[46] Gauchet, 'Les sources du processus d'individualisation', p. 136.
[47] Gauchet, 'Les sources du processus d'individualisation', p. 136.
[48] Slama, 'Democratic Dysfunctions and Republican Obsolesence...', p. 57.
[49] See Philippe Corcuff's article, 'L'individualisme contemporain en question', pp. 126-32.

importance of legitimacy in the *immanence* of the relationship between the individual and the social. French law may need to consult further on this relationship.

Chapter 4

Lesbian and Gay Identity and the Politics of Subversion

At the end of the last chapter, Marcel Gauchet suggested that the crisis in the legitimacy of French law could only be resolved by returning to the founding principles of *les droits de l'homme*, and specifically to what he called the 'immanence' of the relationship between the individual and the 'fait social.' The immanence of this relationship and its connection to the 'fait social' is critical, not only in the context of the law, but also in the context of how lesbians and gays seek to politicise their sexuality within the parameters of French republicanism, and in their perceptions of themselves as sexual 'identities' with political motivations. This chapter will take as its departure point a seminal text by the sociologist Pierre Bourdieu (*La Domination masculine*), the annexe of which addresses the political plight of the lesbian and gay 'movement' in France at the end of the 1990s. Bourdieu reinvigorates the potential for radical gay subversion from within the republic as the site where durable and profound symbolic rupture can take place (as opposed to the more aesthetic and artificial rupture that takes place at the level of passive integrationism). Bourdieu advocates subversion from inside universalism which will take the form of putting difference/particularism to the service of the universal, of re-appropriating the categorising apparatus on which norms of sex and sexuality are instituted, and of reorienting the strategic discourse of power between 'dominant' and 'dominé' (specifically in the context of the perceived passivity of lesbians and gays in the PaCS negotiations). In effect, Bourdieu's hypothesis will be seen to converge (albeit with subtle variations of approach) with the positions of Yonnet, Seidman, Bersani, Pratt and Eribon. In particular, it will follow the broad contours of that of Gauchet in that Bourdieu encourages movement away from symbolic acts of subversion to real, active acts that produce their legitimacy in their immanence.

The second part of this chapter will explore one of Bourdieu's conditions of subversion for lesbians and gays, namely their need to broaden the sexual agenda to incorporate other social and political issues. In this context, I investigate the construction of a gay 'identity' in France, the hypothesis of a core gay identity (on what this core is founded) and how expressions of gay identity communicate with social and political consciousness. In particular, I draw a close connection between the publication of Bourdieu's *La Domination masculine* (and its subversive agenda) and the emergence of a lesbian and gay movement (as evidenced in the

102 *The Gay Republic*

manifestos of ACT-Up Paris) at the end of 1990s. I trace the trajectory of a fledgling gay 'community', emerging out of the dark days of the AIDS crisis, and still steeped in narcissism and one-dimensional sexual politics, towards a deeper and broader movement, whose recognition of its internal diversity (its capacity to reach out and embrace racial and class struggles) was critical to its survival, its subversive credibility, and its fidelity to the 'fait social.' Casting a heavy shadow over this trajectory is the presumption of a cohesive, uniform gay identity with common aims and objectives. To this degree, the critical observations of some leading commentators, notably Didier Eribon, will serve as a salutary reminder that, no matter how far lesbians and gays have advanced in their struggles for recognition and equality of rights, a collective gay identity is not only far off but, for some, an unrealisable utopia and maybe an undesireable one altogether.

In the annex to his influential work *La Domination masculine*, Pierre Bourdieu addressed in substantial detail the crisis that faced, what he calls, the lesbian and gay movement in France at the end of the 1990s. I want to outline his argument for two reasons. Firstly, his comments were addressed to a movement that in the mid to late 1990s was in search of a new direction. Emerging as it had done so, with considerable admiration, out of the traumas of the AIDS crisis and the affair of contaminated blood, the lesbian and gay movement needed to embark on a new stage of its development. What was sure, however, was that the movement had to move on from the preventive mentality adopted in the course of the AIDS crisis. Secondly, the political path advocated by Bourdieu represented a huge challenge to a movement that was on the margins of society and ostracised by widespread homophobia and the stigma of AIDS. Most crucially, politicisation meant transforming a gay community, unified and divided, visible and invisible, into a radical movement with clear political goals and universal clout.

La Domination masculine is primarily focused on masculine heterosexual domination. When Bourdieu speaks about homosexuality there is considerable ambiguity. On the one hand, he views homosexuality as a potential threat to male domination in that it offers the possibility of differentiating 'le rapport sexuel d'un rapport de pouvoir.' But as Reeser and Seifert have suggested, homosexuals have no power within Bourdieu's heterosexual binary, and instead are implicated/subsumed under feminisation by the sexual act of being penetrated. In other words, 'homosexuality is at least in part predicated on a male heterosexual identity.'[1] On the surface, the ambiguity of this position is frustrating because, while Bourdieu affirms the idea that homosexuality can challenge hegemonic constructions of masculinity and femininity, he simultaneously denies homosexuality this power and this denial appears to chime with the advocates of essentialism and specifically 'la différence des sexes.' In short, for Bourdieu, homosexuality can transform heterosexuality but not be part of it. This simplistic overview of Bourdieu's position does, however, belie deeper levels of complexity

---

[1] Todd W. Reeser and Lewis C. Seifert, 'Oscillating Masculinity in Pierre Bourdieu's *La Domination masculine*', *L'Esprit Créateur*, 3 (2003): 93.

Lesbian and Gay Identity and the Politics of Subversion   103

and sophistication.

Bourdieu begins his argument by setting up an important opposition. The lesbian and gay movement is a 'mouvement de révolte contre une forme particulière de violence symbolique [...], qui met en question très profondément l'ordre symbolique en vigueur et pose de manière tout à fait radicale la question des fondements de cet ordre et des conditions d'une mobilisation réussie en vue de le subvertir.'[2] For Bourdieu, lesbians and gays have been caught up in the binary of heterosexual symbolic domination which has denied them visibility, a public existence and stigmatised them when any attempt at visibility is expressed. Hence, lesbians and gays have tended to live discretely, if not hidden within society. Part of the paradox of the gay 'condition', for Bourdieu, has been the fact that, as a result of this domination, the dominated assumes/takes on 'le point de vue dominant', and lesbians and gays are forced to live straight lives and deny their own private sexual identities. The alternative, as made clear in Bourdieu's thematic opposition, is the subversion of the dominant order. At this juncture, things become significantly more problematic, not so much because of what Bourdieu goes to on suggest, but by the socio-political infrastructure of France itself, divided generally along republican (universalist) and democratic (communitarian) lines. I have discussed elsewhere the interplay between these two traditions. Suffice to say now that Bourdieu, in these opening volleys of radicalism, is opposed to the lesbian and gay movement rebelling against the binary of 'la différence des sexes' by itself constituting a constructed category of homosexuality, and thus giving rise to new categorisations and restrictions which the movement itself should be resisting. It might appear from Bourdieu's representation of the lesbian and gay movement that politically and ideologically he is firmly rooted in the republican tradition. To a degree, this would be an accurate assessment. However, Bourdieu's rejection of a communitarian separatism for the lesbian and gay movement is not an indication of a benign capitulation to republican universalism. On the contrary, as I have pointed out in the case of Paul Yonnet, it points in the direction of a potential among lesbians and gays for radical subversion from inside the republic. By the end of the first section of his argument, Bourdieu's alternative to the isolationism of communitarianism is the projection of a utopian 'politique de l'homosexualité', which is represented by the potential subversion of traditional heterosexual constructions of masculinity and femininity.

Bourdieu locates transformative power in the political and symbolic representations of the lesbian and gay movement. In this respect, he embarks on a serious questioning of some of the cherished principles of this movement. He questions the validity of symbolic revolutions, such as Gay Pride festivities or even the PaCS itself. His aim is to make the movement re-evaluate its priorities in terms of whether symbolic gestures, which bestow a certain visible 'catégorie réalisée', are in themselves satisfactory. He asks whether the *belief* in the gendered

---

[2]   Pierre Bourdieu, *La Domination masculine* (Paris: Editions du Seuil, Coll. Liber, 1998), p. 129.

104 *The Gay Republic*

construction of sexuality is fulfilled in visible performances of recognition that make emblems out of stigma. The point Bourdieu wants to make is that through the construction of categorisations ('gay', 'lesbian'[3]) the lesbian and gay movement has bought into the collective fiction of a heteronormative order, which is not only served by the construction of these categories, but reinforced by its perennial opposition to homosexuality. As such, the artificiality of 'gay'/'lesbian' constructions tends to lead the movement away from its true social base. For Bourdieu, the price of visible and symbolic recognition is political aphasia; in short, the movement is contradicting itself in asking the state, cap in hand, for recognition of legal and public status. He sees in this form of capitulation to the state a return to the type of invisibility that lesbians and gays were forced to live under in previous decades: 'tout se passe en effet comme si les homosexuels qui ont dû lutter pour passer de l'invisibilité à la visibilité, pour cesser d'être exclus et invisibilisés, visaient à redevenir invisibles, et en quelque sorte neutres et neutralisés par la soumission à la norme dominante.'[4] Bourdieu concludes the second section of his argument by identifying a structural contradiction within the lesbian and gay movement between exhibition and invisibility, between celebration and suppression, which in turn condemns the movement to a critical balancing act.

Bourdieu's critique dovetails neatly with other theories of lesbian and gay identity (notably Bersani, Eribon and Pratt) that claim that one of the fundamental dangers for lesbians and gays is to allow their sexuality (and identity) to be fashioned by dominant heteronormative structures. Bersani's location of gayness in the desire of sameness, Eribon's creation of an aesthetic of the self and Pratt's state of constant alertness to forces of heteronormative repression are key examples. However, if Bourdieu's suggestion that an integrative strategy (the goal of which is merely social recognition for gays) is the wrong way to bring about subversion, then what is the right strategy? In response, Bourdieu highlights the distinction between the symbolic and the real. Symbolic subversions, he claims, are limited; as 'provocations esthètes', they are useful in so far as they identify what is to be ruptured. However, for symbolic subversions to carry any meaning they must not be limited to symbolic ruptures. On the contrary,

> pour changer durablement les représentations, elle [l'action de subversion symbolique] doit opérer et imposer une transformation durable des catégories incorporées (des

---

[3]   Teresa de Lauretis, who has written widely on feminism and queer theory, has also questioned the validity of 'gay', 'lesbian' terms in the context of the United States. In a queer critique of identities, she claims that these terms are less representative than they might appear, and that notions of gay or lesbian sameness are mythical, preferring to think of any alliance or solidarity within the terms 'gay' and 'lesbian' to be better served by highlighting the differences within them. See in this respect her introduction 'Queer Theory: Lesbian and Gay Sexualities', in *Differences*, 3 (1991): iii-xviii.

[4]   Bourdieu, *La Domination masculine*, p. 132. Bourdieu's critique of integration (where gays merge invisibly into the general populus) is not only a denial of their radical 'raison d'être' but also an implicit critique of Frédéric Martel's 'droit à l'indifférence.'

Lesbian and Gay Identity and the Politics of Subversion 105

schémas de pensée) qui, au travers de l'éducation, confèrent le statut de réalité évidente, nécessaire, indiscutée, naturelle, dans les limites de leur ressort de validité, aux catégories sociales qu'elles produisent. Elle doit demander au droit (qui, le mot le dit, a partie liée avec le *straight*...) une reconnaissance de la particularité qui implique son annulation.[5]

For Bourdieu, the *action* of symbolic subversion implies a long-term transformation of inherited categories of domination. This action involves the imposition and establishment of alternative categories which in turn are conferred, via education and socialisation, a new status. In short, this action amounts to an appropriation of the categorisation process by which society creates norms. It thus produces a realignment of power relations. Several points emerge from Bourdieu's hypothesis. The emphasis on institutions is crucial. Intellectual and educative institutions are key channels by which dissemination of ideas through society are conducted. In this sense, subversion happens at the point of engagement with the institution, and the subsequent wresting of power that a particular institution embodies.[6] For Bourdieu, one of the conditions of subversion therefore is the interaction (and subsequent resistance) between subversion and the dominant order. This is clearly acknowledged in his comments about the role of gay subversion, but only to the extent that he characterises the nature of this interaction as more passive than active. For Bourdieu, the current and contradictory strategy of subversion for the lesbian and gay movement is encapsulated in what he sees as a paradoxical request: 'elle doit demander au droit [...] une reconnaissance de la particularité qui implique son annulation.'[7] Rather than imposing (operating) a transformation of its own, the lesbian and gay movement is perceived to be wanting confirmation of its identity from an institution that consistently denies it.

At different points in the course of this argument, Bourdieu has emphasised the importance of realism and durability to all subversive strategies. This emphasis has meant that we do not lose sight of the empirical dimension to subversion in respect of the clash with institutions, nor of the unique situation of any group asserting its identity in the context of French republican universalism. Whether it be in the form of a heteronormative order or a law which limits the rights of lesbian and gay citizens, universalism is the reality with which the lesbian and gay movement must interact. The key issue for Bourdieu is the challenge represented by the lesbian and gay movement to the universalist doxa and the latter's hypocrisy on lesbian and gay rights. The question for Bourdieu is how to subvert this doxa. We have seen in different chapters thus far how the debate on communitarianism has pitched camp along different stretches of the dividing line between integrationism and separatism, some edging more towards integration (Théry, Agacinski), others more radically subversive (Fassin and Pisier). Bourdieu, in keeping with the logic of

---

[5] Bourdieu, *La Domination masculine*, p. 132.

[6] The sociologist Michel de Certeau has located identity coming into effect at the threshold of engagement with political institutions.

[7] Bourdieu, *La Domination masculine*, p. 133.

106 *The Gay Republic*

realist politics, challenges the perceived hypocrisy of universalism by proposing to 'universalise' the lesbian and gay movement. At a first glance, this may seem contradictory. How can one universalise what is specific and particular to a limited number of people ? Equally, is universalisation not another means of capitulating to the dominant symbolic order ? These are valid questions, but I think Bourdieu's use of universalisation is symbolic and designed to mock and undermine its symbolic namesake (universalism). Symbolic subversion for Bourdieu is an important aspect of subversion itself; part of the subversive strategy is symbolic destruction of the principle of universalism, the other part being the construction of new categories of perception. Both represent interlocking parts of the process. In this light, Bourdieu's case for the universalisation of the lesbian and gay movement would involve, on the one hand, the destruction of the division by which stigmatising and stigmatised groups function and are produced, and, on the other hand, the rehabilitation of the advantages linked to particularism (in this case gay) put to the service of universalism.

In an earlier chapter, I suggested that one of the intractable issues in contemporary French social, political and cultural life is universalism. I also qualified that statement by saying that universalism is a flexible beast, able to adapt to accommodate change without great loss of face. Bourdieu's phrase 'au service de l'universel' has ambiguous overtones. On one level, it points to particularism being at the service of universalism, which echoes the republican ring of a flexible and tolerant integrationism. On another level, the phrase points to particularism being used to facilitate/service universalism. Not withstanding the ambiguity, it is the latter interpretation with which Bourdieu progresses, mainly from the perspective of subversion. In recent debates in France, from parity and the PaCS to the headscarf affair, the concept of universalism has come under intense scrutiny. Previous debates on universalism have been conducted through the prism of sex (parity), sexuality (PaCS) and religious difference (headscarf). All these debates underline the desire for recognition of difference in the context of universal equality. The assumption underpinning these debates is that of the other looking in from the outside and wanting equal and democratic rights. Within each of these debates there have been different degrees of radicalism but the question has remained throughout about the validity of universalism as a unit of citizenship. Universalism, I have argued, conceptualises citizenship as a function of space (public and private). It privileges both public and private as spaces where citizenship is performed. However, while liberating all citizens in their rights to equal citizenship and respect of difference within the confines of private space ('la vie privée'), universalism can only offer full equality and respect for difference on the condition that private expressions of difference (sexual, ethnic, religious) are not only not identified in public space but are not separated out for attention at the expense of public unity and equality. Bourdieu's characterisation of the lesbian and gay movement points to layers and depths of institutional rupture that are necessary for real subversion, both of the sexual order and of universalism itself. In other words, to embed subversion is to integrate it into the universal (with the design of

Lesbian and Gay Identity and the Politics of Subversion   107

subverting universalism 'au service de l'universel'), which Bourdieu says can best be achieved by the creation of a social, avant-garde movement which *embraces the concerns of the particular with the wider interests of society*:

> On peut se demander si la seule manière, pour un tel mouvemnet, d'échapper à une ghettoïsation et à un sectarisme qui se renforcent mutuellement n'est pas de mettre les capacités spécifiques [...] au service du mouvement social dans son ensemble; ou pour sacrifier un instant à l'utopisme, de se placer à l'avant-garde, au moins sur le plan du travail théorique et de l'action symbolique (où certains groupes homosexuels sont passés maîtres), des mouvements politiques et scientifiques subversives, mettant ainsi au service de l'universel les avantages particuliers qui distinguent les homosexuels des autres groupes stigmatisés.[8]

Bourdieu's idea is easier said than done. The lesbian and gay movement in France had difficulty defining itself, let alone bridge gaps with other interest groups. Also, the AIDS crisis had left an indelible mark on the lesbian and gay landscape, with many lesbians and gays forced underground out of fear, or forced to live 'à la discretion.' The AIDS crisis had not only killed many homosexuals but forced a lot more into the closet. The AIDS crisis changed critically the visible/invisible profile of gays. For the more militant AIDS activists, the AIDS crisis facilitated their 'coming out';[9] the cause of the fight against AIDS seemed to matter more than any personal reservations about sexuality. On the contrary, for large swathes of the French population,[10] invisibility remained a preferred option, mainly of out fear and growing homophobia.

On the other side of the Atlantic, increased activism, greater tolerance towards lesbians and gays and Gay Pride marches offered a more accommodating context in which to 'come out' and embrace political activism. Also, the emergence of Lesbian and Gay Studies as an academic discipline on American campuses gave greater articulation to concepts of gay identity and sexuality. To be gay and to be seen to be gay was a matter of duty for many lesbians and gays.[11] In France, given its republican, universalist and academic traditions, homosexual visibility was more problematic. Lesbians and gays were perceived as an integrative part of the social fabric but restricted in terms of rights; acts and displays of difference were tolerated but deeply unrepublican. Gay 'communities' existed, but were forced

---

[8] Bourdieu, *La Domination masculine*, p. 134.

[9] Jean-Sébastien Thirard, then President of the *Centre gai et lesbien* which co-ordinated the Gay Pride march, claimed in 1995 that 'l'engagement dans la lutte anti-sida a aussi permis à certains de sortir plus ou moins discrètement de leur isolement', in 'Les homosexuels veulent constituer une communauté reconnue', *Le Monde*, 24 juin 1995, p. 10.

[10] I am speaking here about Paris and other larges cities, as opposed to the provinces where invisibility was more a condition of integration and acceptability.

[11] It should not be forgotten that this representation of tolerance and acceptability of the gay lifestyle was predominantly a Big City (New York, LA, San Francisco), class (WASP) and educational phenomenon. Among different classes (in the Mid West of America and the South) and ethnic groups, the difficulties of living a gay lifestyle were considerable.

108   *The Gay Republic*

underground (with the exception of Le Marais in Paris). To speak of a separate gay 'identity', while growing in popularity within gay groups, was seen as an affront to universalism and a bridge too far.[12] What Bernard Bosset articulates in his comments about being unable to take pride in his sexuality reflect, I would suggest, the nature of the divide between French and American expressions of gayness from the late 1980s to the mid 1990s. France had experienced Gay Pride marches from 1989 but until 1995 they were festive occasions for a prurient public. The lesbian and gay 'community' was too disparate, too divided, too invisible to rally to an event that produced embarrassment rather than belonging. In the US, 'coming out'[13] was not only a visible celebration of difference, but a statement of one's collective identity, with strong political overtones. In short, Bourdieu's recommendations in *La Domination masculine* were ahead of their time for a gay movement in France that was only just emerging out of a deep and troubled slumber. It would take time, reflection, changes in perceptions of gayness and a willingness to confront the ideology of universalism before the movement could respond adequately to Bourdieu's ideas.

Strategies of Sameness and Difference in the Modern and Postmodern State

The French complex with gay 'identity' in the mid 1990s (and to some extent today) has its roots in the uniqueness of the French socio-political situation. The republican/democratic divide has kept in check the collective pull of a conforming republicanism and the individualist tendencies of American-style identity politics. This divide can also be seen to function as a living model of the modern/postmodern state. Cindy Patton has characterised the *modern* state in terms of 'co-ordinating and integrating different claims on resources and power', of 'making sense to different interests', of 'state management' and of 'achieving representation.'[14] The *postmodern* state 'seems concerned to recede from visibility, to operate blindly as a purely administrative apparatus [...], has to pose itself as capable of administering an incoherent, incommensurable plurality of interests.' In synoptic fashion, she concludes that 'if modernity conceived of power in blocks that operate entropically, postmodern power circulates, disperses, intensifies.'[15] In

---

[12] Bernard Bosset, President of the *Syndicat national des enterprises gaies* (SNEG), states: 'Individuellement, je ne me reconnais pas dans la plupart des revendications identitaires. Je ne suis pas fier d'être gay. Mais tout le monde n'a pas la chance de s'assumer totalement. Certains souffrent et ont besoin de s'exprimer', in 'Les homosexuels se divisent sur la question du communautarisme', *Le Monde*, 15 avril 1996, p. 10.

[13] As we see later in this chapter, 'coming out' has a specific function in queer theory as an articulation of subversion. 'Coming out' rhetoric represents a crisis of *duty* for gays. See in particular Cindy Patton's chapter 'Tremble, Hetero Swine!' in Michael Warner (ed.) *Fear of a Queer Planet* (Minneapolis: University of Minnesota Press, 1994), pp. 143-77, and Didier Eribon's *Réflexions sur la question gay*.

[14] Patton, 'Tremble, Hetero Swine!', p. 172.

[15] Patton, 'Tremble, Hetero Swine!', p. 172.

the context of France, these two representations of the one state are particularly apt given the centralising, institutional blocks where power is stored on the one hand, and the agents of deinstitutionalisation that want to farm power out to constituitive parts in communities and in the free market. These two representations exist in constant tension with each other, often spilling over into political acts in the case of anti-globalisation demonstrations, and more recently politically motivated Gay Pride marches. As the co-existence of these two representations belies an uneasy calm, the tension is heightened at the level of identity, whether ethnic or sexual.

The modern French state is founded on the notion of equality for all citizens regardless of difference. Inherent in this concept is the 'oubli' of difference in favour of a core of common citizenship that is shared by all. As we have seen, this republican position has been found wanting, particularly in the area of gendered identities. Similarly, the notion of a core identity in respect of national identity has been exposed by the more socially and globally adaptive strategies of Anthony Giddens and Manuel Castells. This is not to say that the notion of a core identity is invalid. Mervyn Bendle has recently exposed the lack of core, (social, institutional and psychological) in the theories of Giddens for instance, and resurrected the necessity of an essentialist (embedded, repressed, existential) aspect to identity that has been forgotten in the plastic constructions of identity in response to social and global change.[16] In the area of sexuality, a similar debate is ongoing. While biological difference holds the key to a heteronormative order, the constructionist position has freed up the concept of sexuality and continues to offer a significant challenge to biologism. That said, constructionism itself is under the postmodern microscope, with the concept of a core gay identity in question.

The question of an essential component to constructionism is particularly important in the context of sexual identity politics. We have seen how the French experience of gayness in the early 1990s was not unified. In his history of gay communities in San Francisco in the 1970s and 1980s, Castells has also highlighted the splintering of gay identity into different sexual groups (masochists, sadomasochists).[17] He claims that the visibility of gays living in communities is a source of self-protection and provides a sense of belonging; when gays are scattered and invisible, they tend to lose a sense of identity. Castells distinction highlights the plight of the gay community in asserting an identity, and the difficulty in mobilising gays to think radically about their identity. What Castells infers is that gay identity lacks a core, that there are different versions of gayness out there, with a multitude of articulations and not one broad enough to bring people under one core identity. As de Lauretis has suggested, the terms 'gay' and 'lesbian' are not totally representative; it is what is different, not similar, in these constructions that is significant. If we pursue the idea of a splintered gay identity,

---

[16] Mervyn Bendle, 'The Crisis of "Identity" in High Modernity', *British Journal of Sociology*, 53 (2002): 1-18.

[17] Manuel Castells, 'The End of Patriarchalism: Social Movements, Family, and Sexuality in the Information Age', *The Power of Identity* (Oxford: Blackwell, 1997), p. 219.

110 *The Gay Republic*

we come up against another binary. Mary Bernstein[18] claims that difference within gay identity calls for different political strategies, the latter contingent on goals, access to political structures and interaction with the state. She sets up two models (based on research carried out in gay communities in Oregon and New York City). The first is identity based on difference from the majority. Calling this 'identity for critique', she categorised those lesbians and gays (New York) whose identity was constructed on their distance from the majority, from the establishment, and whose goals were more cultural than political mainly because of their lack of access to the power structures of the city. These gays wished to preserve a critical and communitarian gay identity. Their strategy was one of difference. The second group called 'identity for education' focused on a group of well-heeled white business lesbians and gays in Oregon. They had open access to political institutions, but not with a design for change but more for self-protection. In contrast to the cultural goals of their New York counterparts, their goals were to protect the status quo via political negotiation. Their strategy was one of sameness.

Bernstein's conclusions are significant in respect of future tactics of subversion, with applications beyond the United States. In the context of gay identity politics, the efficacy of the political strategies of lesbian and gay movements can be measured in relation to goals that a movement sets itself (cultural or political), its access to political lobbying and the degree to which it interacts with the state apparatus. And ultimately, the strategies adopted by a movement [a) collective celebration of difference – strategy of difference or b) suppression of difference – strategy of sameness] are the result of goals, political access, interaction with the state and, crucially, alliances with other social movements. While primarily US focused, Bernstein's strategies bear some useful comparisons with a postmodern context and with Bourdieu's prognosis for the lesbian and gay movement in France. Bernstein clearly addresses the splintering of identity within the lesbian and gay community, and attempts to accommodate the plurality of interests in an objective and balanced assessment of respective strategies which are a mixture of both choice and imposition. The strategy of sameness is the one which bears closest resemblance to the process of integrationism in France, where lesbians and gays appear more concerned about inclusion and being accepted as gay, than they do about criticising any normalising heterosexual order.[19] It is this strategy of

---

[18] Mary Bernstein, 'Celebration and Suppression: the Strategic Uses of Identity by the Lesbian and Gay Movement', *American Journal of Sociology*, 103 (1997): 531-65.

[19] I think it is important to clarify a potential confusion over the issue of sameness and its function in this context of gay identity and subversion. What could be perceived as primarily literary representations of sameness, the theories of Bersani and Hocqenghem have privileged sameness, the desire of sameness and the repression of this desire as the 'core' of gay identity. Furthermore, they have located in sameness the 'essence' of gay subversion of the heteronormative order. The particular nature of their positions is that sameness is used to secure the essential difference of gayness which in turn is deployed as an agent of socio-cultural transformation. This is a very clever strategy but, I would suggest, it relies heavily on a narcissism and individualism, coupled with a asociability and unrelationality (Bersani's

Lesbian and Gay Identity and the Politics of Subversion

sameness of which Bourdieu was most critical in his critique of lesbians and gays, accusing them of 'dissoudre en quelque sorte ses propres forces sociales, celles-là mêmes qu'il doit construire pour exister en tant que forces sociales capables de renverser l'ordre symbolique dominant et pour donner de la force à la revendication dont il est porteur.'[20] Bourdieu laments the fact that sameness has brought about the dissolution of lesbians and gays through their inefficacy as a social force. Bernstein is more optimistic, claiming that sameness serves a function. Contrasting the overtly hostile opposition of lesbians and gays to policies in New York, in Oregon 'gay men with insider status by virtue of their race, gender, and class have access to polity, and local anti-discrimination legislation passed.'[21]

Bourdieu's notion that a strategy of sameness represents capitulation to the state and does not bring about change is proved wrong in the case of Oregon. This is not totally surprising given the shape of the American political system with individual states having a degree of autonomy over the passing of legislation. Centralised France is a different case. To a degree, the strategy of sameness has been forced upon the lesbian and gay movement in France by the net of universalism. The PaCS debate has been largely symptomatic of this strategy. The political demand driving the PaCS was recognition by the state of the status of the lesbian and gay couple and equality of rights between gays and straights. While ACT-Up Paris and Aides groups were and remain not satisfied until full equality (marriage, adoption and rights to family law) is guaranteed, the main strategy adopted by PaCS advocates was to gain legal recognition as individuals and couples with rights within the pale of universalism, and then rethink their strategy. There are different ways of interpreting this approach. At the time, it was clearly risky, and some commentators have since claimed that it represented another example of heteronormativity (under the guise of universalism) dictating the lesbian and gay agenda.[22] To have adopted the Bernstein strategy of difference could also have been counterproductive. Strategies of difference adopted by lesbian and gay activists in New York faced a closed and hostile polity: 'Opposition was routine, leaving activists to define their identities in response to state authorities. Negative interactions with the state and the lack of political access

---

terminology) at the heart of gayness. To this extent, I think this strategy has overtones of artistic, aesthetic and academic elitism. It is also different from the way I (Bernstein, Bourdieu) will address sameness as a symptom of complicity with heteronormativity. I am looking to explore the differences within sameness as a way forward in a socio-political and citizenship context.

[20] Bourdieu, *La Domination masculine*, p. 131.

[21] Bernstein, 'Celebration and Suppression...', p. 560.

[22] See Pierre-Olivier de Busscher and Claude Thiaudière, 'Le PaCS: un progrès social ou une avance de l'Etat?', *Mouvements*, 8 (2000): 48-53. They claim that putting gay couples on a par with heterosexual couples is another way of trying to normalise and control lesbians and gays.

112 *The Gay Republic*

led to the deployment of ever more critical identities.'[23] Difference, it would appear, left one vulnerable and subject to manipulation.

Bourdieu's subversion of the dominant symbolic represents a variation on Bernstein's strategy of difference. Bourdieu's strategy is inclusive and integrative but *in a resistant way*. Crucially, it is reappropriative of the structures and discourse by which power relations between 'dominants' and 'dominés' are produced. This variation of difference strategy is clearly more subversive than the cultural model proposed by Bernstein 'to challenge the values and practices of the sex-phobic society.' For Bernstein's 'challenge' read Bourdieu's 'opérer un travail de destruction et de construction symbolique.' The reformist thread in Bourdieu's critique is mirrored in Paul Yonnet's characterisation of the PaCS as 'une matrice révolutionnaire',[24] and in some aspects of queer theory. Bourdieu has been critical of the uses of queer theory and indeed of postmodernity in *La Domination masculine*. He describes both as strategies of evasion of the historical and corporeal rootedness of male/female dualism.[25] Notwithstanding Bourdieu's critique, the advantage, I would suggest, of some elements of queer theory at this juncture is that it brings together two central threads of our discussion thus far, postmodernity and identity, and offers a strategy of socio-political engagement that bears strong comparison with Bourdieu's subversion of the symbolic. Cindy Patton, whom I quoted earlier in the context of the modern/postmodern state, claims that 'the crucial difference' between the 'constitution of governable subjectivities' in a postmodern state and 'the constitution of a governing state' in a modern state 'lies in the constitution of identities.'[26] For Patton, the battle for identity is not simply about democratic representation, as in the PaCS or parity debates in France. Nor is it simply about inclusion and belonging to some notion of a core that the modern state has invented. Rather, for Patton, identity is about wresting control over the discourses concerning identity construction. The opponent, for Patton, is not the state but the other collectivities attempting to set the rules for identity constitution in a 'civil society.' Patton's queer agenda keeps

---

[23] Bernstein, 'Celebration and Suppression...', p. 560.

[24] Yonnet, 'PaCS, un mariage républicain', p. 108. Yonnet defends the integrative approach adopted by those who drafted the legislation for the PaCS. However, like Bourdieu, it is not a passive form of integrationism. For Yonnet, the PaCS has the potential to revolutionise the socio-political infrastructure of French life.

[25] In *La Domination masculine*, Bourdieu says: 'Il contraint enfin et surtout à apercevoir la vanité des appels ostentatoires des philosophes "post-modernes" au "dépassement des dualismes"; ceux-ci, profondément enracinés dans les choses (les structures) et dans les corps, ne sont pas nés d'un simple fait de nomination verbale et ne peuvent être abolis par un acte de magie performative – les genres, loin d'être de simples "rôles" que l'on pourrait jouer à volonté (à la manière des *drag queens*), étant inscrits dans les corps et dans un univers d'où ils tiennent leur force. C'est l'ordre des genres qui fonde l'efficacité performative des mots – et tout spécialement des insultes –, et c'est aussi lui qui *résiste* aux redéfinitions faussement révolutionnaires du volontarisme subversif', p. 110.

[26] Patton, 'Tremble, Hetero Swine!', pp. 172-3.

Lesbian and Gay Identity and the Politics of Subversion 113

her alert to the dangers and abuses of identity construction in the 'field of power.' And in a clarion call to actors of subversion, she announces that 'it is as important to look at the battles taking place within the field of power in which accomplishment of "identities" operates as political capital – say, between the right and gays – as it is to see how their variously constituted identities interact with the administrative units.'[27]

Queer Strategies of Gay Identity: Theory and Practice

While Patton's agenda is clearly the critique of all constructed identities in favour of a post-identity performative construction, the battle is engaged at the levels of discourse, construction and power. Specifically, identity is located, in her echoes of De Certeau and Derrida, at the point of 'the proper', in other words the point at which social and political institutions name and designate. Patton goes on to make two important points in connection with this construction of identity. The first relates to the function of identity as performativity, that is the construction of identity as a reiterative performance within a field of power 'against a backdrop of institutions and spaces.' Queer identity, therefore, is seen to reappropriate the primary strategy by which normalcy is achieved (for queer theorists a matter of citation or constant repetition), and then apply (perform) a form of parody of the normalising structures, often 'male'/'female' 'identities.' The second main point relates specifically to gay identity and politics. For Patton, gay identity in the political sphere is not a given in the sense that rights are not hanging around to be conferred on gay people. As such, the onus is on lesbians and gays to articulate their identity politically. This comes about, for Patton, through the process of 'coming-out rhetoric' which itself creates the demand for gay rights and links it to the institutions of law: 'Coming-out rhetoric, in effect, articulates gay identity to civil rights practices, articulates homoerotic practices to the political concept of minority.'[28]

There are several positives to take from this postmodern social theory. The subversive nature of the tactical operation, for one, and the valid attempt to articulate gay identity politics at the point of 'coming out.' What is also of interest is that Patton's thesis reflects a trend (which this chapter is addressing in part) towards a return to an essentialism within constructionism. We have seen thus far how the idea of a core identity in the modern state has been revitalised by a desire to return to an embedded and existential identity.[29] Postmodernity has splintered

---

[27] Patton, 'Tremble, Hetero Swine!', p. 173.

[28] Patton, 'Tremble, Hetero Swine!', p. 174.

[29] In his article 'The Crisis of "Identity" in High Modernity', Mervyn F. Bendle exposes the emotional and pyschological weaknesses in the identity theories of Giddens and Castells, and highlights, by contrast, the ideas of E. Erikson: 'Erikson recognised the essential need for a subjective sense of continuous existence and a coherent memory, without which a person's self is profoundly weakened and easily threatened [...]. This conception of the

114   *The Gay Republic*

this concept of identity into its constitutive parts, and highlighted the fragmentation of a core gay identity into competing strategic interest groups. Where Patton's theory seems to resist the pluralising trend and ground gay identity is in the very unique and personal experience of 'coming out.' Of course, not all lesbians and gays 'come out.' What Patton claims is that the real issue in the articulation of a gay identity is the incumbent 'crisis of duty' with which gays and lesbians are confronted in relation to themselves and society: 'The innovation of gay identity was not so much in making homosexuality seem acceptable to the homosexual, but in creating a crisis of duty in gays who could "come out."' The idea of 'coming out' is representative of a core that is/was always there, whether articulated repeatedly in silence in anticipation of disclosure, or verbalised as a public statement. Its public airing as a 'rhetoric' is a moment of the 'proper', that is to say when the engagement of gay as 'identity' comes into contact with social and political constructions. I would suggest, furthermore, that as a moment of historical 'instantiation', 'coming out' also represents an act of high modernity for the lesbian and gay individual. It is an act that confirms their place in time and space. It could be argued that 'coming-out rhetoric' (as Patton puts it) is as close as one can get to the definition of a core gay identity.[30]

In the context of queer theory, in which Patton is a leading thinker, her thesis of 'coming out' as a means of 'living' queer and not only 'reading queer', represents an expression of gay 'identity' that is exceptional in its bucking the trend of post-identity queer theory. Judith Butler, another leading exponent of queer theory, is adamant that queer theory cannot accommodate identity politics, let alone fixed or core identity categories. She states:

> As much as it is necessary to assert political demands through recourse to identity categories, and to lay claim to the power to name oneself and determine the conditions under which that name is used, it is also impossible to sustain that kind of mastery over the trajectory of those categories within discourse. This is not an argument *against* using identity categories, but it's a reminder of the risk that attends every such use.[31]

Some points of clarification are necessary at this point. We need to distinguish

---

continuing self-sameness of identity is central to this entire stream of thought', p. 11.

[30] Philippe Muray defines '*le coming out*' as a unique moment of gay identity and 'hyperreconnaissance.' It signals the defining philosophical moment of gay identity (the modern affirmative version of 'je suis'). For Muray, it also represents a significant political moment in which the republican binary of 'vie privée'/'vie publique' is broken: 'L'Empire de la reconnaissance marque l'écrasement de toute vie privée et de tout domaine privé, définitivement précipités dans les poubelles du négatif. Ce qui n'est pas exhibé, donc approuvé, est coupable; ou n'existe pas' in 'Reconnaissance', *Le Débat*, 112 (2000): 131. The philosophical and political overtones of Muray's view on 'coming out' is in stark contrast to the 'banalisation du fait homosexuel' of which Frédéric Martel speaks in his article 'Gay: Chronique d'une émancipation' in the same volume.

[31] Judith Butler, 'Critically Queer', *Bodies That Matter. On the Discursive Limits of 'Sex'* (New York: Routledge, 1993), pp. 227-28.

Lesbian and Gay Identity and the Politics of Subversion

between queer politics (to which Butler subscribes) and identity politics. The former is the totalising effect of the desanctioning and deconstruction of normalising gender categories. Queer politics are queer theories[32] that question the social and political underscoring of 'identity' constructions. Identity politics, on the other hand, is the isolation of any particular identity within this totalising effect to which one might impart a sexual or political significance. For Butler, the latter is particularly problematic because 'queer' is not a fixed, stable or indeed decidable identity. Its undecidability is its critical effect. Butler goes on to say that 'self-naming' (identification with any 'identity') is a conceit because there is no autonomy of the subject, no ownership of the subject, and 'self-naming' is compromised by a history of usage. In addition, to impose will on this process is tantamount to a fiction because the notion of choice is redundant.

On a practical level, Butler's case for the invalidation of identity categories is not absolute as we can see in the above quotation. Queer theory, however, is more absolute; identity categories are insufficient in themselves and the convergence of any political affiliation to a subject is perceived as the 'error of identity.' In reference to identity and politics, Butler states: 'there is no self-identical subject who houses or bears these relations, no site at which such relations converge. This converging and interarticulation *is* the contemporary fate of the subject. In other words, the subject as a self-identical entity is no more.'[33] The gap between practice and theory is, I think, important. Butler does concede a role for identity categories in the pursuit of political demands, albeit with attendant risks. Whether this is political posturing, and a concession to lesbian and gay activists, is debatable. She may also be suggesting that identity categories and politics cannot be distinguished from the overall effect of queer politics. Butler does not rule out identity politics altogether; queer theory can even accommodate them to the point of *assertion of political demands*, laying *claim* to 'the power to name oneself and determine the conditions under which that name is used.' But these practical concerns are unfulfilled by the implications of the theoretical discourse:

> The expectation of self-determination that self-naming arouses is paradoxically contested by the historicity of the name itself; by the history of the usages that one never controlled, but constrain the very usage that emblematises autonomy; by the future efforts to deploy the term against the grain of the current ones, and that will exceed the control of those who seek to set the course of the terms in the present.[34]

In many respects, the theory/practice dialectic mirrors the identity/politics dialectic

---

[32] Or as Steven Seidman, Chet Meeks and Francie Traschen say: 'Queer politics in the 1990s represents a post-identity sexual politics. It does not focus on legitimating identities but on challenging the regulatory power of norms of sexual health and normality', in 'Beyond the Closet? The Changing Social Meaning of Homosexuality in the United States', *Sexualities*, 2 (1999): 31.

[33] Butler, 'Critically Queer', p. 230.

[34] Butler, 'Critically Queer', p. 228.

116   *The Gay Republic*

that is central to much of the critique of queerness; both dialectics reflect the difficulties of translating theory into practice.[35]

And yet, the challenge presented by queer theory to the practice of gay identity politics cannot be underestimated. The nature of this challenge is the relationship between identity as fluidity and identity as core. Queer theory has exposed the myth of identity as core by the continual deferring of its naming.[36] Cindy Patton, however, has shown that there are chinks of light within the theoretical equations that shed light on a political dimension to gay identity. The issue we have raised in this chapter of a modernity within postmodernity, of an essentialism within constructionism, is particularly relevant at this juncture. Mary Bernstein does not dispute the given of a gay identity politics, seeing the issue to be one of strategies of sameness and difference. Mervyn F. Bendle, however, provokes considerable debate in his critique of constructionism's 'tendency to relieve identity of any suggestion of essentialism and to make it fluid and multiple [...]. There has been a hyper-differenciation under high modernity and globalization that makes a stable identity even more desperately sought after and more difficult to achieve.'[37] I should point out at this stage that I am not arguing for a return to nor a nostalgia for modernity and its hegemonic accommodation of difference within a utopian social system. What I want to ask is whether one can speak in terms of a core (of sameness or of difference) gay identity. And, if so, does that core have a political significance?

Queer theory, while useful in its methodological applications, is lacking in part in terms of a coherent and sustained identity framework, and in respect of its political inefficacies. It would be easy to suggest that a core gay identity could be defined by saying that all gays are the same because they are gay. However, as Castells pointed out in his history of the gay 'community' in San Francisco, there are different groups, different aspirations, different lifestyles, different ways of being gay. This divergence prompts us to ask the question whether there is a force of difference in gay identity which is as much a common denominator as is sameness. This question is the subject of an article by Ed Cohen.[38] Cohen takes as

---

[35] Steven Seidman is part of this critical body. In his excellent study *Difference Troubles. Queering Social Theory and Sexual Politics* (Cambridge University Press, 1997), he states as one of the aims of his book: 'I criticize queer theory to the extent that its social perspectives slide into a textual or discursive and have not seriously considered the ethical-political implications of making difference so fundamental to theory and politics', p. 16.

[36] Didier Eribon, while articulating a core of gayness in Sartrean 'authenticité' in which one 'se fait gay' (by 'coming out' as an act of resistance'), is still unconvinced by the notion of a gay 'identity.' He claims that the construct of identity is too mobile and fluid to fix or centre it, and infers that gay politics is ultimately stymied by the assimilationist/separatist binary of the French political system.

[37] Bendle, 'The Crisis of "Identity" in High Modernity', p. 16.

[38] Ed Cohen, 'Who Are "We"? Gay "Identity" as Political (E)motion (A Theoretical Rumination)' in Diana Fuss (ed.) *Inside/Out. Lesbian Theories, Gay Theories* (New York: Routledge, 1991), pp. 71-92.

Lesbian and Gay Identity and the Politics of Subversion

his premise the opposition between gay sameness and diversity within sameness, and then argues how each of these trends might resist (socially and politically) imposed categories, such as normative heterosexuality or heterosexual marriage. The gay sameness trend (the similarities with Mary Bernstein's theory are evident) is characterised as veering towards social inclusion; the integrative or ethnic model that states that there is no difference between gays and straights.[39] The other trend acknowledges difference from the ethnic model and is critical of oppressive norms. Cohen explores the nature of this difference through an analysis of Steven Epstein's celebrated contribution to this debate.[40] Epstein's argument is that gay identity must resist socially imposed categories via the difference trend. Indeed, gay identity must resist collectively and in an organised fashion. Gayness, for Epstein, is a *unifying difference* that should organise a sexual identity politics. As radical as this may seem, there is one major problem for Epstein. While gay identity may assert itself through this difference trend and distinguish itself from the majority, there remains a totalising sameness within the group. He states: 'While affirming a distinctive group identity that legitimately differs from the larger society, this form of political expression simultaneously imposes a "totalizing" sameness within the group. It says this is who we "really are."'[41] For Epstein, difference is partially compromised sameness; in other words, sameness is inevitably destined to return to shape identity politics. The point here is that gay identity politics has difficulty in affirming difference. Cohen picks up on this difficulty and seeks to show how the politicisation of identity politics plays itself out in other areas, like queer theory. He approves of some of queer theory's performative strategies to undermine monolithic structures, but remains unconvinced of the latter's capacity to locate the origin of political commitment, and even sceptical of how subversion actions cohere as strong political and social movements.

One area where gay identity politics (via the difference trend) can function effectively is in its ability to show greater internal diversity. Mary Bernstein reminds us of the need within the strategy of difference to interact 'with opposing movements.'[42] Bourdieu's critique of the lesbian and gay movement in France was that it needed to avoid a politics of sexual ghettoisation, where the successes of the movement were obscured by one-issue politics. Bourdieu called for lesbians and gays to diversify 'au service du mouvement social dans son ensemble [...], de se

---

[39] The 'ethnic model' used and criticised by Steven Seidman, is one that assimilates a 'lesbian/gay to a straight identity' or reduces 'the differences between gay and straight to a minimum [...]. The ethnic model has suppressed differences among lesbian-and-gay-identified individuals, thereby reproducing a repressive politics of identity' in *Difference Troubles*, p. 16.

[40] Steven Epstein, 'Gay Politics, Ethnic Identity: The Limits of Social Constructionism', *Socialist Review* 17 (1987): 9-54.

[41] Epstein, 'Gay Politics, Ethnic Identity: The Limits of Social Constructionism', pp. 47-8.

[42] Bernstein, 'Celebration and Suppression...', p. 560.

118   *The Gay Republic*

placer à l'avant-garde.'[43] And Steven Epstein echoes this solidarity as a solution to 'the peculiar paradox of identity politics': 'A greater appreciation for internal diversity – on racial, gender, class and even sexual dimensions – is a prerequisite if the gay movement is to move beyond "ethnic" insularity and join with other progressive causes.'[44] Returning to our question of how to speak in terms of a core gay identity and engage it politically, the above critics suggest that sameness (in respect of gay identity) is not defined as a *shared identity*, nor is it restricted to the exclusivity of homosexuality. Rather, sameness is *identification with* other identities. As a consequence of this process of identification, wider socio-political alliances are activated.

If sameness can be located at the level of identification with otherness, and identity politics rescued at the point of identification with other social movements, Cohen goes further to locate a core that is at the heart of this identification process. In other words, he sees sexual identification and political commitment originating in the personal. In the same way that Cindy Patton situated a gay identity politics (and Eribon a core of gayness) in the very intimate experience of 'coming out', Ed Cohen claims that gay identity politics is essentially about being able to identify with other people and other politics, and that the origin of this identification is in feeling and emotion, not the 'fetishization of language and image [...], nor acting subjects that are "theoretically" disappeared.'[45] He writes:

> As far as I can tell, political movements are engendered by personal and political (e)motions that impel people – in the parlance of the old "New Left" – to put their

---

[43]   Bourdieu, *La Domination masculine*, p. 134.

[44]   Epstein, 'Gay Politics, Ethnic Identity: The Limits of Social Constructionism', p. 48. Cohen is scathing of the way Epstein relegates the discussion of gay identity politics and other social movements to the end of his argument. He sees it as symptomatic of the privileging of 'sameness over difference and of goals over processes.' Cohen believes that Epstein has prioritised sexual difference over any other social differences, and only comes to an acceptance of this as an afterthought. This issue of the plurality and priority of differences is one that preoccupies Steven Seidman in his book *Difference Troubles*. He states: 'A major issue of contention is less whether or not to acknowledge or seriously consider difference but whether differences of say, ethnicity, race, or religion, penetrate "deeply" into cultural life. If gender or race are differences that shape moral outlook and epistemic values in profound ways, this suggests a world, and a world of thought, fractured and fragmented in ways unimagined, and perhaps unimaginable within enlightenment cultural traditions', p. 2.

[45]   Cohen, 'Who are "We"? Gay "Identity" as Political (E)motion', p. 84. Cohen's distrust of deconstructionist theory in relation to identity politics is shared by Seidman in his article 'Identity and Politics in a "Postmodern" Gay Culture' in Michael Warner (ed.) *Fear of a Queer Planet* (Minneapolis : University of Minnesota Press, 1994). Seidman concludes: 'I am less patient with generalizing, systematizing "theories" in the tradition of Marxism or radical feminism. I favor social sketches, framed in a more narrative rather than analytical mode, as responses to specific social developments and conflicts with specific purposes in mind', p. 137.

Lesbian and Gay Identity and the Politics of Subversion

bodies on the line. If we want to consider what it is that moves people to act together often in the face of manifest danger or violence in order to transform their collective life-worlds, then we must begin to take seriously the notion that political movements cohere only to the extent that they express and make meaningful the shared *feeling and knowledge* that things ought to and can become different than they are – i.e. to the extent that they touch and move people who touch and move each other [...]. Indeed, it would seem that any "movement" which predicates itself on an "identity" dooms itself to fragmentation in so far as it preempts the possibility of being moved by and/or beyond the (somatic) differences presupposed in the very "identity" that it defines. By advocating an understanding of political movements as embodied processes, then, I want to suggest both that bodies do make a (political) difference and that difference is often a matter of (e)motion.[46]

Cohen's deconstruction of theory in favour of a bodily approach to gay identity politics is based on a simple model of human relations. The self (Cohen's alternative to identity) is a human construct effected by others in the most intimate and daily fashion. The self is the unique register through which change comes about; as such it is a highly personal and sophisticated mechanism where opinions are formed in subtle and imperceptible ways. Cohen synthesises this process to the notion of 'feeling', a sensory perception that enables individuals to effect change in one another: 'You see, I *feel* there is something "different" about the body: I *believe* feeling is the difference that bodies make, a difference that *moves* people to action.'[47] In the search for the link between sexual identity and political engagement, both Patton and Cohen find it in the realm of the personal. The *personal as political* connects with other approaches to the postmodern dilemma of how to define the core as difference and engage it politically. Seidman, in similar fashion to Cohen, 'urges a shift away from the preoccupation with self and representations characteristic of identity politics and post-structuralism to an analysis that embeds the self in institutional and cultural practices.'[48] For Cohen and Patton's 'personal' read Seidman's 'cultural practices' and 'social sketches framed in a more narrative than analytical mode.' In a less direct but equally effective way, Bourdieu plays the personal card in his eulogy of lesbian and gay identity. Bourdieu's critique of the lesbian and gay movement is designed to offer an alternative to sameness as integration. The alternative strategy of sameness as difference and its subversive political efficacy with links to other social movements is facilitated by Bourdieu's characterisation of the 'capital culturel' of many lesbians and gays and their high and respected profile in diverse areas of the avant-garde. For Bourdieu, it seems that the very gay disposition (in a personal sense) lends itself to radical and subversive symbolic action. What we see in these representations is that the link between sexual identity and politics is a variation of the personal. Whether articulated in the form of a voluntary act, an act of duty, an

---

[46] Cohen, 'Who are "We"? Gay "Identity" as Political (E)motion', pp. 84-5
[47] Cohen, 'Who are "We"? Gay "Identity" as Political (E)motion', p. 85.
[48] Seidman, 'Identity and Politics in a "Postmodern" Gay Culture', p. 137.

120   *The Gay Republic*

existentialist act, an act of resistance or a natural feeling, the human being ultimately assumes responsibility for their sexuality and engages it. It is in essence a moment of the 'proper' when the union between sexual identity and political conscience is forged.

ACT-Up Paris: AIDS, Communities, Political Manifestos

There are several reasons why ACT-Up Paris should feature at this point in this chapter. Firstly, the brief history of ACT-Up, created in 1989, reflects a political coming of age for an organisation that was founded on strategies to prevent the spread of AIDS in France.[49] Secondly, the crucial decisions to be taken by ACT-Up in respect of its future political commitment came, I would suggest, as a direct response to Bourdieu's critique of the lesbian and gay movement in *La Domination masculine*. Thirdly, the strategies of sameness and difference, discussed in previous sections of this chapter, have had a direct bearing on the political trajectory of ACT-Up through the 1990s and beyond. And finally, the effect of Bourdieu's critique is such that an organisation, split between definitions of community and communitariansim, ends up simultaneously embracing and subverting the cherished republican principle of universalism.

ACT-Up Paris, the brother of ACT-Up New York, became a visible action group at the start of the 1990s. The AIDS crisis defined the group in its early years. ACT-Up functioned as a 'community' against AIDS, and against the isolation and ghettoisation that AIDS produced. The preventive mentality that defined ACT-Up in the early 1990s helped save many lives. It adopted many of the safer sex strategies developed in New York in the 1980s. While gay communities, already diminishing as a consequence of the crisis, were being forced underground, ACT-Up Paris became a focal point for lesbians and gays. Pink triangles, safe sex leaflets and round the clock switchboards ensured a forgotten community that it still existed. However, the first turning point for the gay community was 1995 when Gay Pride, the annual march celebrating gay identity, was changed to the Lesbian and Gay Pride march. The change in name was to coincide with a change in mentality. According to Jean-Michel Normand, a leading gay activist at the time, a new strategy was required to establish, in the aftermath of the early and most devastating effects of AIDS, a more settled and supportive lesbian and gay community. The major obstacle in the way was the perception that an AIDS mindset had already forged itself into its own community spirit. In other words, AIDS, in the absence of a legally recognised gay community, had itself created a community still crippled by the scars of the past. The challenge, according to Normand, was to establish a new community outside of the AIDS problematic. The renaming of the Gay Pride march signalled a start to this challenge. It was

---

[49] I do not propose to outline here the history of this movement. For this, see Didier Lestrade's book *Act-Up, une histoire* (Paris: Denoël, 2000) and Gilbert Elbaz, 'New York ACT-Up' (Ph.D dissertation, City University of New York, 1993).

Lesbian and Gay Identity and the Politics of Subversion   121

significant for several reasons. It represented a move away from the more frivolous and euphemistic connotations of Gay Pride, which had lingered from the 1970s. More significantly, it represented an attempt to break with the past and identify a community by naming it fully and specifically. And intentionally, gay identity was to incorporate both lesbians and gays.[50]

In an attempt to define the parameters of a lesbian and gay community beyond the AIDS epidemic, a new structure and mentality was needed. Up to the mid 1990s, AIDS had dominated not only the way gays thought about sexual activity, but it also contributed to the increasing isolation and ghettoisation of gay men in particular. In response to the first, Normand pointed out that it was necessary to move away from the AIDS preventive mindset, as something fixed and unchangeable, to a different perspective on sexuality that was more positive and focused on the long-term interests of lesbians and gays. Richard Elovich, head of the prevention programme at the Gay Men's Health Crisis (GMHC) in New York in the mid 1990s claimed that 'l'attitude rationnelle qui sous-tend la prévention telle qu'on la pratiquée jusqu'à alors ne fonctionne pas sur le long terme: la sexualité humaine est complexe et irrationnelle et personne n'a convenablement integré ces données dans les campagnes de prévention [...]. Il faut briser le sentiment d'isolement et se concentrer sur la communauté.'[51] For Elovich, the rationale of prevention, whilst effective at the time of a crisis, could not work as a long-term strategy for lesbian and gay sexuality. In order to break out of the prevention/isolation binary, Elovich suggests that a way forward could be found by looking to a community structure which would have the consensual support of lesbians *and* gays.

Up to 1995, preoccupation with the AIDS crisis also determined strategy in the wider context of communitarianism. Organisers of Gay Pride marches claimed that, in the absence of any structured gay community outside the militancy of ACT-Up and Aides, the message of AIDS awareness was the only way to 'parvenir à construire une véritable communauté.' However, the monopolisation of the gay voice by ACT-Up and Aides betrayed sincere reservations about an AIDS

---

[50] Despite the renaming of the Gay Pride march and the recent increased political dimension to the march, some feminist commentators have remained convinced that it continues to glorify masculine domination (regardless of the drag and feminisation of men), and that as a political march the link between sexuality and politics is the aesthetic effacement of women. For more on this view, see Véronique Nahoum-Grappe, 'Le cortège des sexualités', *Esprit*, 273 (2001): 254-60. Marie-Jo Bonnet has also criticised the gay movement for its strategy of mimesis (integration with the established order as a measure of self-protection), and for having sacrificed lesbians to this integration. Similarly, she sees the Lesbian and Gay Pride march as a misnomer because lesbians are not fully represented: '[The marches] resemble mimetic parades [...], where the male sex is omnipresent [...]. The female sex is grotesquely caricaturised' in 'Gay Mimesis and Misogyny: Two Aspects of the Same Refusal of the Other', *Journal of Homosexuality*, 41 (2001): 265-80.

[51] In Jean-Michel Normand, 'Les homosexuels veulent constituer une communauté reconnue', *Le Monde*, 24 juin 1995, p. 10.

122   *The Gay Republic*

dominated strategy,[52] and also opened up a crucial debate about the nature of a gay community within the French republican state. Emeric Languerrand, editor of the *Journal du sida*, stated at the time: 'Grosso modo, nous avons le choix de deux modèles: le ghetto américain, véritable contre-société, ou l'intégration absolue, comme en Europe du Nord. La seule issue me paraît être la voie choisie aux Pays-Bas. La constitution d'un ghetto, même considérée comme une étape, se situerait à contre courant de l'intégration.'[53] Languerrand's comments were timely for three reasons. Firstly, they took the debate about gay identity out of the claustrophobic space of the AIDS discourse and politicised it as a debate between republican universalism and communitarianism. Secondly, they moved the definition of community away from ACT-Up's equivalence between AIDS and community, and repositioned it at a political and ideological level which, with the publication of Frédéric Martel's book *Le Rose et le noir* several months later, ensured wider coverage and more serious reflection about definitions of community and communitarianism. Thirdly, Languerrand's preference for the integrative approach to gay sexuality in 1995 is a useful barometer against which to measure Bourdieu's subsequent critique of the passive integrative strategy of the lesbian and gay movement in *La Domination masculine*.

In the context of passive integrationism, the publication of Martel's *Le Rose et le noir* in 1996 was a defining moment in the history of gay sexuality at this time. Scathing in his treatment of gay associations that denied the existence of the AIDS crisis up to 1984, Martel also preached a passive 'droit à l'indifférence', a form of invisible dissolved integrationism that denounced communitarianism as an American import. Martel saw in this communitarian development a trend towards identity politics that was far removed from the then divided and depoliticised gay communities in France, themselves held in check by anti-communitarian universalism. It could be said that gay 'identity' was a foreign concept in the late 1980s and early 1990s in France, and that communitarianism was anathema to French integrative republicanism. In short, Martel was part of a wider body of opinion that defended lesbian and gay rights within the confines of republican universalism. A separate and culturally defined gay identity (in the American model) was played down by Martel. He described talk of gay identity as 'un débat très luxueux.' Martel argued that to foster the idea of a gay identity was to encourage separatism from the universalism of republican citizenship. It is clear, therefore, that the notion of a community for lesbians and gays was highly contentious at this time. Community seemed synonymous with either AIDS or identity politics, neither of which commanded the unconditional support of lesbians and gays.

However, three comments from people working at the forefront of lesbian and

---

[52]   Jean-Michel Normand details some of these reservations, from the inefficacy of Gay Pride as a mobilising force against AIDS to Gay Pride's openly provocative content which only harms the communication and sincerity of gay issues.

[53]   In Normand, 'Les homosexuels veulent constituer une communauté reconnue', p. 10.

Lesbian and Gay Identity and the Politics of Subversion 123

gay associations at the time serve to highlight some key concerns. In a debate conducted in the pages of *Le Monde* about what defined a gay 'community', Alexis Meunier, director of the *Centre gai et lesbien* in 1996 stated: 'Le communautarisme est un faux débat, la priorité aujourd'hui est de s'attaquer au quotidien des gens, de se battre sur le terrain des droits, de l'incompréhension et de l'injustice.'[54] Philippe Mangeot, then head of ACT-Up, described the community as a place of belonging, particularly for young people who 'come out' for the first time: 'La communauté s'est aussi structurée à partir d'une expérience commune de la discrimination. Tous les adolescents homosexuels ont eu un jour le sentiment de n'être pas chez eux. Or, arriver à ne plus avoir peur, cela se passe par le groupe [...]. Une communauté, c'est un lieu de convivialité, d'échanges, de pratiques sexuelles et sociales partagées, mais ce n'est pas beaucoup plus que cela.'[55] Bernard Bosset, President of the *Syndicat national des entreprises gaies* (SNEG) stated that 'une minorité d'homosexuels est dans le modèle identitaire. On ne voit que la partie visible de l'iceberg. 60% des homosexuels ne fréquentent pas les établissements gays.'[56] What these comments reveal is that abstract notions of communitarianism and gay identity were the stuff of academics and intellectuals. A gay 'community', defined as a space where people could talk through social and sexual issues, was more in tune with lesbian and gay daily experience. And yet what is noticeable and ironic about the above characterisations of the French gay community at this time is the presence of a common and fledgling gay 'identity', forged around the personal and the political, and a merging equilibrium between the respective values of integration and separateness: 'une communauté parfaitement intégrée et qui conserve sa spécificité.'[57]

The renaming of Gay Pride in 1995, the transition from AIDS prevention under ACT-Up to the emergence of other gay associations and a supportive community ethos, accompanied by an increased politicisation of lesbian and gay rights, forced ACT-Up to re-evaluate its direction in the late 1990s. By 1998, ACT-Up was in crisis. AIDS had been partially controlled through years of campaigning and was no longer the number one priority. Recruitment to the organisation had dropped considerably and there was a sense of political immobilisation. Philippe Mangeot characterised the crisis in terms of an 'absence de désir politique.'[58] Bourdieu's invitation to the lesbian and gay movement to become 'une avant-garde politique' was circulating in the wings of the movement, but of course Bourdieu's conditions of engagement with politics were very strict. The idea of a perfectly integrated gay

---

[54] In Laurence Folléa, 'Les homosexuels se divisent sur la question du communautarisme', *Le Monde* 15 avril 1996, p. 10.

[55] In Folléa, 'Les homosexuels se divisent...', p. 10.

[56] In Folléa, 'Les homosexuels se divisent...', p. 10.

[57] Mathieu Verboux, member of Arcat-Sida, in Laurence Folléa, *Le Monde*, 15 avril 1996, p. 10.

[58] In Ariane Chemin, 'Le dilemme d'Act-Up, désenchantée et courtisée', *Le Monde*, 19 août 1998, p. 5.

124 *The Gay Republic*

community that preserves its specificity, as described above by Mathieu Verboux, was not what Bourdieu had in mind. Bourdieu's agenda involved the action of symbolic subversion, the transformation of categories of thought and structure, and the capacity of the lesbian and gay movement to ally itself with a wider social movement. In the course of 1998, 'la question du politique' within ACT-Up showed signs of addressing Bourdieu's agenda. Firstly, ACT-Up's spectacular, media-seeking stunts of political disaffection were challenged by new ideas that underpinned the need for real political action and not pranks. In a risky but ground-breaking move, ACT-Up decided to promote itself as a political alternative to leftist politics in the lead up to the legislative elections of 1997. With its slogan 'Nous sommes la gauche', the campaign did not get off to a promising start, with hardly a thousand people attending its demonstration under the slogan 'la gauche réelle.' However, this event was important for two reasons. It represented the first steps in what was to be a more pronounced political involvement for the organisation. And secondly, it signalled a shift away from one-dimensional sexual politics and a new identification with other political causes. Philippe Mangeot's reaction to these early brushes with politics was the following: 'On s'est plantés, mais on a gagné au moins sur deux points. D'abord, nous avons pris à cette occasion l'habitude de travailler avec d'autres associations […]. Ensuite, la gauche officielle a répondu à notre convocation, et nous a reconnus.'[59]

The theme of the 1998 Lesbian and Gay Pride march in Paris was 'Gays et Lesbiennes ont des droits: les droits de l'homme.' It was more a militant than festive occasion, reflecting the urgency of the organisation to respond to what it perceived to be the government's stalling tactics in passing legislation relating to gay concubinage. And, lest we forget, the PaCS debate was beginning to gain momentum. While the Lesbian and Gay Pride marches became more politicised and could be viewed as the measure by which the lesbian and gay movement was transforming itself,[60] I would suggest that it is within the ACT-Up organisation and more specifically in a series of manifestos that it produced, that we can best evaluate the extent of this transformation, and how the imprint of Bourdieu is very visible in its strategic realignment. In its first mainfesto entitled 'PaCS: du droit à la politique' and published in *Le Monde* on 9 October 1998, ACT-Up Paris takes some giant leaps into the realm of socio-political engagement. In a synthesis of past, present and future, it sets out an agenda for a political response to the PaCS. What is noticeable from the outset, is that the PaCS is not about gays or straights. It is about all of society. Taking the AIDS crisis as its starting point, the manifesto makes clear that its demands are presented in the form of requests made by the families of AIDS victims, HIV carriers, friends of HIV carriers and the dead themselves. Divided into three parts, the first part pays indirect homage to Bourdieu's invitation to evangelise the social and political dimensions of lesbian

---

[59]   In Chemin, 'Le dilemme d'Act-Up, désenchantée et courtisée', p. 5.

[60]   One has only to compare the 1998 Gay Pride slogan with the 2001 slogan ('Parentalité, Séjour, Travail, Couple') to gauge the extent of this politicisation.

and gay sexuality. The PaCS, it states 'ne deviendra droit commun que si elle s'adapte aux conditions de vie concrètes d'une multitude d'autres groupes sociaux qu'on ne saurait réduire à la catégorie des "hétérosexuels." Pour juger le PaCS, il faut quitter le sexuel pour le social et le symbolique pour le reel.' Bourdieu, we recall, highlighted the dangers for the lesbian and gay movement of limiting its agenda to sexual goals. He asked: 'Comment, en termes plus réalistes, c'est-à-dire plus directement politiques, éviter que les conquêtes du mouvement n'aboutissent à une forme de ghettoïsation?'[61] The alternatives, he suggested, included the imposition 'de nouvelles catégories de perception et d'appréciation', the destruction of 'le principe de division même selon lequel sont produits et le groupe stigmatisant et le groupe stigmatisé.' And critically, Bourdieu's key strategy for lesbians and gays was to bring together their subversive potential, their stigmatised status and cultural capital 'au service du mouvement social dans son ensemble.'

The second part of the manifesto spells out in detail the nature of the demands sought, underpinned by a request for equality, and fairness of treatment between gays and straights. The demands include the right of a surviving gay partner to remain in the apartment or home owned by the gay couple, including the right to inherit material goods and financial assets. The PaCS has partially addressed this issue in respect of legal status for lesbian and gay couples where surviving partners no longer have to reapply for a lease to a home occupied while living as a couple. The legislation is however more cumbersome in respect of assets, introducing a process of 'indivision' at the point of separation, or death. Other demands focus on the legal inequalities between gays and straights in respect of immigration and residence of foreign partners, as well as an end to discriminatory practices against lesbians and gays who automatically lose other benefits once they become 'pacsé.' In short, the ACT-Up agenda is about addressing the personal details and everyday life experiences of lesbians and gays, confronting the powers that make discriminatory laws and trying generally to exercise change. The final part of the manifesto is a testament to this approach:

> C'est pourtant là, à l'intersection des lois et des vies, que le débat doit porter car c'est là, précisément, qu'il devient politique. Pour notre part, comme les chômeurs ou les sans-papiers (qu'ils y réflechissent: nos inquiétudes sur le PaCS les concernent), c'est ainsi que nous luttons: en opposant le détail de nos inquiétudes aux majorités tranquilles, aux lois rigides et aux administrations mécaniques. Nous continuerons [...]. Mais la vraie bataille, en vérité, commencera après le vote du texte. Qu'on se le dise: nous avons l'intention de mettre en place un Observatoire du PaCS, avec tous ceux qui le voudront: non pas un "comité de sages", moral et pseudo-compétent, mais des "groupes d'usagers" revendiquant un droit de surveillance sur l'application du texte et une participation active à sa jurisprudence. C'est ainsi, disait le philosophe Gilles Deleuze, qu'on passe du droit à la politique.

In the course of the latter half of 1998 and deep into 1999, the struggle for lesbian

---

[61] Bourdieu, *La Domination masculine*, p. 134.

126   *The Gay Republic*

and gay rights reached a new intensity in the lead up to the PaCS legislation in November 1999. While gay rights were of primary significance to the gay interest groups, the PaCS legislation had a wider brief that effected heterosexuals and homosexuals, individuals and couples, single and married, and families. ACT-Up, let alone Aides or Arcat-Sida, was no longer fighting an isolated battle; lesbian and gay rights had now become part of a social movement. In a demonstration under the slogan 'égalité des droits', co-ordinated by ACT-Up Paris for the 17 October 1998, no less than eighty organisations 'à gauche de la gauche' rounded at the intersection of the Odeon in Paris to protest once again against the government's slow progress on the PaCS legislation, and specifically against the government's reluctance to involve lesbian and gay organisations in its deliberations. The organisations present at the demonstration covered a wide section of leftist protest groups, from the obvious gay groups to women's groups, family planning groups, students and lawyers groups, youth and communist groups, greens and anarchists. This new social dimension to the lesbian and gay movement was reflected months later in a second manifesto, again published in *Le Monde* on 26 June 1999 under the title 'Pour l'égalité sexuelle', but which this time had the combined support of ACT-Up, Aides Fédération et Aides Ile-de-France, Sida Info Service, SOS Homophobie and ten other associations.

The comparisons with the first manifesto were clear; a more focused political agenda and a need to bring into the frame of reference other social causes. The first manifesto brought the concerns of ACT-Up and 'les sans-papiers' closer together. In the second manifesto the concerns of women (in the context of the parity debate) were merged with those of lesbians and gays. Under the principle of equality, the manifesto sought to unite the interests of *paritaires* and 'pacsés.' As an opening gambit, this represented an initial shock tactic. *Paritaires*, as I have mentioned in the course of this book, had been roundly criticised for what appeared to be a regressive policy of using biological difference (highlighting women as a separate category in the republic as opposed to a part of the human species) to secure 'special' (equal) treatment during municipal elections. However, it was becoming increasingly clear that ACT-Up had a wider agenda. Significantly, however, it intended using a strategy deployed by *paritaires*. From the start, the signatories were adamant that they did not want to get bogged down in the politics of the parity debate, and that their overarching concern was sexual equality, 'à la fois entre les sexes, et entre les sexualités.' Their aim was to bring together the concerns of women and lesbians and gays, not in terms of their mutual 'particularismes' but in order to 'généraliser la revendication d'égalité contre toutes les discriminations.'

In uniting the issue of parity (as a tactical weapon, and not strictly as a particularism in itself) to the cause of lesbian and gay rights, ACT-Up and co. decided to mirror the strategy of *paritaires* in their claim that abstract universalism could not be defended on a practical basis as it concealed inequality and discrimination between men and women. With the backing of the wider social movement in its claim to 'parler d'autres discriminations et d'autres inégalités', and by addressing the issue of sexual equality from universalist and practical perspectives, the lesbian and gay lobby was in a strong position to present a forceful, radical and realistic case. This strategy was not without risks. Universalism had not been a good friend to lesbians and gays,[62] and the accusation of communitarianism undermined continually any attempts at self-determination outside of the universalist model. The difference with this present strategy was that it was not a call for reform of universalism from the margins of the political institutions, but a call to *engage* with the structure of universalism, expose the weaknesses of abstract universalism, and, on the basis of the parity model, make a case for a corrective to universalism that would be more accommodating to the everyday life of French citizens. The notion of engaging and subverting the institutions of power from within is indicative of the influence of Bourdieu and Yonnet. The force of this engagement can be detected in one of the many rallying calls of the manifesto: 'Mais prenons-le (universalisme) au mot: comment l'universalisme s'accommoderait-il de la discrimination, qu'elle vise les femmes ou les couples de même sexe? La République ne saurait rester indifférente à l'égalité. Et l'amour de l'égalité ne doit pas demeurer platonique: il faut lui donner les moyens d'arriver à ses fins.'

Positive Discrimination: Pros and Cons

The invitation to help find a solution to the inadequacies of abstract universalism comes in the form of a distinction, deployed in the parity debate, between 'égalité de droit' and 'égalité de fait.' The former is described as a 'condition nécessaire'; that is to say that equality in law is the most cherished and necessary principle in any society. It is a condition which, ACT-Up confirms, should enable lesbians and gays to marry and raise families as heterosexuals do. But realistically (the echo of Bourdieu), the second manifesto makes clear that it is not enough to simply aspire to such an ideal and abstract 'condition', and that a practical accommodation, or 'égalité de fait', is itself necessary to maintain faith in the principle of equality: 'C'est pourquoi, quand le monde politique s'obstine à fermer ses portes aux femmes, l'égalité de fait requiert une politique volontariste.' In the context of parity, this 'politique volontariste' translated into a form of positive discrimination. Positive discrimination is described by ACT-Up as a positive development, better than living *with* discrimination. While not full equality, or a substitute for

---

[62] Hugues Montouh claims that 'les homosexuels, comme toutes les minorités par ailleurs, sont aujourd'hui les victimes de l'universalité du droit, de ses effets égalisateurs et homogénéisants. Ils ne luttent plus seulement désormais pour la non-discrimination, c'est-à-dire pour le droit de ne plus être persécuté, mais aussi pour la reconnaissance de leur pleine et entière identité. La question posée aujourd'hui aux démocraties libérales est celle de la reconnaissance non plus d'une dignité universelle, mais d'une égale dignité de tous les citoyens' in 'L'esprit d'une loi: controverses sur le Pacte civil de solidarité', *Les Temps modernes*, 603 (1999): 191-92.

128   *The Gay Republic*

discrimination, positive discrimination is seen as 'un instrument qui corrige.' Applied to lesbian and gay rights, parity 'doit être non un principe mais une stratégie au service d'un principe: l'égalité.' Strategically, there are pros and cons with the parity analogy. ACT-Up's interpretation of parity as a form of positive discrimination needs clarification. *Paritaires* would defend women's rights to equal representation as a matter of respect for the duality of the human condition; to this degree, positive discrimination is seen to address sexual discrimination, imbalances and illegalities under the principle of universal equality. The benefit of positive discrimination in this respect is that it cannot only highlight inadequacies of legal principle but that it can also effect change. As Gwénaële Calvès states: 'Cette notion a en effet pour fonction de faire tomber sous le coup de la loi des différences de traitement qui, *de jure* irréprochables, s'avèrent, *de facto*, génératrices d'inégalités.'[63]

Positive discrimination is a form of engagement with the structure of universalism. It subverts the homogenising effects of universalism and forces a shift in the balance of institutional power. Crucially, in the context of Bourdieu, strategies such as positive discrimination represent a prised foothold inside the universalist logic, in which a strong, rehabilitated and undominated 'particularisme' can be put to the service of a better universalism. Bourdieu writes: 'Ce travail [de subversion symbolique], les homosexuels sont particulièrement armés pour le réaliser et ils peuvent mettre au service de l'universalisme, notamment dans les luttes subversives, les avantages liés au particularisme.'[64] Calvès also points out that positive discrimination has the benefit of being 'une démarche volontariste'; as such, 'elle signale la volonté d'agir plutôt qu'attendre et voir venir. Elle ne désigne rien d'autre qu'une [...] recherche active de solutions concrètes à des problèmes dont il est illusoire d'attendre qu'ils se résolvent d'eux mêmes.'[65] In short, positive discrimination can bring about change in the *here and now* without having to wait for constitutional or legislative changes. Its subversive effect is practical and immediate.

It is significant, however, that ACT-Up is careful to distinguish between the strategy of positive discrimination and the principle. It appears to distance itself from the latter which suggests that it disagrees with the principle of positive discrimination. As the second manifesto states, positive discrimination is conditional on 'une politique volontariste' which suggests that as a practice it is subject to the control and vagaries of political powers. The quantative approach to discrimination, with the use of quotas and arithmetic, may also point to tokenism and the accusation of gesture politics.[66] But the manifesto also makes clear that

---

[63] Gwénaële Calvès, 'Pour une analyse (vraiment) critique de la discrimination positive', *Le Débat*, 117 (2001): 169.

[64] Bourdieu, *La Domination masculine*, p. 134.

[65] Calvès, 'Pour une analyse (vraiment) critique de la discrimination positive', p. 167.

[66] See Anne-Marie Le Pourhiet, 'Pour une analyse critique de la discrimination positive', *Le Débat*, 114 (2001) 166-77. Setting the agenda for Calvès' response, Le Pourhiet

Lesbian and Gay Identity and the Politics of Subversion　　129

positive discrimination is a means to an end.

The alliance with other social causes, the re-appropriation of universalism via a strategy adopted by *paritaires* seems, on the surface, an indirect way for ACT-Up and the lesbian and gay movement to make progress. However, we have seen how these three pathways have been necessary rites of passage in terms of a move way from the stagnating agenda of AIDS prevention and the frivolous excess of Gay Pride, towards a movement with a solid social base and a realistic political identity. In identifying with other inequalities and other discriminations, the lesbian and gay movement widened its support base and, as a result, strengthened its lobbying power. The effects of the PaCS legislation solidified this base and provided a platform on which to take the core agenda of rights and equality to the institutions of government.

In terms of Bernstein's strategies of sameness and difference, it could be argued that the alliance struck between gay and other social movements was a strategy of sameness designed to pursue inclusion within the established order. It is a critique that one could level at Bourdieu's indirect involvement in the lesbian and gay movement. In other words, the strategy of allying the cause for gay sexual identity with wider political associations brought clear benefits in the form of the PaCS and, as we see today, new legislation against homophobia and the possibilities for gay marriage. But, have these benefits brought with them the normalisation of gayness? Is not universalism doing what it was designed to do, accommodate and integrate gayness? In short, have lesbians and gays fallen into the trap of selling their specificity and subversive potential for the prize of legal recognition and equality? These are criticisms that hold sway among many lesbians and gays. However, in defence of Bourdieu, they may be harsh criticisms. The strategy of sameness, which Bourdieu condemned, was a strategy of passive acquiescence, a form of sacrifice of particularism for the sake of social inclusion. In the context of the lesbian and gay movement, sameness of socio-political message should not be confused with a strategy of sameness where the balance of power has not moved.

On the contrary, I would argue that the lesbian and gay movement and its affiliated organisations have united their differences in the common pursuit of a strategy of difference, the aim of which, as Bourdieu states, is to 'opérer un travail de destruction et de construction symbolique visant à imposer de nouvelles catégories de perception et d'appréciation, de manière à construire un groupe ou, plus radicalement, à détruire le principe de division même selon lequel sont produits et le groupe stigmatisant et le groupe stigmatisé.'[67] In tackling universalism ('le principe de division') head on, and divesting parity of its

---

highlights the dangers of positive discrimination in its reinforcement of the stereotypes it seeks to combat, its deformation of the idea of democratic representation and its privatisation of the *res republica*. In particular, she sees positive discrimination as being at the mercy of subjectivism, moral relativism and what she sees as the nefarious influence of 'le droit-de-l'hommisme.'

[67]　Bourdieu, *La Domination masculine*, p. 134.

130 *The Gay Republic*

principle and advocating it as *strategy* with a positive outcome, the lesbian and gay movement declared its opposition to 'l'orthodoxie' and signalled its intention to subvert universalism by putting it to the service of the particular. Detractors of this strategy will no doubt question the voluntarism of the politics and the discomfort of sharing a bed with *paritaires* who, it is claimed, turned their back on the lesbian and gay movement by denying the concept of gendered sexuality and essentialising, for their own gains, sexual difference to 'la différence des sexes.'[68] The response to such detractors can be found in the second manifesto and is a testament to the transformation undergone in the brief history of ACT-Up Paris and the wider lesbian and gay movement: 'Nous revendiquons l'égalité. Non pas pour les femmes, non pas pour les homosexuels, mais pour tous, et donc pour toutes: il n'est d'égalité qu'universelle. Il en va de l'intérêt général. Nous sommes les universalistes.'

Conclusions

This chapter opened with a detailed analysis of Bourdieu's characterisation of the lesbian and gay movement in France in the mid 1990s. Bourdieu called for a subversive and radical politics from the movement if it was to avoid the ghettoisation of sexual politics. Flagging up the dangers of capitulation to a heteronormative order via recent government legislation (CUC and subsequently the PaCS), Bourdieu suggested that the best way the movement could advance itself was to subvert the main principle of universalism, in effect to put the use and advantages of the particular (gayness, sexual difference) to the service of the universal, rather than have the universal determine, dominate and stigmatise the particular. One way to achieve this aim was to politicise sexual identity, and link the aspirations of sexual equality with the broader aims of other organisations in a common politics of the 'avant-garde.' I have shown in this chapter that Bourdieu's recommendations, as characterised in *La Domination masculine* in 1998, mirror the transformations that were taking place in ACT-Up Paris and the broader lesbian and gay movement at this time. So much so that we can see subtle connections between the drafting of manifestos by ACT-Up and how Bourdieu saw the future for lesbian and gay activism. Nevertheless, Bourdieu's assimilation of sexual identity and politics belies tensions about the validity, origin and function of this assimilation in modern and postmodern debates.

Mervyn F. Bendle has claimed that all approaches to identity are either essentialist or constructionist. The essentialist approach, associated primarily with modernity, gave us the concept of identity as a core, a unified entity that was oppressive in its inflexibility. The constructionist approach, associated with postmodernity, offered a fragmented concept of identity that was valorised as progressive, adaptable and ongoing. The trajectory of this sequence, from

---

[68] I address this issue in detail in the chapters on universalism and 'la différence des sexes.'

Lesbian and Gay Identity and the Politics of Subversion 131

oppressive modern to progressive postmodern, has been challenged in recent debates (particularly by Bendle) by the idea of a need to return to a more essentialist, personal and modern version of identity. In respect of *sexual* identity, this trajectory has been similar up to a point. The essentialist position of biological difference as the determining factor of sexual identity has been challenged by the constructionist notion of gendered identities that are the product of social forces. However, rather than a nostalgia for the essentialist 'différence des sexes',[69] the trajectory has stopped at constructionism and focused on the question of whether there is a need for a new *essentialism within constructionism*.

This question could be rephrased in more concrete terms by asking whether, in the postmodern age, there is such a thing as a core gay identity. In this chapter, we have unearthed sufficient evidence of the diverse history of lesbian and gay communities in the US and France to suggest that it is unrealistic to claim that gays are the same by virtue of their sexual preference. By extension, the search for a core to gay identity is, on the one hand, to recognise that there is difference within sameness but, on the other hand, to recognise that difference is equalised through a shared *personal* heritage. Queer theory challenges biological essentialism as a normalising effect, and this is one of its valid contributions, but it also pushes constructionism into overdrive where any notion of a stable identity is undermined. Similarly postmodern theories seem content to decentre identity and accommodate its proliferation *ad infinitum*. Hence certain critics' attempts to rescue gay identity through philosophy (Eribon), through desire (Bersani and Hocquenghem) or through the personal. Cindy Patton speaks of the 'coming-out rhetoric' that essentialises lesbian and gay identity both sexually and politically. Ed Cohen speaks of the importance of 'feelings' as signifiers of sexual identity and political motivation. The net effect of these contributions is to relocate the personal in the postmodern, to retrieve a semblance of a forgotten and fragmented subject.

In his invocation of Michel Foucault at the end of his article, Ed Cohen implies that labels of essentialist, constructionist, gay, or queer are not important.[70] What matters is how sexuality can be used to alter the society in which one lives. This may not further our immediate objective of locating a core to gay identity, but what it does suggest is that sexuality can make a difference, socially and politically. Bourdieu makes this connection in his eulogy of the innately subversive disposition that is being lesbian or gay. And yet, recent debates have contested the durability and relevance of the link between sexual identity and politics. While acknowledging the 'empowerment' of politics and gay identity, Steven Seidman has claimed that because of the normalisation and routinisation of homosexuality in the United States, a decentering of gay identity politics has occurred and has been encouraged by queer theory.[71] The latter, subversive in its methods and

---

[69] The parity debate is an exception here, in that *paritaires* used biological difference to effect political change.

[70] Cohen, 'Who Are "We"? Gay "Identity" as Political (E)motion', p. 88.

[71] Steven Seidman, Chet Meeks and Francie Traschen, 'Beyond the Closet? The Changing

132   *The Gay Republic*

tactics, has been unable to accommodate identity politics because of the absence of ownership in any identity construct.[72] The 'costs attached to identity politics', as Seidman calls them, are 'the repression of differences among lesbians and gay men, a narrow focus on legitimating same sex preference, the isolation of the gay movement from other movements and as queer perspectives argue, normalizing a gay identity leaves intact the organization of sexuality around a hetero/homosexual binary.'[73]

I would argue that normalisation of homosexuality and the perceived 'costs' of identity politics are more symptomatic of the American context. In France, the notion of moving 'beyond the closet' must be viewed within the perspectives of legislation that only recently recognised lesbian and gay couples, and a republican base of institutionalised anti-communitarianism and universalism. As unsettling as Seidman et al.'s globalisation of the normalisation of homosexuality must appear to any self-respecting lesbian or gay, Henning Bech imparts a more balanced vision in which 'these developments [...] take different shapes and speeds in different national contexts.'[74] In France, the 'normalisation' (or 'banalisation') of homosexuality is not by and large a desirable objective, even though one of France's leading gay figures, Frédéric Martel, has suggested that 'banalisation' is the endgame in the history of gay emancipation. Marie-Jo Bonnet has also interpreted the PaCS as a way for lesbians and gays to normalise their private lives along the same lines as heterosexuals. But a significant number of critics on the French context, whose ideas I have addressed in this book (notably Bourdieu), have decried normalisation as capitulation to heteronormativity and have thus cautioned against it. The thrust of this chapter has been to show that, given the politicisation of ACT-Up and the increased political focus of the lesbian and gay movement, normalisation is not a realistic option, and only ever could be on homosexual terms. Furthermore, I would suggest that the perceived 'costs' of identity politics in the US have been factored into the French context under Bourdieu's recommendations. The latter warned against ghettoisation of a one-dimensional sexual agenda, political isolation and heteronormative normalisation. Seidman's suggestion that the link between identity and politics is under threat may have some relevance in the US. In France, it is more the case that this link has been intensified by a new politics of the avant-garde. What Ed Cohen, Pierre Bourdieu, Cindy Patton and Didier Eribon confirm is that, in the plurality of interests that compete for space in the postmodern age, there is a place for gay

---

Social Meaning of Homosexuality in the United States', *Sexualities*, 2 (1999): 9-34.

[72] As I hope to have shown in this chapter, queer theory has been particularly effective in deconstructing the homogenising models of sexual norms in a postmodern context. Where it has been less effective is in rivalling the power of traditional, personal, modernist visions of identity, whether in the area of community politics or individual rights.

[73] Steven Seidman, Chet Meeks and Francie Traschen, 'Beyond the Closet? The Changing Social Meaning of Homosexuality in the United States', p. 10.

[74] Henning Bech, 'After the Closet', *Sexualities*, 2 (1999): 344.

Lesbian and Gay Identity and the Politics of Subversion

identity politics in an *ethics* of the personal. To speak of a core to gay identity is to set in train a sequence beginning with the verbal act of 'coming out', the freedom and subversive responsibility this act bestows on its enunciator, and its conditional socio-political engagement. In this way, the personal becomes the political.

PART TWO
PRACTICAL CONCERNS

Chapter 5

Adoption and Filiation: The New PaCS Pact

> Quatre personnes peuvent être à l'origine de la naissance d'un enfant: un couple de parents biologiques, composé d'une mère lesbienne et d'un parent gay, et leurs partenaires respectifs […]. Cette coparentalité, souvent pratiquée aux Etats-Unis, pose le problème de la place de chacun des acteurs, de la construction des différentes parentalités, de ses rapports avec la filiation de sang et la co-résidence.[1]

In the second part of this book, we will look at the practical problems facing lesbians and gays living in contemporary France. The context is the social space of the family, couple and kinship where issues of equality, rights and legal recognition, in short gay sexual citizenship, will be contested. The social space will also allow us to establish some key principles of sexual citizenship in the living social space, such as the accommodation between diversity and common value, between individuality and social responsibility, and the *rapprochement* between private and public demands of traditional republican citizenship. The social space will also serve to refine our perceptions for a legitimate sexual citizenship that is born out of rational claims to sexual difference and an accommodation inside the democratic infrastructure of republicanism.

The social is a space shared by both republican and democratic claims to citizenship. However, by opening up these respective claims to closer examination, we will see how each claim reflects certain political, ideological and sexual preconditions. Specifically, we will be examining current debates on adoption and filiation, and comparing how these debates are argued, the terminology deployed and the assumptions made. We will then be in a position to say how they feed into respective republican and democratic models. In the context of republican citizenship, we will see how the institutions of the family, marriage, 'la différence des sexes', paternal and maternal referents, and genealogical filiation produce a discourse in which sexual citizenship is predetermined, exclusive, and resistant to the legitimacy of Gauchet's model of social immanence. Democratic citizenship, by contrast, will be defined by its capacity to forge new social, relational lines of filiation and familial connection out of traditional republican discourse, in order to respond to the contingent, temporal and elective demands of the social space. In this way, the social will be revalidated as a democratic space which questions

---

[1] Agnès Fine, 'Vers une reconnaissance de la pluiparentalité', *Esprit*, 3-4 (2001): 51.

138 *The Gay Republic*

received notions (medical, judicial, scientific) of 'appartenance' and generates new meanings that are culturally and socially produced. Gay sexual citizenship will compete for credence, equality and legitimacy within this resignified social space.

Throughout the 1990s, during the course of the debate on the PaCS legislation and right up its implementation in November 1999, one of the sources of political tension between the political left and right centred on whether legal recognition of same-sex couples would eventually give way to demands by homosexual couples to adopt children and live as families. At the time, and given the controversy of the debate, the terms of the PaCS legislation was clearly confined to the couple. What is equally clear, however, is that since the legislation was passed, the PaCS agenda has moved on to address issues relating to children and most specifically adoption and 'filiation.' At the Lesbian and Gay Pride march in Paris 2001 (attended by the newly elected and first-ever openly gay Mayor Bertrand Delanoë), the slogan used to define the direction of this new agenda was 'Parentalité, Séjour, Travail, Couple.' New 'co-parentalité' legislation was passed in 2002, regulating the custody of children (and the relationship between biological parents and children) in situations where parents split up, and new parents (straight or gay) enter the recomposed family unit. In 2004, the 1881 Press law was modified, making it a crime, as in ethnic or religious cases, to discriminate by hatred or violence against a person on the basis of sex or sexual orientation. And with the recent case of Mayor Noël Mamère of Bègles endorsing a civil marriage between two gay men in 2004 (only for it to be subsequently annulled), it is clear that the PaCS legislation of 1999 has set in train a series of shock waves through the French legislature and cultural landscape. Furthermore, the increased politicisation of the post-PaCS agenda has brought into sharp focus conflicts between democracy and republicanism, France and the European Courts, opposing models of family unit, blood ties versus social ties, and internal disputes within scientific and judicial fields about the role of heterosexuality ('la différence des sexes' and 'l'ordre symbolique') at the heart of the family.

On the right of French politics, the introduction of the PaCS and its legal recognition of lesbian and gay couples represented confirmation of the misgivings many politicians had in the first place about the legislation and where it was leading.[2] On the other hand, for many gay pressure groups and militant activists the politicisation of the post-PaCS debate was only a natural consequence of legal recognition of their unions. While legal recognition through the PaCS represented a significant breakthrough in terms of rights of kinship and a range of socio-economic privileges, it did not represent full equality with heterosexual couples. Even for many lesbians and gays, the PaCS was and remains a cop-out, a half-measure that created nothing more than an in-between status. It is my contention in

---

[2] See the range of letters that form the substance of Roselyne Bachelot's useful synopsis of the PaCS debate in *Le PaCS entre haine et amour* (Paris: Plon, 1999). For example, one letter states: 'Le PaCS évoluera un jour ou l'autre pour intégrer les aspects de l'adoption', p. 119.

this chapter that the *politicisation* of this new post-PaCS agenda (with its emphasis on adoption and new rights of 'filiation') seeks to re-engage French social, political, judicial and philosophical thought with the central issue of equality of citizenship. However, where this politicisation appears even more radical than a pre-PaCS agenda (with its specific focus on rights of status), is in its attempt to address equality, not from the communitarian and disenfranchised margins of the republic, but from within the republic and from the perspective of one of its cherished institutions, the family. To this degree, post-PaCS politicisation is a continuation of the subversive intent inspired by Bourdieu in *La Domination masculine*.

A further dimension to this new politicised agenda has been the way in which the post-PaCS debate has sought to situate itself firmly within a democratic republican framework, as opposed to the republican and universalist traditions of integration and assimilation. Some commentators like Paul Yonnet and Frédéric Martel have been very measured in situating the debate as a debate *within* republicanism. Paul Yonnet, as we have seen, talks of the PaCS as 'une matrice révolutionnaire' and 'un oeuf fécondé'[3] inside republicanism. Martel refers to the legislation as 'une position intermédiaire, restant à définir précisément – sinon à inventer –, qui combinerait multiculturalisme avec défense de l'Etat républicain.'[4] Other commentators, who have written widely on the subject of the PaCS (Eric Fassin, Marcela Iacub, Daniel Borillo, Irène Théry, François de Singly to name but a few), have embraced the legislation *as a model for the democratisation of private life*, where they explore the links between the aspirations for equality, respect and identity (belonging to the private world of the individual) and the socio-political structures that exist to accommodate these aspirations. The move within a *democratic* republican framework to bridge the gap between public and private space (an idea which a traditional representation of republican citizenship has sought to keep distinct) is a significant development. We have seen in the first part of this book how, under the concept of universalism, traditional republicanism responded (via resistance) calls for change, evolution and amendment to the definition of citizenship. The democratisation of republicanism provides a clear rationale for a re-negotiated sexual citizenship and a socio-political context for the *rapprochement* between private and public. In other words, if a potential model of sexual citizenship is to be born out of this *rapprochement*, there needs to be a fundamental and mutual recognition of the rationality of sexual difference as a core of citizenship, and the implementation of flexible social, political and legislative structures for difference to exist.

Firstly, the concept of the democratisation of private life needs further articulation. In the context of lesbian and gay rights, it can be expressed in the notion of sexual citizenship. This can be defined in terms of 'bringing to the fore issues and struggles [sexuality] that were only implicit or silenced in earlier notions

---

[3] Yonnet, 'PaCS, un mariage républicain', p. 108.
[4] Frédéric Martel, in 'Repères, Controverse', *Esprit*, 10 (1998): 216.

of citizenship.'[5] In the context of France, sexuality ('le sexuel' (orientation) as opposed to 'le sexué' (male/female dichotomy)) has been subsumed under the notion of republican universalism. Increasingly, however, universalism has come under threat from claims to difference and particularism, which democratic claims for equality and right to difference have reinforced. Jeffrey Weeks, in his illuminating article on the 'Sexual Citizen', has identified important components to the notion of the sexual citizen such as the democratisation of relationships, which he characterises as being based on detraditionalisation, egalitarianism and autonomy. He also identifies the emergence of new subjectivities (narrative quests, life projects, biographies, hybrids), which challenge traditionally fixed concepts of the self and identity. What is key to Weeks' contribution to the debate on the democratisation of the sexual citizen is the link he makes between the private and the public; the sexual citizen, he explains, is one who incarnates a balance between his diversity and the common values of society.[6] This link is the linchpin of the sexual citizen's participation and acceptance as a social citizen. We can draw many useful conclusions from Weeks' theories, not least the notion that difference 'is also a claim to inclusion, to the acceptance of diversity, and a recognition of and respect for alternative ways of being, to a broadening of the definition of belonging. This is the moment of democratic citizenship.'[7]

Given Weeks' observations and with reference to contemporary France, the general perception of republicanism as integrative and to society's overall benefit (in contrast to democratisation with its emphasis on difference and the perception of fragmentation), is questioned by a vision of democratic citizenship that is at once individualistic and altruistic, for one and for all. Weeks' theory of *responsible* democratic citizenship is useful for several reasons. It challenges a myth of democracy as being solely differentialist and individualist. It also helps us rethink the relationship between republicanism and democracy, less in terms of an opposition and more in terms of core common values which have been framed to suit different political agendas. Equality of all citizens is ensured from both republican and democratic perspectives. But it is the way in which these respective traditions interpret equality that creates conflict. What Weeks' theory indicates is that sexual democratic citizenship is a force that has a universality and rationale that are increasingly difficult to overlook. It has a language that reflects with subtlety and sensitivity the inter-relationships between individual and social experiences. It is also underpinned by a discourse of freedom that is invested primarily in the individual, and which he can use to subvert the political and social institutions that may seek to control individual expression. The impression that

---

[5] Jeffrey Weeks, 'The Sexual Citizen', Special issue on Love and Eroticism, *Theory, Culture & Society*, 15 (1998): 39.

[6] Jacques Commaille and Claude Martin examine in detail this balance between citizenship and 'le bien commun' in their article 'Les conditions d'une démocratisation de la vie privée' in Eric Fassin and Daniel Borrillo (eds) *Au-delà du PaCS*, pp. 61-78.

[7] Weeks, 'The Sexual Citizen', p. 37.

Adoption and Filiation: The New PaCS Pact   141

Weeks' advocacy may give is that freedom in the name of individual and sexual citizenship is more important that republican values, namely the principle of universal equality. This would be an oversimplification of Weeks position, given his qualifications on responsibility and respect for core common values. However, this relationship between freedom and equality has been raised in recent debates in France on homophobia. I will discuss this relationship in a later chapter, suffice to say now that this is a very sensitive issue among lesbian and gay activists. In particular, they do not want to be seen to be advancing an agenda of putting their own freedoms or equality first, especially if it is done so at the expense of wider equality.[8] It is important that we view the Weeks contribution and that of the lesbian and gay movement within a democratic republicanism that balances out these respective demands.

In the light of these preliminary remarks, this chapter will examine the politicisation of the post-PaCS agenda. Specifically, it will question legal arrangements in respect of adoption by single and married persons, forms of discrimination on the basis of sexual orientation, and the use of maternal and paternal references as pre-requisites for approval to adopt. In all these areas, there are inconsistencies of treatment across the board. In the light of these inconsistencies, and with the perception that the defining and universal horizon of the traditional family is being challenged by a deinstitutionalised, denaturalised and less prescriptive alternative (what Eric Fassin, echoing Pierre Bourdieu, has termed as the movement from 'la famille' to 'la famille des familles'[9]), I propose to examine how conventional biological lines of filiation are being questioned by new social and generational actors.[10] I will compare the traditional pillars of

---

[8]   To read more on this debate, see Nathalie Heinach, 'Lorsque le sexe paraît: de quelques confusions dans des débats brûlants', *Le Débat*, 131 (2004): 170-78; Alain Piriou, 'Homos, l'égalité démocratique', *Libération*, 28 juin 2004, p. 39; Alain Policar, 'Reproductions homosexuelles et droits de l'homme', *Libération*, 11 août 2004, p. 27.

[9]   See Eric Fassin's article 'Usages de la science et science des usages: A propos des familles homoparentales', pp. 391-408.

[10]   The debate on the crisis of the family in the context of filiation is extensive. The following references may prove useful: Eric Fassin, 'L'illusion anthropologique: homosexualité et filiation', *Témoin*, 12 (1998): 43-56; Jean Hauser, *La Filiation* (Paris: Dalloz, 1996); Françoise Héritier, 'La cuisse de Jupiter. Réflexions sur les nouveaux modes de procréation', *L'Homme*, 94 (1985): 5-22 and *Masculin/Féminin. La pensée de la différence* (Paris: Odile Jacob, 1996); Pierre Legendre, *L'Inestimable objet de la transmission: étude sur les principes généalogiques en Occident* (Paris: Fayard, 1985); François de Singly, *La Famille: état des savoirs* (Paris: La Découverte, 1991); Irène Théry, 'L'homme désaffilié, *Esprit*, 12 (1996): 50-54, *Couple, filiation et parenté aujourd'hui. Le droit face aux mutations de la famille et de la vie privée* (Paris: Odile Jacob, 1998), 'L'un et l'autre sexe', *Esprit*, 3-4 (2001): 57-69; see also the section entitled 'Filiations', in Eric Fassin and Daniel Borrillo (eds), *Au-delà du PaCS. L'expertise familiale à l'épreuve de l'homosexualité* (Paris: PUF, 1999); The following exchange of articles in *Le Monde* can also serve as a way into this complex subject: Eric Fassin, 'Homosexualité, mariage et

142 *The Gay Republic*

republicanism (family and marriage) with alternative versions of them. On the legal front, changes and amendments to current legislation on adoption and filiation will be the subject of political and institutional debate, with the objectivity of the law coming under scrutiny. The current position of the legal profession is that greater institutional and juridic links must be put in place to protect filiation from the vagaries of social change, parental voluntarism and bioethics. However, recent high profile legal cases have opened up the debate to further democratic scrutiny in which the impartiality of the law and the legal system have been seen to have been undermined, leading to conspiratorial accusations being levelled at science (in particular certain branches of anthropology) and the judiciary in their attempts to stifle democratic deliberation.

Adoption: Two Case Studies and Their Implications

The phenomenon of adoption first became apparent in western Europe in the 1920s, after the Great War. Then it was presented as a way of giving a family to an orphaned child. In this way, a child would be brought up and cherished by his adopted parents as if they were blood parents. In the inter-war period, it was possible, particularly in France, to hide adopted children under the benevolent and uncontroversial umbrella of 'une filiation de seconde zone.'[11] A change in French law in 1966 introduced the notion of 'adoption plénière' where the integration of the adopted child into the new family was conditional upon the child breaking all ties with the original family. Agnès Fine writes: 'L'enfant perd son nom d'origine, entre dans une autre lignée et perd aussi éventuellement son prenom. Dans l'adoption plénière, l'état civil de l'enfant est modifié et son extrait d'acte de naissance affirme qu'il est "né" de ses parents adoptifs, favorisant ainsi la fiction de la naissance naturelle.'[12] 'Adoption simple', by contrast, (where ties with biological parent(s) are maintained) is still available in France today. Since 1966, there have been amendments to the adoption legislation in the light of medical advancements. A law on bioethics dated 29 July 1994 places conditions on adoptive parents and, for instance, their access to medically assisted procreation: 'l'assistance médicale à la procréation ne peut bénéficier qu'à des couples composés d'un homme et d'une femme vivants, en âge de procréer, mariés ou en mesure de d'apporter la preuve d'une vie commune d'au moins deux ans.'[13] That same law prohibits any form of surrogacy in France.

Amendments to the original legislation have provoked debate and controversy, particularly in respect of unmarried couples and gay couples in the context of

---

famille', *Le Monde*, 5 novembre 1997; Serge Bakchine, 'Homosexualité, mariage, famille; et la nature', *Le Monde*, 19 novembre 1997; Eric Dubreuil et Maud Grad, 'Homosexualité, famille, filiation', *Le Monde*, 12 décembre 1997.

[11] Fine, 'Vers une reconnaissance de la pluriparentalité', p. 42.

[12] Fine, 'Vers une reconnaissance de la pluriparentalité', p. 42.

[13] Quoted in 'Le cadre légal', *Le Monde*, 15 mars 1999.

'adoption plenière' and bioethics legislation, and the fact that single people can adopt while unmarried couples cannot. Indeed, the debate has intensified since the introduction of 'la loi Mattéi' in July 1996. This law fixed the minimum age for prospective adopters at twenty-eight. Furthermore, this law does not stipulate what the sexual orientation of a single person adopting should be, but if one's homosexuality is publicly declared then this could be viewed as a reason to reject the request to adopt. On the issue of marital status, couples must have been married for a minimum of two years before adoption can take place. As a way of addressing some of the vagaries of this legislation (single people can adopt but cohabitants cannot, a single gay or lesbian who keeps their sexuality discrete can adopt[14]) and the thinking that underpins it, I would like to study two case examples of recent times. On 24 February 2000, the administrative court in Besançon overturned a decision by the Conseil Général of Jura which had rejected a request for adoption made by Emmanuelle B (the surname was withheld for reasons of privacy), a single gay woman of thirty-eight who did not hide the fact she lived with another woman. The Conseil Général's case against Emmanuelle was based on the grounds of 'défaut de repères identificatoires dû à l'absence d'image ou de référent paternel' and of 'ambiguïté de l'investissement de chaque membre du foyer par rapport à l'enfant accueilli.'[15] A subsequent decision to overturn the decision of the Besançon court was founded on the lack of substantial reasons to justify the refusal to adopt, and on the good character of the adopter.[16] With the intervention of the Département of Jura and the Appeal Court of Nancy in the form of an 'arrêt' on 21 December 2000, the original decision to refuse adoption was reinstated, making it clear that its decision had nothing to do with the 'choix de vie' of the interested party.

What followed as a result of this case were two petitions inviting interested parties to support the views of either the APGL (L'Association des parents et futurs parents gays et lesbiens) or of the deputé (RPR) des Bouches-du-Rhône, Renaud Muselier. The APGL claimed that its petition was not a call for legislation to provide access for 'pacsés' couples to adopt, but was designed to highlight the discrimination against gays on the basis of their sexual orientation against the

---

[14] Anne F. Garréta has pointed out interestingly that 'entering into a "pacs" with a same-sex partner still leaves you, civilly, single, and as such theoretically entitled to seek to adopt. But entering into a "pacs" shows you to be engaged in a same-sex relationship; the law may be blind, but the administration may peer from under the blindfold' in 'Re-enchanting the Republic: "PaCS", *Parité* and *Le Symbolique*', p. 158.

[15] Pascale Krémer, 'La jurisprudence exclut les homosexuels au nom de leurs "choix de vie"', *Le Monde*, 3 mai 2001, p. 10.

[16] 'Ces motifs ne sont pas par-eux-mêmes de nature à justifier légalement un refus d'agrément' [à Mlle B.] 'dont les qualités humaines et éducatives ne sont pas contestées, qui exerce la profession d'institutrice et qui est bien insérée dans son milieu social, qu'elle présente des garanties suffisantes sur les plans familial, éducatif et psychologique pour acceuillir un enfant adopté.' Quoted by Pascale Krémer in *Le Monde*, 3 mai 2001, p. 10.

144   *The Gay Republic*

backdrop of the legal rights of single people who want to adopt.[17] Even *Le Monde* became involved in the debate, siding in its editorial of 3 May 2001 with the APGL, reinforcing the central point of discrimination, but also going further and responding indirectly to some judicial inconsistencies. In particular, it highlighted the fact that the suitability of a person to adopt should be based on the character of the individual and not on prejudice or the prior exclusion of a category of citizens. Most pointedly, it revealed the paradox of a law which may, on the one hand, allow a single person to adopt, but, on the other hand, deny adoption rights to a single lesbian or gay on the grounds that there is an absence of a maternal or paternal referent. In the case of Renaud Muselier, whose petition was bolstered by the RPR network and the association of Catholic families, he managed to present the arguments in his favour by side-stepping the discrimination issue and focusing his attention on the potential harm to the child, the family institution and the social order of a homoparental family.

The second case involved a single gay male called Philippe Fretté who wanted to adopt a child in 1991. The Conseil Général in Paris rejected his request in 1993 on the basis of his 'choix de vie.' He appealed to the administrative tribunal in Paris in 1995 which decided in his favour, stating that lifestyle could only be justified as a reason to reject his request if it were accompanied by a form of behaviour that was in some way prejudicial to the child. This judgment was annulled a year later by the Conseil d'Etat on the grounds that it would be in the child's interests to be situated in a stable family (i.e. heterosexual) environment (the child had been deprived of his family of origin and had experienced emotional trauma as a consequence). M. Fretté appealed subsequently to the European Court of Human Rights where a decision against him was reached on 26 February 2002. There are obvious comparisons here with the Emmanuelle B case (rejection followed by approval followed by rejection; also the discrimination against lesbian and gay persons in respect of adoption on the basis of sexual orientation or 'choix de vie'). Where the Fretté case differs is that the claimant took his case to the European Court and lodged an appeal against the French Republic. Forced to defend its position against claims of discrimination on grounds of sexual orientation, against violations of Articles 8 of the European Convention (right to a private family life) and 14 (the assurance of this right without discrimination), and against being one of only two of the 43 member states of the Council of Europe to allow adoption for single persons but exclude non-heterosexuals, lawyers for the Republic offered the following response. Firstly, refusal to grant adoption to a lesbian or gay individual did not infringe any *existing* right but only 'une virtualité de parenté adoptive.' Secondly, refusal to grant adoption, while not motivated *solely* by the client's homosexuality (admission of discrimination is self-evident

---

[17] 'Depuis la loi de 1966, les célibataires de plus de vingt-huit ans peuvent adopter plénièremnet un enfant. La loi ne spécifie pas qu'elles doivent vivre seules ou être hétérosexuelles.' Quoted by Pascale Krémer in 'Une pétition sur l'adoption relance le débat sur l'homoparentalité', *Le Monde*, 3 mai 2001, p. 10.

here), had more to do with concerns over the adopter's suitability to adopt a child. Thirdly, admitting 'ingérence' (interference) in the private life of the adopter (a 'but légitime' according to lawyers), it was deemed that the latter action was warranted in the interests of the child in order to 'protéger le bien-être psychologique de l'enfant susceptible d'être adopté.'[18] While accepting that there was a 'différence de traitement en raison de son homosexualité', lawyers for the republic claimed that this difference in treatment was founded on 'des motifs raisonnables en vue de l'état actuel des connaissances.'

The two cases raise some controversial issues. General confusion within the legal system is reflected in one court approving claims by lesbians and gays to adopt and another court overturning this decision. In the Emmanuelle B case, the use of male or female (mother/father) 'référents' to deny adoption to lesbian and gay couples is inconsistent with approval for adoption by single people who may be biologically neither a mother or father. The insistence on a 'couple différencié' is therefore contradictory. However, lawyers distinguish between 'une image de père absent' (in the context of single (gay) woman) and 'une image de père nié' (in the context of a lesbian or gay couple). From a legal perspective, it would appear that the image of an *absent* father is less detrimental to a single female adopter who may be gay, the logic being that the potential for this absence to be filled by a 'father' is always possible. Therefore, adoption is deemed safe (regardless of the secret lesbianism of the mother). In the second case, the image of a denied or rejected father is more final and permanent, thus adoption is legally prohibited on the 'différence des sexes' principle. The open gayness of the couple further compounds the illegality of the adoption. As Evelyne Pisier has highlighted in respect of this case: 'Dans les deux cas, il y a un risque pour l'enfant. Mais, dans le premier cas, le risque est "légal" et le juge doit appliquer la loi. En revanche, dans le cas de l'adoption par un homosexuel, l'effrayante négation du "père" justifie le refus de l'agrément. Dans le passage de l'absence de père à sa négation, il construit son postulat.'[19]

Pisier's analysis highlights a latent discrimination within the law against adoption by lesbians and gays, couched in the psychoanalytic discourse of 'absence' and 'nié.'[20] She goes on make some key points in respect of this case and the legal implications. She claims that if the concept of risk is critical in placing children with single persons or married couples, the very *sexuality* of a potential 'parent' does not negate risk or increase it (unless the presumption that married

---

[18] Pascale Krémer, 'La Cour européenne des droits de l'homme appelée à statuer sur l'adoption par les homosexuels', *Le Monde*, 4 octobre 2001, p. 38.

[19] Evelyne Pisier, 'Adoption: la justice du divan?' *Revue des deux mondes*, mai (2001): 90.

[20] These terms are highly charged in Freudian and Lacanian psychoanalysis, and are open to much conjecture when used in a legal sense. On a more general note, there is a body of opinion within psychoanalysis which maintains that maternal and paternal functions are always present in couples, regardless of their sexuality. See Elisabeth Roudinesco, 'Psychanalyse, famille, homosexualité', *Revue des deux mondes*, mai (2001): 103-7.

146   *The Gay Republic*

status implies heterosexuality). Risk, she claims, is an issue for all parents, whether biological or adopting parents. The difference, however, is that biological parents have total rights over their children and the state is, in large measure, powerless to intervene. By contrast, adoption is one area where the state is seen to be given authority to control private life and intervene (where needs be) in the interests of the child 'au nom du principe de précaution.'[21] In the Fretté case for example, the law is seen to be able to ride rough shod over one of the sacrosanct principles of the republic (the right to privacy) in order to justify its claim that the interests of the child are paramount. But what is the meaning of the term 'the interests of the child'? New legislation on 'co-parentalité' stipulates that children have rights to relations with their parents (biological) and parents have obligations to maintain relations with their children. This legislation guarantees a continuity of relations between parent and child. But it also reveals inadequacies in the case of uncooperative children and parents, or children who want to escape abusive biological parents. Again, the law, in this particular legislation, appears to promote a certain heteronormative order of the family, where biological ties have supremacy over affective ties. Pisier states that the interests of the child reside in that child's very interests (*'ses* propres conditions de vie' by which she means the child's physical, psychological situation). For Pisier, the interests of the child are separate from the interests of the parents, hence her reluctance to consider the imposition of a model of behaviour on family arrangements. Critically, she exposes what she sees as the weak logic of the French courts and state in setting up a relation between a child's interests and those of the adoptive parents on the grounds of precaution. This creates, she claims, a parental imbalance between biological parents and children, and adopters and children. Such an imbalance is open to the creation of a hierarchy of parent and the perceptions that a biological parent is free from criticism if the child goes astray, whereas it is the fault of the adoptive parent.

Pisier's views are quite radical in that she wants to loosen the legal and state grips on adoption and give more power to individuals to make their own choices. Part of her strategy is to expose the legal machinery to closer scrutiny. This strategy falls within the pale of the democratisation of sexuality and citizenship. However, Pisier's approach to democracy via a critique of the law and an increase in more power to individuals is not the only way democratic citizenship can be expressed. The psychoanalyst Jean-Pierre Winter presents a different view in which democracy is on the side of the law, and must be seen to resist social trends and personal fixations which run contrary to the principles of universalism. In his article, he highlights the dangers of the law legalising what he calls the 'phantasme' of 'homoparentalité.'[22] His argument is based on three main concepts. The first is political. He plays down the idea that not to accept lesbian and gay

---

[21]   Pisier, 'Adoption: la justice du divan?', *Revue des deux mondes*, p. 91.

[22]   Jean-Pierre Winter, 'Du phantasme à la loi: la question de l'homoparentalité', *Revue des deux mondes*, mai (2001): 92-102.

parents through adoption is to be anti-democratic and reactionary. He undermines the homosexual argument of equality of all citizens *before the law* by saying that the law is not the real arbiter in this context. Rather, the notions of mother and father are 'le résultat d'un acte simultanément physique et psychique fondé sur le Réel de la différence de sexes.'[23] Winter's second concept builds on the psychoanalytic foundation of 'la différence des sexes' and lays claim to the idea that 'homoparentalité' is a denial of the 'Réel' in 'la différence des sexes' in favour of 'le vrai.' The distinction is significant because it raises and questions the validity of our perception of democratic citizenship, namely that the law should evolve to reflect wider social, political and cultural change. Winter argues that what is frequent, popular or desirable within society may have the allure of being 'vrai' and acceptable, but that does not make it necessarily 'universalisable.' Winter scotches any notion of a *rapprochement* between public and private space. His argument condemns the private to the realm of fantasy ('vrai') whereas the public is the 'Réel' (republican) space of universal citizenship. His third concept is to oppose two identity structures, one a 'imaginaire identificatoire' and the other a 'identité symbolique.' The former belongs to the category of fantasy (even 'phantasme') in that children build around them a wide range of imaginary models to emulate. The symbolic structure is the key structure for Winter because for the child 'ses premières identifications concernent ceux avec qui il est lié par un lien significatif et par un lien de désir.'[24] As the key structure in identity development, Winter argues that the role of law is not to determine who has the right to have children (biological parents or gay parents) but that the law should not legitimise 'la disjonction du Réel et du Symbolique.'

Winter's study raises some important and contentious issues. His argument brings together the heavy weights of republican universalism and the expertise of psychoanalysis and presents the evidence as a case study of how real, as opposed to subjective, democracy works. The combination of a political constitution and scientific expertise is bound by a legal system, itself shored up by the power invested in it by republican principles and the knowledge of science. However, Winter's theories are far from full proof. We have seen in the course of this book that psychoanalysis and science (anthropology notably) have been questioned in respect of their 'expertise' and political applicability. Winter's implication that republicanism is superior in its democratic credentials because of its historical and eternal values is also questionable. He appears to suggest that social change (and by implication the claim for the democratisation of citizenship based on difference) is subject to the vagaries of cultural change. He couches change and difference in terms of 'le fréquent', 'le vrai', 'le quotidien', all of which are described as manifestations of a desire to overturn the universality of 'le Réel' and 'contourner la loi.' The delicate issue here is where does the law situate itself in respect of these social, political and scientific differences.

---

[23] Winter, 'Du phantasme à la loi: la question de l'homoparentalité', p. 98.
[24] Winter, 'Du phantasme à la loi: la question de l'homoparentalité', p. 100.

148   *The Gay Republic*

Winter's distinction between 'le Réel' and 'le vrai' may help us untangle some of the knots of perception. Approaching it as a socio-political model (and not the more obvious psychoanalytic model), the concept of the 'Réel' can be equated with a perception of the world founded on *a priori* model of universal and abstract equality. 'Le vrai', on the other hand, is a perception of the world founded on the necessity to update the structure of universal equality, make it less abstract and more relevant to contemporary society. Negotiating this difference of perception is the task for the legal system in the way it deals with justice. As we have seen in the cases above, the legal system is ambivalent in its decision-making. In both cases mentioned, the outcome has favoured the perception of the 'Réel' where the republic has been seen to stand firm on traditional values and issues. But the temporary satisfaction of the outcome has come at a cost with haemorrhaging of the legal system over issues of impartiality, technical obfuscation and breaking rules on spurious grounds.

The exposure of the inconsistencies of treatment between heterosexual and homosexual couples within the legal system is not only linked to the democratisation of the issues (the perception of 'le vrai') but also to the expectation that democratic citizenship, if it is to work effectively, must be representative of all citizens. The respective positions of Evelyne Pisier and Jean-Pierre Winter highlight the gulf that still exists in France today between conflicting versions of citizenship. For Pisier, citizenship is founded on equality of treatment for all parents in adoption cases, irrespective of sexual difference, risk or the presence or absence of paternal referents. She deconstructs the legal structures that create the obstacles to fairness of access by equalising opportunity to all citizens, and providing the opportunity for all citizens to engage their individuality, difference and separateness in a responsible and positive fashion. In effect, by bridging the gap between private and public, Pisier creates the conditions where sexual citizenship can thrive in the democratisation of access of citizens of difference to adoption by valuing them meaningfully and socially in the all-embracing structures of parenting and the family.

Given the current legal loopholes that lesbians and gays need to circumnavigate and interpret in order to avail of their limited rights (and in the case of Fretté, the argument in favour of the interests of the child has only a measure of validity in its applicability to *all* applicants who want to adopt), it is incumbent on society and its democratic structures to secure the means by which *all* its citizens have *equal* rights. The impartiality of the law is crucial in the management of this process. However, an opposition opens up here (as we have seen) between individual expectations and the legal system. If the law is seen to be behind the times, slow to act or suspiciously partial to a political system, then democratic expectations can come into conflict with lawmakers. The dangers here are multiple. People lose trust in the law because they feel alienated, unequal, marginalised and unrepresented. A dangerous and more immediate consequence is that, given the aforementioned legal inconsistencies, if decisions about adoption, and as we will see filiation, are left entirely within the remit of the courts, then there is the risk of the judiciary

Adoption and Filiation: The New PaCS Pact

making decisions about society, and the society that *it* wants, and not its citizens.[25] All the more need, I would suggest, for a democratic republican model rather than the purely republican model of citizenship in France. That said, the democratisation of issues such as adoption and filiation should not be perceived as *carte blanche* for unlimited freedoms. Democracy is not an open invitation to a policy of 'anything goes', nor is it a process in isolation. The democratisation of private life, as Weeks pointed out earlier, is a negotiation between private and public. What may serve the interests of individual freedom may also collide with established notions of common good. For Weeks, it is the search for the common good that is the key to the full democratisation of private life.

A recent example of the democratisation of private life in the service of a common good can be further seen in the case made by Geneviève Delaisi de Parseval for 'homoparentalité', AMP ('assistance médicale à la procreation', and also referred to as PMA) and adoption, on the grounds of a global ethics that has at its core 'la justice des échanges humains.'[26] Broadening the debate on adoption as exemplified by Mlle B. and M. Fretté, Parseval constructs a framework whereby in the case of 'homoparentalité', the child is nurtured not only by his/her gay parents but in an environment where a plurality of 'appartenance' is respected, where transparency about past biological links is respected where applicable, and where in fact the model of the new family is as much conditional on the love of the parents as it is on the responsibility of all branches of the wider family. She maintains: 'L'histoire de ces enfants se structure ainsi sur une double loyauté: ils appartiennent au système familial dans lequel ils ont été acceuillis et reçus; mais ils sont aussi liés au système familial dont font partie ceux qui ont contribué à leur mise au monde ou qui fait partie de leur capacité procréatrice.'[27] Essentially, Parseval's approach to 'homoparentalité' is one founded on lesbian and gay difference making its democratic claim to inclusiveness and citizenship, combined with the participation of other citizens in the elaboration of parental links and deployed in the best interests of the adopted child. No doubt there are complex issues to consider within this approach, particularly on the level of filiation and the legal status of multiple parents, but the basic principle of wresting control of a child's future from the courts and investing it in a knitted structure of family ties (the vertical/horizontal compromise as she calls it) ensures that there is a wider and more negotiated support base for the child's interests than any imaginary structure imposed by the courts. The democratic underpinnings of this approach fuse the language of obligation and duty to the interests of the child (public concern), with

---

[25] This notion underpins the work of both Eric Fassin and Daniel Borrillo.

[26] Geneviève Delaisi de Parseval, 'La construction de la parentalité dans les couples de même sexe', in Eric Fassin and Daniel Borrillo (eds), *Au-delà du Pacs*, p. 237.

[27] Delaisi de Parseval, 'La construction de la parentalité dans les couples de même sexe', p. 238.

150 *The Gay Republic*

the language of negotiation, love and commitment which comes from the private sphere.[28]

The Maternal/Paternal Axis and the Child's Rights of Origin

As mentioned earlier, one of the most controversial aspects of the case studies discussed is the reference to the maternal/paternal axis on which the judiciary (philosophers,[29] sociologists,[30] and renowned anthropologists[31]) place great faith. This issue also captured the attention of academic and medical professions, and was played out in sensational form in a national newspaper. In a flurry of letters to *Le Monde* over a two year period (1997 to 1999) between Serge Bakchine, Eric Dubreuil and Eric Fassin (among others), Serge Bakchine, an eminent neuro-psychologist, defends the importance of the maternal/paternal axis by claiming that the fact that many homosexual couples already have children from previous heterosexual unions is not a valid reason for approving adoption for lesbian and gay couples.[32] Furthermore, he disputes the validity of studies carried out in the USA and elsewhere that indicate that children are not adversely affected by

---

[28] For more on this approach to filiation, see Claude Sageot, 'Aux sources de l'adoption', *Libération*, 13 août 2004, p. 33.

[29] I refer here to one notable feminist philosopher who has contributed to these debates, namely Sylviane Agacinski who, in *Politique des sexes* (Paris: Seuil, 1998), claims that 'homoparentalité' is undesireable because a child is denied 'la mixité du genre' and there is a 'effacement de la différence sexuelle.' Agacinski, however, does say that if 'monoparentalité' can exist there should be no reason to discriminate against individuals on the basis of their sexual orientation.

[30] Irène Théry who has been a prolific contributor to debates on the PaCS and related subjects, insists on the centrality of 'la différence des sexes' as key to a child's development and well-being, whether it be in visible form or communicated symbolically: 'En l'absence d'un ordre symbolique de référence, chacun devient une menace pour chacun, quand tous peuvent se sentir rejetés ou spoliés. C'est pourquoi, l'ouverture de la famille au temps et à l'espace suppose aussi que soient réinstitués, au sein d'un ensemble ordonné, les places de la parenté' in 'Différence des sexes et différence des générations. L'institution familiale en déshérence', *Esprit*, 12 (1996): 86.

[31] I refer specifically to Françoise Héritier and Pierre Legendre. Héritier has been the main exponent of a prohibition on access to homosexual parenthood. See her contributions on this issue to the National Assembly during the PaCS debates, and her book *Masculin/Féminin. La pensée de la différence* (Paris: Odile Jacob, 1996). For a detailed analysis of their anti-PaCS sentiments and opposition to filiation on the basis of 'la différence des sexes' see Elisabeth Zucker-Rouvillois' chapter 'L'expertise familiale ou la perte du doute scientifique', in *Au-delà du PaCS*, pp. 111-28.

[32] The context is a series of letters under the title 'Homosexualité, famille, filiation' to *Le Monde* in the autumn of 1997, where each 'expert' set out his position on adoption by lesbian and gay couples.

Adoption and Filiation: The New PaCS Pact

growing up with lesbian and gay couples/parents.[33] Bakchine accuses Fassin and Pisier of reducing the problem to 'une pure question de droit' and, more pointedly, of skirting the fundamental issue of 'la différence des sexes' which he equates with 'un ordre symbolique des sexes et de la sexualité, aussi un ordre des choses immémorial et intangible.'[34] The comparisons with Jean-Pierre Winter's position are striking.

Bakchine's position is defended with equal force by child psychiatrist, Frédéric Jésu, and leading child representative Jean-Pierre Rosenczveig in a letter to *Le Monde* a year later. Writing at a time when the movement towards the implementation of the PaCS was at full speed, the co-writers contest the spirit of the adoption process, which they believe has been overly-politicised to serve the interests of lesbian and gay couples: 'l'adoption vise à donner de nouveaux parents à un enfant ne disposant plus juridiquement de ses parents de sang et non pas à "servir" un enfant à ceux qui ne peuvent ou ne veulent biologiquement en avoir.'[35] They go on to highlight the fears of paedophilia, incest, psychological trauma for vulnerable youngsters, and the conflicts that may arise between the interests of the child and what they characterise (with pejorative emphasis) as the 'projet d'avenir' of the gay couple in question. They reserve their most powerful argument to the end of the article when they return to what they perceive to be the true spirit of adoption, which is to provide security and certainty, not doubt, to the child. This, they claim, applies as much to general family circumstances as it does to the issue of gender:

> L'adoption ne laisse la porte ouverte à aucune fiction, à aucun déni portant sur la réalité biologique de la procréation. Elle reste symboliquement, primitivement et définitivement inscrite dans le postulat biologique et social de la différence des sexes comme condition de reproduction et de survie de l'espèce humaine.[36]

The views of Bakchine and the above psychiatrists form part of a wider debate about the role of science in political and legal circles (see my chapter on 'la différence des sexes'). The expertise that science brings to political and legal debate is considerable but, as we have seen in the field of psychoanalysis, it is not without its shortcomings. Freudian psychoanalysis is founded on the relationship between child, mother and father. There is a strong traditional lobby within psychoanalysis which is opposed to lesbian and gay parents on the basis of their 'reproductive sterility', and which highlights the dangers for children whose identity and concept of role model is damaged by symbolic modifications

---

[33] The website devoted to the issue of 'Homoparentalité' and on which one can find a host of information (articles, case studies) and debate is: www.homoparentalite.free.fr.

[34] Serge Bakchine, 'Homosexualité, mariage, famille; et la nature', *Le Monde*, 19 novembre 1999, p. 17.

[35] Frédéric Jésu and Jean-Pierre Rosenczveig, 'Le fallacieux épouvantail de l'adoption', *Le Monde*, 9 octobre 1998, p. 15.

[36] Jésu and Rosenczveig, 'Le fallacieux épouvantail de l'adoption', p. 15.

152   *The Gay Republic*

introduced by same sex parents.[37] However, in the context of recent scientific developments in France and internationally (medically assisted procreation, anonymous donors and the mother's right to give birth anonymously), traditional concepts of role models and maternal/paternal origins have already been thrown into question. For psychoanalysis, the primary concern remains 'l'importance de l'accès à l'origine, à la vérité de l'origine pour l'enfant. Mais on sait que le modèle procréatif actuellement dominant a organisé, bien avant que l'homoparentalité doive soulever ce problème, un déni de l'accès à l'origine parfaitement légal avec l'IAD ou l'accouchement sous X.'[38] Traditionally, the consensus in psychoanalysis has been that origin ('lieu de parenté') for the child is vital. But as the controversial psychoanalyst Michel Tort infers, to make 'homoparentalité' the scapegoat for this loss of origin is misguided. He identifies two other sources. The first is medical science which he believes has endangered the validity of the concept of origin, and the second is the law which has legalised medical advances. In spite of, and indeed because of, these scientific developments, Tort claims that traditional psychoanalysis is driving forward its key message of the importance of a child to know their origins. The psychoanalyst Elisabeth Roudinesco remains steadfast that, even though an adopted child can be spared the details that led to their birth, 'il est capital pour l'enfant de connaître la vérité de ses origines.'[39] For Michel Tort, on the other hand, the break in the parental/procreative link and the dilution of the direct line of filiation has two fundamental but different consequences.

Firstly, it represents a regression for psychoanalysis in that the principle of origin is undermined. But, secondly, it represents a potential breakthrough for lesbian and gay parents who want to adopt. However, the precedent that origin can be medically blurred is soon qualified in respect of gay parents, whose desires to adopt are denied by the law on the grounds that procreation (or potential procreative capability) determines 'parenté.' The legal discrimination may seem unfair and deliberately obstructive, but it would seem that the victim of this qualification could be the child, with the law being seen to hold not only a very rigid line but also a selective and discriminatory one in respect of who can be a parent. Evelyne Pisier brings to our attention three concerns in this respect.[40] In favour of lesbian and gay parents and adoption by homosexuals, she claims that the law, in demanding all adopting parents to 'faire la preuve du deuil de l'enfant biologique', has infantilised parents, damaged the identity construction of adopted

---

[37] Jean-Pierre Winter, 'Gare aux enfants symboliquement modifiés', *Le Monde des débats*, 12 (2000): 21-34; Christian Flavigny, 'L'enfant n'est pas un bien social', *Le Monde*, 16-17 juillet 2000, p. 20; Aldo Naouri, 'Maintenir la fonction paternelle, même artificiellement', *Libération*, 3 août, p. 27.

[38] Michel Tort, 'De la différence "psychanalytique" des sexes', *Les Temps modernes*, 609 (2000): 178.

[39] Elisabeth Roudinesco, 'Psychanalyse, famille, homosexualité', *Revue des deux mondes*, mai (2001): 103.

[40] Evelyne Pisier, 'Sexes et sexualités: bonnes et mauvaises différences', *Les Temps modernes*, 609 (2000): 156-75.

children who in later life may wish to know their real origins, and generally made the task of rearing adopted children significantly more difficult. Secondly, and linked to the first, she circumvents the conflicting and subjective research about the perceived instability of children growing up with lesbian and gay parents. Instead, she redirects the debate towards the issue of children's rights, which she claims are not relevant in respect of choice of parents, as this is not the case in a heterosexual couple, or a single mother or father raising children. Where a child's rights are particularly relevant, is where the real parent(s) are not present at all, as with anonymous donors. Pisier's third concern, which gives hope to law reform, is that the law has acknowledged the advances in medical science and introduced some legal measures in response. But Pisier is fearful that these laws can be changed at any given time. What is interesting in Pisier's contribution, and which links her symbolically to Tort and Roudinesco, is that she contextualises her concern for the child in terms of their democratic rights to know their origins, *if that is what they want*. In this way she removes the authority of the law over the child, which is presumed to act in that child's interests, and reinstates authority in the rights of the child: 'La question est tout autre que celle de son "intérêt" et de la capacité de ses parents à l'éduquer. La question se rapporte *à ses droits*'[41] (my italics).

The concerns of psychiatrists and psychoanalysts in adoption cases are considerable and need to be taken seriously. However, suspicious of a bias in the way psychoanalysis and science appeared to defend the maternal/paternal axis at the expense of lesbian and gay parents, Eric Fassin, Daniel Borrillo, Marcela Iacub and Eric Dubreuil mounted a campaign in the press, in books and in academic journals to contest and to expose what they perceived to be a medical/judicial conspiracy against lesbian and gay couples forming families.[42] In a letter signed by Fassin, Iacub and Borrillo to *Le Monde* on 16 February 1999, they crystallised their

---

[41]   Pisier, 'Sexes et sexualités: bonnes et mauvaises différences', p. 173. The debate on adoption, and specifically the issue of the child's rights and access to biological origins, has captured the headlines in contemporary gay debates in France, and is an indication of how far the politicisation of the post-PaCS agenda has infiltrated the wider French consciousness. The issue of right to origins is split into two camps. The first is represented mainly by Martine Gross (President of the APGL), who, in the interests of legal transparency, maintains that knowledge of origins in respect of biological filiation needs to be restored in the interests of the child, and as a point of equality. The second is represented by Marcela Iacub who rejects the argument that biology needs naming, or should have supremacy over other filial ties. Specifically, she claims that biological naming has been oversignified and that knowledge of origins is an issue of the 'will' of the child, if or when the child wants to research the issue. To read more on this debate, see Martine Gross, 'Séparer les trois volets de la filiation', *Libération*, 10 août 2004, p. 23. Further articles by Claude Sageot and Serge Tisseron complement the discussion (see bibliography).

[42]   Daniel Borrillo has written widely on this subject. See his contribution to his co-edited collection with Eric Fassin, in *Au-delà du PaCS*, and his article 'L'orientation sexuelle en Europe: esquisse d'une politique publique antidiscriminitoire' in *Les Temps modernes*, 609, (2000): 263-282.

154 *The Gay Republic*

response. The *point de départ* in their approach to the PaCS, gay adoption and lesbian and gay marriage has remained equality of sexuality and the end in law to discrimination against lesbians and gays. They see in the PaCS one of the great advances of the recent period, but also point to the fact that beyond equality of the individual is equality between couples and, beyond that, equality between homosexual and heterosexual marriage and gay and straight families. Their argument is threefold and what is of particular interest to us is how the maternal/paternal axis is addressed. Their premise is the recognition of the importance of marriage and the family in society. They expose what they see as the hypocrisy of society in its exclusion of homosexuals from marriage and the family by invoking the norm of 'la différence de sexes'; in other words, 'la différence des sexes' can be enrolled in the service of equality (for feminists, for example, in their debate on parity), but it can then be used as an arm against equality in the context of equal rights for gay marriage and adoption.[43] The second hypocrisy is what Fassin has termed elsewhere in his writings as the 'illusion anthropologique.'[44] Scotching the idea that 'la différence des sexes' is 'le principe anthropologique qui fonde l'institution du couple, de la famille et de la parenté',[45] the co-writers invoke the social sciences (as opposed to *les sciences humaines*) and claim that societies, laws and cultures evolve and, in the process, new models of living are invented: 'C'est pourquoi il est impossible de proposer, du couple, de la famille ou de la filiation, quelque définition anhistorique: dans le temps et dans l'espace, les sociétés remodèlent les institutions qui les définissent.'[46]

The role of 'la différence des sexes' in the debate on the family is a pivotal one because at its centre is the concept of the heterosexual model of the family. We have seen how and why the medical and legal professions have defended this model in the context of adoption and the interests of the child. In fact, this concept has also been invoked by Irène Théry in her critique of adoption by lesbians and gays, including the status of the homosexual couple as we shall see later. Despite indications of more progressive thinking on adoption and filiation elsewhere, Théry's essentially biological position on 'la différence des sexes' has itself become a source of debate in the French academy. Fassin and Théry have exchanged views on this issue in the journal *Esprit*, and it has also provoked comment from the American feminist Joan Wallach Scott who has denounced what

---

[43] Garréta has exposed the 'fabulous regression' of the parity debate (*Yale French Studies*, p. 162), and Evylene Pisier has underlined its fundamental hypocrisy: 'La même norme de nature qui accepte la parité au nom d'une différence convenable interdit qu'on reconnaisse au couple homosexuel des droits semblables à ceux du couple hétérosexuel' in *Le Monde*, 20 octobre 1998, p. 18.

[44] Eric Fassin, 'L'illusion anthropologique: homosexualité et filiation', pp. 43-56, and 'Usages de la science et science des usages: A propos des familles homoparentales', pp. 391-408.

[45] Borrillo, Fassin and Iacub, 'Au-delà du PaCS: pour l'égalité des sexualités', *Le Monde*, 16 février 1999, p. 17.

[46] Borrillo, Fassin and Iacub, 'Au-delà du PaCS: pour l'égalité des sexualités', p. 17.

Adoption and Filiation: The New PaCS Pact

she sees as Théry's regressively essentialist position. Scott deflates the importance of the biological unit that underpins the family, and reproaches Théry's indirect 'homophobia', suggesting with forceful evidence that the notion of 'la différence des sexes' has now become a 'sexual difference that is socially, culturally, linguistically produced' and thus subject to change.[47]

From these short exchanges, it is clear that the issue of 'la différence des sexes' is central in the debate on adoption and, particularly, filiation. In one camp (democratic), we have those, like Pisier, for whom 'la différence des sexes' is a fiction of the past, overtaken by social constructionism and new conjugal links. In the other camp (republican), there are those who fear the loss of the institutionalisation of 'la différence des sexes', and who are in favour of greater controls in verifying filiation in order to avoid 'la dépendence relationnelle' of which Théry speaks. Catherine Labrusse-Riou has voiced similar concerns by stating that filiation is not simply a matter of private life, but needs to be viewed in its historical context:

> son enjeu individuel et collectif, concerne l'identification de chaque individu, à une place unique et interchangeable, au sein d'un ordre généalogique culturellement construit; cet ordre inscrit, en outre, la personne dans le temps et dans l'espace et dans la longue lignée des vivants et des morts. Or de ce point de vue, il n'y a pas d'autofondation de la personne par elle-même.[48]

Labrusse-Riou's views have a conservative and republican imprint. She situates filiation in an individual and collective binary but the collective (genealogical order) is dominant. As such, the contemporary and alternative notion that filiation can be constructed *ad hoc* is dismissed. In order to preserve her interpretation of filiation, Labrusse-Riou resorts to the law as principle arbiter. Unfortunately for Labrusse-Riou, the law has been too fickle on the issue of filiation. It has buckled under pressure from social change and ceded priority of filiation to the vagaries of individual choice. In so doing, parental will (in cases of adoption and filiation) and the transformations in modern life have challenged crucial juridic institutions, and created a crisis of 'appartenance.' In short, Labrusse-Riou's argument comes down to two central points. The first is that recognised institutionalised structures of 'parenté' and 'filiation' must be protected by the law from the climate of contestation and voluntarism. Secondly, filiation can only be defined as a dependent of marriage and 'la différence des sexes': 'le mariage et l'alliance font équilibre à la toute puissance du lignage et de la parenté [...]. Restera cependant à faire entendre, à défaut de rite civil préalable, que soit respecté le principe de la différence des sexes, comme loi sociale autant que naturelle, nécessaire à la constitution de liens de famille.'[49] One of the problems with Labrusse-Riou's

---

[47] Joan Wallach Scott, 'Feminist Family Politics', *French Politics, Culture and Society*, 17 (1999): 29.

[48] Catherine Labrusse-Riou, 'La filiation en mal d'institution', *Esprit*, 12 (1996): 92.

[49] Labrusse-Riou, 'La filiation en mal d'institution', p. 109.

156   *The Gay Republic*

argument is that she wants the law to be harsh on some issues while soft on others. She expresses fears about the law's quick fire response to social change, opening up inequalities of treatment between 'parenté légitime' and 'parenté naturelle', as well as inequalities between maternity and paternity, in the context of the 'accouchement sous X' phenomenon.[50] Then, she calls for changes to the law in respect of rights for step-parents (compare Théry). It could be argued that her appeasement to step-parents is a strategy to convey a soft (integrationist) side to her republican sympathies because where she is uncompromising is in her refusal to extend a debate on filiation outside of marriage and 'la différence des sexes.' Both, according to her, dictate the institutional link that founds filiation. Hers is a safe, uncompromising and conservative position. It also has a very powerful support base. However, in relation to the opposing democratic camp, we will see that while these institutional (genealogical) roots of filiation are cultivated and reinforced where possible, they must also be seen to be flexible enough to reform themselves in response to alternative conjugal ties.

After digesting this exchange of viewpoints, it is clear we are at a political crossroads between the forces of conservatism/republicanism and democracy. We are also at an ideological crossroads between the institutions and values that have shored up the traditional socio-cultural and political infrastructure, and the forces of deinstitutionalisation. Many commentators have couched this opposition in the binary of French republicanism and democracy.[51] Alain Finkielkraut, one of the exponents of the republican school, has characterised the opposition in terms of a decline of republican values (what he has called 'une crise de la transmission'[52]), where the links between past, present and future (albeit in a cultural and literary context) have been lost. The democratic counter to this republican humanism would be to question not only the origin of such idealism and its relevance to contemporary France, but also to contest the concept of the republican community and its message of a collective, unified national heritage. It cannot be denied that both these ideologies are in constant tension within current French socio-political thought. However, in the context of the new debates on adoption and filiation (and their related issues), it is clear that democratic models of thinking have responded more creatively to what are serious issues in contemporary France. The sociologist Irène Théry subscribes to this view in the context of her 'democratic' response to the decline of the family, but she does not absolve democracy from a degree of culpability for the role it has played in creating a culture of individualisation, which she has described as partially responsible for 'démariage', and 'la

---

[50]   A law, dating from 9 January 1993, was passed in France giving the right to a mother to give birth without revealing her identity, thus depriving the father and the child the possibility of establishing maternal and paternal links.

[51]   For an overview of the extent to which this opposition permeates French society, see John Marks and Enda McCaffrey (eds), *French Cultural Debates* (Monash Romance Studies, Monash, 2001).

[52]   Alain Finkielkraut, 'La crise de la transmission', *Esprit*, 12 (1996): 55.

Adoption and Filiation: The New PaCS Pact

désarticulation de la conjugalité.'[53] In the case of Théry, it may be justifiable to suggest that democratisation is in some measure responsible for the decline in valued state institutions like the family or marriage. But this critique needs to be couched not only within the bosom of democracy's gifts but also within the very nature of democracy itself. As Fassin and his co-writers in the letter to *Le Monde* in 1999 remind us, democratic societies are not one-track political structures. They are societies traversed by time and history, not resistant to them.

'Filiation', 'Désaffiliation' and 'Pluriparentalité'

> Or, de façon croissante, l'institution de la filiation devient incertaine, fragile, incohérente, contradictoire, soumise à une double pente; celle de la tyrannie des volontés privées d'un côté, celle de la tyrannie du biologisme de l'autre. Ces deux pentes, paradoxalement, ne s'équilibrent pas mais se nourrissent mutuellement. [54]

In her introduction to a section of the journal *Esprit* entitled 'Le Malaise dans la filiation', Irène Théry cast a shadow over Finkielkraut's theory on the crisis of transmission by claiming that the links between identity, filiation and transmission were more alive today than ever. [55] What she meant was that in society today where the traditional family is no longer the norm, and where divorce has opened up new conjugal arrangements post marriage, the need for stabilising links between the individual and parentage is even more acute. What makes this stabilisation difficult to sustain is not only the unravelling of parental and genealogical ties, but also a decline in the very meaning of the concept of 'parenté.'[56] In addition, some of the institutions of filiation (nature, marriage, procreation) through which individuals have given meaning to their lives and identified themselves, have themselves come under threat from shifts in thought, behaviour and science.

As a first example, the institution of the family has been under attack from two fronts: as an institution, and as a unit with an identifiable 'parenté' (or set of blood relationships). As an institution, the family has always been seen as one of the safeguards of the state: 'La défense de la famille est devenue [...] une cause d'Etat.'[57] Remi Lenoir contextualises the inter-dependent nature of the relationship between family and state, from the social categories that were put in place to

---

[53] Irène Théry, 'Différence des sexes et différence des générations. L'institution familiale en déshérence', *Esprit*, 12 (1996): 65-90.

[54] Théry, 'Filiations', *Couple, filiation et parenté aujourd'hui. Le droit face aux mutations de la famille et de la vie privée* (Paris: Odile Jacob, 1998), p. 169.

[55] Théry, 'L'homme désaffilié', *Esprit*, 12 (1996): 50-53.

[56] *L'Homme* devoted a recent issue to the question of kinship: 'Question de parenté', *L'Homme*, 154-155 (2000).

[57] Remi Lenoir, 'Le familialisme et le PaCS', in *Au-delà du PaCS*, p. 48. For more on the historical links between family, church and state see Lenoir's article 'La question familiale: familialisme d'Eglise, familialisme d'Etat', *French Politics, Culture and Society*, 17 (1999): 75-100.

158   *The Gay Republic*

defend the family in the late nineteenth century to the state's mobilisation of other factions from the dominant classes, like 'la gestion des affaires civiles' and most crucially, 'la mouvance nataliste.' The latter, in particular, was seen to defend a certain conception of the family, which was primarily ethico-religious. As Lenoir goes on to suggest, with the separation of church and state at the beginning of the twentieth century, this ethico-religious vision was substituted by a more technocratic vision of rationalist and scientific inspiration, which was designed to counter depopulation in the inter-war period. Post Liberation, the political institutionalisation of the family took shape in the form of legitimate bodies of public power and state grants. In short, as Lenoir concludes, 'Le familialisme [...] est une conception générale du monde social qui fait de la famille le principe de toute chose.'[58]

At the root of this embedding process of the family was marriage, and of course heterosexual marriage. It is not within the remit of this chapter to chart the decline of marriage in western societies over recent decades.[59] As the bedrock of the family and, by extension, society, marriage has become the central conduit of filiation. However, the links between birth (in a married or unmarried context) and 'parenté' in France provide some interesting insights into the transmission of ties of descent. In a fascinating study on reproduction and bioethics,[60] Marcela Iacub highlights the shaky foundations on which the maternal/paternal bond is currently established. In French law, it is the birth act itself ('accouchement') which makes the mother the biological mother. The mother's name on a birth certificate is only relevant and legally binding to the birth act, and not to 'engendrement' (conception, gestation, ownership, blood ties). Of course, we assume proof of 'engendrement' is evident in the birth act. We can see here, however, the possibility of breakdown in filial ties, and also in cases of *in vitro* fertilisation or when a mother receives eggs from an anonymous donor, or in rape when a child is born. While the birth act is irrefutable proof of maternity for the mother, in the case of the father, written confirmation on a birth certificate is the only legal measure of paternity. Without teasing out the intricacies of these configurations, it is plain to see that, without scientific or genetic proof of filiation, there are not only inequalities in the foundations of maternal and paternal links, but plenty of room for agents of 'désaffiliation.'

Such a scenario may appear to justify the concerns of Labrusse-Riou and her call for the institutionalisation of marriage and the family to reinforce the natural

---

[58]   Lenoir, 'La question familiale: familialisme d'Eglise, familialisme d'Etat', p. 77.

[59]   For a brief analysis of marriage in the context of France, see my own article 'The PaCS debate and the Implications for Universal Equality in France', *French Cultural Debates* (Monash Romance Studies, Monash, 2001), pp. 22-36.

[60]   Marcela Iacub, 'Reproduction et division juridique des sexes', *Les Temps modernes*, 609 (2000): 242-62.

Adoption and Filiation: The New PaCS Pact

processes of filiation and 'parenté.'[61] However, for Théry, the modern forces of divorce, 'démariage', 'cohabitation' and 'homoparentalité' have dented irrevocably the foundations of these institutions. Similarly, sociological critique, in the work of Pierre Bourdieu, has exposed the illusion of the 'naturalité' of the family institution by stripping it of its institutional credentials. The family, Bourdieu claims, is no longer an institution but a category ('la famille cellule de base de la société'[62]). This deinstitutionalisation is important for two reasons. Firstly, as exemplified by Bourdieu, the family as category (as opposed to intangible or mythic institution) becomes subject to examination within a system of classification. In his sociological analysis of class, Bourdieu sets up for critique the 'normal' bourgeois family which the dominated classes find impossible to emulate. Social change in the shape of homoparental families and a plurality of different family forms has challenged this bourgeois norm, and destabilised the dominant heterosexual model of the family founded on marriage. Secondly, deinstitutionalisation exposes the role of the state in its sponsorship of the 'normal' bourgeois family structure. Bourdieu claims that agents of the state (statisticians, certain sociologists, magistrates)

> contribuent à reproduire la pensée étatisée qui fait partie de ces conditions du fonctionnement de la famille [...]. La famille est bien une fiction, un artefact social, une illusion au sens le plus ordinaire du terme, mais une "illusion bien fondée", parce que, étant produite et reproduite avec la garantie de l'Etat, elle reçoit à chaque moment de l'Etat les moyens d'exister et de subsister.[63]

Irène Théry has elaborated a similar thesis on the deinstitutionalisation of the family, with a particular focus on filiation. Claiming that 'la famille contemporaine n'est plus une institution, c'est un réseau relationnnel',[64] Théry's critique differs from Bourdieu's critique of the hierarchical norm of the family by locating a crisis within the family at two key points. The first is the ideological battle that democratisation appears to be winning over republicanism, and specifically where the push towards the individualisation of the family has produced an idea of the family locked in the present, unaware of its origins and without a window on the future (the allusion to Finkielkraut's 'crise de la transmission' is significant).[65] The

---

[61] As Garréta has pointed out, there exist strong parliamentary and academic lobbies who want to keep 'the axis of filiation straight' (*Yale French Studies*, p. 158).

[62] Pierre Bourdieu and Jean-Claude Passeron, *La Reproduction* (Paris: Editions de Minuit, 1970).

[63] Bourdieu, *Raisons pratiques. Sur la théorie de l'action* (Paris: Editions du Seuil, 1994), pp. 137-45.

[64] Théry, 'Différence des sexes et différence des générations. L'institution familiale en déshérence', p. 65.

[65] For more on the individualisation of the family, see François de Singly, 'Questions de famille', *Libération*, 1 août 2004, p. 31, and Serge Hefez, 'La vraie crise, celle de la fusion', *Libération*, 2 août 2004, p. 30.

160 *The Gay Republic*

second, linked to the first, is the collapse of notions of affinity, solidarity and biology that were once considered central to a definition of the family.

Let us consider two examples to measure the nature of these shifts. The first is a very common situation affecting many family contexts, namely the breakdown of a marriage and family, followed by divorce where each partner either remarries or cohabits with a new partner (in both cases heterosexual partners). The consequences of the break between conjugality and filiation (experienced in many difficult and traumatic ways) are also felt at the institutional level with the loss in meaning of once very obvious terms and words. Théry makes some pertinent remarks in this regard:

> La précarisation du lien entre père et les enfants est la manifestation la plus inquiétante de ce problème [...]. Comment institue-t-on le père, hors du mariage? Comment évoquer que la famille ne se maternalise? [...]. L'un des effets de la crise de l'institution familiale les moins compris est qu'elle a créé une situation tout à fait inédite: désormais les mots même de père, de mère, de fils ou de fille sont devenus incertains.[66]

We can see here how Labrusse-Riou's nostalgia for a pure marriage-filiation link is out of touch with this context. Alternatively, in her attempt to reinstitute the concept of filiation along new lines, Théry and others have widened the net of relational connections and sought to include the identities of old and new parents in a redefinition of 'parenté.' Théry has set up a triumvirate of 'composantes' ('biologique', 'domestique' et 'généalogique'), but the central thrust of her thesis is to push through the democratisation of this relationship, inviting participants 'à la prendre en charge eux-mêmes, négociant comme une affaire personnelle l'univers symbolique de la parenté.'[67] It is clear that part of Théry's strategy on filiation is to link traditional lines of filiation with new social/relational lines. Her concerns, therefore, for Finkielkraut's crisis of transmission are not totally misplaced. Her argument in favour of a different 'parenté' is expressed as a respect for both the genealogical root of parental responsibility, and for the responsibility of the citizen to reinvent new levels of intimacy:

> Ce qui nous menace désormais, comme l'ombre portée de l'aventure démocratique, est l'insignifiance d'un présent sans attaches, purement résumé à lui-même. Là prend tout sens l'enjeu de l'institution. Le besoin de lier l'un à l'autre le temps horizontal de la citoyenneté et le temps vertical de la transmission des générations a longtemps fait concevoir la famille comme l'institution qui devait *résister au temps*, opposant à l'écoulement incertain des jours et à la futilité de l'être voué à disparaître, la promesse de la fixité des statuts et des places. Entré à son tour en temporalité, le lien familial

---

[66] Théry, 'Différence des sexes et différence des générations. L'institution familiale en déshérence', pp. 75-6.
[67] Théry, 'Différence des sexes et différence des générations...', p. 80.

Adoption and Filiation: The New PaCS Pact 161

contemporain nous confronte à la question inédite de penser la famille comme *l'institution qui construit le temps.*[68]

The second example, which links Théry's notions of responsibility, reinstitution and citizenship, is that of 'homoparentalité.' As French law stands, homosexual couples ('pacsés' or not) cannot adopt children, but a single (and gay) person can adopt, providing they keep their sexuality hidden. Similarly, artificial insemination and PMA are forbidden to lesbian and gay individuals and couples. The APGL has sought to redress what it sees as a denial of these rights, as well as an end to discrimination against a lesbian or gay parent who wants to keep their children in the case of divorce or separation.[69] Where its agenda links in with that of sociological and academic debate is in its call, firstly, for legal status for the co-parent in a homosexual context (a status that Agnès Fine has equated with the status of step-parent[70]), and secondly, for a new institutional framework for the parent-child link. We have seen in the course of this chapter how conventional roles of parenting have been determined by the institution of the traditional family. These roles served a particular post-war function *within* the structure of a generation that was for the most part untouched by the fragmentation of family life that is prevalent today. What the APGL (and Fine) have proposed is an *inter-*generational approach to contemporary 'parentalité', which respects horizontal and vertical lines of filiation. What at first glance may appear radical and even impractical begins to gain some validity in the wider, relational notion of parenting as espoused by Théry, and which may be in the long-term interests of the child. Eric Dubreuil (former President of the APGL) has commented wisely that while the couple (heterosexual or homosexual) is provisional and subject to collapse, 'c'est le lien parent-enfant qui est pérenne, intemporel et indissoluble.'[71] His observations echo the threefold 'composantes' of Irène Théry and the call for the type of 'pluriparentalité' espoused by Agnès Fine:

> Reconnaître un statut distinct à ces trois filiations permettrait à tous les enfants d'avoir accès à leurs origines (filiation biologique), d'avoir une place dans la chaîne des générations (filiation légale/généalogique), d'être élevés par tous leurs parents (filiation

---

[68] Théry, 'Différence des sexes et différence des générations...', pp. 89-90.

[69] The Green Party in France (Les Verts) has also called recently for a change in family law to end what it sees as discrimination against gays wanting to adopt. It also supports new rights for homosexual parents. Its proposals are founded on a 'éthique de la responsabilité et sur la co-parentalité, afin d'offrir à l'enfant une réelle protection de ses liens en le faisant appartenir à un cercle familial plus élargi' in 'Les effets pernicieux de l'arrêt de la cour européenne en ligne de mire', *CityGay*, 1 mars 2002.

[70] Fine, 'Vers une reconnaissance de la pluriparentalité', p. 51.

[71] Eric Dubreuil and Maud Grad, 'Homosexualité, famille, filiation', *Le Monde*, 12 décembre 1997, p. 23.

162   *The Gay Republic*

sociale). Cela permettrait aux enfants de bénéficier d'un "plus": l'autorité parentale partagée de manière consensuelle par plus de deux personnes.[72]

Some would say that this is what in practice really happens in many such circumstances; parents, step-parents and grand parents all chip in in the upbringing of a child. This may well be the case, but it is important to highlight the fact that the law recognises only one line of filiation, not three.

Nevertheless, this 'horizontal' reconfiguration of filiation does belie some tensions. Clearly, good practice (stable environment for child, healthy relations between parents, transparency about biological past, education about 'facts of life'[73]) is encouraged where needs be. But, in most cases of 'familles recomposées' and homoparental familes (and except situations of 'adoption plénière'), the dubious and vulnerable status of the 'other' arises (in the cases of step-parent or co-parent).[74] Taking its inspiration from 'adoption plénière' (or adoption on the basis of artificial insemination from an anonymous donor where the line of filiation is invented (so to speak)), the APGL pursued initially the controversial path that filiation did not need to be fixed exclusively on a knowledge of origin. In other words, filiation could be construed in terms of difference of origin (Iacub, as we have seen, has shown that French law is open to this re-interpretation of filiation) and could therefore be constructed for the benefit of same-sex parents seeking to adopt.[75] Michel Tort, we recall, foresaw this development in his idea that out of the debate on the crisis of origins for the adopted child, induced by medical advancement, there was a ray of light for adoption by lesbian and gay parents. However, under the current Presidency of Martine Gross, the position of the APGL has shifted. Its current position is that filiation must have an accountable biological and transparent context, where there is an ethics of responsibility to the child, to biological parents and future parents, and where an official 'livret de l'enfant' is written up registering all personal, birth and parentage details. The APGL insists that its turn of face is not a sign of wanting to *locate* parentage but rather a sign of wanting to give the adoption process a greater legal and voluntary significance. As things stand, therefore, there is a face-off. The official position of the APGL is to say that gay adoption is made easier and legal if biological ties of filiation are made transparent. The alternative view is that gay adoption is easier if lines of filiation are left to the discretion of the individuals concerned.

This characterisation of the APGL as more legally focused in its insistence on biological transparency is not designed to paint the APGL as an organisation that bends easily to the rule of law. There is clearly much to be gained through the

---

[72]   Fine, 'Vers une reconnaissance de la pluriparentalité', p. 23.

[73]   Delaisi de Parseval, 'La construction de la parentalité dans les couples de même sexe', pp. 242-43.

[74]   I refer here to practice in France and not Britain or the USA where legal practice is different.

[75]   We have seen in the course of this chapter that there is substantial support from Evelyne Pisier and Michel Tort for the modification of lines of filiation.

Adoption and Filiation: The New PaCS Pact   163

legalisation of gay adoption than via the more voluntary approach. That said, the APGL has not abandoned the values of a voluntary approach to gay adoption. Indeed, it has some imaginative ideas in respect of the absence of a legal status for a gay step-parent or co-parent in the new age of consenusual filiation. The APGL has underlined the primacy of what it terms 'le lien social', a concept which has significant parallels in anthropology. Notwithstanding the problems in social parenting (particularly the tensions between biological status of one parent versus the socially recognised 'status' of another), the arguments in favour of recognition of legal status for the social parent appear to outweigh the negatives. Firstly, as Irène Théry has pointed out in her study of recomposed families, it is imperative that the status of step-father and co-parent be recognised by law in order to prevent 'désaffiliation' and to avoid people inventing rules of filiation for themselves: 'Faute de le faire, c'est-à-dire de s'efforcer de penser la règle et l'exception, la société soumet les individus à la pire des dépendences: la dépendance relationnelle.'[76] Her insistence on the need for recognition of status for step or co-parent is founded on the responsibility of parents to act in the best interests of the child. In this respect, she emphasises the importance of a *language of negotiation* based on the experience acquired in the aftermath of the breakdown of traditional ties of kinship. As Théry suggests, the terms of 'step children' and 'step parents' (within the same recomposed family) may not lie comfortably together from legal or familial perspectives. But, within the broader context of the term 'family' (Bourdieu's notion of 'la famille des familles'), the reconfiguration of familial ties along new lines of 'attachement' and 'génération' needs speedy legal acknowledgement:

> Sans inscrire l'enfant dans sa lignée, sans lui donner son nom, sans que son lien à celui-ci relève de l'inconditionnalité et de la perpétuité de la filiation, le beau-parent est pourtant lié à l'enfant dont il prend soin et auquel il est attaché. Autrement dit, beaux-parents et beaux-enfants appartiennent à la même famille mais pas à la même parenté généalogique. En ce sens, la place du beau-parent est une place *générationnelle.*[77]

In her defence of social parenting, or 'pluriparentalité', Agnès Fine contextualises the debate in anthropological terms, and sets up an opposition between traditional European models of filiation (based on blood and exclusivity) and African models, where social interaction and inclusivity are the norms. She sees the recent fragmentation of the parental role in western family structures as reflecting trends in non-European countries, where the child is not only a property of its parents but also that of its 'récipiendaires potentiels.'[78] Filiation, among African tribes, is perceived as a dual 'droit de la parenté ascendante ou collatérale (consanguine et

---

[76] Théry, *Couple, filiation et parenté aujourd'hui. Le droit face aux mutations de la famille et de la vie privée*, p. 210.

[77] Théry, *Couple, filiation et parenté aujourd'hui...* ', p. 214.

[78] Fine, 'Vers une reconnaissance de la pluriparentalité', p. 45.

164 *The Gay Republic*

alliée.)'[79] With further evidence from the USA and Canada, she presents a case in favour of social parenting, founded on the mutual interests of the child and step-parent/co-parent and on the increasing need to take into account 'la question identitaire.' While in many European countries, including France, where anonymity of biological origin in the case of adoption is still the most favoured option, we have seen that there is a considerable weight of opinion behind the idea of the right of the child to know their origins in the interests of the psychological stability of the child. Evelyne Pisier and the APGL has called for a reform of French law allowing, where possible, the names of biological parents to be recorded on the adopted family's certificate, with the clarification 'qu'ils sont, non pas nés de, mais fils ou fille de [...], par adoption survenue à telle date et en tel lieu.'[80] For Pisier, in particular, such a simple addition to a certificate would rid society of the culture of secrecy that undermines the adoption process. She also believes that such an innovation could facilitate adoption by lesbian and gay couples, and take away the pain and confusion that often accompanies a child's lifelong search for their roots.

Conclusions

Transformations in filiation and adoption have pushed the traditional institutions of marriage and family beyond breaking point. There are, naturally, concerns about how these transformations are being processed in law. Labrusse-Riou has raised real fears about voluntarism overriding juridic law, and 'vérité biologique' being undermined by the existence of multiple parents. I think there is no disputing the value of an institutional foundation of filiation in law. However, to ground this foundation in marriage and 'la différence des sexes' is to fly in the face of contemporary society, and to undervalue the increasingly diverse needs of people to establish new and alternative meaningful relations. Whether it be termed social parenting, 'pluriparentalité' or 'multiparentalité', the notion of the family in the postmodern age has acquired a new historical form. Once defined as a community of need held together by 'the obligation of solidarity',[81] the traditional ties linking the family together have weakened under the cumulative strain of socio-cultural change (divorce, separation, individually designed lives, rights to live differently). Elisabeth-Beck Gernsheim claims that the family today is freely chosen by individuals who decide their own boundaries in respect of parenting and filiation. However, as Irène Théry has pointed out, it is vitally important in these new elective relationships that certain legal markers are laid down, in particular the need for the recognition of status of step-parent/co-parent (in both heterosexual and homosexual contexts) so that the security of the link between filiation and 'co-

---

[79] Fine, 'Vers une reconnaissance de la pluriparentalité', p. 45.

[80] Pisier, 'Sexes et sexualités: bonnes et mauvaises différences', p. 174.

[81] Elisabeth Beck-Gernsheim, 'On the Way to the Post-Familial Family: From a Community of Need to Elective Affinities', *Theory, Culture and Society*, 15 (1998): 57.

Adoption and Filiation: The New PaCS Pact 165

parentalité' is ensured. That said, in the case of adoption, we should be careful not to turn exclusively to the law for answers. We have seen in a previous chapter how the law has problems addressing its own legitimacy. A dual biological/voluntary approach (in short an open policy) to adoption is perhaps a sensible way forward, where biology is seen not to impose or oversignify parentage but records a legal framework, and where voluntarism is free to have a role in this framework at any time without penalty or discrimination.

At the heart of these debates on adoption and filiation is the question of what defines a parent in our culture today. Is a parent the one who gives of their genes, or the one who gives birth? Or is a parent the one who takes care of a child and rears that child? And regardless of their sex or sexuality, can all these parents be instituted equally as 'mothers' and 'fathers' (or 'co-parents') in respect of filiation? And for that matter, should filiation be linked to birth, or desire to have children or to a voluntary declaration of two individuals who have decided to have children? Indeed, should one be able to change or invent filiation? There are no simple answers to these questions. What we have determined in this chapter is that the rule of law is under more scrutiny today than it has been in recent generations, and as such its function has become more and more critical. Firstly, the law needs to examine its role in society as either objective arbiter of values or a complicit enforcer of traditional institutions. Secondly, it needs to find a measured balance between the necessary demands of the 'Réel' and the urgent calls of the 'vrai.' Thirdly, it needs to address the culture of inequality of treatment between straight and gay couples, and draught legislation that is seen to be fair and equal to all sexes and sexualities. And fourthly, it needs to look at ways of redefining links of filiation and 'parentalité.' The PaCS legislation was designed to give legal status to heterosexual cohabitees and homosexual couples. In this it has largely succeeded. In targeting rights to gay adoption and gay parenthood (with gay marriage also on the agenda), the post-PaCS debate has now become a truly democratic and socially inclusive debate. What was perceived at the outset as a piece of insignificant gay legislation has in effect become the prism through which to examine the affective and elective choices that many of us face in our private lives today.

Chapter 6

Between Marriage and Concubinage: The Dilemma of the Lesbian and Gay Couple

La France reste structurellement attachée à un trait de mentalité historique qui lui interdit de rendre égal autrement qu'en rendant identique.[1]

In chapter one, we characterised France in terms of a political opposition between republicanism and democracy. This opposition has served us well in contextualising the theoretical debates that were central to the first part of this book. However, with the emergence of the conflictual reality of the social space, the lines of division between republic and democracy have become more blurred. Instead of clear dividing lines between republic and democracy, we have a socio-political and cultural organism made up of relations that are complex, interconnected, mutually exclusive and contradictory. This transformation from theoretical to organic model is useful from several perspectives. It is a more accurate model to reflect the interactive dimensions of sexual citizenship in the republic. Born out of the social realisation of political principle, this organic model feeds into the lived experience of the individual in the social space and gives oxygen to the social immanence of the decision-making process.

By way of exploring the organic nature of the republican/democratic relationship, this chapter will examine the discourses of leading sociologists and academics in their analyses of debates on the couple, concubinage and marriage. I aim to show that via the art of argumentation (including the wide range of discursive devices, ruses, tactics of persuasion and deferral), we can see reflected the shifting and deceptive sands between republican and democratic positions. In other words, the contours of debates will be seen to mirror the complex, sophisticated and intricate relationship between visions of republic and democracy. We will see how commentators project opinions, qualify them, and then place conditions on qualifications. This discursive tug of war within argumentation will be seen to reflect the political slippages between universalism and separatism, between public and private, between 'la différence des sexes' and sexual diversity. Two crucial points will emerge from this approach. The first is that the organ of the state that is the republic, perceived as sufficiently flexible in its accommodation of difference of all types under the principle of universalism, will also be seen to compromise its impartiality and democratic egalitarianism when placed under the spotlight of social pragmatism. As such, the model of republicanism will be seen to

---

[1] Paul Yonnet, 'PaCS, un mariage républicain', p. 108.

168   *The Gay Republic*

revert to type as final arbiter of corroboration and self-justification. The second point is that by exposing the ruses, bluffs, carrots and sticks that 'justify' the discourse of republican citizenship among some commentators, others will lay claim to an alternative and authentic equality of citizenship by subverting these tactics and other republican provisos of conditionality and tolerance.

The quotation by the cultural historian Paul Yonnet that opens this chapter identifies what he sees as the dilemma of French republican universalism: everyone is equal, regardless of differences. Difference, whilst assumed in the concept of 'la vie privée', is subsumed in the public concept of equality for all. Yonnet's representation of this dilemma as a feature of the nation's historical mentality suggests that we are dealing with a phenomenon that is not simply a distant legacy of the past, but rather a mindset that determines current policy decisons taken at the *Bercy* and National Assembly, and impacts on the ways in which the French interact as citizens. The impression left by this mentality on debates on sexuality and the couple (particularly in the light of the implementation of the PaCS legislation) has been divisive and symptomatic of a deepening crisis within the republic about how it represents sexual difference. Two of the leading players in the PaCS debate reflect the two poles of this crisis. In the context of the legal recognition of gay marriage, the sociologist Eric Fassin has campaigned in favour on the basis of sexual equality between homosexuals and heterosexuals. Without this equality, Fassin claims that a perception of the superiority of the heterosexual couple is reinforced socially, culturally and legally. In short, the issue underlying the PaCS for Fassin is one of a political struggle for equality between homosexuality and heterosexuality. Fassin's call for the legal recognition of gay marriage on the grounds of equality and via the acknowledgment of a strong communitarian lesbian and gay identity, runs contrary to the ideas of the sociologist Irène Théry. Théry (who advocates a debate on the notion of the specificity of the gay couple, what she calls 'un contrat de vie couple'[2]) claims that there is only one human sexuality which is equal. This one sexuality does not differentiate between homosexuality and heterosexuality, and is sufficiently flexible to accommodate a form of self-reflexivity in which there is the mutual recognition of each sexuality in the other, what Théry calls the recognition of 'l'autre en soi.'[3]

The divisive nature of Yonnet's characterisation of the French mentality (framed as it often is within a democratic – republican opposition) has also left its mark on recent attempts to define the nature of the couple. Since the instigation of civil marriage in France in 1792, marriage has been and remains the state's approved form of couple, created no less 'dans le souci de la laïcisation conforme aux idéaux de la déclaration des droits de l'homme, mais aussi au nom de l'égalité de tous les citoyens devant la loi.'[4] Alongside marriage has been the oft ill-

---

[2]   Irène Théry, 'Le contrat d'union sociale en question, *Esprit*, 236 (1997): 185.

[3]   Théry, 'PaCS, sexualité et différence des sexes', *Esprit*, 257 (1999): 172.

[4]   Théry, 'Le contrat d'union sociale en question', p. 170.

Between Marriage and Concubinage

approved but increasingly common 'situation de fait' known as concubinage or *union libre*. Concubinage has enjoyed a dubious status in French society in the course of the twentieth century. In post-war France, it was referred to as a form of sub-marriage, with pejorative implications for offspring of such a union. In the latter half of the twentieth century, it was rehabilitated particularly in the aftermath of 1968 and acquired a certain allure from its associations with bohemia, artists and celebrities. It also enjoyed a radical appeal because of its anti-state 'non-status.' In the eyes of non-conformists, radicals and certain intellectuals, the simplicity of *union libre* (with its no frills, lack of ceremony and 'liberté d'esprit') made it appear a more authentic, freer form of emotional attachment than the state-sponsored ritual that was marriage. Of course, the major distinction between marriage and concubinage was legal status, and particularly the social benefits that accrued from being married. On the one hand, therefore, there was marriage, endorsed by the republic, and accessible to all citizens. Marriage became the unique way of institutionalising the couple in the common values of citizenship. On the other hand, there was concubinage which was a form of second-class contract, characterised by libertarian models of freedom, individualism and difference.

In the multitude of governmental research carried out in the run-up to the implementation of the PaCS in 1999, it was clear that a process of fundamental restructuring was under way in respect of the couple. In the late 1980s, Professor Jean Hauser was commissioned to write a report on the state of the couple. His report entitled *Le Pacte d'intérêt commun* (PIC) was designed to address the nature of relationships between pairs of persons. The use of the term 'pairs' was deliberate in that it embraced different types of pairs, both heterosexual and homosexual, as well as familial and amical pairs. The central thrust of this pact was that it united a pair on purely fiscal and material levels, without any affective or legal relationship presumed. The reception of this proposal was generally negative, with commentators outlining a myriad of confusions, not least in the area of inheritance and filiation.[5] The report was shelved, on the grounds that it dealt with the notion of the couple in terms of assets and not as people.[6]

What followed from the PIC was an amalgamation of several propositions ('contrat de partenariat civil' (1990), 'contrat d'union civile' (1992), culminating in the 'contrat d'union sociale' in 1997. The CUS, as it was known, aimed to plug the gap between marriage and concubinage, by extending the social and legal rights of marriage to 'concubins.' Furthermore, it planned to lift the ban on homosexual

---

[5]   Théry states: '[Le PIC entraîne] une confusion symbolique et une injustice puisqu'en matière successorale, ce ne sont plus les liens humains qui sont pris en considération mais les liens financiers' in 'Le contrat d'union sociale en question', p. 173.

[6]   For more on the PIC, see the following two articles by Michèle Aulagnon, 'Une reconnaissance du concubinage homosexuel sans PaCS ni PIC', *Le Monde*, 15 mai 1998, p. 9, and Laurent Cheno and François Vauglin, 'Couples ou paires?', *Le Monde*, 9 octobre 1998, p. 14.

'concubins.' By leaving the status of marriage untouched, the proposal sought to address the formalisation of the couple from the perspective of concubinage. This approach was initially well received by lesbians and gays because, firstly, it abolished the longstanding discrimination against homosexual unions, and secondly, it represented a sincere effort to enshrine the legalisation of lesbian and gay unions outside of marriage. In this regard, the CUS had a strong republican imprint in that the concerns of lesbians and gays were broached within the wider concerns of heterosexual concubinage, and not separately. On the negative side, it was perceived that the free-standing status of *union libre* would become redundant, forced as many new 'concubins' would be into signing up to this new legislation in order to avail of the obvious material benefits, and in order not to avoid total banishment into third class citizenship. The second negative was in relation to some lesbian and gay groups who believed that they had been given 'reconnaissance' by the side door, in the form of an amendment to the law on heterosexual concubinage. Despite these misgivings (elaborated in particular by Irène Théry[7] and Eric Fassin,[8] and which we will discuss in detail later), the CUS of 1997 evolved in large measure into the PaCS of 1999. There are considerable differences between the CUS and the PaCS, but on the central issues outlined above (particularly marriage, concerns over the demise of concubinage, and the oblique format by which lesbian and gay unions were to be recognised), there is strong continuity of thinking from the CUS proposal to the eventual PaCS legislation.

Before examining in more detail these coupling configurations, we need to sketch in the socio-political currents in which these debates are taking place. We saw in the chapter on adoption and filiation how the political and ideological underpinnings of republicanism and democracy shaped the nature of a mainly divisive debate. The presumption often made about these two political structures is that that they irreconcilable; they stand for the political right and left, conservative and liberal, and as such there is no common ground between them.[9] On issues of political economy and the role of the state, these categorisations may prove useful in delineating broad ideological differences. Where they become less accurate forecasters is in relation to issues of sexuality and identity because in these areas we are dealing with individual perceptions of place, self and citizenship. We have seen in the debates on adoption, filiation, identity and citizenship that the purely oppositional approach not only polarises issues and individuals but militates against resolution and progress. Bourdieu's subversive strategies, Yonnet's

---

[7] Théry, 'Le contrat d'union sociale en question', pp. 159-87.

[8] Eric Fassin and Michel Fehr, 'Parité et PaCS: anatomie politique d'un rapport', in Eric Fassin and Daniel Borrillo (eds), *Au-delà du PaCS,* particularly pages 30-33.

[9] Régis Debray's question, 'Etes-vous républicain ou démocrate?' (Le Nouvel Observatuer, 30 novembre-décembre 1989, p. 49) served to heighten the debate about republican citizenship, but also framed the debate simplistically as an either/or, for/against issue.

'matrice révolutionnaire', ACT-Up's socialisation and politicisation of the sexual agenda, Lefort's and Gauchet's agency of social awareness and Fine's inter-generational language of negotiation demonstrate that the democratic/republican divide may serve as a useful framework from which to observe perspectives on French citizenship, but that alone it does not reflect the complexity and sophistication of sexual behaviour, nor does a divide bear witness to the degrees of cross over between these respective structures. For instance, the traditional opposition between integration and communitarianism which has dominated the gay agenda from the 1970s has been transformed in recent years by the politicisation of the lesbian and gay movement. This has opened up splits within this movement between integrationists (who see the only fulfilment of a gay identity within the full equality defined through republican universalism) and separatists, who see the creation of a separate identity as the only way of addressing democratic rights to sexual difference and ultimately equality defined through a radicalised universalism. And then there are those who want a bit of both, that is to be simultaneously a universal subject with a separate sexual identity.

In the recent edition of his work *Le Rose et le noir*, Frédéric Martel countenances such a *rapprochement*. In his reflections on the future of communitarianism, he states: 'Un courant universaliste coexiste souvent avec un courant identariste et culturaliste, une demande de différence et de particularisme avec une demande d'indifférence.'[10] For Martel, the transformations in lifestyles in French and European society over the last thirty years have blurred the boundaries between republican universalism and democratic difference. Far from being mutually exclusive, both universalist and 'identitaire' tendencies have come closer to a mutual recognition, to the point that it is possible today to have a foot in both camps, depending on the nature of the debate. But how realistic or desireable is this *rapprochement* envisaged by Martel? Decriminalisation of homosexuality, the containment of the HIV virus and the PaCS legislation represent some of the biggest advances in the lives of French lesbians and gays over recent decades, but as Marie-Jo Bonnet has pointed out, there is still not full equality between gay 'individuals' and heterosexual 'subjects' in the republic, nor does the contract signed in a PaCS carry the same institutional clout as the 'union' designated in marriage.[11] It would seem that, from Bonnet's perspective, to want to integrate within republican universalism must bring something more meaningful and subversive than fading into the normalising and unequal indifference envisaged by Martel. The 'trouble-free' option of integrationism (in which the potential divide between republican and democratic versions of citizenship is softened and normalised) can itself be seen as part of the republican model's subtle agenda of bringing in from the cold the marginal voices of dissent and difference. Bonnet's

---

[10] Frédéric Martel, *Le Rose et le noir* (Paris: Editions du Seuil, 1996), p. 404.

[11] Marie-Jo Bonnet, 'Gay Mimesis and Misogyny: Two Aspects of the Same Refusal of the Other', *Journal of Homosexuality*, 41 (2001): 265-80.

172   *The Gay Republic*

rejection of Martel's vision is therefore very timely and serves as a constant reminder that attempts at reconciliation between dissenting voices of republicanism and communitarianism must be evaluated within the embracing but discriminating clutches of universalism. The utopic/dystopic dichotomy of Martel's vision, however, highlights another key thread of this book. Despite the perception of a blurring of boundaries between republicanism and democracy, there are still deep-seated and divisive forces at work which militate against reconciliation. Parity, for example, may give women equal representation in municipal elections, but women remain symbolically unequal in the 'system of symbolic representation in which only the male has been universalised.'[12] Boundaries may be less pronounced, but they do remain in subtle and sinister forms. This has been particularly evident in the debate on the sexual orientation of individuals and the definition of the couple.

In the light of these preliminary remarks, a simple question arises. How do we define the couple in France today? Is the couple an entity itself, or is it the sexuality of the persons involved that defines the couple, or is it what the couple stands for in the republican tradition that matters? The difficulty in giving a clear answer to these questions has been reflected in the recent glut of legislations to try to define the gay couple. The use of terms such as 'contrat', 'partenariat', 'projet de vie' and 'organiser la vie' reveal not only the clinical nature of the terminology, but also the absence of more obvious terms such as fidelity or commitment. Some critics (Marie-Jo Bonnet, Evelyne Pisier and Irène Théry) have picked up on this as one of the major flaws of the PaCS legislation. Their argument is that an opportunity to define the lesbian and gay couple (in its social, cultural and political separateness) was missed. Furthermore, in the absence of a definition of the lesbian and gay couple *per se*, they claim that legislators deliberately took the easy (political) option of using language of an ultra legal nature. In defence of the legislators and of the PaCS, it could be argued that defining the legality of the lesbian and gay couple had to take precedence over any overtures to acculturate or sentimentalise a gay relationship. In other words, ascribing any affective or overly political terminology to a legislative process could have been interpreted as inappropriate and threatening to the republican mindset. That said, even the rather technical and 'safe' terms of 'projet' and 'contrat' did not spare the PaCS (and lesbians and gays) being seized on by opponents and ridiculed because of the clinical and sterile nature of the legislation. However, what is overlooked in this debate is that the significant issue of marriage stood in the way of the acculturation of the lesbian and gay couple. Marriage is clearly the institutional model of the couple, uniquely and implicitly invested with love, fidelity and commitment. With lesbians and gays still denied marriage, it was clear to see (and the then socialist leader Lionel Jospin was under pressure to differentiate between marriage and the PaCS) that legislators were under political pressure not to formulate the PaCS in a way that could be confused with marital union. In short, the outcome of this

---

[12]   Bonnet, 'Gay Mimesis and Misogyny…', p. 275.

Between Marriage and Concubinage

political 'nobbling' was a sanitised piece of legislation, rushed through to accommodate the pressure for legal status for lesbians and gays.

By contrast, marriage has its vows. The married couple is fêted, ritualised and enters into a mutual bond of love, commitment and fidelity. Marriage institutionalises the couple as a unit with obligations and benefits. Similarly, the heterosexuality of the couple through marriage institutionalises a symbolic order (heterosexual, 'la différence des sexes'), which is in turn linked to a generational order (both republican and civil). The institution of marriage, its sexual referents, and the institutions of the state that it upholds, confirm it as the unique standard by which the couple is defined. However, we have seen across Europe in recent years that this matrimonial and heterosexual institutionalisation of the couple is being challenged by the demands of lesbian and gay couples not only for legal status as a couple (partnerships, contracts with rights and benefits), but also for equal status in respect of gay marriage itself. In an editorial entitled appropriately 'La démocratie des moeurs', *Le Monde* put the case for the democratic right to question not only the institution of marriage but also the definition of the couple:

> Aujourd'hui, le mariage n'est plus la norme, mais un choix, à côté duquel d'autres choix sont possibles pour deux personnes désirant vivre ensembe. L'homosexualité n'est heureusement plus considérée comme une tare inavouable, et la diversité des orientations sexuelles est une dimension évidente et reconnue de l'humanité. Le couple ne peut plus être exclusivement défini par l'union entre deux personnes de sexe opposé. Le droit doit définir les conditions dans lequelles la constitution juridique d'un couple, quel qu'il soit, ouvre droit à un régime spécifique au regard de la fiscalité, des successions et des autres règles attachées jusqu'à maintenant au seul mariage.[13]

Concubinage: Definitions and Drafting Legislation

Technically, the term concubinage is difficult to pin down. It is a specific form of human relationship which is linked to the idea of the couple. But at what point does concubinage become defined in terms of a couple? French law defines concubinage as 'une situation de fait', in other words a social arrangement between a man and a woman but without legal foundation. But it also goes further in defining concubinage in respect of 'une communauté de vie.' According to Françoise Dekeuwer-Défossez, there are two components to this 'communauté de vie'; 'la communauté de toit' (cohabitation) and 'la communauté de lit' (socially acceptable sexual relations).[14] Of course, none of these components are enforceable by law. Instead, they represent a way for society to attempt to formalise

---

[13] Quoted in 'La démocratie des moeurs', *Le Monde*, 16 septembre 1998, p. 15. *Le Monde* may not admit openly to be in favour of lesbian and gay marriage, but in its reporting of the PaCS and other social and sexual issues, it has shown itself to be very progressive on these debates.

[14] Françoise Dekeuwer-Défossez, 'Couple et cohabitation', Colloque de l'Université de Reims, 20-21 juin 1997, (Presses Universitaires de Reims, 1998).

174 *The Gay Republic*

concubinage in the context of a couple. In a report to the Ministre de l'Emploi et de la Solidarité in 1998, (a pre-PaCS report, but the contents of which would have been available to the government before legislation on the PaCS was passed), Irène Théry proposed new ways of defining concubinage. Recognising the difficulties of formalising a relationship which is generically independent of rules and law, Théry put forward several proposals. The first was to introduce a contract 'inscirt dans le droit des personnes', designed to authorise 'concubins' to sign a contract, attesting to their status, and providing limited rights. However, problems of status were rightly identified by Théry, ('concubins' by definition have no legal status), and the concept of a contract in such an open and fluid context was misjudged. In short, as Théry admitted, to impose a contract on a couple whose status is outside of marriage and any juridic control is to destabilise concubinage itself.

Her second proposal, designed to avoid any form of institutionalisation of the couple via a contract, was to approach formalisation of the couple through their combined material assets: 'Si un simple pacte financier privé, accessible à tous, accorde à ses signatures des droits qui traditionnellement sont issus de liens personnels (et non financiers), on ne peut sans doute éviter de créer à la fois une confusion symbolique et une injustice sociale.'[15] The problems here, as she forewarned, were, firstly, to avoid the scenario of a brother or sister (where a financial pact had been established) assuming the social rights of a surviving 'conjoint' in the event of death. The second and more immediate concern was the inequality that could emerge between a couple who would sign the pact and a couple who would refuse, preferring to remain 'free.' Théry went on to make two final recommendations. The first was the recognition of homosexual couples (which we will come to later) within the broader remit of concubinage. The second was to seek a more lasting and binding definition of concubinage as 'une possession d'état': 'Le concubinage, autrement dit, en tant qu'il est communauté de toit et de lit, peut s'appréhender par la possession d'état de couple naturel.'[16] By means of an extreme and partial appropriation of the law, Théry appeared to force a structure on concubinage as a state asset, from which would accrue, admittedly, a wide-range of benefits and privileges.

It cannot be denied that the changes envisaged by Théry address some of the fundamental concerns of 'concubins' over the years. The denial of transfer of a lease on a property to a surviving 'concubin' (a hangover of unofficial *union libre*) is rescinded in her proposals, as is a proposed reform to rights of succession, bringing an end to outlandish and discriminatory tax impositions on surviving partners. Furthermore, as she claims, her recommendations address directly the issue of concubinage, not as an equivalent to marriage or sub-marriage but as an

---

[15] Irène Théry, 'Concubinage', *Couple, filiation et parenté aujourd'hui. Le droit face aux mutations de la famille et de la vie privée* (Paris: Odile Jacob, 1998), p. 147.

[16] Théry, 'Concubinage', p. 150.

Between Marriage and Concubinage

independent couple, retaining its new status as a 'fait juridique.'[17] In this respect, Théry's proposals differ from those of the CUS which recognised concubinage as a new 'cadre jurdique', closer in status to the 'acte juridque' of marriage. Not surprisingly, Théry takes issue specifically with the ways in which the CUS defines concubinage in the shadow of marriage, as if marriage were the benchmark by which concubinage is only definable. In a predictive swipe at future PaCS legislation (which according to many commentators has effectively replaced concubinage), Théry's critique of the CUS reads like a valediction to traditional concubinage: 'Or, à ces centaines de milliers de concubins par choix, le CUS ne propose rien que de cesser de l'être, de renoncer à leur union libre, à leur volonté de vivre et de vieillir ensemble sans autres droits qu'assurés par la certitude d'être aimés, sans autres devoirs que dictés par la morale des sentiments.'[18] The sociologist François de Singly would dispute this exaggerated characterisation of the demise of concubinage, claiming that the latter has become even more popular as a result of the decline of marriage.[19] Regardless of these projections, it is quite evident from both sets of proposals by Théry and the CUS that, in their attempts to redefine concubinage, the shadow of state institutions has loomed heavy. Whether in the shape of Théry's appropriation of 'concubins' as a 'possession d'état' or the CUS's approximation of concubinage to marriage via a change in juridic status, the state has been seen to leave its imprint on a definition of concubinage.

It would be inaccurate to over-exaggerate Théry's republican sympathies in this regard. Her interest in preserving the independence of concubinage has also a semi-communitarian echo. However, as we see in other areas, a deep-seated republicanism is subtly enforced.[20] On the one hand, she laments the decline of concubinage as one of the last vestiges of 'choix de vie' (her choice of words), but, on the other hand, she praises the CUS for its strong republican ethos in being consensual and open to all couples. Lesbian and gay couples are also included within this ethos but in a discrete and invisible form: 'En outre, le CUS est apparu "républicain" au sens du consensuel, modéré et sage, dans un contexte d'évolution très rapide mais très inégale des esprits. Consensuel et modéré parce qu'il évite de se prononcer sur la signification de l'homosexualité, noyée dans l'ensemble flou de la cohabitation ou du plus vague encore "projet de vie."'[21] This comment is not

---

[17] Théry states: 'La démarche proposée veut respecter le concubinage comme situation de fait: les droits proposés reconnaissent simplement que la communauté de vie est un fait social, qui doit être reconnu en tant que tel. Mais l'union libre demeure un engagement personnel et privé' in 'Concubinage', p. 156.

[18] Théry, 'Le contrat d'union sociale en question', pp. 167-68.

[19] Véronique Darde Muñoz and François de Singly state: 'Le dévelopment de l'union libre correspond à un type de relation, reposant moins sur la définition des rôles et sur le support d'une institution et, en contrepartie, plus sur une attention à l'autre en tant que personne' in 'Pour le pluralisme des formes de la vie privée', *Le Monde*, 25 septembre 1998, p. 16.

[20] Théry would dispute such a charge, but her abuse of the notion of 'possession d'état' has strong republican overtones.

[21] Théry, 'Le contrat d'union sociale en question', p. 164.

176 *The Gay Republic*

anti-gay, despite the undertones. Théry is in favour of lesbian and gay concubinage. The crux of the issue, however, is why is homosexual concubinage perceived as something that has to be attached to heterosexual concubinage? Why, as Théry states, is it preferable to introduce legislation that is sufficiently general that the homosexual question does not need to be addressed directly? Why is this 'question' better hidden, 'noyée dans l'ensemble flou de la cohabitation'? Before trying to answer these questions, I think it would be useful as a preamble to reflect further on Théry's stance on concubinage and marriage in the context of the republic. Théry has not disputed the recognition of concubinage for lesbians and gays. However, in framing this process of recognition within consensual republicanism, her approval is contingent on a definition of equality where all citizens are equal before the law even though there are apparent inequalities of treatment of lesbian and gay citizens within that law (openly admitted by Théry as we see in the quotation to come). For example, in the context of lesbian and gay concubinage and the CUS, Théry sees the framework of universal equality as having a double lock on the expression of a gay identity:

> Que le CUS soit un contrat ouvert à tous a été valorisé comme une double conquête de la valeur "République": parce qu'elle préserverait les homosexuels de l'éventualité qu'on leur applique un droit particulier, en soi porteur d'un risque d'inégalité et de discrimination de la part de l'état, et aussi parce qu'elle combattrait chez les homosexuels eux-mêmes la tentation du repli communautarien, incarnée par la revendication d'un droit spécifique.[22]

We saw earlier how Théry criticised the CUS on legal technicalities. She also saw the CUS as leading to the demise of concubinage because of its approximation to marriage. In this instance, however, she is politically in agreement with the CUS because, as a contract open to all citizens, it reinforces the republican ethos. But she then undermines the universal applicability of this legislation by saying that it serves the more sinister purpose of preventing lesbian and gay couples seeking specific rights for themselves. What may seem for Théry a triumph of republican universalism in embracing all couples, is a no win situation for the particularity of the lesbian and gay couple, best summed up in the familiar adage that what is given with one hand, is taken away with the other.

Théry's adherence to republican universalism in the context of gay concubinage is further evident in her own proposals to the government on concubinage and in subsequent comments on the CUS. As the PaCS has borne witness, Théry approved a recognition of the lesbian and gay couple within the framework of heterosexual concubinage. But her recognition needs further clarification. Théry is not saying that the lesbian and gay couple had a right to exist *per se*, independent of concubinage or marriage. Her recognition of gay concubinage is not expressed as a recognition of the legitimacy of a different sexual identity, but rather as an acknowledgement of this variation within

---

[22] Théry, 'Le contrat d'union sociale en question', p. 164.

heterosexual concubinage. Her proposition to the government was phrased thus: 'Le concubinage se constate par la possession d'état de couple naturel, que les concubins soient ou non de sexe différent.'[23] This statement appears to suggest that the sexuality of the couple is irrelevant in the definition of concubinage, although her use of the term 'couple naturel' is vague in the context. By contrast, in her response to the CUS, her position appears ambiguous. In an allusion to her own propositions on concubinage, she sees recognition of the homosexual couple via 'le non-couple homosexuel';[24] in other words, heterosexual concubinage is the only route by which gay concubinage can be accepted. In effect, lesbian and gay concubinage is conditional on heterosexual concubinage.

Based on these observations, one could be justified in claiming that a major strand in Irène Théry's approach to lesbian and gay concubinage is via an integrative, heteronormative republicanism. But this would be to underestimate a radically communitarian streak in her thinking that goes further in articulating the context of the lesbian and gay couple than the PaCS legislation presumed to do. Théry, among others, rejected the PACS legislation because it did not address the 'spécificité du couple gai.' What Théry meant by this comment was that gay couples are unique and as such deserve separate legislation that addresses their specificity. The PaCS, for Théry, lumped gay couples in with all other couples, thus producing a half-baked solution to the particularity of gay couples. From a political and republican perspective, she approved of this consensual approach. However, from the gay perspective, the PaCS, for Théry, appeared to have missed a significant opportunity. Théry's alternative was to introduce a 'contrat de vie de couple', specific to homosexuals, *equal in status to marriage* and 'une façon de s'engager beaucoup plus clairement dans la reconnaissance légale du couple homosexuel, au nom de l'égalité, tout en disant clairement non à l'assimilation, au nom de la différence.'[25] What strikes one immediately is the contradiction in Théry's ideological position in respect of lesbian and gay couples. On the one hand, she advocates gay concubinage via the side door of heterosexual concubinage. On the other hand, she goes out on a limb to promote specific legislation to address the specificity of lesbian and gay couples.

What seems a contradiction may belie a hidden strategy in this complex thinking. What might explain this difference in thinking are the respective terms of concubinage and the couple. Théry has already stated that concubinage, whether heterosexual or homosexual, is essentially a triumph for the republic because it limits the scope for gay communitarian radicalism within the republic. Therefore, whether gay concubinage comes at the expense of heterosexual concubinage is ultimately an irrelevance in that both are recognised, although with different symbolic significations. The couple, on the other hand, is a different concept in that for lesbians and gays, the couple (prior to the PaCS) is not legalised. With marriage

---

[23] Théry, 'Concubinage', p. 151.

[24] Théry, 'Le contrat d'union sociale en question', p. 168.

[25] Théry, 'Le contrat d'union sociale en question', p. 185.

178 *The Gay Republic*

the only route to the legalisation of the couple, and it being denied to lesbian and gay couples, the specificity of a gay couple as an alternative couple to the married couple becomes a valid notion for consideration. Crucially, whilst concubinage has sought to integrate lesbian and gay couples, marriage has not. Théry's analysis of the implications of the two situations is more complex, therefore, than we supposed at first. Her thinking reflects a sensitivity to the dilemma of the lesbian and gay couple in respect of the limits of integrative universal equality, and the need to accommodate alternative communitarian strategies.

And yet, there are limits within her communitarian discourse that beg serious questions. For example, Théry claims that the 'contrat de vie' specific to lesbian and gay couples is equal to marriage. *It is not* marriage, she claims, because of its difference and specificity. But equally, because this 'contrat de vie' is not marriage it is perceived to be secondary to marriage. Marriage, as we have ascertained, is the model *par excellence* of the couple. For many lesbians and gays, it represents the holy grail of full equality because of its institutional and symbolic status. Théry's proposals for the lesbian and gay couple are thoughtful and her intentions seem sincere. However, her overall analysis, as we will see later, resides on some fundamental ground rules about the role of sex and sexuality, and in particular the centrality of 'la différence des sexes' as the essentialist social, filial and familial model. In denying marriage to lesbians and gays, under the ruse of an alternative contractual model for lesbians and gays, Théry is implicitly nailing her colours to the high mast of republican idealism. She is content to propose a benign separate contract for lesbian and gay couples, with all the difference that it may denote. But for her detractors, like Eric Fassin for example, this contract represents a sop to difference, 'une reconnaissance symbolique, mais qui n'affecte rien l'ordre symbolique.'[26] It seems that, despite her communitarian sympathies, Théry's adherence to a republican vision of sexual homogeneity is unshakeable ('il n'y a qu'une sexualité humaine'[27]). This adherence intimates the 'mentalité historique' invoked by Yonnet at the beginning of this chapter. It is an adherence to a fixed, universalist principle of sexual equality that is immune to, what Joan Wallach Scott called, 'sexual difference that is socially, culturally, linguistically produced.'[28]

---

[26] Eric Fassin and Michel Fehr, 'Parité et PaCS: anatomie politique d'un rapport', in *Au-delà du PaCS*, p. 31.

[27] Théry, 'PaCS, sexualité et différence des sexes', p. 174. Théry's theory on sexuality is that the 'masculin' and the 'féminin' are the two principal categories. Each category has the potential to experience the other in itself (what she calls the experience of 'l'autre en soi). This is not a form of androgyny but a sense of being able to put oneself socially, politically and sexually in the situation of the other sex so that an understanding of (b)idenity provides one with a wider awareness of one's responsibility to the other sex. This forms part of Théry's wider concept of 'mixité.' Her comment that there is only one human sexuality is designed to show that sexuality is derived from these two interlocking categories and not from exclusive or gendered constructions of sexuality.

[28] Joan Wallach Scott, 'Feminist Family Politics', *French Politics, Culture and Society*, 17, (1999): 29.

Concubinage, PaCS and the Couple

The conclusions to be drawn from the Théry proposals and the CUS is that both provoked radical thinking about gay concubinage and the lesbian and gay couple, but that any effective legislation would have to address the respective and competing demands and needs of republicanism and democracy, and also face the uncompromising structures within both. But what is the relationship between the PaCS and gay concubinage? Both legislations were passed on the 15 November 1999. The PaCS was defined as a contract concluded between two individuals of legal age, of either sexes or the same sex, in order to organise their life together. Concubinage was defined as a *de facto* union, characterised by a stable and continuous life together, between two persons of different sexes or the same sex who live together as a couple. From an initial reading of the respective definitions, it could be construed that concubinage placed greater emphasis on the quality of the relationship. Marie-Jo Bonnet has pointed to the differences in terminology between 'union' and 'contrat.' She appears to suggest that concubinage focuses on the individual rather than the fiscal: 'In the case of concubinage, the law recognises individuals who are subject to the legislation; in the case of the PaCS, the law recognises them as property owners.'[29] While Bonnet might favour and prioritise the quality aspect of the relationship in concubinage, with its emphasis on the stability and continuity of the union, other commentators point to the contractual and fiscal aspect of the PaCS as giving the partners in the 'pacsé' couple greater negotiating power, and subsequently more legal clout.

The first point to make is that Théry's proposals and the CUS merged almost seamlessly into the PaCS negotiations and subsequent legislation. There are clear technical differences between 'pacsés' partners and 'concubins', in relation to 'fiscalité', 'patrimoine', 'filiation' and 'séjour.'[30] And opinions on the respective merits of each continue. Bonnet appears to privilege concubinage, while Théry has predicted that 'concubins' have come off worse in relation to social benefits, and also in relation to status. For Théry, concubinage, as a consequence of its new-found legal tenure, has lost not only its neutrality but also its cultural 'effet.' In general, the consensus to be taken from the PaCS/concubinage alternative, is that one would be better off financially (as a lesbian/gay or heterosexual couple) to be 'pacsé.' However, some would argue that, by virtue of its better financial incentives, the PaCS not only demeans concubinage but also forces heterosexual and gay 'concubins' to conform to a strict contractual agreement. Irène Théry has said as much in her suggestion that the PaCS, as an intermediary status between concubinage and marriage, represents a humiliation for lesbians, gays and 'concubins.' But outside the relative merits and disadvantages of each status, a wider debate has opened up about the introduction of choice in respect of types of

---

[29] Bonnet, 'Gay Mimesis and Misogyny...', p. 273.

[30] For a detailed account of these differences see Clarisse Fabre's article 'Mariage, PaCS, concubinage: trois régimes différents pour les personnes vivant en couple', *Le Monde*, 17 mars 1999, p. 6.

180   *The Gay Republic*

couple, and how what is perceived as a democratic initiative has been received within the republican tradition. What is of particular concern from the republican perspective is the creation of a hierarchical structure of the couple within the republic. This perception, it is claimed, can only serve to chip away at republican marriage by virtue of the variety of choices on offer. It also can be seen to render the management of the concept of universal equality even more problematic.

The bishops of France, who are opposed to any formulation of the couple outside of marriage, have expressed alarm at this development: 'Il serait prejudiciable de voir une législation entériner une hiérarchie d'unions, au gré des tendances subjectives des personnes, accentuant, de fait, les disparités de droits et de devoirs.'[31] Are we presiding over a situation where new legislations offering choice of lifestyles are questioning the republic's capacity to adapt to social change and to remain faithful to the universal in the growing clamour for the specific? For answers, we need to take a closer look at how the republic has accommodated the PaCS. There is a significant body of opinion that believes that on the surface, and despite the democratic inspiration of the PaCS, the legislation is rooted within a republican ethos. Paul Yonnet, for example, has characterised the PaCS as 'un mariage républicain', highlighting the notion that those who scripted the legislation did nothing more than conform to the principle of individualism within assimilationist republicanism: 'la stratégie [...] s'est lovée dans le cadre de l'assimilationnisme républicain français, de nature individualiste.'[32] Jan-Paul Pouliquen and Denis Quinqueton have also outlined the PaCS's republican credentials: 'Il reconnaît la sphère publique de la vie de chaque citoyen, ses relations avec le reste de la société et l'organise dans l'équité et la justice. Il conçoit la sphère privée inhérente à chacune de nous, nos relations intimes, comme un élément constitutive de la liberté individuelle qui ne saurait servir à nous classer.'[33] In both these representations, the republic is characterised theoretically as a malleable institution, capable of respecting the particularity of the individual in the collective.

From a republican perspective, the homosexual aspect of the PaCS is accommodated but strictly within the confines of 'la vie privée.' Any expression of homosexual union outside of this condition has no legal, social or political validity. Republicans therefore can be seen to tolerate, without loss of face, the legal recognition of lesbian and gay couples as long as the couple is expressed as an issue of privacy, and not as a wider expression of communitarian difference. What

---

[31] Quoted in 'La société n'a pas à reconnaître toutes les associations affectives qui relèvent de l'expérience de chacun', *Le Monde*, 18 septembre 1998, p. 34.

[32] Paul Yonnet, 'PaCS, un mariage républicain', p. 106. Yonnet's position is nevertheless more complex than it appears. He interprets the location of the PaCS within republican assimilation as the beginning of a revolutionary strategy from within. See the end of chapter one.

[33] Jan-Paul Pouliquen and Denis Quinqueton, 'Le PaCS est-il républicain?', *Le Monde*, 12 octobre 1999, p. 19.

I called the malleability of republicanism serves a very clever and dual function in its ability to simultaneously welcome and reject sexual difference. It could be argued forcefully therefore that any subscription to this view of republicanism would come at a severe cost for a wider gay identity. The question one asks, however, is why Yonnet and in particular those who drafted the legislation are keen to argue its republican credentials? The simple answer, as Pisier intimated in her analysis of universal equality, is that republican universalism is the only realistic framework in which the PaCS can ever have a chance of succeeding. The republic, in other words, is the only show in town. However, as Bourdieu reminds us, there is room for manoeuvre within the republic at the levels of passive and subversive integration. Yonnet, for example, predicts that the PaCS is the beginning of a 'matrice révolutionnaire' within the republic. Pouliquen and Quinqueton speak of the PaCS as a bridge between the private and the public. In short, what on a surface level may appear as the 'republicanisation' of the PaCS is not an expression of acquiescence to rigid republicanism. Rather, the 'republicansation' of the PaCS can be interpreted as a ruse by undercover democrats to infiltrate republican networks and exploit from within what they see as sexual inequalities, discrimination and the hypocritical tyranny of private/public seduction.

'La Différence des sexes': 'Mixité', 'Vie privée', 'Vie publique'

The private/public dialectic is the real sticking point in the republican mentality because it effects people at the core level of who they are and how they live their lives. In the context of the couple and individual lives, this dialectic is felt most acutely because of the perception that what can be applicable privately and universally (in a theoretical sense) can be denied a socially sexual and visible reality. While the republican logic for this is based on the repression of any communitarian split within universal equality, one also has to question the validity of a democratic logic that tries to universalise sexual emotions and desires. In the context of the threat to marriage by different types of couple arrangements, the bishops of France at their Annual Conference on 15 September 1998 highlighted the dangers of French law creating new legislation to suit the whims of individual desires: 'la loi peut s'édifier sur des réalités universelles et non sur des désirs, voire des représentations affectives singulières.'[34] The difficulty in trying to legislate people's desires is particularly controversial on the issue of sexual orientation. We have seen examples up to now of how legislative proposals have sought to integrate recognition of lesbian and gay couples within the republic. As it stands at the moment, lesbian and gay couples are presented with three pathways: concubinage or PaCS, integrationism or communitarianism (with the possible consequences of increasing homophobia and marginalisation), or militancy. In the

---

[34] Quoted in 'La société n'a pas à reconnaître toutes les associations affectives qui relèvent de l'expérience de chacun', *Le Monde*, 18 septembre 1998, p. 34.

182 *The Gay Republic*

case of the first, the issue is, by and large, a *fait accompli* because the choice is no longer one of recognition or status but one of financial and social security. In the second and third cases, the stakes are higher because the choice is one of individual perception, sexual identity and political conviction with respect to rights, privileges, status, and equality. These personal choices are vital because they have long-term implications in determining the visibility and deeper contours of the lesbian and gay cartography.

The militant option is the preferred *modus operandi* of pressure groups like ACT-Up. As we have seen, its tactics were highly effective in bringing key issues to the attention of the lesbian and gay movement and the wider public. But some of its strategies were counter-productive, as we will see in the practice of 'outing.' The one area, however, where the militant faction has been effective in a democratic way is in highlighting for public attention the main parameters of the crucial debate on 'la différence des sexes', which has raged in academic circles over the last decade, and which remains the key debate for contextualising the direction of sexual difference in comtemporary France.[35] The debate itself asks the question how is sexuality defined? There are two conflicting responses. The essentialist response places emphasis on biological alterity, rooted in the sexual difference between masculine and feminine. The constructionist response replaces the binary of sexual difference with sexuality as a social and cultural construction defined by homosexuality and heterosexuality. In a largely conservative and republican France, the latter response has been met with much derision, on the ground and within academia. The lobby in favour of 'la différence des sexes' is powerful. It has in its ranks, the Catholic church, thousands of mayors across the hexagon,[36] rural France, large swathes of the legislature, and some eminent psychoanalysts and sociologists. Their views crystallise around notions of attachment to republican marriage, the terrorism represented by modernity, and the defence of 'la différence des sexes' as essential to the family, reproduction, stability and the social and psychological well-being of citizens.

In sociology, Sylviane Agacinski and Irène Théry, in developing extensive theses on 'la différence des sexes', bear witness to the significance of this issue in

---

[35] ACT-Up's increased politicisation from 1998 onwards coincided with a higher media profile and the publication of a series of manifestos in *Le Monde*. Two of these manifestos which debate the issue of 'la différence des sexes' are 'Du droit à la politique' (9 October 1998) and 'Pour l'égalité sexuelle' (26 June 1999). See my chapter on 'Lesbian and Gay Identity and the Politics of Subversion' for an analysis of these manifestos. My treatment of 'la différence des sexes' here is confined to two of the main feminist players Sylviane Agacinski and Irène Théry. For a wider and historical contextualisation of the issue, see my chapter on 'La Différence des sexes: Difference or Distinction.' On a separate point, one should not underestimate either the role of the printed media in educating the public about a debate that was conducted mainly in the academic journals of *Esprit* and *Les Temps modernes*.

[36] Quoted in '18 845 maires affirment dans une pétition leur attachement au "mariage républicain"', *Le Monde*, 24 septembre 1998, p. 37.

Between Marriage and Concubinage 183

determining not only an individual's sexual identity but where they fit in the republican/democratic spectrum. In the case of Agacinski, 'la différence des sexes' (or 'l'opposition du masculin et du féminin') is the central and unique duality of existence, underpinned by the law of fertility. Homosexuality, she claims, is confined to the law of pleasure. She goes on to state that to define oneself in terms of the 'masculin/féminin' opposition is to concretise one's sexual identity. This opposition, she states, 'concerne l'identité sexuelle du sujet, alors que l'homosexualité reste une question de "choix d'objet", de structuration du désir.'[37] While her psychological thesis on homosexual desire makes interesting reading,[38] the key to her interpretation of sexual orientation within the republican mentality centres on three key ideas. Firstly, she classifies homosexuals as 'objets de désir' as opposed to heterosexuals who are classed as 'sujets de désir':

L'une des conséquences de ce glissement [glissement de sens qui a fait passer d'une classification des objets de désir à une classification des sujets] a été de construire une nouvelle classification sexuelle des individus, qui ne concerne ni leur sexe ni leur genre, mais leurs goûts, et qui enferme chacun dans une détermination fixe et définitive.[39]

Secondly, she acknowledges that homosexuality today is considered more in terms of a form of sexuality and not a transgression (although it is possible to trace a note of concern in her argument that the homosexual/heterosexual opposition could, if unchecked, become a substitute for the 'masculin/féminin' opposition). Thirdly, she sees homosexuals within the republic as facing a choice of strategies which will determine their sense of belonging. This choice is between a strategy of what she describes as tolerance of all sexual practices *within the private sphere* (the integrationist model), or a strategy which would recognise new models of life, and recognise the existence of new communities (the communitarian model). To no surprise, Agacinski favours the former. As a threat to the integrationist model, the legalisation of the homosexual couple, she claims, 'constitue en effet une nouvelle façon de vivre et d'assumer l'homosexualité; de l'autre, il représente une expression officielle de l'homosexualité, calquée sur le modèle de l'hétérosexualité et sur la figure du couple mixte [...]. Cette figure permet de revendiquer pour les couples homosexuels les mêmes droits que les couples hétérosexuels.'[40]

Agacinski's tolerance of homosexuals and the choices they have to make is clearly conditional on them integrating into the private/public dialectic. Her

---

[37] Sylviane Agacinski, 'Identité et homosexualité', *Politique des sexes* (Paris: Editions du Seuil, 1998), p. 131.
[38] With the aid of examples from literature (Gide, Colette, Genet), Agacinski defines male homosexual desire as a schism between soul and body, and a 'culte fétichiste de l'organe mâle séparé de sa fonction génitrice.' She goes on to describe the death of sublime homosexual desire (the Platonic tradition of the love of young boys and external ideas), and the emergence in modernity of pleasure and sexual identity.
[39] Agacinski, 'Identité et homosexualité', p. 132.
[40] Agacinski, 'Identité et homosexualité', pp. 134-35.

184   *The Gay Republic*

tolerance is also conditional on the centrality of 'la différence des sexes' and on the opposition to equality between homosexuals and heterosexuals on the basis of sexuality. In short, Agacinski's tolerance of lesbians and gays is not unconditional in terms of an appreciation of sexual diversity. It is tolerance conditional on a political structure that appears to deny the full and unconditional expression of sexual diversity. Agacinski's argument is another example of the duplicity of the private/public republican stricture which is content to theorise tolerance and equality as universal abstractions but reluctant to realise these abstractions as social and sexual realities. In the case of Irène Théry, the trajectory of her argument is the same in respect of choices for the homosexual couple, although there are significant differences between her and Agacinski that appear to point to a more compromising and compassionate republicanism. The first part of Théry's thesis is to make a distinction between 'le sexué' and 'le sexuel.' The former is the 'masculin/féminin' distinction, the latter refers to behaviour and orientation. The 'sexué' for Théry is the symbolic order of the couple and society. However, as Agacinski saw in the homosexual couple ('objet de désir') a potential threat to the heterosexual order ('sujet de désir'), Théry explores the space that exists for confusion between the 'sexué' and the 'sexuel', where the politicisation of sexuality through the PaCS for instance has moved the centre of gravity away from the 'sexué' (or 'la différence des sexes') to the 'sexuel.' Speaking of the PaCS, she writes:

> Le paradoxe fondamental de ce débat, c'est à quel point il *dévaluait les enjeux symboliques de la différence des sexes* [...]. Il *déplaçait la question de la différence des sexes sur la sexualité*, alors même que nous affirmons qu'il est essentiel aux libertés démocratiques qu'elle reste hors champ du droit, dont le seul rôle en la matière est de veiller aux interdits fondateurs de civilisation.[41]

Here, Théry alerts liberal democracies to the danger of the 'sexuel' subverting the 'sexué'; bluntly, for Théry, the 'sexué' is non-negotiable.

With the concept of the 'sexué' set in stone, Théry turns her attention to 'le sexuel' which she divides into the standard integrationist/'identitaire' elements. Whereas Agacinski left us at this juncture with a simple choice between strategies, Théry opens up a new route towards recognition of the homosexual couple. Via an allusion to Greek Antiquity, she pursues tentatively a psychoanalytic approach to sexuality, suggesting that the issue with homosexuality is not sexual orientation in itself, but the capacity in all human beings to appreciate what she calls 'l'autre en soi.' This self-reflexive sexuality where one can recognise 'le masculin en elle, le féminin en lui',[42] is used cleverly by Théry to show, on the one hand, that she is open to a debate on the issue of uncertainty in sexuality, but, on the other hand, she also uses this uncertainty to deflect attention away from the rigidity of her position on 'la différence des sexes.' This tendency to elaborate the 'sexuel' extends to the

---

[41]   Théry, 'PaCS, sexualité et différence des sexes', p. 159.
[42]   Théry, 'PaCS, sexualité et différence des sexes', p. 173.

Between Marriage and Concubinage

185

final strand of her argument, which is the essence of her position. For Théry, what is central (as it is for Agacinski) is 'la différence de sexes' and the establishment of equality between men and women on the basis of 'la différence des sexes.' However, for Théry, 'la différence des sexes' is not simply a biological issue. Coupled with it is social responsibility, what Théry calls 'mixité'; in other words, 'mixité' is the social component of sexuality. It is the capacity of both sexes to empathise with each other.

'Mixité' is Théry's way of moving beyond the mimesis of biological difference and elevating a responsibility of action within each sex to care and respect the identity of the other. In short, 'mixité' is 'le pari d'une nouvelle civilité.'[43] It is the recognition that biological difference is not the only defining characteristic in identity construction, and that other cultural and historical elements contribute to the narrative of identity. 'Mixité' enables Théry to rethink the importance of the social in the 'sexuel', and this is particularly evident in some of her thoughts on adoption and homosexuality.[44] In the context of the latter, 'mixité' represents a way of lifting homosexuality out of the secondary realm of the 'sexuel' and into the primary space of a new reflexive sexuality: 'Cesser de renovoyer l'homosexualité au "sexuel", comme le faisait le modèle organique, suppose alors d'approfondir encore cette démarche démocratique de mixité, qui pose le vis-à-vis de l'un et de l'autre, non pour enfermer chacun dans sa spécificité, mais à l'inverse pour dépasser l'assignation à l'étrangeté mutuelle.'[45] Is it therefore possible to see in Théry's concept of 'mixité' an indication of a tolerance, if not conversion, to a type of communitarian democracy? Not exactly, because 'mixité' is not only a social value but a reciprocal value with obligations and responsibilities that require all citizens to embrace 'l'étrangeté mutuelle.' As such, heterosexuals and homosexuals have a mutual responsibility to tolerate each other's contexts, both privately and publicly. 'Give and take' and reciprocity are the touchstones of this process of 'mixité.' But as we have seen with filiation, 'parenté' and adoption, unconditional mutual recognition is not an easy process to manage within a formulaic republic.

Théry's concept of 'mixité' is clearly full of good intentions and verges towards an open door policy between private and public. But it remains an idealistic notion, mainly because of the difficulties of legislating for responsibility, empathy and civility. More worryingly in the case of Théry, I suspect that there is a

---

[43] Théry, 'L'autre en soi: l'intolérance à la mixité', *La Revue des deux mondes*, novembre-décembre (1999): 148.

[44] In her defence of the concept of 'pluriparentalité' for adopted children, Théry claims that 'mixité' provides a framework to include a wider social milieu for an adopted child in order to replace the loss of biological parents and encourage a construction of identity that prioritises social relations over biological mimesis: 'En affirmant le droit de l'enfant à *ne pas être privé de sa propre histoire*, la démarche de la mixité suppose de repenser l'adoption comme une institution non mimétique du biologique, et d'imaginer aussi les formes d'une pluriparentalité' in 'L'autre en soi: l'intolérance à la mixité', pp. 151-52.

[45] Théry, 'PaCS, sexualité et différence des sexes', p. 177.

186   *The Gay Republic*

catch in her idealism that puts pay to any democratic expectations in the concept of 'mixité.' It is important to remind ourselves that, while Théry has constructed a tolerant space beyond 'la différence des sexes' in 'mixité', she has not abandoned altogether the idea of 'la différence des sexes.' In fact, she has inscribed 'la différence des sexes' in a symbolism that has even more social and political significance than it had as a biological construct. Whether 'mixité' is a realisable eventuality or not, the conditions that Théry lays down for lesbian and gay couples are that, in order to embrace the ideals of 'mixité', they must subscribe to the basic logic of 'la différence des sexes', and furthermore accept its symbolism. For many lesbians and gays with strong convictions, this is one step too far. But what is significant in Théry's strategy is the way in which it mirrors not only Agacinski's duplicitous tolerance but also the way in which it abuses the private/public dialectic; 'mixité' is the carrot for lesbian and gay couples, the symbolism of 'la différence des sexes' is the stick.

Théry's 'compassionate' republicanism has merit in its desire to expand the parameters of the 'sexuel' on the issue of homosexuality. However, the levels of this compassion are controlled by the extent to which the concept of 'la différence des sexes' is threatened. This is particularly apparent in the distinction she goes on to draw between homosexuality (as an orientation) and homosexual couples. Théry is opposed to discrimination against homosexuals in respect of their sexual preference. But like Agacinski, she perceives sexual preference as a way of assuming a sexual identity on a par with heterosexuality; sexual preference is seen to be part of what she calls the 'passion de désymbolisation' that threatens the symbolic order of 'la différence des sexes.'[46] In respect of lesbian and gay *individuals*, Théry is less forceful in highlighting this 'threat' as her articulation of 'mixité' shows. In respect of the lesbian and gay *couple*, the situation is different. She states: 'En effet, le couple, qu'il soit homosexuel ou hétérosexuel, n'est jamais réductible à une relation sexuelle. Il s'agit aussi d'un lien sexué, au sens où il s'inscrit dans cet ordre symbolique de la différence des sexes qu'on nomme la différence des genres.'[47] For Théry, a couple is defined not in terms of a sexual relation but in terms of the *symbolic link* between the male and female sex. Homosexuals are recognised (both individually and as couples) within the 'sexuel', but they are different from heterosexuals because of their unsymbolised status (in the republic) which in turn alienates them from access to family law.[48] Once again, the *relational* connotation of 'le sexuel' is devalorised, while the *link* that unites 'la

---

[46]   Théry, 'Le contrat d'union sociale en question', p. 176.

[47]   Théry, 'Le contrat d'union sociale en question', p. 178.

[48]   Anne F. Garréta claims that 'in Europe, the sequence of rights' recognition thus starts from individual rights, may be extended to couples' rights, but stops at the line of family rights. Homosexuals, as individuals, might be allowed to enter into state-sanctioned unions; however, gaining recognition for the families they found turns out to be the limit' in 'Re-enchanting the Republic: "PaCS", *Parité* and *Le Symbolique*', p. 157.

difference des sexes' is not only inscribed in the symbolic order but utopian in aspiration. Théry states:

> N'est-il pas essentiel de reconnaître, à l'inverse, que la différence des genres est l'horizon de sens qui inscrit les rapports sexuels dans l'univers de la différenciation, du même et de l'autre? En réalité, la différenciation symbolique régit et passionne tout le monde, aussi bien les hétérosexuels (qui désirent l'autre sexe/genre) que les homosexuels (qui désirent le même) ou bien les bisexuels (qui alternent, mais ne sont certainement pas indifférents à l'identité de genre de l'objet de leur désir). Le nier au nom d'une mythique émancipation de l'individu, c'est au bout du compte renoncer à inscrire dans la culture humaine la pulsion sexuelle, au risque d'y perdre les sources même de l'érotisme.[49]

It is fair to suggest that Théry's defence of 'la différence des sexes' has its corollary in a defence of universal equality in the republic, particularly given the way in which 'la différence des genres', represented above as the universal 'horizon de sens', is the source from which all equally diverse 'rapports sexuels' derive. The problem with this analogy, as demonstrated in the course of this chapter, is that the derivation of equality from its source is not expressed as equally as it might or should be. But this is how the principle of universal equality works in the republic. It is a principle constructed on a dialectic, on symbolic signification and on a mechanism of simultaneity that invites equality for lesbians and gays on one level and then withdraws it on another level. Looking in from the outside, the task facing republicanism today is the credibility of this principle. The PaCS and parity legislations have come and gone without effective and meaningful examination of this principle. However, republicanism is under the growing critical eye of democratic and neo-liberal forces in contemporary France. And the progressive consensus is that concepts like universal equality need urgent modification.

This is not to suggest, however, that conservative republicans are for turning. If anything, the convergence of these two political traditions has given rise to a flurry of partisan literature, most of it extolling the virtues of the republic.[50] It is not within the remit of this chapter to debate the merits of this literature, suffice to say, from an objective viewpoint, that better cohabitation between republicans and democrats might serve well the competing demands of all citizens. Democracy should not be seen as a danger to the republic but rather as a reality check with the concrete demands of equality. Democracy can act as a safeguard for republicanism. It can restrain republican presumption, be a foil for some of the excesses of

---

[49] Théry, 'Le contrat d'union sociale en question', p. 179.

[50] See for example Régis Debray, *Que vive la république!* (Paris: Odile Jacob, 1989); Christian Jelen, *La France éclatée, ou les reculades de la république* (Paris: NIL Editions, 1996); Blandine Kriegel, *Philosophie de la république* (Paris: Plon, 1998); Pierre Rosanvallon, *Le Peuple introuvable* (Paris: Gallimard, 1998); Pierre-André Taguieff, *La République menacée* (Paris: Textuel, 1996).

188 *The Gay Republic*

universalism, and balance out some of the inequalities and inconsistencies outlined in this chapter. Put another way, democracy can be a complement to the ideals of republicanism. It can argue the case for the legitimacy of the 'le sexuel' in conjunction with 'le sexe.' It can make space for the diverse human culture of 'la pulsion sexuelle' alongside the procreative purity of 'la différence de sexes.' It can press home the idea that the legalisation of couples established as a result of the PaCS and concubinage legislations does not represent a threat to marriage, the family or the future of the human species. But rather, variety represents freedom to choose with impunity the way one wants to live one's life.[51] Democracy can bring to light the hidden and often offensive discriminations within the 'heterosexism' of 'la différence des sexes.' Democracy can expose the intransigent tendency in universalism's governance of the 'sexué', as well as the tactical bluffs used by clever sociologists to placate the 'identariste' tendency.

The framing of the debates on 'la différence des sexes', 'le sexe' and 'le sexuel' in biological and sociological terms clearly help us understand the nature of the sexual debate in France. We need to be aware, however, that this expertise can be used to promote certain essentialist or constructionist positions, which can then be exploited politically and legally. Ultimately, neither the expertise nor the political lobbying should deflect us from the equality of each human being in society. In the wider context of this debate, equality of citizenship (regardless of race, ethnicity, sex or sexuality) must not only be the barometer by which a society is judged, but it must also be seen to be independent of any dialectic or symbolic structure that inhibits its full expression. In the cases of Agacinski and Théry, it could be argued that the biological and sociological models have been prioritised over an engagement with the sexual debate on the political level of equal rights. By contrast, where communitarians, lesbian and gay activists and certain academics have stolen a march on science is in pitching camp at the political doorstep of equal citizenship. Eric Fassin, one of the figureheads of this tendency, praises the PaCS as a law 'qui n'ouvre que des droits limités',[52] but he also highlights the measure of equality that strengthens these rights. He speaks of the PaCS in terms of 'une logique d'égalité entre les orientations sexuelles', and as a law 'qui fait bouger l'ordre symbolique [...], qui touche à la norme conjugale [...], à la norme hétérosexuelle.'[53] For Fassin, it is state and republic influenced norms, and the promotion of 'la différence des sexes' over other sexually diverse expressions, which are at the root of inequalities among citizens. This is particularly the case with marriage.

---

[51] Véronique Darde Muñoz and François de Singly see a virtue in the pluralism of lifestyles that the PaCS has initiated. For a balanced analysis and reasoned interpretation of the respective merits and weaknesses see their joint article 'Pour le pluralisme des droits de la vie privée', *Le Monde*, 25 septembre 1998, p. 16.

[52] Eric Fassin, 'Les pacsés de l'an I', *Le Monde*, 14 octobre 2000, p. 20.

[53] Fassin, 'Les pacsés de l'an I', p. 20.

Between Marriage and Concubinage

Marriage: 'Unicité' and 'Égalité'

Why would gay couples want to get married in the first place? Does a desire to want to get married reveal a desire to be straight?[54] Or does it represent a desire to be brought in from the margins of society, to be institutionalised, to imitate the heterosexual norm?[55] Or less cynically, does marriage represent a form of fulfilment to which all human beings aspire?[56] Alternatively, would the PaCS not represent a sensible compromise, a new institutionalised milieu between the obligations of marriage and the open-endedness of concubinage? Eric Fassin extols the virtues of the PaCS, claiming that it puts freedom back into sexuality, that it liberates the couple from the constraints of fidelity and duty, and points the way to the sexual relationship of the future without the state or anyone else dictating its terms.[57] Given such a recommendation for the PaCS, why does Eric Fassin continue with the idea that 'la bataille du mariage n'est pas gagnée'?

In order to respond to this question, one has to unpack some of the historical baggage linked to civil marriage in France. Founded in 1792, civil marriage conferred on citizens two privileges. The first was the recognition by the state of the singular and highest union between a man and a woman. The second was the creation of this union 'au nom de l'égalité de tous les citoyens devant la loi.'[58] From the outset, the establishment of marriage created two precedents: uniqueness (what has been called 'unicité') and equality. Enshrined in French law, these two concepts were perceived to represent a triumph for the republic in its quest to tame the vagaries of individual choice and free will, and forge links in law between the universal and the private. As Irène Théry states: 'L'unicité du mariage civil est une conquête de la République: celle d'un lien voulu et maintenu entre le débat démocratique, les valeurs de la citoyenneté et la vie privée.'[59] Procréation, children and family are also given legal status and protection under this 'lien.' Republican marriage is seen to define the couple and what the couple stands for. In this regard, marriage is perceived to have the interests of the majority of citizens and future generations ('l'intérêt général') at heart. In the context of all of the above, marriage has justifiably acquired a symbolic status over time.

---

[54] A view expounded by Hadley Arkes, 'The Closet Straight' in Andrew Sullivan (ed.) *Same-Sex Marriage: Pro and Con* (New York: Vintage Books, 1997).

[55] Joseph Landeau is in favour of gay marriage on the basis that it institutionalises gay unions and counters segregation of gay couples. See his article 'Marriage as Integration' in Andrew Sullivan (ed.) *Same-Sex Marriage: Pro and Con.*

[56] Andrew Sullivan is a strong advocate of gay marriage on the grounds of the emotional stability it provides the couple, and because it scotches notions that gays are by nature promiscuous. He has written widely on these issues. See, in particular, his two books *Virtually Normal: An Argument about Homosexuality* (London: Picador, 1995), and *Love Undetectable: Reflections on Friendship, Sex and Survival* (New York: A.A.Knopf, 1998).

[57] Fassin, 'Les pacsés de l'an I', pp. 2-4.

[58] Théry, 'Le contrat d'union sociale en question', p. 170.

[59] Théry, 'Le contrat d'union sociale en question', p. 171.

190 *The Gay Republic*

But in western societies today, marriage is no longer what it was. As we have seen, the choice between marriage, concubinage and PaCS has given more freedom to couples and individuals with different lifestyles. Choice has meant that marriage has lost its cachet (not its uniqueness) as the 'acte fondateur du couple.'[60] The crisis for marriage today is that the conjugal link has been undermined by feminism, equality of rights between men and women, greater recognition of private sexualities, and new types of domestic arrangements. Coupled with the decline in religious belief and faith, people are more cynical of monogamy and fidelity. In his 1895 introduction to the groundbreaking work *On the Sociology of the Family*, Georg Simmel dismissed conjugal fidelity as having 'nothing at all to do with marriage [...].'[61] 'Individual qualities and elements of marriage', he claims, 'arose from separate and often very superficial causes and, in turn, it was they which brought about love as an individual relationship of the heart.'[62] As for monogamy, he claims that 'strict monogamy in marriage has probably only emerged out of the victory of the democratic principle' and has become 'an inner moral law for everyone as social levelling grows.'[63] Having shaken these two central pillars of traditional marriage, Simmel proceeds to question the purpose of marriage by arguing that it has only acquired significance over generations through a desire to care for offspring and that 'over time, marriage has created a direct superiority of the group with respect to a group without marriage, in which the younger generation is abandoned either to the isolated powers of the mother or to a communistic care that is devoid of personal interest.'[64] Simmel's vision of marriage is that of a phenomenon that owes its socio-cultural purchase to increased social levelling, and is sustained by the idea that the more people get married, the more people do not want to be left outside of marriage. This sociological representation casts a shadow over codified, sacramental and time-honoured republican marriage.

Indeed, recent interpretations of the PaCS and concubinage reflect Simmel's organic vision of contemporary relationships where there are greater elements of choice, freedom and fluidity.[65] What we are witnessing here are two interconnected trends. Firstly, Simmel's observations at the end of the nineteenth century can be interpreted as prophetic of current transformations in the conjugal link, and therefore worthy of serious reflection on the nature and expression of love and fidelity. In this respect, they serve as a challenge to the symbolism of marriage

---

[60] Pascale Krémer, 'Le mariage a cessé d'être l'acte fondateur du couple', *Le Monde*, 9 décembre 1999, p. 10. See also Irène Théry's work *Le Démariage. Justice et vie privée* (Paris: Odile Jacob, 1993).

[61] Georg Simmel, 'Introduction to "On the Sociology of the Family"', trans. by David Frisby in *Theory, Culture & Society*, 15 (1998): 277-81.

[62] Simmel, 'Introduction to "On the Sociology of the Family"', p. 280.

[63] Simmel, 'Introduction to "On the Sociology of the Family"', p. 280.

[64] Simmel, 'Introduction to "On the Sociology of the Family"', p. 281.

[65] Fassin and Singly have written widely about the ways in which the PaCS opens up new possibilities for those who cannot marry and those who do not want to marry.

today. Secondly, despite current legislations that have led, for some observers, to the 'désymbolisation' of marriage, marriage remains the measure against which other couples are defined (at least by the state and its socio-fiscal benefits). Why is it that, throughout the debate on the implementation of the PaCS, Lionel Jospin was keen to reassure the republic that the PaCS was not equal to marriage?[66] Why is it that Irène Théry has labelled the CUS a 'mariage-bis', and the PaCS a 'sous-mariage'? Why is that Eric Fassin and François de Singly have been careful to point out that the PaCS is not a threat to marriage?[67] Why does Eric Fassin repeat his desire for gay marriage?[68] The answer to these questions is that marriage matters, not because of fidelity, monogamy, children or future generations (although important), but because of its uniqueness within the republican mentality.

The uniqueness of marriage (its 'caractéristique fondamentale'[69]) is a notion that has guaranteed non-exclusion of citizens. However, in the politicised climate of sexual rights today, this interpretation of uniqueness has given way to uniqueness as a form of privilege and separation. The uniqueness of marriage today is subject to certain conditions, namely a heterosexual couple and the link therein to family life.[70] These conditions are reinforced, by and large, in the national courts and European Court. For lesbian and gay activists, militants and gay marriage campaigners, what makes these conditions unacceptable is the state's 'méreconnaissance' of the link between 'unicité' and 'égalité.' The French state's position on this is twofold. Firstly, marriage is tied intrinsically to 'la différence de sexes' which is in turn linked to reproduction and filiation. To permit gay marriage would be to undermine this universal message. Secondly, by introducing the PaCS in recognition of lesbian and gay couples, the state believes that it has gone as far as it can to address and respect lesbian and gay couples. Its greater priority is to serve the 'intérêt général', which is the protection and continuity of the species.[71] It is in the interest, therefore, of the state not to confuse the two issues.

From the perspectives of 'l'intérêt général' and the future of the species, it is difficult to disagree with the state's position. But we can still ask some awkward

---

[66] See 'Le PaCS n'est pas un mariage' and 'Le gouvernement veut distinguer rigoureusement le PaCS du mariage', *Le Monde*, 2 septembre 1998, pages 1 and 8 respectively.

[67] Fassin, 'Les pacsés de l'an I', *Le Monde*, 14 octobre 2000, p. 20, and Véronique Darde Muñoz, and François de Singly, 'Pour le pluralisme des formes de la vie privée', p. 16.

[68] Fassin, 'Une égalité qui reste à conquérir: ouvrir le mariage aux homosexuels', *Le Monde diplomatique*, 6 juin 1998, p. 22.

[69] Irène Théry, 'PaCS, sexualité et différence des sexes', p. 152.

[70] Gay marriage (blessing) does exist in certain American states, and has been legislated in some European countries. In France, the PaCS is the nearest lesbians and gays get to legalised marriage.

[71] For an insight into a republican defence of social values, read Jean-Pierre Chevènement's interview in a recent issue of the gay magazine *Têtu*, no. 65, mars 2002, pp. 57-59.

192 *The Gay Republic*

questions. For example, in what way is homosexuality a threat to heterosexuality? In what way can the legalisation of a lesbian or gay 'marriage' be seen to threaten the 'intérêt général', except to presume that there are more homosexuals in society than anticipated, or that legalisation would see a rapid conversion from heterosexuality to homosexuality? Irène Théry reminded us earlier that 'il n'y a qu'une sexualité humaine.' She may have meant this in the context of an argument on 'mixité', underpinned by the premise of 'la différence des sexes.' But this statement also has a meaning that calls into question the very division of the sexes, and, as she claims, points to the interaction of the sexes not in a strictly (bi)sexual way but as a subconscious acknowledgement of the presence of one sex in the other. Freudian psychoanalysis has also hinted at the latency of homosexuality in heterosexuality. As part of the one human sexuality (as characterised by Théry), homosexuality is not a threat to heterosexuality *per se*. Rather, homosexuality is perceived as a threat to what heterosexuality symbolises as an institutional, social, political, religious and sexual order. If 'la différence des sexes' (and its link to 'droit à la vie familiale') is the basis on which lesbian and gay marriage is denied, then a crucial dimension to this denial (outside of the reproduction issue) is the social and symbolic creation of a fundamental inequality between homosexuality and heterosexuality. This perception of inequality as a function of symbolic and social construction has been the focus of the writings of Eric Fassin and some notable American scholars.[72] For Fassin in particular, denial of gay marriage (whether in the interests of the child, the family or biology) represents the denial of equality with heterosexuals, which in turn is expressed in the form of a denial of access to full citizenship defined by the family, the social and the symbolic:

> l'interdiction du mariage signifiée aux homosexuels n'est pas seulement le résidu insignifiant d'une discrimination en voie d'effacement, elle est au principe même de cette discrimination, dès lors qu'elle renvoie l'homosexualité hors de la famille, autrement dit aux marges de la société. Les effets de notre ordre symbolique sont terriblement réels.[73]

By politicising the debate on gay marriage as an issue of equality, Fassin deflects attention away from the sociological and anthropological cul-de-sac of 'la différence des sexes', towards an engagement with marriage on its own terms, namely on the principles of 'unicité' and 'égalité' on which it was founded. Then his strategy is to show how the state and society create inequalities in their classification and segregation of individuals vis-à-vis marriage. But what is most significant about Fassin's argument is the way in which he advocates *the right* to

---

[72] The right to same-sex marriage in the USA can be expressed in terms of the denial of constitutional and equal protection under the law, which amounts to sex discrimination. For more on this and related issues see Morris B. Kaplan's study *Sexual Justice. Democratic Citizenship and the Politics of Desire* (New York, Routledge, 1997), and in particular chapter seven, 'Intimacy and Equality: The Question of Lesbian and Gay Marriage.'

[73] Fassin, 'Une égalité qui reste à conquérir', p. 22.

Between Marriage and Concubinage

lesbian and gay marriage. It is not described as an automatic, unconditional right that lesbians and gays be allowed to marry. Rather, lesbian and gay marriage is contextualised in relation to the rights of other citizens, not independent of or separate from them. As such, his advocacy of lesbian and gay marriage is conditional on the rights of access of heterosexuals to marriage. This clause of conditionality places the equality of gay marriage on a par with straight marriage. It conveys the notion that lesbians and gays are not seeking different, preferential or exceptional treatment, just the same treatment as everybody else:

> Il n'est pas, il n'est plus nécessaire (ni pour l'Etat ni pour la société) de séparer des classes d'individus (hétérosexuels d'un côté, homosexuels de l'autre), auxquelles s'attacheraient des droits différents et une légitimité inégale. D'ailleurs, les revendications actuelles portent non pas sur quelque droit inconditionnel des homosexuels au mariage ou à l'enfant, mais sur un droit égal (et donc également conditionnel) pour chacun, indépendamment de son orientation sexuelle, de se marier, d'adopter ou de recourir à la procréation médicalement assistée.[74]

Conclusions

I think it is fair to say that, from a socio-political perspective, equality is what matters to most lesbians and gays today; equality of sexes, equality of sexualities, equality as individuals and equality as couples. And the crucial issue underlining these demands is strategy. Within the context of a universal republic, passive or apolitical communitarianism cannot deliver these demands. It withers on the vine of equal inequality. The alternative is to seek change from within the republic. Frédéric Martel half anticipated this idea in his notion of a 'droit à l'indifférence.'[75] This was a space beyond difference, beyond the need for recognition of difference, a neutralised difference blending into sameness; in short, a space where universalism and the specificity of identity could co-exist. But Martel's integrationism is more passive than active. It reflects a tendency towards the normalisation and routinisation of homosexuality within a heteronormative order. It seems the political drive for equality of citizenship is not represented with enough conviction in Martel's concept of 'indifférence.' By contrast, Pierre Bourdieu, Eric Fassin, Paul Yonnet and notable others share the common view that subversion from within, as opposed to indifference from within, is the way forward for the lesbian and gay movement. Yonnet's representation of the PaCS as a marriage with republicanism and a revolutionary embryo growing within the republic, is complemented by Fassin's conditional equality that locks lesbians and gays into equality of citizenship with other universal and symbolic heterosexual subjects. Bourdieu, similarly, proffers duplicitous integration with the ulterior motive of institutional re-appropriation.

---

[74] Fassin, 'Les pacsés de l'an I', *Le Monde*, 14 octobre 2000, p. 20.
[75] Frédéric Martel, *Le Rose et le noir* (Paris: Editions du Seuil, 1996), p. 405.

The subversion of the instruments of power (as detailed by Bourdieu and implied by Eribon, Fassin, Pratt and Yonnet) does not imply an end to universalism. It implies a reconfiguring of it in order that universalism is seen to serve all citizens rather than citizens serving it. As things stand, the PaCS and concubinage have made significant inroads into republican territory. The PaCS has legalised the lesbian and gay couple with accruing fiscal and social benefits. Concubinage has undergone a republican makeover in the shape of a new 'cadre juridique.' But marriage still remains the gold standard by which all couples are measured. It is in the absence of full equality of citizenship (and the perceptions of discrimination) that democratic/subversive levers need to be engaged to address some specific areas. Firstly, lesbian and gay individuals and couples, in the context of the above legislations, are still closeted within the restrictive space of 'la vie privée.' Legally recognised they may be, but this recognition comes with a spatial compromise. Secondly, lesbians and gays are denied marriage on the grounds of family law, reproduction of the species and the symbolic primacy of the male/female union (in short the dual 'decrees' of 'la différence des sexes' and 'l'intérêt général'). Social, religious and political institutions are seen to combine with sociological and biological expertise to universalise these decrees. All serve to reinforce a stereotype of marriage as intrinsically heterosexual. The republican principle of universal equality rubber-stamps these institutional, sexual and symbolic logics, and in the process creates marginalisation and disenfranchisement among lesbians and gays. However, the recent politicisation of equality by lesbian and gay groups has rescued this debate from the untouchable heights of abstract universalism. With the advent of the PaCS and lesbian and gay concubinage, coupled with gay adoption and the prospect of gay marriage, it is becoming increasingly evident that equality is no longer the preserve of 'l'intérêt général.'

Chapter 7

Homophobia: Mimesis, Legislation and 'Outing'

One of the constant features of this book has been the relationship between, on the one hand, subversion from within the republic (advocated by many commentators thus far), and, on the other hand, the eternal capacity of the republic to accommodate degrees of subversion but then always find a way to revert to type. It is a relationship predicated on the eternal supremacy of the republic to simultaneously respond to change and revert to the timeless principle of perfectibility. It would seem that democratic change is impotent in the face of untouchable universalism. How can personal chronology compete with Real chronology, how can history compete with History? In short, how can democratic 'immanence' (Gauchet's terminology) challenge republican transcendence? The answers to these questions lie inside the republic and inside subversion. In other words, for the democratisation of sexual citizenship to gain any currency, the premise of subverting the republican model from within must still be viable. What must follow is that the methods and strategies of subversion need to engage effectively with the institutions of power that create, categorise and manage the parameters of discourse in the republic. In effect, this subversive strategy is akin to Bourdieu's legacy to the lesbian and gay movement, although we have seen variations on this thematic throughout this book.

This chapter will proceed, therefore, on two fronts. Firstly, I will explore the phenomenon of mimesis in which lesbians and gays are portrayed (through the adoption of the PaCS) as pursuing a strategy of sameness to a heterosexual order. In the case of male homosexuals, they do this in order to be seen as (hetero) male universal and symbolic subjects (as this is perceived to be the only way to be fully and equally valued within the universal model), or out of fear of homophobia which has rooted them in a form of symbolic domination. I contend that mimesis can be questioned by arguing that the PaCS and parity legislations are introducing new symbolisms, where specificity (much maligned in republican discourse) can be seen as an effective contribution to universalism, and not as a threat to it. Similarly, I proceed to share the assumption of Marie-Jo Bonnet that mimesis and its attenuating symbolism do not spare lesbian and gays from homophobia, not because, as she claims, the latter are not universal and symbolic citizens, but precisely because the PaCS legislation confronts the conditioning and categorising of homophobia through the language of difference, equality of rights and the

196   *The Gay Republic*

legitimacy of political visibility (closely linked to the notion of 'coming out'). The situation has also been improved as of 2004 with legislation in France making homophobic hatred and violence a crime.

Secondly, the theme of subversion, first posited as a theoretical debate in Part One, is revisited in reality in the second half of this chapter. At the end of chapter six, we concluded with Eric Fassin's justification for lesbian and gay marriage. His justification was not advocated as an automatic, unconditional or separate right, but rather as a right in relation to the rights of other citizens. Fassin's advocacy of gay marriage was perceived as conditional, in as much as heterosexuals have the right to marry. He couched this argument within the notion of equality of law and thus the conditionality of the law for all citizens regardless of sexual orientation. Fassin's appropriation of the law as the barometer of equality (which he applies to advocate gay marriage) is mirrored in this chapter by different and inventive attempts (by lesbians, gays and sympathisers) to breed insurrection within the republican guard, in particular by re-appropriating words and concepts, such as tolerance, outing and the closet, in order to challenge pre-conceived definitions and perceptions. Evelyne Pisier will expose the hypocrisy of the republic's reaction to the PaCS as an issue of tolerance and try to restore faith in the idea of tolerance through a radicalisation of universalism. The closet, long-standing symbol of repression and control, will be revalorised as a space *inside* heteronormativity, capable of collaboration, subterfuge and resistance. Finally, the concept of 'outing' will be explored as a tactic of equivalence between the widespread license to insult lesbians and gays and the insult and violence inflicted on them right up to the recent passing of legislation on homophobia.

In a recent and special issue of the *Journal of Homosexuality* on 'Homosexuality in French Literature and Culture', Marie-Jo Bonnet seeks to redress some of, what she sees, as the misconceptions and misrepresentations of women in the debate surrounding the PaCS. In a feminist critique, she argues that the lesbian and gay movement in France (and like other feminists, she questions the validity of the use of the term 'lesbian' in this title), in approving the PaCS legislation, has sacrificed lesbians to a model of republican and conservative integration based on mimesis. The term 'mimesis', as defined by Bonnet, 'is the ability of certain animal species, in order to assure their own protection, to give themselves an appearance similar to their environment, to another creature in this environment, or to a member of a species that is better protected or more feared.'[1] By applying this term to the lesbian and gay movement, Bonnet implies that the latter has followed what Mary Bernstein has identified elsewhere as a strategy of sameness.[2] In other words, Bonnet argues that the lesbian and gay movement has acquiesced to a patriarchal, universal and republican order by assuming that there

---

[1]   Marie-Jo Bonnet, 'Gay Mimesis and Misogyny: Two Aspects of the Same Refusal of the Other?', *Journal of Homosexuality*, 41 (2001): 265-80.

[2]   Mary Bernstein, 'Celebration and Suppression: the Strategic Uses of Identity by the Lesbian and Gay Movement', pp. 531-65.

Homophobia: Mimesis, Legislation and 'Outing' 197

is value to be gained in bridging gaps between itself and a heterosexual order. Indeed, Bonnet speculates whether 'gay mimesis is not a new way to restructure and reinforce the masculine sexual order so brutally challenged by the women's movement revolt of the 1970s.'[3]

In order to follow better Bonnet's argument, it is important to understand the reasons why she believes that women and in particular lesbians have felt betrayed by the lesbian and gay movement. Bonnet charts the history of the homosexual group FHAR (*Front Homosexuel pour Action Révolutionnaire*) in the 1970s and the role that women played in inspiring this group, a solidarity appreciated on both the gay and women's sides. However, according to Bonnet, all was not as it seemed. There were growing differences between the two movements, of both a personal and ideological nature. Feelings of misogyny and vengeance were surfacing from within the gay camp. Bonnet writes: 'Misogyny reappeared with such force that women, who were in the process of challenging the very foundations of male domination, found it intolerable [...]. The pleasure derived from this situation came more from a desire for vengeance on other men than from a veritable love for women.'[4] Despite the personal differences, there was a degree of solidarity between the two now distinct movements (FHAR and MLF (Mouvement de la Libération des Femmes)). However, for Bonnet, there was the perception that this solidarity was built more on what the FHAR could get out of the MLF (in terms of support) than on what the MLF really stood for. It seemed more like an alliance of convenience than one of equals. Bonnet describes the alliance as seeming 'so self-evident [...]. FHAR adopted feminist slogans, such as "our body belongs to us" [...]. FHAR organized itself along the same anarchist lines as the MLF [...]. FHAR participated in all of the MLF's demonstrations, and its members were the only men whom the founders of a women's only movement were willing to accept as allies.'[5] So close were the movements that the FHAR even went as far as to distance itself from the seductive appeal of 'fascist virility.'[6] In reality, for Bonnet, the solidarity between gays and feminists seemed more like gesture politics than a substantial shift in ideological commitment. And indeed, it was in the domain of ideology where the real and inevitably divisive splits surfaced. Bonnet goes on to suggest that, despite the semblance of harmony and cooperation, there were substantial differences of ideology culminating in disputes over the role of men in a patriarchal society. While women questioned the centrality of men (a male/female issue) in this ideological order, homosexuals placed more emphasis on the repression of male sexuality. Quoting one of FHAR's members from 1971, Bonnet writes:

---

[3]   Bonnet, 'Gay Mimesis and Misogyny...', p. 266.
[4]   Bonnet, 'Gay Mimesis and Misogyny...', pp. 268-70.
[5]   Bonnet, 'Gay Mimesis and Misogyny...', p. 269.
[6]   Bonnet, 'Gay Mimesis and Misogyny...', p. 267.

198   *The Gay Republic*

> We homosexual men cannot accept the "deconstruction of roles" unless we have the right to every role, not when certain roles (being the object of desire, for example) are forbidden to us [...]. The fact remains that as far as the ideology of FHAR is concerned, I have reached the conclusion that it is indeed rather different from that of the MLF, even if we are natural allies. Sexuality is central to the revolt of homosexuals [...]; it is principally in this respect that we have been repressed.[7]

The accusations of misogyny followed and the FHAR broke with the MLF. For these and other historical reasons, Bonnet believes women and in particular lesbians have been 'instrumentalised' by the mainly gay movement today, and she characterises this instrumentalisation in the form of a mimesis in which women (whether feminist or lesbian) are subsumed in a male (gay) universalism. Today, the animosity between feminists and gay groups shows little sign of abating, despite the inclusion of the word 'lesbian' in the name lesbian and gay movement. As though to prove Bonnet's point of mimesis, in the recent parity debate, the lesbian and gay movement was perceived to have 'sold out' its historical feminist ally. By adopting the positive discrimination approach to equality of representation in municipal elections, feminists were perceived to 'categorise' women and give women a special 'communitarian' status whilst denying it to other 'categories', such as lesbians and gays. On this level, the lesbian and gay movement felt betrayed by *paritaires*. On another level, it could appear that the cohesion of the lesbian and gay movement seemed to carry more influence than any solidarity between lesbians and *paritaires*. Despite the fact that women, lesbians and gays have achieved separate legislation to address their specific contexts (PaCS and parity legislations), debate and conflict between both camps continue. The reasons for this continuing conflict relate, I would suggest, to the differences in principle and strategy of both movements, and most crucially to the perceived integrity of principle and strategy adopted by both. Both seek equality of representation but both have been seen to have deployed strategies of duplicity. The parity strategy, for example, seeks equality for women at the expense of other 'minorities.' The lesbian and gay movement, in the guise of ACT-Up Paris, has endorsed the tactic (not the principle) of positive discrimination deployed by *paritaires* as a means of self-promotion and equality, despite this tactic's 'association' with discrimination of other groups. That said, it should be stressed that, in the case of the lesbian and gay movement, the tactic of positive discrimination has been used also to garner support from the wider social movement in its desire to put the particular to the service of the universal.

What this historical coverage reveals is that the ideological debate that characterised the split between the FHAR and the MLF back in the 1970s bears some resemblance with current PaCS and parity debates. On a strategic level, ACT-Up's approximation to parity in the promotion of lesbian and gay rights, but differenciation from it on the level of principle, mirrors the trajectory of sameness followed by difference that identified the relationship between FHAR and the

---

[7]   Bonnet, 'Gay Mimesis and Misogyny...', p. 269.

Homophobia: Mimesis, Legislation and 'Outing' 199

MLF. Solidarity in exclusion brought the lesbian and gay movement and feminism together during the PaCS and parity debates, but more substantial differences surfaced over time. Ideology and strategy separated the two camps. Ideologically, women challenged a masculinised and symbolically male universalism that misrepresented women in the political classes, while lesbians and primarily male gays demanded recognition of their separate sexualities. Strategically, this translated into a feminist strategy that focused on 'égalité des sexes', while for lesbians and gays the strategy was to target 'égalité des sexualités.' For Bonnet, the strategy adopted by the lesbian and gay movement has been to avoid the debate on equality of the sexes (thus eschew the controversy of 'la différence des sexes'[8]) and to shift the debate from sex to sexuality, in short from male/female to homosexual/heterosexual. In doing so, homosexuality is not only validated in this opposition as a starting point for debate, but it is male homosexuality and not lesbianism that is symbolically universalised. For Bonnet, women (both straight and lesbian) lose out.

Bonnet goes on to qualify mimesis in terms of 'egalitarian mimesis' where, lesbian and gay couples, now universally accommodated under the PaCS, compete for equality with heterosexual couples. From a feminist perspective, this ideological shift from 'sexe' to 'sexualité' is worrying on several fronts. It shifts the parameters of critique from patriarchy to heterosexuality. It forces feminism to debate on the alien ground of egalitarian mimesis (heterosexuality). Feminist critique is thus made to reroute its critique of patriarchy via heterosexuality, which indirectly forces feminists to look at their role in the construction of heterosexuality and related debates on its subjugation of homosexuality. On both ideological and strategic grounds, feminist critique is undermined. There are further fears of disempowerment in feminist circles under this new dynamic of 'sexualité', where gay couples and specifically male gay couples compete for control with other heterosexual males in the universal republic. Equally, the lesbian couple, although nominally part of this gay mimetic hegemony, is relegated to play second fiddle in the symbolic and universal stakes to men (gay or straight) in the French republic. And there is the real fear that parity, as the new arm of contemporary feminism, is being outflanked in importance by the PaCS because of the former's limited focus on *individual* women's rights and the latter's 'universal' appeal to the rights of the new institutionalised *couple* (both gay and straight). Bonnet states:

> egalitarian mimesis of gay men has enabled them to obtain a new law giving them equality with heterosexuals without having to engage in any debate on equality between the sexes. They thus followed an institutional logic very different from a symbolic logic

---

[8] We saw in a previous chapter how part of ACT-Up's transformation to a political strategy involved negating difference between groups in order to form alliances and, specifically, promote its agenda of equality of sexualities.

200 *The Gay Republic*

necessary for the recognition of homosexuals, because the latter implies a recognition of the other as Other, and not merely as an equal.[9]

This is where Bonnet's critique of egalitarian mimesis begins. She claims that while recognition of homosexuality has been achieved through the PaCS, the fallacy of this recognition is to believe that it has been achieved in terms of equality with heterosexuals. The absence of symbolic recognition, as opposed to recognition via equality, condemns the PACS to an 'illusory legal recognition.' For Bonnet, the importance of symbolic recognition is central to women as it is to lesbians and gays. She claims that PaCS and parity legislations

> will be in vain as long as women and/or homosexuals are not recognized as universal subjects to the same extent as others. It is the articulation between the one and the other that is missing in these laws on equality, just as it is missing in the gay movement, which is not even conscious of its denying the existence of lesbians when its speaks of feminist demands.[10]

Essentially, Bonnet's argument is based on the hypothesis that the strategy of promoting 'égalité des sexualités' will backfire on the lesbian and gay movement because the only way, according to her, that an individual can be universalised symbolically is as a heterosexual male. Firstly, claiming that universalism is a male sexual order, Bonnet states that women remain ostracised (although parity has questioned this but only within the confines of political representation in elections), and lesbians and gays are merely recognised and tolerated. Secondly, and most importantly, the institutionalisation of the gay couple via the PaCS legislation, previously feared by feminists and perceived politically to be an effective strategy against feminist individualism, is seriously undermined because, in the absence of symbolic recognition, institutional equality between heterosexuals and homosexuals is not guaranteed in the PaCS. In her conclusion, Bonnet highlights how the lesbian and gay movement misjudged the implications of the PaCS legislation. But she is particularly scathing of the way egalitarian mimesis, through a strategy of 'égalité des sexualités', has not only negated women but also the entire notion of the Other, and left as a residue a misogyny at the heart of the gay movement.

I have used Bonnet's fascinating article to address several points. The issue of symbolic recognition within universalism, for both women and gays, is critical. And their permanent exclusion inside universalism is an issue for serious concern. I also agree that symbolic recognition for gays and women does not come about as a direct result of legislation. This is a regrettable reality of the French context. However, Bonnet's argument on mimesis appears to demonise the lesbian and gay movement, in the context of its history, and particularly in respect of misogyny. While Bonnet uses the example of the PaCS to support the view that 'gay

---

[9] Bonnet, 'Gay Mimesis and Misogyny...', p. 275.
[10] Bonnet, 'Gay Mimesis and Misogyny...', p. 275.

egalitarianism obliterates the women's dynamic of autonomy and emancipation', denies 'the existence of lesbians' and 'brings about a return to normative male views', I would point out that the post-PaCS debate, as evidenced in one of ACT-Up's manifestos, sought to engage all people 'pour l'égalité sexuelle – à la fois *entre les sexes*, et entre les sexualités.' My italicisation is deliberate for two reasons. Firstly, it indicates how the strategy post-PaCS was designed to bring together feminists and lesbians and gays, and not just in terms of strategy (as suggested prior to the PaCS legislation) but in terms of principles as well. So much so that the term 'la différence *entre* les sexes' as opposed to 'des sexes' (a qualification introduced by *paritaires*) is incorporated into ACT-Up's second manifesto.[11] Also, this manifesto goes further, and states: 'Au nom de la différence des sexes, même à gauche, on nous demande trop souvent aujourd'hui de choisir entre les droits de l'homme et les droits des gays et des lesbiennes. Pour notre part, au lieu de les opposer, nous voulons marier les revendications du féminisme et du mouvement homosexuel.'[12] The explicit nature of this intention to reconcile homosexual and feminist positions flies in the face of the sentiments of anti-lesbianism and misogyny that Bonnet identifies with the gay movement.

Nevertheless, Bonnet's construction of mimesis to describe the lesbian and gay movement's response to the PaCS has some positive points, corroborated by the consensus that in order for lesbians and gays to avail of any rights they need to be willing to integrate. Other reactions have been less favourable. In seeking integration into a heteronormative universalism via the institutionalisation of the couple and not the individual, some critics (Bourdieu, Théry, Pisier to name but a few) have accused the movement of conformism, of settling for second class citizenship, or, as Bourdieu claimed, betraying its subversive potential. Similarly, the argument in favour of integrationism is not fully proved by Bonnet either, since institutional recognition fails to prove the acid test of symbolic recognition. It is not one of the aims of this chapter to evaluate how far the lesbian and gay movement has 'sacrificed' itself as a mimesis of republican universalism. What I want to highlight at this point is the connection that Bonnet makes between mimesis as a self-protection mechanism and homophobia. Bonnet makes reference to homophobia twice in her article. In the first instance, she states: 'And it is not only because the gay movement seeks "sexual indifference" (i.e. the right to be treated "indifferently", just like everyone else), as people used to say in the 1980s; it is because mimesis is a way for it to protect itself against homophobia while avoiding its own dissolution into the wider society.'[13] In this instance, Bonnet sees the function of mimesis as a strategy of avoidance; in order to protect themselves

---

[11] Evelyne Pisier articulates this distinction: 'La parité annoncerait une nouvelle ère, un changement de civilisation, la reconnaissance d'une différence égale. Pas n'importe quelle différence: la différence entre les sexes. On change de paradigme. On remet l'universel sur ses deux pieds' in 'Sexes et sexualités', *Les Temps modernes*, 609 (2000): 161.

[12] ACT-Up in *Le Monde*, 'Pour l'égalité sexuelle', 26 juin 1999, p. 17.

[13] Bonnet, 'Gay Mimesis and Misogyny...', p. 265.

202   *The Gay Republic*

against homophobia, lesbians and gays must deny their sexuality, and act like heterosexuals so that they won't stand out and be victimised. As a strategy of avoidance it may be effective. But rather than protection against homophobia, it allows the latter to go unchallenged. Within the conditions of Bonnet's mimetic egalitarianism, wanting 'to be treated like everyone else' would also mean that male homosexuals, having negated women, would only have to deal with other male heterosexuals in respect of homophobia. This representation of mimesis would hardly function as an effective protection against homophobia, since it is generally acknowledged that male heterosexuals, whose sexuality can often be threatened by homosexuality, are the common source of homophobic violence.

On the contrary, mimesis, as defined by Bonnet, would encourage homophobia for two reasons. Firstly, the idea that gay males would be able to be treated like straight males because of the male heterosexual sexual order underpinning French universalism is contentious; sameness of sex is not sameness of sexuality and the space for conflict is considerable. In this respect, mimesis could only accelerate (not avoid) the 'dissolution' of gays into wider society. Secondly, it would seem that the only effective protection against homophobia in the concept of gay mimesis is women, the 'other half' of the heterosexual constituency. I would contend that in her argument to show how women have become victims of the lesbian and gay movement, Bonnet has underestimated the role of women in the function of gay mimesis. Women and lesbians counteract homophobia within gay mimesis.[14] They are often perceived as the *natural* allies of gay males (was naturalness of affiliation not one of the founding features of the FHAR and the MLF?), and as Bonnet has stated, both share a symbolic rejection from the category of universal subjects. It is in this context of universal subjects that Bonnet makes her second reference to homophobia: 'The PaCS is a victory for male mimesis because it achieves an illusory legal recognition, on the basis of property and not of a relationship between two individual subjects, who remain as exposed as ever to homophobia and social violence.'[15] Bonnet appears to make a key distinction between universalism and institutionalisation, with respect to homophobia. She implies that as a universal subject (heterosexual man or woman), the individual is elevated to a superior status of citizen, immune to insult and homophobic violence. On the other hand, regardless of legislation that institutionalises the lesbian and gay couple for example, such legislation is not enough to protect these individuals from insult and violence because it is founded on the 'unsafe'/illegitimate ground of sexuality and not universal sex.

---

[14] In studies carried out in the USA, it has been shown that males are more prejudiced than females. This difference was greater towards gay males than lesbians, and prejudice increased over time. See Janet G. Baker and Harold D. Fishbein, 'The Development of Prejudice Towards Gays and Lesbians by Adolecsents', *Journal of Homosexuality*, 36 (1998): 89-100.

[15] Bonnet, 'Gay Mimesis and Misogyny...', p. 275.

The implications of Bonnet's analysis are not only worrying but have an effect on how French society evaluates and deals with homophobia. If we pursue Bonnet's thesis further, homophobia is given free license against sexual identities defined outside the pale of 'sexe.' For lesbians and gays, only full equality (not legal recognition) will confer the necessary status of universal subjects. Most alarmingly, given the fact that 'we live in a system of symbolic representation in which the male has been universalised',[16] violence and sexism against women is seemingly permitted to circulate unpunished. If we review together the situations of lesbians and heterosexual women, we come up against a paradox. With the prospect (remote in reality) of full equality for gay males only possible because of their maleness and not their sexuality, there is a theoretical chance that they will be spared homophobia and violence on the basis of their maleness. However, *all* women (for whom full equality is denied in the symbolically male universal) are condemned to second-class citizenship and therefore become 'legitimate' targets of 'social violence' because neither their sexuality nor their femaleness protect them. This paradox contributes to Bonnet's depression about the value of the parity legislation ('it will all be in vain'), and her critique of the philosophy of gay egalitarianism and its myopic focus on equality and masculinity. Despite the widespread perception of equality between men and women, it can be argued that, symbolically, this equality is invalid on the basis of the privileged heterosexual male precedent within universalism. Returning to the issue of homophobia, if the symbolic status of the subject is that which expels homophobia and violence, then legislation that does not give equality to gay males, for instance, is in part seen to encourage, if not, condone homophobia. And women, in the absence of a revision of universalism, are eternalised not as 'universal subjects' (in Bonnet's usage) but as eternal subjects of violence. We can deduce from these projections that homophobia in the context of France is not only a complex issue but one which threatens the lives of gay men and women.

In the remainder of this chapter, I propose to look at the notion of homophobia in France in a more socio-political context, and specifically from four main angles. Firstly, by locating my discussion from the end of 1999 to the present, I want to show how the PaCS legislation has awakened a latent homophobia within French society, and most noticeably within the political classes. Secondly, the increase and threat of homophobia has made it one of the main priorities of the lesbian and gay movement, so much so that the theme of the Lesbian and Gay Pride march of 1999 was the fight against homophobia under the slogan 'L'homophobie, fléau social.' In the light of this threat, new legislation has been introduced under the recent 'projet de loi de modernisation sociale', not to tackle homophobia as such but to address one its manifestations, namely discrimination against sexual orientation in the work place and in some areas of society, notably housing. Thirdly, I want to explore the contours of the homophobic debate in its more subtle and intellectual forms, as a force of opposition to social and sexual change. And finally, given the

---

[16] Bonnet, 'Gay Mimesis and Misogyny...', p. 275.

204 *The Gay Republic*

recent legislation against incitement to homophobic hatred, I aim to examine the pros and cons of the strategy of 'outing' as a means by the more militant factions within the lesbian and gay movement to confront homophobic aggression. Firstly, however, some working definitions are in order.

Some Defining Markers

The literature on the causes and manifestations of homophobia is extensive.[17] The term itself is misleading, given that a phobia is characterised generally in terms of fear and avoidance, not confrontation and violence with the object of fear. Given the looseness of the term for all anti-homosexual feelings, some psychologists prefer the term homoprejudice, which locates anti-homosexual responses within the realm of prejudice.[18] My working definition of the term homophobia is any form of discrimination, prejudice or hostility (including physical abuse and social stigma) towards lesbian and gay people or homosexuality. However, definitions do not paint the full picture of how the homophobic mindset functions as a psychological and sociological phenomenon. By way of an introduction to a better understanding of this mindset (the complexities of which, we will see later, are played out in socio-political debates), I propose a brief analysis of an article by Peter Redman which appeared recently in the journal *Sexualities*.[19] The particular value of Redman's analysis is that he couches the debate on homophobia between psychological and sociological origins. Within the psychological origins, he opposes two strands. The first is the Freudian strand which locates the origin of homophobia 'in the presence of homosexual desires within the phobic person.'[20] The displacement of anxiety on to an external object can be explained, according to Redman, in Freud's origins of sexual desire, in which the displacement of the father as a desire for the mother is the classic Oedipal complex. However, as Freud himself pointed out, and Redman reconfirms, displacement of the father entails some identification with the father. Redman suggests, echoing Freud, 'that we have all made a homosexual (and, by implication, heterosexual) object-choice at the level of the unconscious.'[21] A second strand within the psychological origins picks up on the pre-Oedipal processes that articulate desire. Here Redman, echoing Kaja Silverman, opens up a more fluid structure of identification:

---

[17] Of this literature I would point the reader to the following sources: *The Journal of Homosexuality*; Gregory M. Herek and Kevin T. Berrill (eds.) *Hate Crimes – Confronting Violence Against Lesbians and Gay Men* (London: Sage, 1992); K. Plummer (ed.) *Modern Homosexualities: Fragments of Lesbian and Gay Experience* (London: Routledge).

[18] For more on the history and (mis)uses of the term 'homophobia' see Colleen R. Logan, 'Homophobia? No, Homoprejudice', *Journal of Homosexuality*, 31 (1996): 31-53.

[19] Peter Redman, '"Tarred with the same Brush": "Homophobia" and the Role of the Unconscious in School-based Cultures of Masculinity', *Sexualities*, 3 (2000): 483-499.

[20] Redman, '"Tarred with the same Brush"...', p. 486.

[21] Redman, '"Tarred with the same Brush"...', p. 486.

The pre-Oedipal infant desires the father and identifies with the mother, identifies with the father and desires the mother, and indeed, desires and identifies with the self [...]. The multiple, contradictory and simultaneous nature of these identifications mean that the child is not restricted to the conventional binary structure – wanting to be the father and desire for the mother/wanting to be the mother and desire the father – but can also straddle and combine the binaries. For example, it may identify with the father while simultaneously desiring him.[22]

The first conclusion Redman's draws from the psychological origins of homophobia is that male/male desire is continually present and repudiated. As such 'homophobia can be understood as a defensive strategy, never fully achieved, deployed against the subject's own pre-Oedipal identifications.'[23] The second origin for homophobia is sociological. Based on interviews with boys in schools, Redman interprets behavioural patterns in other boys as part of a wider construction of gender roles, in which the assumption of heterosexuality (or any hegemonic version of gender) is validated and homosexuality constructed in opposition to heterosexuality. This sociological 'dialogic' challenges the psychological construction of homophobia as 'reducible to repressed homosexual desire.' In assessing these two origins to homophobia, Redman sees weaknesses in the psychological model on the grounds of what we alluded to at the beginning of this discussion, namely the incompatibility between phobia and violence. Redman states: 'homophobia understandably directs our attention towards the unconscious but, in implying phobic avoidance rooted in a repressed homosexual object-choice, it risks overlooking much else that is of relevance.'[24] Furthermore, repressed homosexual desire is by its nature a *repressive desire*, which negates both expression and rage. Given these reservations, Redman appears to favour an explanation to homophobia that has its roots in a sociological construction of heterosexuality. Building on theories by Simon Watney and Leo Bersani, Redman offers a sociological explanation to homophobia where the key issue is gay sex. Gay sex is seen to threaten men's phallocentrism by dissolving the boundaries of heterosexual male self-construction. Phallocentrism is not the sole denial of power to women; in its denial, it also signifies the 'denial of the value of powerlessness [...] a radical disintegration and humiliation of the self.'[25] For heterosexual men, gay sex can thus imply their disempowerment, the dispossession of the phallus and

---

[22] Redman, '"Tarred with the same Brush"...', p. 486.
[23] Redman, '"Tarred with the same Brush"...', p. 487.
[24] Redman, '"Tarred with the same Brush"...', p. 493.
[25] Leo Bersani, 'Is the Rectum a Grave?', in Douglas Crimp (ed.) *AIDS: Cultural Analysis, Cultural Activism* (London MIT, 1988), p. 217. Bersani continues this debate on homophobia in his work *Homos*. He claims that homophobia is grounded in a political anxiety about the subversive and potentially revolutionary social arrangements with which lesbians and gays are experimenting. In this context, he alludes to that now celebrated reference to Foucault in which the latter recounted the incident of two young gay males who were seen going to bed together. The subversive quality of this incident was not the act of sleeping together but the fact that they woke up happy.

206 *The Gay Republic*

the celebration of this dispossession. Redman goes on to suggest that in refusing to recognise the heterosexual value of phallic possession, gay sex assumes *a real threat*, the response to which 'is a murderous, narcissistic rage.'[26]

It would be inaccurate, as Redman makes clear in his conclusion, to side exclusively with either a psychological or sociological analysis of homophobia. Both complement each other and cover a variety of manifestations of homophobia. As theoretical models, they help us configure the processes at work in the homophobic mindset. But as theories, they also require the gel of application to be effectively representative. In this respect, Redman makes a valid case for the consideration of cultural dynamics that underpin both models and which determine the expression of homophobia in particular contexts. The cultural exceptionalism of France, for instance, is a case in point. As we have seen in the discussion by Bonnet, any analysis of homophobia needs to be contextualised within the sociological/psychological constructions of heterosexual masculinity, but this analysis in turn needs to be inflected with the unique discourse of universal and symbolic representation in the French republic.

Homophobia: The Silent/Verbal Dialectic

Two events in recent contemporary French life have awakened homophobia from the slumbers of the French subconscious. Throughout 1998 and 1999, there were many passionate contributions to the debate on the PaCS legislation in the National Assembly. For many lesbians and gays, however, the passion and rigour of the debate will be forever eclipsed by the overwhelming stink of homophobia. Indeed, what has captured public and political attention since the passing of the PaCS legislation has been the indelible mark left by homophobic insult. Led primarily by conservative and right-wing republicans, their outbursts have since led to a damage limitation exercise by the right, a crisis of identity and a concerted strategy to excise this episode from its political dossier. Brought together in the title *Les Anti-PaCS, ou la dernière croisade homophobe*, published ironically by Editions Prochoix in 1999, we can sample the following comments: 'Jacques Myard (RPR, Yvelines): "Il y a aussi les zoophiles!"; Pierre Lellouche (RPR, Paris): "Il n'y a que les stériliser"; Philippe de Villiers (RPR, Vendée): "En guise d'innovation, le PaCS annonce le retour à la barbarie"; François Vannson (RPR, Vosges): "Et les animaux de compagnie?"; Michel Meylan (DL, Haute-Savoie): "Les homos, je leur pisse à la raie."' The 1999 annual report by SOS-Homophobie described these comments as 'des réactions ouvertement homophobes d'une violence qu'on aurait crue d'un autre âge [...], une homophobie plus larvée mais tout aussi dangereuse, s'abritant derrière la défense de la famille et de l'enfant. Il aura révélé la survivance des préjugés homophobes dans le monde politique.'[27] The second major

---

[26] Redman, '"Tarred with the same Brush"...', p. 492.

[27] Quoted in 'La Gay Pride 1999 fêtera le PaCS et dénoncera l'homophobie', *Le Monde*, 26 juin 1999, p. 10.

event took place on the streets of Paris on 31 January 1999. Approximately 100,000 people attended an anti-PaCS demonstration organised by Christine Boutin (UDF, Yvelines). With banners proclaiming 'Pédés au bûcher', 'PS=PD' and 'Pas de neveux pour les tantouzes', this demonstration sent shock waves through French society.

Firstly, what is particularly remarkable about these two events is that, while tolerance towards homosexuals has increased in France in recent years with greater visibility of lesbians and gays, the term 'homophobie' (until now recently unused) has re-entered public discourse and instances of homophobia have been on the rise. Caroline Fourest, President of the *Centre gai et lesbien* in 1999, commented on this phenomenon: 'C'est justement parce que l'homophobie recule qu'elle commence à s'exprimer. Quand elle était tellement évidente, on n'avait pas besoin de la dire.'[28] Fourest, I believe, identifies a central mechanism of the way in which homophobia operates in relation to two key oppositions. The first opposition relates to homophobia in its silent and verbal forms. One implication of her statement is that there is a sort of inevitability about the existence of homophobia; once threatened with extinction, it keeps coming back. A related but perhaps more sinister implication is the idea that homophobia has been engrained in the French subconscious for so long that it has been taken for granted. So much so that one doesn't have to mention it. In other words, the perceived widespread acceptability of homophobia has rendered redundant any verbal expression of it. Homophobia, literally, goes without saying. And the worrying implication of this is that homophobia seems so deep-seated that it does not need to be spoken to be expressed.

The second opposition that Fourest's statement points to is that characterised by visibility and invisibility. What links the two events described above is the PaCS legislation which was designed to give legal recognition to lesbian and gay couples. The socialist government under Jospin, in taking the pulse of social change and the 'évolution des moeurs', was convinced that this legislation would find a welcome reception not only from the lesbian and gay community but from the wider public. However, given the volume and nature of the dissent at the time, the conclusions to be drawn are different and can be interpreted in two contradictory ways. Firstly, it would appear that large swathes of the French population do not agree with the legal recognition of lesbian and gay *couples* because it makes homosexuality *visible* and 'threatening', hence the intensity of the verbal diatribe and public outcry. Secondly, it could be argued that this same swathe agrees to tolerate lesbian and gay *individuals* as long as the latter remain *invisible* (without legal recognition as couples). In other words, homophobia may be latent in both circumstances but its intensity and public expression are commensurate with the levels of visibility and legal recognition given to lesbians and gays in the republic. Bonnet's prophecy that legal recognition will not spare lesbians and gays from homophobia rings true. While tolerance of lesbians and

---

[28] Quoted in 'La Gay Pride 1999 fêtera le PaCS et dénoncera l'homophobie', p. 10.

gays as the invisible constituency is expressed silently and with 'approval' (*not* as a threat to mainstream society), this same tolerance may also be an expression of hidden homophobia and may give way to overt homophobia once the gay constituency becomes visible and legal.

Put another way, in the first instance, homophobia does not need to be verbalised in order to perform its function as an agent of repression and control. In fact, one could argue that homophobia is potentially more dangerous when expressed silently. In silence, it can acquire an unchecked universal approval. Its silence is conditional on the contract negotiated in response to the invisibility of lesbians and gays. In the second instance, that unspoken contract, conditional on respective silence and invisibility, is broken and spoken homophobia becomes an expression of rage and betrayal at the collapse of the contract. However, rage and betrayal are also symptomatic of a deeper concern within the homophobic mindset which is characterised in terms of a shift in the balance of power. In other words, what may really be at stake as a consequence of contractual breakdown is that the power invested in silent homophobia is undermined (and externalised in insult and rage) by the new power invested in gay visibility, recognition and rights to self-determination. The very visibility of homosexuality takes away from verbalised homophobia a justification for its existence because the legitimacy established in the recognition of lesbians and gays in the PaCS disempowers homophobia of any coherent or expressive logic. More crucially, legal gay visibility serves to isolate the discourse of open invective for what it is, a discourse founded on repression, fear and self-loathing. One could also argue that Bersani's depiction of homophobia as phallocentric disintegration at the loss of phallic power is mirrored here by homophobic implosion at the loss of its power of silence.

The conclusion we can draw from these hypotheses is that once homophobia is externalised verbally it goes automatically into decline. This may seem a contradiction given the venom of the insults expressed above by French politicians. For the latter, the verbalisation of homophobia clearly remains a powerfully political expression of disapproval and exclusion. However, Redman has demonstrated that, psychologically, homophobia is incompatible in respect of phobia and violence, and sociologically, it is an expression of sexual instability and fear of loss of sexual identity. It is my contention that the verbalisation of homophobia is an expression of self-reflexive angst, of sexual confusion, and of the fear of self-'disintegration.' In short, verbalised homophobia has little to do with the 'other' and a lot to do with the self. For these reasons, our silent/verbal and visible/invisible approach to homophobia has some merit because it enables us to contest the underlying symptoms of the homophobic mindset and not underestimate (or become complicit with) it as a subliminal 'universal.' By exposing homophobia to democratic scrutiny, one is able to address, understand, challenge and oppose it. One obvious way of achieving this is through legislation. After years of struggle, the French parliament amended the 1881 Freedom of the Press law in 2004, making it a crime to discriminate against individuals on the basis of their sexual orientation, and a crime to defame a person on the basis of their sexual orientation. Both crimes come with a one year jail term and a fine of 45,000 euros, and six months jail and a fine of 22,500 euros respectively. Some would argue that legislation against homophobia sends it back underground and re-invests it with its silent power. I tend to dismiss this argument on the basis that once homophobia is verbalised and then denounced by legislation, it becomes a damaged and corrupted condition, stripped of any power, value, consensus or credibility.

Homophobia and Anti-Discrimination Legislation

Anti-homophobia legislation has been generally welcomed in France. However, the means by which it was achieved were arduous and complicated. Strategists developed a twin track approach by which they pushed for legislation against homophobia on the basis of discrimination against sexual orientation. This was then used to pave the way for legislation relating to defamation of character. If we consider the first track approach, we can see that sexual orientation legislation had been on the political agenda for some time, and support for it was growing in the workplace, and in the wider legal and political contexts of freedom of expression and equality of rights. The European parliament had already devolved protective legislation in respect of sexual orientation to member states in the late 1990s. The next step was for these member states to apply it to their own contexts.[29] In October 2000, the Socialist government in France tabled legislation to address discrimination in the work place. The independent anti-homophobia group SOS-Homophobie had registered a significant increase in complaints from lesbians and gays, ranging from personal threats and insults to threats of dismissal from work and non-renewal of working contracts.[30] This new legislation was therefore a way of addressing this rise in discriminatory practices. It was also part of a wider

---

[29] As we will see in the case of France, protection of sexual orientation is now enshrined in the new 'projet de loi de modernisation sociale.' In Britain, the new Bill of Human Rights has addressed the problem to some degree, but only indirectly and as part of a wider package of social measures. Section 28, which prevents local authorities from intentionally promoting homosexuality or promoting the teaching of homosexuality in their schools, remains on the statute books in England and Wales. For many of its critics, this statute is one of the main reasons for continuing homophobia particularly in schools. Current New Labour attempts to repeal this legislation have failed. Strategies of appeasement have included the introduction of specific non-discrimination legislation, the amendment of the Sex Education Act and the promotion of the importance of marriage. All appear to have failed to appease many Tories, Church leaders and members of the House of Lords who do not want to see Section 28 repealed.

[30] It may be worth pointing out at this juncture that until the recent adoption by Britain of the recent Human Rights Act (HRA) in October 2000, it was legal to sack someone for being gay and employers had no legal duty to protect people from homophobia at work. It remains to be seen, of course, how this legislation has been received and interpreted at the working level.

'projet de loi de modernisation sociale' that the government had decided on from 1999 to look at all forms of discrimination effecting foreigners and young people of immigrant parents in the areas of work, housing, leisure and access to public services. In a significant move, the government introduced three amendments to existing legislation. As it stood, Article 122-45 of the *Code du travail* stipulated: 'Aucune personne ne peut être écartée d'une procédure de recrutement, aucun salarié ne peut être sanctionné ou licencié en raison de son origine, de son sexe, de ses moeurs, de sa situation de famille, de son appartenance à une ethnie, une nation ou une race, de ses opinions politiques [...], de ses convictions.' The first amendment was to expand the frame of reference of the code by incorporating other discriminatory practices relating to job applications, qualifications and promotion. A second amendment would remove the burden of proof of discrimination solely from the victim, and require an employer or landlord (in related cases) to prove also that they were *not* guilty of discriminatory practices. And finally, in a move to address explicitly sexual orientation and by extension homophobia, the new legislation proposed the replacement of the word 'moeurs' in the existing code with 'orientation sexuelle.'

What is significant about these legislative changes is the nature of the shift from a culture of centralised power to greater transparency and accountability. Looking at these changes closely, one can see that this shift in culture is pursued through a doubling process designed to ensure that no aspect of discrimination is overlooked. In this regard, the accommodation of legislation to visible and invisible forms of discrimination is indicative of the scope of the legislation to root out discrimination in its silent and verbalised forms. Similarly, victim and agent of discrimination must now prove their respective innocence and lack of guilt. The doubling process is also in evidence at a linguistic level in the symbolic transfer of power from 'moeurs' to 'orientation sexuelle.' The word 'moeurs' is an all-inclusive term connoting a wide range of beliefs, customs and practices, including sexual preference. The unspecificity of the word, however, lends itself to abusive reference in that, in making no particular practice explicit, it can be construed that some practices are tacitly condoned and others not. 'Moeurs' can be seen to belong to the terminology of silent complicity where homophobic collusion thrives in the shadows of generality and imprecision. 'Orientation sexuelle', on the other hand, reinstates the power of language as a crucial arbiter in the silent/verbal stakes already discussed. Its denotative, as opposed to connotative, power targets the source of homophobic aggression in sexual prejudice. This denotative power is then reinforced by the specificity of the language of law.

With the law amended to address many discriminations and particularly of a sexual nature, where does this leave the debate in respect of legislation to tackle specifically homophobia? François Vauglin, from the group *Homosexualité et socialisme*, suggested that a debate on 'les structures d'études des discriminations'

Homophobia: Mimesis, Legislation and 'Outing' 211

could lead to proposals for the penalisation of homophobia.[31] Similarly, in their 2001 parliamentary report on the PaCS legislation, Jean-Pierre Michel and Patrick Bloche proposed a law against 'l'injure et la diffamation homophobes.'[32] The introduction of the word 'diffamation' into the debate on homophobia triggered the second part of the twin track approach for lesbian and gay strategists which, as we will see in the course of this chapter, would have an impact on the particularly controversial strategy of 'outing.' In fact, the beginnings of this strategy could be said to reside in an earlier strategy developed in 2001 by a group of lesbian and gay associations (made up of the associations 'de lutte contre le sida', 'de défense des droits des homosexuels' and 'de défense des droits de l'homme') in response to constant vilification of lesbians and gays in the press. Adopting a strategy 'en deux volets, un volet répressif et un volet préventif,'[33] the associations repeated Vauglin's call for an inquiry into the wider applications of anti-discriminatory legislation, with specific focus on the press and the Press law of 1881. In 2001, the press, and specifically the journal *Présent*, had become the target of a lawsuit by the *Centre gai et lesbien* in which the journal had published drawings of gay men. One of these drawings showed two gay men extending their hands to a young boy, and exclaiming in a caption below: 'Viens mon petit, nous allons t'accueillir à draps ouverts.' The association of homosexuality with paedophilia was conveyed through a play on the words 'draps' and 'bras.' The lawsuit failed because the 1881 Press law, not having been modified, did not allow for lesbian and gay individuals or associations to bring civil suits against the press.

To be exact, the 1881 Press law condemns crimes of discrimination, as a result of hatred or violence towards an individual or a group of individuals on the basis of ethnic origin, national identity or religious affiliation. However, this law does not cover incitement to hatred towards individuals on the basis of their sexual orientation. In other words, gay associations could not bring lawsuits against newspapers in France, in contrast to antiracist groups that could. Libel suits, highlighting defamation of character, did not work either because sexual orientation was not considered 'un critère d'aggravation des peines.' Before the current legislation of 2004, one could freely and publicly insult a gay person without risk. The logic of the 1881 Press law was built on freedom of expression and this freedom could be used to discriminate against a minority group unprotected by the law and whose right of redress to it was denied. The new 2004 legislation has addressed some of these glaring inadequacies in the French legal system. However, these changes have not been universally welcomed, and some of the criticism on sexual orientation and homophobia legislations has been

---

[31] Quoted by Pascale Krémer in 'Inscrite dans la loi, la notion d'"orientation sexuelle" devrait permettre d'améliorer la lutte contre les discriminations', *Le Monde*, 24 juin 2000, p. 12.

[32] Quoted by Pascale Krémer in 'Un rapport parlementaire dresse un bilan très positif des deux ans d'existence du PaCS', *Le Monde*, 15 novembre 2001, p. 11.

[33] *Têtu*, juin 2001, p. 60.

212 *The Gay Republic*

unfavourable to lesbians and gays. The latter have been criticised for being part of a wider social movement that has sought to undermine the law, and in which micro problems are perceived to be resolved by the creation of new micro legal categories.[34] For example, Marcela Iacub, a leading researcher in the legalities of biotechnology at the CNRS (and defender of lesbian and gay rights), has highlighted the inconsistency of inscribing within the law 'une minorité homosexuelle' in the fight against homophobia when homosexuals themselves have struggled for years to 'sortir de cette assignation.'[35] What these critiques reveal is that French law today faces two different directions forward. One direction is traditional, reflective of an earlier time and place, generally inclusive, sufficiently broad and open-ended in its characterisation of society; in short, the law of general interest. The other direction is postmodern and hyper differentialist, where communities and individuals are seen to negotiate their own exceptionalism.

Homophobia and the Threat to New Ideologies

In a special issue of the journal *La Revue des deux mondes* on 'Les nouvelles intolérances' published in 1999, Irène Théry and Evelyne Pisier extend the discussion on homophobia to include its more ideological dimensions, and specifically the threat posed by homophobic ideas in the intellectual arena. In her article 'L'autre en soi: l'intolérance à la mixité', Théry presents her philosophy on 'mixité.' For Théry, it is a philosophy based on the idea of the recognition of 'l'autre en soi.' She develops this idea from Greek Antiquity and the work of Nicole Loraux who, in her book *Les Expériences de Tirésias*, identifies the two sites of bed and war as the point of coming together of femininity in masculinity and vice versa. Théry states:

> La façon dont le féminin et le masculin se rejoignent par cela même qui les définit et les sépare l'un de l'autre: le lit et la guerre. La souffrance du guerrier blessé au combat lui fait atteindre, à l'extrême de l'épreuve virile, la féminité qui est en lui: il souffre comme une femme qui accouche. La douleur de l'accouchement, où toute femme risque sa vie est aussi le moment où la féminité extrême, toute de force et de courage, rejoint la virilité.[36]

Théry builds a model of mutual respect in male/female relations that is founded on the recognition of the presence of mutual sexual characteristics in men and women

---

[34] The intolerant/homophobic argument is that creation of new legal categories to recognise new affective unions muddles the whole 'lien social' and imposes an unnecessary burden on the legislature when other possible solutions to sexual representation could be addressed.

[35] Quoted by Pascale Kremer in 'La Gay Pride 1999 fêtera le PaCS et dénoncera l'homophobie', *Le Monde*, 26 juin 1999, p. 10.

[36] Irène Théry, 'L'autre en soi: l'intolérance à la mixité', *La Revue des deux mondes*, novembre-décembre (1999): 143.

(not a biological androgyny but a social empathy). Hence she concludes that there is only one human sexuality. The organic model, which she rejects, promotes the essentialist difference of the sexes, without any socially responsible mutual inflection. This is not to imply that Théry goes off on a limb to suggest that the fundamental asymmetry of the male/female bodies (and the implications for sexual procreation and primary sexual roles) is abolished. Rather, her model of 'mixité' respects certain biological givens, but, on the level of social roles, she claims that there are *a priori* precedents. This attempt to reconfigure traditional roles for men and women allows her to open up to women traditionally masculine spheres (work and politics for instance), and to men traditionally female spaces (domesticity). The reasoning behind Théry's model of 'mixité' is twofold. She highlights the changing nature of society and sexuality in the context of the impact of traditional roles for men and women. She claims that the 'imposition' of traditional roles as the only model of 'truth' is suspect and needs adapting. She envisages the replacement of a traditional 'vérité' with renewed values of responsibility and civility. She explains thus: 'En faisant primer le principe de reponsabilité sur la dictature du biologique, ou celle des sentiments, la mixité pose une borne fondatrice à la passion d'évincer l'autre ou de l'utiliser à son gré, qui peut saisir un parent et met en inégalité *a priori* les femmes qui accouchent et les hommes qui n'accouchent pas. Cette mixité est le pari d'une nouvelle civilité.'[37] In other words, 'mixité' eschews attempts to segregate the sexes, and allows an individual to accommodate his/her other.

Théry's model of 'mixité' makes many assumptions about sexual difference and how social interaction should be conducted. As a model for civil responsibility, it has positive aspects. Also the notion of one's sexual (b)identity provides some interesting philosophical and psychological insights in respect of the human condition. However, it is the relation between the sexual and the social, and particularly the construction of a social model on a perception of mutual recognition that causes concern. Furthermore, the sexual concept 'l'autre en soi' is premised on 'sexe', as opposed to the 'sexuel.' In other words, in promoting the notion of the recognition of sexual difference within 'le sexe', Théry privileges the masculine/feminine 'différence des sexes' as the only valid sexual construct, and sidelines the whole issue of sexuality. This is the cornerstone of Théry's model of 'mixité' and it is on this basis that she criticises other ideologies as intolerant and homophobic.

For example, she perceives as intolerant any formulation of sexuality that is not grounded in the male/female binary. In particular, she highlights the identity

---

[37] Théry, 'L'autre en soi: l'intolérance à la mixité', p. 148. The term 'mixité' has gained considerable currency in contemporary feminist debates. In a footnote to her analysis, Théry contrasts her definition with that of another prominent feminist Sylviane Agacinski. Théry states: 'Elle [Agacinski] constate la mixité comme un fait (qu'elle valorise) et fait de la parité l'objectif politique. Pour moi, le fait est la nature sexuée de l'humanité, et la mixité est l'objectif politique', p. 152.

214 *The Gay Republic*

movements of Lesbian and Gay Studies which claim that male and female opposites are artificial constructions, imposed by the masculine domination of women and by the heterosexual domination of homosexuals. Similarly, the PaCS legislation is blamed for moving the sexual debate away from the masculine/feminine opposition to the homosexuality/heterosexuality agenda. However, Théry is careful not to come across as too restrictive or conservative in her views. For these reasons, she distances herself from what she calls a neo-organic trend that seeks to naturalise 'la différence des sexes' and deny any concept of the couple outside of its procreative function. Also, she distances herself from other voices of intolerance that describe homosexuality as a form of pathological behaviour. This type of intolerance, which situates lesbians and gays 'dans le sexuel', outside of 'la différence des sexes', in a pregenital and primitive wasteland, foments, according to Théry, the homophobic fantasies of irrationality and paedophilia. This latter comment is a direct attack against the outspoken homophobia of the priest and psychoanalyst Tony Anatrella who has put on the record that 'qu'on le veuillle ou non, l'homosexualité reste le symptôme d'un problème psychique et d'un en-deçà de la différenciation des sexes.'[38]

In the context of homosexuality, and even given her rejection of homophobia, I cannot but detect elements of duplicity and self-deception at work in Théry's argumentation. Her argument about the innate intolerance of homosexuality on the grounds that it is pathological and 'engluée dans le sexuel' is suspect given the fact that she has already invalidated 'le sexuel' as a basis on which to construct sexual identity. She undermines 'le sexuel' and then uses this category in an argument to preach the intolerance of homosexuality. Overall, I would suggest that Théry's article is a subtle manipulation of intolerance, the end result of which is her own naïvité. She promotes positive and socially responsible ideas on 'mixité' but her adherence to the symbolic 'différence des sexes' can be interpreted as a sexist and political posture. On the one hand, she wants to highlight the levels of intolerance to her ideas on 'mixite' from lesbians and gays and gender groups. On the other hand, this strategy backfires on her because in reality her argument against intolerance reveals her own intolerance, particularly in respect of her opposition to social constructions of identity.

In the second and more radical article, Evelyne Pisier locates intolerance and homophobia in the institutions of government and power.[39] Her argument follows three main lines. First, she claims that the sexual order of heterosexuality has been reinforced by theological and political institutions. The elevation of heterosexuality as the norm, through the hierarchy of 'la différence des sexes', has eternalised the power of masculinity in this difference, which in turn has been universalised in the republican ideal. This representation is solidified by a moral code of good and bad. The good are the 'intégristes' who participate in this order, the bad are the

---

[38] Tony Anatrella, 'A propos d'une folie', *Le Monde*, 26 juin 1999, p. 17.

[39] Evelyne Pisier, 'Du PaCS et de l'ambiguïté d'une tolérance', *La Revue des deux mondes*, novembre-décembre (1999): 163-61.

marginalised and disenfranchised, among whom Pisier situates lesbians and gays. The second strand to Pisier's argument is to demonstrate that the PaCS legislation is a form of intolerant tolerance. In other words, given the heterosexual nature of the sexual order in which they are 'désintégristes', Pisier argues that the best that lesbians and gays can expect is a tolerance of their weakness, marginality, abnormality and inferiority.[40] The PaCS, therefore, is demeaning and intolerant and merely inscribes lesbians and gays in their 'tolerated' difference. The third, and most interesting strand to this argument, pursues this dynamic of tolerance. We have seen in the earlier context of Marie-Jo Bonnet that silent tolerance of lesbians and gays can translate into a sinister form of homophobia, more powerful and threatening than its verbalised alternative. Bonnet argued that legal and visible recognition of lesbians and gays would not spare them from homophobia and violence, a point of view I have tried to redress in this chapter. Pisier also claims that the PaCS has caused homophobia to resurface because the heteronormative sexual order has been contested by the legal and visible recognition of lesbians and gays. She states:

> S'ils se cachent, dans la honte et pour éviter l'insulte, alors, par définition, les homosexuels sont tolérés. Mais l'invisibilité est le prix de cette tolérance intolérante. Un prix que, depuis les années soixante, ils refusent de payer. Une invisibilité dont ils ont décidé collectivement de sortir. En rendant leur différence politiquement visible. En exigeant l'égalité en droit.[41]

Pisier shows that the assumption that silence equals tolerance is misguided, and one for which homosexuals have paid a high price in terms of their invisibility. But both Bonnet and Pisier also appear to confirm that visibility has brought with it the prize of equality. Whereas Bonnet stopped at this juncture in her argument and accepted in defeatist fashion the status quo of 'symbolic representation in which the male has been universalised' and women disenfranchised, Pisier proceeds to turn the tables on the hypocrisy of universalism and its abuse of tolerance. In a subtle twist to her argument, Pisier follows the republican logic of tolerance towards lesbians and gays in its introduction of the PaCS legislation to accommodate lesbian and gay couples. However, as Pisier has argued throughout, there is no way this legislation could be perceived as tolerant ('sa belle signification') in respect of full equality of rights for all citizens. It is, as she has said, tolerance ('condescendence') of communitarian difference. Pisier then goes on to suggest that if the republic is to restore faith in the concept of tolerance, it must radicalise the concept of universalism. Pisier states:

---

[40] Daniel Borrillo in his article on sexual orientation legislation in Europe says that the motivation behind gay decriminalisation and demedicalisation has only ever been about tolerance or minimum protection of gays and never full equality. See 'L'orientation sexuelle en Euroope: esquisse d'une politique antidiscriminatoire', *Les Temps modernes*, 609 (2000): 263-82.

[41] Pisier, 'Du PaCS et de l'ambiguïté d'une tolérance', p. 157.

216   *The Gay Republic*

Pourtant, en leur proposant le PaCS, que fait-on d'autre, par hypocrisie ou inconscience, que d'inscrire, dans un statut juridique particulier, leur différence communautaire? Ces républicains tolérants se contredisent. Si l'on veut débarrasser la tolérance de ses relents de condescendence et lui rendre sa belle signification, il n'est d'autre solution qu'universaliste. Un universalisme exigeant, intransigeant sur ses exceptions dérogatoires. Un universalisme au nom duquel la différence entre un homosexuel et un hétérosexuel ne justifie ni des statuts inégaux ni même le refus d'un égal accès aux droits.[42]

In exposing the sham of tolerance within republican universalism, Pisier calls for a new democracy to come along and replace the beleaguered concept of good with justice. In both articles, we have different approaches to homophobia and intolerance/tolerance. Irène Théry focuses on competing definitions of sex and sexuality as the source of intolerance. The real value of her article is in showing the ideological capital to be gained by winning the battle of 'la différence des sexes'; however, the essentialist/constructionist dialectic that underpins this battle can be seen to shape attitudes of homophobia and intolerance. Evelyne Pisier takes on homophobia and the institutionalised intolerance that masquerades as tolerance in the republic. She demonstrates that, in order to remove sources of intolerance, the principle of universalism needs to be adapted to reflect individual circumstances and not abstract ideals.

Homophobia and the Practice of 'Outing'

On the 10 February 1999, the militant group ACT-Up Paris sent a letter to a *député* (gay, but not openly) that, unless he declared publicly his homosexuality, the group would 'out' him. The reason for this unprecedented move was that the politician in question had attended the anti-PaCS demonstration of 31 January, which was reported to be violent, offensive and deeply homophobic. Given that the *député* in question had not condemned the demonstration, ACT-Up interpreted his silence as legitimising the demonstration and its message. As the moment of his 'outing' approached, ACT-Up forwarded a communiqué to the national press. This communiqué wished the *unnamed député* a happy birthday. In effect, his date of birth signalled his 'outing.' In deferring the final 'dénonciation' of the politician's name, the group succeeded in 'outing' him by not naming him. The reason for this last minute change in strategy was based on legal advice; were a name to released, the politician would sue for defamation of character. The threat of 'outing', with a twist of ingenuity, secured its goal, despite the efforts of other politicians to persuade ACT-Up to renounce its practice in the interests of the freedom of the individual.

I have used this incident to illustrate some of the issues that the practice of 'outing' raises for discussion. I propose to look at this phenomenon from three perspectives; the problematic of naming, the private/public debate and the pros and

---

[42] Pisier, 'Du PaCS et de l'ambiguïté d'une tolérance', p. 158.

cons of the practice of 'outing.' In another of its manifestos from June 1999,[43] ACT-Up sought to justify why it was going to borrow a strategy used by its American and Anglo-Saxon branches. The central reason was in response to increased homophobia and lack of protection from the law for lesbians and gays: 'tant qu'un délit d'incitation à la homophobie ne sera pas institué, il sera possible de nous insulter tous sans insulter personne.' The encoded message of this statement revealed a reversal of logic that played on the law of defamation. That law, as it stood prior to the 2004 legislation which has since changed everything in this regard, meant that to insult anyone by name was to incur risk, penalty or imprisonment depending on the nature of the insult. In claiming, in the absence of a law against homophobia, that lesbians and gays could still be insulted collectively and not individually, ACT-Up was flagging up several important points. Firstly, as named individuals, lesbians and gays were still immune from insult, hence the law on defamation was to their advantage. However, the problem with this was that, as a group (unlike until recently ethnic or racial groups), 'lesbians' and 'gays' remained targets of verbal and written abuse. As the recent invective in the National Assembly and on the streets showed, one could with impunity call 'gays' (collectively) anything one liked but one could not name/call an individual 'gay' without recrimination.

ACT-Up conceded that the practice of 'outing' was hurtful, threatening and violent. But it qualified its position by claiming that the 'logic' of 'outing' was linked to homophobia and that the violence was not in the 'outing' itself but in the act of naming. What gave this practice its particular 'logic', according to ACT-Up, was the asymmetry of the law: 'Et pourtant, l'impossibilité de nommer est au coeur du problème. Aucun de nos détracteurs ne s'est en effet interrogé sur cette embarrassante dissymétrie du droit: il n'est pas possible de dire d'une personne qu'elle est homosexuelle, en revanche il est possible de dire des homosexuel(le)s qu'ils sont des animaux.'[44] In other words, the justification for 'outing' was based on an *equivalence* between, on the one hand, the license to insult 'gays' (as a group) and, on the other hand, the nominal insult/violence of 'outing.' For ACT-Up, naming in the act of 'outing' was a way of reclaiming control through the power game of words. In a linguistic exposé of the homophobic insult, ACT-Up identified a preference among homophobes for the generic or abstract term (such as 'gays') over the 'incarné' term (or named individual). This genericness was then perceived to structure 'un ensemble de discours parascientifiques – psychanalytique, anthropologique, sociologique, juridique, etc. – qui, sous le régime douteux de l'expertise bienveillante, n'hésitent pas à juger nos vies.'[45] The emergence of terms such as 'groupes à risque' (gays after the AIDS crisis) and 'stigmatisés' was seen to perpetuate a form of linguistic homophobia in which language was the instrument of manipulation. Homophobes, it claimed, had been

---

[43] ACT-Up, 'Votre vie privée contre la nôtre', *Le Monde*, 26 juin 1999, p. 26.
[44] ACT-Up, 'Votre vie privée contre la nôtre', p. 26.
[45] ACT-Up, 'Votre vie privée contre la nôtre', p. 26.

218   *The Gay Republic*

able to exploit this genericness by categorising individuals via sexual preference, and by hiding behind the abstraction of the insult in the knowledge that they remained protected as individuals from insult. 'Outing' turned this logic on its head by saying that insult would be met with insult and that there was nowhere to hide.

The second 'logic' of 'outing' characterised by ACT-Up was the public/private debate, which was linked to the problematic of naming. As the title of the manifesto ('Votre vie privée contre la nôtre') suggests, ACT-Up made a distinction between the private lives of gays and the private lives of other citizens. In France, 'la vie privée' is sacrosanct for everyone, politicians and celebrities alike. It is one of the foundation stones of tolerance and an area where the state has been reluctant to extend its centralising tentacles. According to ACT-Up, the perception of private life is different for lesbians and gays. The difference of perception is that the absence of full equality of rights (and, prior to the PaCS, lack of legal recognition) has forced lesbians and gays to open/'out' their private lives to public scrutiny and intrusion in order to avail of social benefits:

> En matière de ve privée, l'Etat n'a jamais été un allié. Nous appartenons, avec d'autres, à ces populations dont la vie privée, loin d'être "protégée", est l'objet d'intrusions fréquentes de la part des administrations; [...] homosexuel(le)s obligé(e)s de subir une enquête de moeurs meneé par les DDASS pour accéder au droit pourtant reconnu à l'adoption individuelle; allocataires du RMI soumis aux "visites domiciliaries" des contrôleurs des Caisses d'allocations familiales; sans-papiers tenus, pour obtenir un titre de séjour, de produire les preuves – et le détail – de leur "vie privée et familiale."[46]

ACT-Up argued the forced 'outing' of lesbians and gays on two fronts. Firstly, the lesbian and gay community initially resisted the state's prurient desire to 'out' gay people (by lying, cheating or hiding the fact that they were gay), but eventually the public pressure was too strong. However, rather than atrophy under this imposed 'outing', ACT-Up argued that lesbians and gays put their new visible 'status' to effective use by rallying together in the struggle for equal rights and by preventing the state dictating how they live their lives. From the perspective of ACT-Up, therefore, the state's 'volonté de savoir' about the private lives of lesbians and gays became the catalyst for a new era of gay openness and self-determination. However, the positivity to which the lesbian and gay community put this new self-imposed 'outing' must be balanced against the earlier resentment felt by many lesbians and gays to being publicly exposed and humiliated. In short, it was within this context of gays being forced to live their private lives publicly, with the accompanying levels of intolerance and voyeurism, that ACT-Up couched an historical justification for the 'outing' of others: 'L'outing s'inscrit dans cette stratégie d'occupation, avec des visages et des noms, d'un espace public habitué à parler de nous sans nous.' In a connected argument of justification, ACT-Up attempted to gain some moral high ground for a highly controversial practice by claiming that 'outing' was a strategy 'de pauvres [...]. Pauvres en droits, là où

---

[46]   ACT-Up, 'Votre vie privée contre la nôtre', p. 26.

Homophobia: Mimesis, Legislation and 'Outing' 219

d'autres sont mieux lotis.' Again, the perception of being disenfranchised underpinned the 'outing' strategy. Previously, the violence of naming through 'outing' was in response to the freedom to insult gays. Now, a similar 'tit for tat' strategy operated according to the logic that if lesbians and gays have no private life, then closeted ones who insult them won't either.

Apart from the militant tendency within ACT-Up and perhaps clusters of lesbians and gays who relished the vengeful aspect of 'outing', there was not widespread support for this strategy, despite the 'logic' underpinning it. Even the President of ACT-Up at the time condemned the practice as 'indéfendable', but added that the practice would persist as long as there was no law against homophobia.[47] Daniel Borrillo reinforced this position by saying that it was for the French state to condemn homophobia, and not for individuals to seek vengeance.[48] Some questioned the political value of the practice,[49] and others contemplated how a community that had suffered so long could inflict suffering on others.[50] One of the more reasoned critiques of 'outing' came from the journalist Laurence Folléa in *Le Monde*.[51] She condemned unreservedly the practice of 'délation' ('informing') as an affront to the principles of French society. She equated the practice to a form of 'terrorisme communautariste' that did not serve the interests of the lesbian and gay community. Addressing the case of the 'outed' *député*, she made two significant comments. She suggested that even though the *député* did attend the anti-PaCS demonstration, this in itself did not justify him being 'outed', except to imply that one could not be gay and also anti-PaCS. Similarly, homophobic slurs from a pumped-up crowd did not justify him being 'outed' except to imply that a person's sexuality constitutes his complete identity and convictions, or that he assumes on himself the actions of others.

These caveats raise crucial issues about ACT-Up's aims and objectives at this time and particularly the ethics of 'outing.' ACT-Up would argue that a gay politician should not attend an anti-PaCS demonstration (itself not necessarily anti-gay). If they attend, then some explanation should be forthcoming. Furthermore, for ACT-Up, the case of politicians is unique; as elected representatives, the divide between public and private is not as protected as it is for other citizens because an electorate has a right to know who they have voted for, including aspects of a private life in the event of a conflict of interests with political ramifications. This type of reasoning forms part of ACT-Up's defence of 'outing', if not a blanket justification for it on the grounds of the hypocrisy of a closeted politician condoning homophobia. However, the questions to be asked are twofold. What gave ACT-Up the legitimacy to act in this way, and who did it presume to

---

[47] Quoted in 'On a peur d'être aggressés', *Le Monde*, 13 mars 1999, p. 39.

[48] Quoted in 'L'association ACT-Up Paris menace de dévoiler l'homosexualité d'un député', *Le Monde*, 13 mars 1999, p. 39.

[49] François Vauglin in 'L'association ACT-Up Paris menace de dévoiler...', p. 39.

[50] Catherine Tasca in 'L'association ACT-Up Paris menace de dévoiler...', p. 39.

[51] Laurence Folléa, 'Délation', *Le Monde*, 13 mars 1999, p. 39

220 *The Gay Republic*

represent? The level of consultation on policy with the broader lesbian and gay movement is difficult to assess and therefore a matter of concern. However, what ACT-Up achieves with success is to make it seem that it is the only audible and representative gay voice 'out there.' And it achieves this by claiming to act on behalf of all lesbians and gays. The title of the manifesto mentioned above 'Votre vie privée contre *la nôtre*' (my emphasis) is a measure of its manipulation of the lesbian and gay agenda. In characterising itself as the embodiment of the history of gay struggle and gay rights, ACT-Up's strategy, despite been disowned by its President, has been to drive through an agenda (in the case of 'outing') founded on vengeance and an 'ethics' of presumption.

To 'come out' and 'to out' are very different concepts. For Didier Eribon, 'coming out' is key to the expression of gay identity in that, as a public affirmation, it takes back control of identity from the stigmatising discourse of gayness produced by heteronormativity. To 'come out' for Eribon, is to escape the mental ghetto of the closet. He also says that to 'come out' is either an essential rite of passage for all lesbians and gays, or the very culmination of being gay, both notions predicated on a necessary coming to terms with one's sexual identity. Critically, in the context of homophobia, he describes 'coming out' as a way of highlighting the fact that homophobia cannot control the terms of its own inferiorising strategies.[52] ACT-Up, on the other hand, presumes that to 'come out' is to share the universal burden of all lesbians and gays; in other words, to 'come out' is to stop the shame of being gay, and thus all lesbians and gays are perceived to have a responsibility to respond to this call. Where ACT-Up appears to have stretched the meaning of 'coming out' is to assume, in the wider struggle for solidarity and equality, that 'coming out' can translate into (have an equivalent in) 'outing.' I dispute the validity of this thinking because of its assumption of a united, collective gay voice. I dispute it also on the grounds that sharing a collective and historical burden of gayness is a valid or the only way to experience gay identity. One of the threads running through this book has been the idea that sameness is in reality the toleration of difference. 'Coming out' of the closet has been part of the lesbian and gay cartography for several decades now. But to 'come out', let alone to be 'outed', is not the only, nor should it be the only, way of valorising gayness. The history of recent lesbian and gay struggle has focused on the closet as a repressive space, and dismantling the closet has been central to gay liberationism.[53] The idea of 'coming out' of the closet has therefore been privileged as a personal coming of age and as a political act of sexual definition. The closet, on the other hand, has been demonised as a place of secrecy, isolation and complicity with normative heterosexuality: 'The closet has served as a marker of

---

[52] Didier Eribon, *Réflexions sur la question gay* (Paris: Fayard, 1999).

[53] In this respect, see Steven Seidman's, Chet Meek's and Francie Traschen's article 'Beyond the Closet? The Changing Social Meaning of Homosexuality in the United States', *Sexualities*, 2 (1999): 9-34. In particular, see the brief history of the sociology of the closet (pp. 12-13).

Homophobia: Mimesis, Legislation and 'Outing'

the lack of homosexual legitimacy, while coming out has symbolized progress.'[54] To remain in the closet is to betray oneself and one's difference. The closet has been described as 'ahistorical ground for gay life'[55] but recent debate on the concept of the closet has opened up a renewed interest in its foundational function.

Eve Sedgwick in her work *The Epistemology of the Closet* has stated that 'the gay closet is not a feature only of the lives of gay people. But for many gay people it is still the fundamental feature of social life.'[56] Quoting other contributors to this debate, in their joint article, Seidman, Meeks and Traschen point to the closet as a space where lesbians and gays have been able to create imaginatively their gay lives through strategies of concealment, protection, passing and the *jouissance* of leading a double life. In the same way that Seidman et al. and Sedgwick argue for a revalorisation of the closet, I think there is a case to made for the rehabilitation of the closet as a constructive space of 'self-management' for lesbians and gays, and also as a space of radical and subversive expression contiguous with the space of being 'out.' The closet, as I have suggested, has become synonymous with complicity with heteronormativity and self-denial. Eribon equates the closet with gay invisibility and the imposition of the heterosexual veto.[57] These critiques of the closet are important in that they form part of the wider debate about strategy and subversion. And while not wishing to undermine their significance, there is a trend within them to demonise the closet, view it in negative terms, and, crucially, underestimate its subversive potential. Politically, the closet has and continues to occupy a valuable place on the *inside* of heteronormativity. As such it can be a place of cooperation and fulfilment, but also a Bourdieu styled 'habitus' of subterfuge and resistance.

In its monopolisation of the lesbian and gay voice and its presumption of the wisdom of 'outing', ACT-Up misjudged the multi-faceted nature of sexual identity. Its attempt to universalise lesbian and gay identity under the banner of 'out' was simplistic, and it reduced the complexity of sexual identity, and particularly gay identity, to a linguistic triviality. In the late 1990s, ACT-Up believed that it was acting in the interests of lesbians and gays. It believed that the system of equivalence between one form of violence and another was justified, that closeted lesbians and gays should be forced to share the collective heritage of gay 'occupation', and that there should be no shame in 'coming out' and expressing one's sexuality. The problems with these 'justifications' are the following. Where does ACT-Up's legitimacy come from to empower it to act on behalf of lesbians and gays? Secondly, the strategies of meeting violence with violence (in the context of insult and naming) or force with force (in the context of 'outing' lesbians and gays to make them realise the voyeurism to which their sexuality has

---

[54] Seidman, Meek and Traschen, 'Beyond the Closet?...', p. 30.

[55] Seidman, Meek and Traschen, 'Beyond the Closet?...', p. 14.

[56] Eve Sedgwick, *The Epistemology of the Closet* (Berkeley: University of California Press, 1990), p. 68.

[57] Eribon, *Réflexions sur la question gay*, pp. 74-5.

222   *The Gay Republic*

been subject) are, as ACT-Up has confessed, the strategies of the poor 'en droits.' The distorted 'logic' that ACT-Up used here was to presume that, because lesbians and gays had not yet acquired legal rights and there was no movement on anti-homophobia legislation, it had a moral authority and justification to 'out' other closeted lesbians and gays. The implication is that ACT-Up had no choice in this decision and so it absolved itself of any responsibility. This strategy was a cynical manipulation of the position of the disenfranchised and the poor. Instead of pursuing its agenda of equality of rights for all, ACT-Up abused its lack of rights to deny the rights of other lesbians and gays to lead their lives as they wished. The poverty of ACT-Up's position in this respect is illustrated in the idea that 'outing' is only hurtful to a lesbian or gay if homosexuality is still deemed to be an unacceptable way of living. The implication that there should be no shame in 'coming out' misses the point altogether of lesbian and gay identity. The real issue, I would suggest, is respect for sexual diversity, and respect for the diversity *within the word 'gay.'*

Conclusions

Neither Seidman et al. nor myself advocate a return to the closet. The former make clear in their article that the closet is only half of the homosexual narrative. As the title of their article implies, they see an end to the age of the closet. Henning Bech, similarly, sees beyond the closet to the rebeginning of a new era of 'normalization' and 'routinization' of homosexuality in which Americans (and the American context is significantly different) 'are not dominated by shame, fear and guilt, and [...] have integrated their homosexuality into their conventional social worlds in ways that differentiate according to the level of intimacy they consider appropriate and desired.'[58] Bech's characterisation of Seidman et al.'s position is interesting for several reasons. She tends to agree that the closet needs to be reconfigured in the light of 'changes that *are* going on', although not necessarily in terms of an 'end' to the closet. My reading of this process of normalisation and routinisation (albeit in an American context) is that, while it can be equated with the notion of 'coming out', the implication of normalisation lies somewhere more 'in' as defined by integration than 'out' as defined by communitarianism. This opens up a whole new debate about definitions and conditions of coming out, and what one is coming out into. But Bech suggests that the dangers of normalisation, as we saw with the illusion of legislation for Marie-Jo Bonnet, are that they overlook and even 'belittle the continued existence of repression and homophobia, fear and guilt.'[59] This chapter has shown that homophobia in France works on many levels, including personal prejudice, insult, gender role constructionism, legislation, institutions, (in)tolerance and violence itself. The introduction of legislation against sexual discrimination in the work place and beyond has been welcome in making the law

---

[58]   Henning Bech, 'After the Closet', *Sexualities*, 2 (1999): 343.
[59]   Bech, 'After the Closet', p. 343.

more explicit and bringing the issue of sexual orientation out into the open. And new anti-homophobia legislation, while welcomed, has yet to be fully tested. In the context of France, however, more radical legislation is needed, particularly full equality of rights for lesbians and gays. Marie-Jo Bonnet reminded us that the symbolic status of universal subjects may help expel homophobia. However, while homosexuals and women remain individual citizens and not symbolic universal subjects, then institutional homophobia may well continue regardless of recent legislative change.

Conclusion

In his recent article 'Malaise dans la République', Alain Bertho claims that the French republic still thinks of itself as 'un idéal construit socialement et historiquement, une conception du monde et de la vie commune.'[1] He agrees that one of the great assets of republicanism has been its capacity to make a production out of the 'commun.' In the same issue of journal, the eminent feminist Françoise Collin also acknowledges the 'commun' thinking underpinning republicanism (she refers to it as a tendency to 'ramener l'autre au même'[2]). But both confirm that the 'commun' focus of French republicanism can no longer capture the multiple claims for equal representation within the republic. Bertho states that the republic 'n'est pas un régime politique *concret et tangible*'[3] (my italics); in other words, the republic is still caught in a time warp in which the idealism of republican values makes it blind to the realities of ordinary life. He says as much in his assertion that 'quand l'Etat républicain concret est mis en difficulté pratique de gouvernementalité, son interpellation ne peut plus se faire au nom de ses anciens principes.'[4] Collin, from the perspective of equality between the sexes, highlights the failings of 'commun' thinking by arguing that variations of the 'commun' (universalism, 'mêmeté', 'égalité') merely hide inequalities: 'Vendre de la mêmeté au prix de l'égalité est un marché de dupes. La mêmeté recouvre mais ne résout pas l'inégalité. On ne peut avoir le même sans l'égal.'[5] In different ways and with different objectives in mind, both are calling for the redefinition of the 'commun.' Bertho wants to move beyond the homogenising opposition between universalism and subjective singularity, to a 'commun' that is never complete or closed, to a collective that is never unifying, what he terms 'le dynamisme paradoxal d'une incomplétude.' Collin, similarly, seeks to transcend the binary between 'indifférence des sexes' and 'différence des sexes', and embrace a Derridean 'Différance' which she locates 'dans le movement actif de différ-a-ance, faisant avec le donné de la nature et de l'histoire indissociables, sans en être cependant prisonnier(e)s.'[6]

I have used the examples of Bertho and Collin for several reasons. As recent commentators on the state of French republicanism, their ideas represent some of the most adventurous thinking on the subject. It is also significant that in both their redefinitions of the 'commun', they look beyond the binaries of republicanism, and

---

[1] Alain Bertho, 'Malaise dans la République', *Mouvements*, 38 (2005): 15.
[2] Françoise Collin, 'Le comme un', *Mouvements*, 38 (2005): 8.
[3] Bertho, 'Malaise dans la République', p. 14.
[4] Bertho, 'Malaise dans la République', p. 17.
[5] Collin, 'Le comme un', p. 13.
[6] Collin, 'Le comme un', p. 13.

226   *The Gay Republic*

reposition their alternatives in a context of continuous suspended animation, deliberately free from attempts to control, define and identify them within the conventional paradigms of republican citizenship. Not only is this an innovative strategy, but it is also indicative of the lengths thinkers feel they have to go to resist what they see as the homogenising and hegemonic structure of republicanism. To relocate citizenship in a post-republican suspension is also designed to liberate the citizen from the more subtle and sophisticated means by which republicanism can draw citizens into the pale of universalism. We have seen throughout this book how universalism can be expressed in diffuse ways, with difference being subject to diverse forms of controlled tolerance, placating integrationism or principled compromise. While respecting and admiring the respective theoretical hypotheses of Bertho and Collin, I have sought to go back *pre* and *intra* republic in this book, not least so because the issue of lesbian and gay citizenship is one circumscribed by rights, equality, identity and political representation, all of which have a direct impact on the real lives of French citizens. This is not to suggest that I absolve myself of finding solutions to what might be seen as the intractability of 'gay citizenship' in French republicanism. On the contrary, as the title of this book underlines, my intentions have been to expose the paradoxes of the relationship between sexuality and republicanism, as well as identify a range of subversive strategies that point to a *real and concrete* redefinition of the 'commun.' In short, the direction of this book has been to find ways of breaking the mould of republican universalism, whilst highlighting simultaneously the traps of complicity with dominant universalism and its multiple manifestations (as expressed in 'la différence des sexes', 'l'indifférence des sexes', symbolic order, mimesis, normalisation, collaboration, heteronormativity, relationality, heteroisation).

By focusing on the social (a space contested by universal idealism and a 'universalisme en acte'[7]), I have demonstrated that control of this space determines how citizenship is bestowed on individuals. The social is either a pre-existent order in which citizens are anchored legally, politically, sexually and culturally, or a space where individuals are at the centre of the social, capable of shaping their lives legally, politically, sexually and culturally. Stéphane Breton and Yan Thomas debate this very issue in chapter three of this book. Breton claims that the social is a pre-requisite to individual agency, whereas Thomas claims that individual agency is a pre-requisite to the social. I have argued throughout in favour of the latter. The social is not a status quo, nor can it be a space where individuals are forced to conform to a preset mould of universalism in order to avail of laws and citizenship rights. Universalism (to which Bertho and Collin have alluded in their discussion of the 'commun' and 'mêmeté' in the French context) conceals pitfalls of complicity with the status quo for lesbians and gays in particular, but it also challenges us to think of ways of avoiding these pitfalls. The social, therefore, is a space of agency. It is a space where the law moulds its legitimacy, not through the

---

[7]   Patrick Simon and Sylvia Zappi, 'La politique républicaine de l'identité', *Mouvements*, 38 (2005): 7.

Conclusion 227

exclusive and sometimes arbitrary observance of norms, but through the 'fait social' (Marcel Gauchet's phrase) and its 'immanence.' The crisis in French law (and by extension in French political life in respect of citizenship) is that it has become detached from its social and representative roots. The expression of the social as a real and concrete space can therefore serve as a new testing ground for the validity of norms, symbolic axioms and the processes of acculturation on which many of the latter are predicated.

I claimed earlier that the central direction of this book was to find ways of breaking the mould of republican universalism. One of the pre-conditions of universalism, as alluded to by Bertho and Collin, is that universalism is indifferent to difference as long as citizens do not express their difference. This contract of citizenship is part of the republic's historical and social legacy. However, a more recent interpretation of this pre-condition is that the indifference (neutrality) of the universal citizen forces minorities (lesbians and gays for example) to identify themselves and seek socio-political and legal recognition. Patrick Simon and Sylvia Zappi state: 'L'indifférenciation formelle qui tient lieu de garantie d'un traitement équitable aboutit de fait à visibiliser, par contraste, les identités minoritaires. Pour faire état de ruptures d'égalités qu'elles subissent dans l'ordinaire du contrat social, ces identités minoritaires doivent se manifester et se déclarer.'[8] In fact, it could be argued that universalism obliges lesbians and gays to declare themselves publicly. To pursue this interpretation, one could suggest that this obligation subverts radically the received wisdom that it is difference which is seen to fragment republican universalism. To turn the tables and suggest that it is universalism itself that produces potentially its own break up is an ideological and theoretical leap that not only encourages subversive thinking, but also absolves lesbians, gays and other minorities from the guilt/shame they sometimes feel (and are forced to feel) as disenfranchised and marginalised citizens. Needless to say, this sense of guilt soon dissipates with the realisation that republican universalism finds its justification not in explaining discrimination and the absence of legal rights to lesbians and gays but by sanctioning them as transgressors.

However, it is this spirit of subversion and transgression that underpins another aspect of the social and of this book. Subscription to the social as a space of agency and immanence is itself conditional on the development of real strategies that target the core of universalism's authority. These strategies come in different forms and degrees of subversion. On a theoretical level, Pierre Bourdieu and Michel Foucault locate subversion at the level of and inside republican structures. They target the institutional structures that create the universal and particular categorisations of dominant and dominated. In Bourdieu's address to the lesbian and gay movement, he calls for a move away from symbolic acts of subversion to real acts. Foucault, whilst recognising that power and its institutions repress individuals, also calls for individuals to subvert that mindset and produce power for themselves. We might include here the recent insights of Patrick Simon and

---

[8] Patrick Simon and Sylvia Zappi, 'La politique républicaine de l'identité', p. 6.

228 *The Gay Republic*

Sylvia Zappi who challenge universalism as a value system that bestows supremacy but which, they claim, can be overthrown:

> Proposons ici une autre lecture des fonctions de la norme universaliste: installer et justifier un système de domination fondé sur une conception de la supériorité de certaines valuers, et de ceux qui les incarnent, sur d'autres qu'il convient d'éclaircir et de régénérer. La supériorité des valeurs valide la suprématie du groupe majoritaire qui s'identifie alors dans la transcendence de l'universel.[9]

In similar fashion, Didier Eribon identifies the oppressive structures of integrationism and separatism, preferring a more interactive approach between them, with the condition that gay 'culture' preserve its destabilising potential. Eribon places conditions on belonging to the social but refuses to withdraw from it altogether because he thinks that the social has a cultural and transformative potential for both gays and straights. Paul Yonnet highlights the individualist tendency within communitarianism as a revolutionary cell that can effect change over time. Another key subversive strategy, which is no less proactive, is the constancy of the critique of complicity with heteronormativity and its myriad forms. In his use of the phrase 'strategic practicality', Murray Pratt highlights the need for strategies of awareness that caution lesbian and gay activists against dropping their guard in their pursuit of real social change. What underpins many of these types of strategies is the acute sensitivity shown by lesbian and gay sympathisers to being hijacked by universalism, by the seductions of 'mixité' or the allure of 'l'autre en soi', all of which are predicated on universalism's core binary of 'la différence des sexes.' In the light of the earlier comment by Eribon in relation to the need for lesbians and gays to retain their separateness as a way of creating 'espaces de liberté' and a subversive 'rôle perturbateur' inside universalism, Leo Bersani and Guy Hocquenghem similarly see in strategies of sameness and the essentialism of homosexual desire a subversiveness that, by its very self-reflexivity, eschews the pitfalls of universalism, heteronormativity and Martelian indifference.

On a final and practical note, the example of ACT-Up Paris at the end of the 1990s illustrates the effective and controversial aspects of subversion. On the positive side, ACT-Up Paris succeeded in moving away from a one-dimensional strategy of addressing gay sexuality in the aftermath of the AIDS crisis, to embracing a wider social movement in the common cause of equality of rights for all minority groups. More controversially, the *strategy* of using positive discrimination (the strategy of *paritaires*) to promote lesbian and gay citizenship and undermine universalism was approved only as strategy but not as principle. Most controversial of all was the strategy to 'out' gay politicians, a move which took subversion to a new personal and vengeful level. To 'out' as a form of punishment or in the 'logic' of forcing all lesbians and gays to face up to their homosexuality, was to misunderstand gay identity, pervert the meaning of

---

[9] Patrick Simon and Sylvia Zappi, 'La politique républicaine de l'identité', p. 7.

Conclusion 229

sameness, and to confuse gravely 'outing' with 'coming out.' To 'come out', as Eribon says, is a spoken act, a personal act of resistance against the repression and domination of universalism. He goes on to describe it as a Sartrean choice between the 'liberté' of 'authenticité', and the 'mauvaise foi' of 'inauthenticité.'[10] To 'out', on the other hand, was and remains a betrayal of the real, personal and authentic subversiveness of gayness.

Subversion manifests itself in many forms, from theories, strategies and tactics to real acts of danger. But subversion is not confined to acts of insurrection, threat or resistance. There is a tendency to (mis)understand subversion as a condition of inferiority and minority. As part of a binary, it is often perceived in negative terms, and this perception conceals any potential for meliorism. In this context, it may be worth recalling an anecdote in which Foucault recounted the story of two young gay males who were seen going to bed together after a party. For Foucault, the subversive quality of this scene was not the act of sleeping together but the fact that they woke up happy. In other words, there was something in the *attitude* of these two gay males that made them happy. Eribon attributes this attitude to the transformative power of gay 'culture', while Foucault locates it in a 'style de vie' and in the creation of an 'esthétique de l'existence' which brings a sense of self-sufficiency and self-awareness. For both, and I tend to concur, subversion may have its true measure in a self-conviction in a gay asceticism which transcends the binary of politics and citizenship and, as Bertho and Collin imply, is always in a state of becoming.

---

[10] Didier Eribon, *Réflexions sur la question gay* (Paris: Editions Fayard, 1999), p. 156.

Bibliography

Adkins, L., 'Risk, Sexuality and Economy', *British Journal of Sociology*, 53 (2002): 19-40.

Agacinski, S., *Politique des sexes* (Paris: Seuil, 1998).

Anatrella, Tony, *La Différence interdite* (Paris: Flammarion, 1998).

___,'A propos d'une folie', *Le Monde*, 26 juin 1999, p. 17.

Bach-Ignasse, G., 'Le contrat d'union sociale en perpsective', *Les Temps modernes*, 598 (1998): 156-70.

Bach-Ignasse, G. and Roussel, Y., *Le PaCS juridique et pratique* (Paris: Denoël, 2000).

Bachelot, R., *Le PaCS entre haine et amour* (Paris: Plon, 1999).

Bakchine, S., 'Homosexualité, mariage, famille; et la nature', *Le Monde*, 19 novembre 1997, p. 17.

Baker, J.G. and Fishbein, H., 'The Development of Prejudice Towards Gays and Lesbians by Adolescents', *Journal of Homosexuality*, 36 (1998): 89-100.

Barraud, C., 'La distinction de sexe dans les sociétés', *Esprit*, 273 (2001): 105-29.

Bastard, B. and Cardia-Vonèche, L., 'La coparentalité fige la famille dans le "tout-biologique"', *Libération*, 4 août 2004, p. 27.

Baudoux, C. and Zaidman, Cl., *Egalité entre les sexes. Mixité et démocratie* (Paris: L'Harmattan, Collection Logiques Sociales, 1992).

Bauman, Z., *In Search of Politics* (Cambridge: Polity Press, 1999).

Bech, Henning, *When Men Meet. Homosexuality and Modernity* (Chicago: University of Chicago Press, 1997).

___, 'After the Closet? The Changing Social Meaning of Homosexuality in the United States', *Sexualities*, 2 (1999): 9-34.

Beck-Gernsheim, Elisabeth, *The Normal Chaos of Love* (Cambridge: Polity Press, 1990).

___, 'On the way to a Post-Familial Family: From a Community of Need to Elective Affinities', *Theory, Culture and Society*, 15 (1998): 53-70.

Bell, L. and Flood, C., *Political Ideologies in Contemporary France* (Pinter Press, 1997).

Bendle, M., 'The Crisis of "Identity" in High Modernity', *British Journal of Sociology*, 52 (2002): 1-18.

Bersani, Leo, *Homos* (Oxford: OUP, 1995).

___, 'Is the Rectum a Grave?' in D. Crimp (ed.) *AIDS: Cultural Analysis/Cultural Activism* (London: MIT, 1998).

Bernstein, M., 'Celebration and Suppression: the Strategic Uses of Identity by the Lesbian and Gay Movement', *American Journal of Sociology*, 103 (1997): 531-65.

232 *The Gay Republic*

Bertho, A., 'Malaise dans la République', *Mouvements*, 38 (2005): 14-18.

Blais, M.-Cl., 'Une libération problématique', *Le Débat*, 121 (2002): 140-8.

Bonnet, M.-J., 'Gay Mimesis and Misogyny: Two Aspects of the Same Refusal of the Other?' *Journal of homosexuality*, 41 (2001): 265-80.

Borne, D., *Histoire de la société française depuis 1945* (Paris: Armand Collin, 1992).

Borrillo, Daniel, *Homosexualités et droit: de la tolérance à la reconnaissance* (Paris: Presses Universitaires de France, 1998).

___, *L'Homophobie* (Paris: Presses Universitaires de France, 2000).

___, 'L'orientation sexuelle en Europe', *Les Temps modernes*, 609 (2000): 263-82.

Borrillo, Daniel and Lascoumes, P., *Le PaCS, les homosexuels et la gauche* (Paris: Editions de la Découverte, 2002).

Bourcier, M.-H., *Queer Zone* (Paris: Balland, 2001).

Bourdieu, P., *La Distinction. Critique sociale du jugement* (Paris: Editions de Minuit, 1979).

___, *La Domination masculine* (Paris: Seuil, Coll. Liber, 1998).

Bourdieu, Pierre and Passeron, Cl., *La Reproduction* (Paris: Editions de Minuit, 1970).

Bozon, Michel, *Sociologie de la sexualité* (Paris: Nathan, 2002).

___, 'Révolution sexuelle ou individualisation de la sexualité', *Mouvements*, 20 (2002): 15-22.

Breton, Stéphane, 'De la nécessaire clarification du langage juridique', *Esprit*, 285 (2002): 25-54.

___, 'Norme juridique et normalité sociale', *Esprit*, 285 (2002): 56-79.

Brown, M.P., *Replacing Citizenship: AIDS Activism and Radical Democracy* (New York: Guildford Press, 1997).

Busscher, P.O. de and Thiaudière, C., 'Le PaCS: un progrès social ou une avance de l'Etat', *Mouvements*, 8 (2002): 48-53.

Butler, Judith, *Gender Trouble. Feminism and the Subversion of Identity* (New York: Routledge, 1990).

___, *Bodies that Matter. On the Discursive Limits of 'Sex'* (New York: Routledge, 1993).

Butlers, R., McClun, J. and Moon, M., *Displacing Homophobia: Gay Male Perspectives in Literature and Culture* (Duke University Press, 1989).

Cadoret, Anne, *Parenté plurielle, anthropologie du placement familial* (Paris: L'Harmattan, 1995).

___, *Des Parents comme les autres. Homosexualité et parenté* (Paris: Odile Jacob, 2002).

Calvès, G., 'Pour une analyse (vraiment) critique de la discrimination positive', *Le Débat*, 117 (2001): 163-74.

Caron, D., *AIDS in French Culture: Social Ills, Literary Cures* (University of Wisconsin Press, 2001).

Carter, G.M., *ACT-Up, The AIDS War and Activism* (New Jersey: Westfield Press, 1992).

Bibliography

Carrington, C., *No Place like Home. Relationships and Family Life among Lesbians and Gay Men* (Chicago: Univeristy of Chicago Press, 2002).

Castells, M., *Power and Identity: The Information Age. Economy, Society and Culture* (Oxford: Blackwell, 1997).

Chambon, L., 'Le placard universaliste: quand la République se fait particulariste contre les gays', *Mouvements*, 38 (2005): 34-40.

Cohen, E., 'Who are "We"? Gay "Identity" as Political (E)motion', in D. Fuss (ed.) *Inside/Out. Lesbian Theories, Gay Theories* (New York: Routledge, 1991).

Cohen. Ph., *Le Bluff républicain* (Paris: Arléa, 1997).

Cohen-Tanugi, L., *La Métamorphose de la démocratie* (Paris: Odile Jacob, 1989).

Collin, F., 'Le comme un', *Movements*, 38 (2005): 8-13.

Corcuff, Ph., 'L'individualisme contemporain en question', *Le Débat*, 119 (2002): 126-32.

Darmon, M., 'Les "enterprises" de la morale familiale', *French Politics, Culture and Society*, 17 (1999): 11-26.

Debray, Régis, 'Etes-vous démocrate ou républicain?' *Le Nouvel Observateur*, 30 (1989): 49-55.

___, *Que vive la République* (Paris: Odile Jacob, 1998).

Deleuze, G. and Guittari, F., *L'Anti-Oedipe* (Paris: Editions de Minuit, 1972).

Delph, E., *The Silent Community. Public Homosexual Encounters* (London: Sage, 1978).

D'Emilio, John, *Making Trouble. Essays on Gay History, Politics and the University* (New York: Routledge, 1992).

___, *The World Turned. Essays on Gay History, Politics and Culture* (Duke University Press, 2002).

Demorand, N. and Jallon, H., *L'Année des débats 2000-2001* (Paris: Editions de la Découverte, 2000).

Dubreuil, E., *Des Parents de même sexe* (Paris: Odile Jacob, 1998).

Dubreuil, Eric and Gross, M., 'Homosexualité, famille, filiation' *Le Monde*, 12 décembre 1997.

Dumont, Louis, *Homo hierarchicus* (Paris: Gallimard, 1979).

___, *Essais sur l'individualisme* (Paris: Seuil, 1983).

Duvert, C., 'Le droit jetable?: A propos des débats sur l'homoparentalité', *Le Débat*, 131 (2004): 179-92.

Edley, N. and Wetherall, M., *Men in Perspective. Power, Practice and Identity* (New Jersey: Prentice Hall. 1995).

Eliacheff, C., 'Malaise dans la psychanalyse', *Esprit*, 3-4 (2001): 62-76.

Elias, N., *La Civilisation des moeurs* (Paris: Calmann-Lévy, 1973).

Epstein, Steven, *Impure Science. AIDS, Activism and the Politics of Knowledge* (Berkeley: University of California, 1986).

___, 'Gay Politics, Ethnic Identity: The Limits of Social Constructionism', *Socialist Review*, 17 (1987): 9-54.

Eribon, Didier, *Les Etudes gay et lesbiennes: un débat* (Paris: Editions du Centre Georges-Pompidou, 1998).

234 *The Gay Republic*

___, *Réflexions sur la question gay* (Paris: Fayard, 1999).

Fassin, Eric, 'Homosexualité, mariage, famille', *Le Monde*, 5 novembre 1997, p. 21.

___, 'L'illusion anthropologique: homosexualité et filiation', *Témoin*, 12 mai 1998.

___, 'Le savant, l'expert, et le politique. La famille des sociologues', *Genèses*, 32 (1998): 156-69.

___, 'PaCS socialista, la gauche et le "juste milieu", *Le Banquet*, 5 (1998): 12-13.

___, 'Le mariage des homosexuels', *French Politics, Culture and Society*, 17 (1999): 165-79.

___, 'Usages de la science et science des usages: à propos des familles homoparentales', *L'Homme*, 155 (2000): 391-408.

___, *Liberté, actualité, sexualités* (Paris: Belfond, 2003).

Fassin, Eric and Borrillo, D., *Au-delà du PaCS. L'expertise familiale à l'épreuve de l'homosexualité* (Paris: Presses Universitaires de France, 1999).

Fine, Agnès, *Parrains et marraines; la parenté spirituelle en Europe* (Paris: Fayard, 1994).

___, *Adoptions. Ethnologie des parents choisis* (Paris: Editions de la Maison des Sciences de L'Homme, 1998).

___, 'Vers une reconnaissance de la pluriparentalité', *Esprit*, 3-4 (2002): 40-52.

Finkielkraut, Alain, *La Défaite de la pensée* (Paris: Gallimard, 1987).

___, 'La crise de la transmission', *Esprit*, 12 (1996): 54-65.

Flood, C. and Hewitt N., *Currents in Contemporary French Intellectual Life* (Macmillan, 2000).

Flynn, G., *Remaking the Hexagon. The New France in the New Europe* (Westview Press, 1995).

Foucault, M., *Histoire de la sexualité* (Paris: Gallimard, 1976-1984).

Furet, F., Julliard, J. and Rosanvallon, P., *La République du centre* (Paris: Calmann-Lévy, 1988).

Fuss, D., *Inside/Out. Lesbian Theories, Gay Theories* (New York: Routledge, 1991).

Galleotti, A.E., *Toleration as Recognition* (Cambridge: Cambridge University Press, 2002).

Gallo, M., *L'Amour de la France expliquée à mon fils* (Paris: Seuil, 1999).

Garréta, A.F., 'Re-enchanting the Republic: "PaCS", *Parenté* and *Le Symbolique*', *Yale French Studies*, 100 (2001): 145-66.

Gauchet, Michel, *Le Désenchantement du monde* (Paris: Seuil, 1985).

___, 'Les deux sources du processus d'individualisation', *Le Débat*, 119 (2002): 133-37.

Giddens, A., *The Transformation of Intimacy. Sexuality, Love and Eroticism in Modern Societies* (Cambridge: Polity Press, 1992).

Gilbert, G., *Sexuality* (Cambridge: Polity Press, 2004).

Godelier, Michel, *La Production des grands hommes* (Paris: Fayard, 1982).

___, *L'Idée et le matériel* (Paris: Fayard, 1984).

Bibliography 235

___, 'La sexualité est toujours autre chose qu'elle même', *Esprit*, 3-4 (2001): 96-104.

Gross, Martine, *Homoparentalités, état des lieux. Parentés et différence des sexes* (Paris: ESF Editeur, 2000).

___, 'Séparer les trois volets de la filiation', *Libération*, 10 août 2004, p. 23.

Hargreaves, A., *Immigration, Race and Ethnicity in Contemporary France* (London: Routledge, 1995).

Hauser, J., *La Filiation* (Paris: Dalloz, 1996).

Hefez, S., 'La vraie crise, celle de la fusion', *Libération*, 2 août 2004, p. 30.

Heinach, N., 'Lorsque le sexe paraît: de quelques confusions dans des débats brûlants', *Le Débat*, 131 (2004): 170-78.

Herek, G.M. and Berrill K., *Hate Crimes: Confronting Violence against Lesbians and Gay Men* (London: Sage, 1992).

Héritier, Françoise, 'La cuisse de Jupiter. Réflexions sur les nouveaux modes de procréation', *L'Homme*, 94 (1994): 5-22.

___, *Masculin/Féminin, la pensée de la différence* (Paris: Odile Jacob, 1996).

___, 'Articulations et substances', *L'Homme*, 154-155 (2000): 391-408.

Hermet, G., *La Trahison démocratique: populistes, républicains, et démocrates* (Paris: Flammarion, 1988).

Hocquenghem, G., *Le Désir homosexuel* (Paris: Editions Universitaires, 1972).

Howarth, J. and Ross G., *Contemporary France. A Review of Interdisciplinary Studies* (Pinter Press, 1988).

Humphrey, J., 'To Queer or not to Queer a Lesbian and Gay Group? Sexual and Gendered Politics at the Turn of the Century', *Sexualities*, 2 (1999): 223-46.

Iacub, Marcela, 'Le couple homosexuel, le droit et l'ordre symbolique', *Le Banquet*, 12-13 (1998): 111-24.

___, 'Homoparentalité et ordre procréatif' in E. Fassin and D. Borrillo (eds), *Au-delà du PaCS* (Paris: Presses Universitaires de France, 1999).

___, 'Reproduction et division juridique des sexes', *Les Temps modernes*, 606 (2000): 243-62.

___, 'Les fécondations artificielles, le droit et la nature,' *Vacarme*, 14 (2000): 33-6.

___, 'Légaliser la gestation pour autrui', *Libération*, 10 août 2004, p. 23.

Jackson, S. and Scott, S., *A Sociological Reader* (New York: Routledge, 2002).

Jallon, H. and Mounier P., *Les Enragés de la république* (Paris: Editions de la Découverte, 1999).

Jelen, C., *La France éclatée, ou les reculades de la république* (Paris: NiL Editions, 1996).

Jordan, M.D., *The Silence of Sodom. Homosexuality in Modern Catholicism* (Chicago: University of Chicago Press, 2002).

Kandel, L., 'Sur la différence des sexes et celle des féminismes', *Les Temps modernes*, 609 (2000): 283-306.

Kaplan, M.B., *Sexual Justice. Democratic Citizenship and the Politics of Desire* (New York: Routledge, 1997).

Kaufmann, J.-Cl., 'L'expression de soi', *Le Débat*, 119 (2002): 116-25.

Kosofsky Sedgwick, E., *Epistemology of the Closet* (Berkeley: University of California Press, 1990).

Kriegel, B., *La Philosophie de la république* (Paris: Plon, 1998).

Labrusse-Riou, C., 'La filiation en mal d'institution', *Esprit*, 12 (1996): 91-110.

Lara, Ph. de, 'Une anthropologie du point du vue juridique', *Le Débat*, 121 (2002): 149-53.

Larouche, J.-M., *Reconnaissance et citoyenneté: au carrefour de l'éthique et du politique* (Sainte-Foy: Presses de l'Universite du Québec, 2003).

Laudet, Cl. and Cox. R., *Le Peuple de France aujourd'hui* (Manchester University Press, 1995).

Lauretis, T.de, 'Queer Theory: Lesbian and Gay Sexualities', *Difference*, 3 (1991): iii-xviii.

Le Bitoux, J., 'The Construction of a Political and Media Presence: The Homosexual Liberation Groups in France between 1975-1978', *Journal of Homosexuality*, 41 (2001): 249-64.

Lebovics, H., *True France. The Wars over Cultural Identity 1900-1945* (Cornell University Press, 1992).

Legendre, Ph., *L'Inestimable objet de la transmission; études sur les principes généalogiques en Occident* (Paris: Fayard, 1985).

Le Goff, J.-P., *Mai 68, l'héritage impossible* (Paris: Editions de la Découverte, 1998).

Léobon, A., 'La communauté homosexuelle: processus d'intégration et dynamique sociospatiales' in C. Bard (eds) *Le Genre des territoires: féminin, masculin, neutre* (Presses de l'Université d'Angers, 2004).

Lestrade, D., *ACT-Up, une histoire* (Paris: Denoël, 2000).

Le Pourhiet, Anne-Marie, 'Pour une analyse critique de la discrimination positive', *Le Débat*, 114 (2001): 166-77.

___, 'Deux conceptions du droit', *Le Débat*, 117 (2001): 175-8.

___, 'Egalité et différence dans la France contemporaine', *Revue politique et parlementaire*, 1017-18 (2002): 44-9.

Leroy-Forgeot, Françoise, *Histoire juridique de l'homosexualité en Europe* (Paris: Presses Universitaires de France, 1997).

___, *Les Enfants du PaCS; réalités de l'homoparentalité* (Paris: L'Atelier de l'Archer, 1999).

Leroy-Forgeot, Françoise and Mécary, C., *Le Couple homosexuel et le droit* (Paris: Odile Jacob, 2001).

Lipovetsky, G., *L'Ère du vide: essai sur l'individualisme contemporain* (Paris: Seuil, 1983).

Livia, A., 'Public and Clandestine: Gay Men's Pseudonyms on the French Minitel', *Sexualities*, 5 (2002): 201-17.

Logan, C.R., 'Homophobia? No, Homoprejudice', *Journal of Homosexuality*, 31 (1996): 31-53.

Maniglier, P., 'L'humanisme interminable de Claude Lévi-Strauss', *Les Temps modernes*, 609 (2002): 216-41.

Bibliography

Marks, J. and McCaffrey, E., *French Cultural Debates* (Monash Romance Studies Series, 2001).

Martel, Frédéric, *Le Rose et le noir* (Paris: Editions du Seuil, 1996).

___, 'Gay, chronique d'une émancipation', *Le Débat*, 112 (2002): 78-80.

Mason, A. and Palmer, A., *Queer Bashing* (London: Stonewall, 1998).

McGhee, D., 'Beyond Toleration: Privacy, Citizenship and Sexual Minorities in England and Wales', *The British Journal of Sociology*, 3 (2004): 357-75.

Mécary, C., *Droit et homosexualité. Etat de droit* (Paris: Dalloz, 2000).

Mendès-Leite, R., *Le Sens de l'alterité. Penser les homosexualités* (Paris: L'Harmattan, 2000).

Merin, Y., *Equality for Same-Sex Couples* (Chicago: University of Chicago Press, 2002).

Montesquieu, baron de, *De l'Esprit des lois* (Paris: Garnier Frères, 1748).

Montouh, H., 'L'esprit d'une loi. Controverses sur le Pacte civil de solidarité', *Les Temps modernes*, 603 (1999): 190-204.

Muray, Ph., 'Reconnaissance', *Le Débat*, 112 (2000): 128-31.

Murphy, T. and Poirier, S., *Writing AIDS: Gay Liberation, Language and Analysis* (New York: Columbia University Press, 1993).

Nadaud, S., *Homoparentalité. Une nouvelle chance pour la famille?* (Paris: Fayard, 2002).

Nahoum-Grappe, V., 'Le cortège des sexualités', *Esprit*, 273 (2001): 254-60.

Naouri, A., 'Maintenir la fonction paternelle, même artificiellement', *Libération*, 3 août 2004, p. 27.

Noiriel, G., *Le Creuset français* (Paris: Seuil, 1998).

Ory, Pierre, *L'Entre deux mai. Histoire culturelle de la France, mai 1968-1981* (Paris: Seuil, 1983).

___, *L'Aventure culturelle française 1945-1989* (Paris: Flammarion, 1989).

Patton, C., 'Tremble, Hetero Swine!' in M. Warner (ed.) *Fear of a Queer Planet. Queer Theory and Social Theory* (University of Minnesota Press, 1993).

Piriou, A., 'Homos: l'égalité démocratique', *Libération*, 28 juin 2004, p. 39.

Pisier, Evelyne, 'PaCS et parité: du même et de l'autre', *Le Monde*, 20 octobre 1998, p. 18.

___, 'Du PaCS et de l'ambiguïté d'une tolérance', *Revue des deux mondes*, décembre (1999): 153-61.

___, 'Adoption: la justice du divan?', *Revue des deux mondes*, mai (2001): 88-92.

___, 'Sexes et sexualités: bonnes et mauvaises différences', *Les Temps modernes*, 609 (2000): 157-75.

Plummer, Ken, *The Making of the Modern Homosexual* (London: Hutchinson, 1981).

___, *Modern Homosexualities. Fragments of Gay and Lesbian Experience* (London: Routledge, 1992).

Policar, A., 'Revendications homosexuelles et droits de l'homme', *Libération*, 11 août 2004, p. 27.

Poulantzas, A., 'Du PaCS à la famille homoparentale: quel avenir pour la parenté?' in N. Demorand and H. Jallon (eds), *L'Année des débats 2000-2001* (Paris: Editions de la Découverte, 2000).

Pouliquen, J.P. and Quinqueton, D., 'Le PaCS est-il républicain?', *Le Monde*, 12 octobre 1999, p. 19.

Pratt, Murray, 'The Defence of the Straight State: Heteronormativity, AIDS in France, and the Space of the Nation', *French Cultural Studies*, 27 (1998): 263-80.

___, 'Post-Queer and Beyond the PaCS: Contextualising French Responses to the Civil Solidarity Pact' in K. Chedgzoy, E. Francis and M. Pratt (eds), *In a Queer Place. Sexuality and Belonging in British and European Contexts* (Ashgate, 2002).

Prokhoris, S., *Le Sexe prescrit. La différence sexuelle en question* (Paris: Aubier, 2000).

Redman, P., '"Tarred with the Same Brush": 'Homophobia' and the Roles of the Unconscious in School-Based Cultures of Masculinity', *Sexualities*, 3 (2000): 438-99.

Renault, A., 'L'enfant dans la dynamique de la modernité', *Le Débat*, 121 (2002): 167-75.

Reubach, A., *Intellos précaires. La culture gaie et lesbienne* (Paris: Fayard, 2004).

Rosanvallon, P., *Le Peuple introuvable* (Paris: Gallimard, 1998).

Roudinesco, Elisabeth, 'Une parité régressive', *Le Monde*, 11 février 1999, p. 12.

___, 'Psychanalyse, famille, homosexualité', *Revue des deux mondes*, mai (2001): 103-7.

Sageot, Cl., 'Aux sources de l'adoption', *Libération*, 13 août 2004, p. 33.

Schor, N., 'The Crisis of French Universalism', *Yale French Studies*, 100 (2001): 43-64.

Segal, N., *André Gide: Pederasty and Pedagogy* (Clarendon Press: University of Oxford, 1998).

Seidman, Steven, 'Identity and Politics in a "Postmodern" Gay Culture: Some Historical and Conceptual Notes', in M. Warner (ed.) *Fear of a Queer Planet. Queer Theory and Social Theory* (University of Minnesota Press, 1993).

___, *Queer Theory/Sociology* (Oxford: Blackwell, 1996).

___, *Difference Troubles. Queering Social Theory and Sexual Politics* (Cambridge University Press, 1997).

___, *Beyond the Closet: The Transformation of Gay and Lesbian Life* (New York and London: Routledge, 2002).

Seidman, Steven, Meeks, C., Traschen, F., 'Beyond the Closet? The Changing Social Meaning of Homosexuality in the United States', *Sexualities*, 2 (1999): 9-34.

Simmel, G., 'On the Sociology of the Family', *Theory, Culture and Society*, 15 (1998): 283-93.

Bibliography

Slama, Alain Gérard, 'Democratic Dysfunctions and Republican Obsolescence: The Demise of French Exceptionalism' in G. Flynn (ed.) *Remaking the Hexagon: The New France in the New Europe* (Westview Press, 1995).

___, *La Régression démocratique* (Paris: Fayard, 1995).

Steinberg, S., 'L'inégalité entre les sexes et l'égalité entre les hommes', *Esprit*, 3-4 (2001): 23-39.

Stychin, C.F., 'A Queer Nation by Rights: European Integration, Sexual Identity Politics, and the Discourse of Rights', in K. Chedgzoy, E. Francis and M. Pratt (eds), *In a Queer Place. Sexuality and Belonging in British and European Contexts* (Ashgate, 2002).

Sullivan, Andrew, *Virtually Normal. An Argument about Homosexuality* (London: Picador, 1995).

___, *Same-Sex Marriage: Pro and Con* (New York: Vintage Books, 1997).

___, *Love Undetectable: Reflections on Friendship, Sex and Survival* (New York: A.A. Knopf, 1998).

Singly, Francois de, *Le Soi, le couple, la famille* (Paris: Nathan, 1996).

___, *Sociologie de la famille contemporaine* (Paris: Nathan, 1998).

___, 'Famille démocratique ou individus tyranniques', *Libération*, 27 juillet 2004, p. 31.

Taguieff, P.-A., *La République menacée* (Paris: Editions Textuels, 1996).

Théry, Irène, *Le Démariage. Justice et vie privée* (Paris: Odile Jacob, 1993).

___, 'Différence des sexes et différence des générations. L'institution familiale en déshérence', *Esprit*, 12 (1996): 65-90.

___, 'Le contrat d'union sociale en question', *Esprit*, 236 (1997): 159-87.

___, 'L'homme désafillié', *Esprit*, 12 (1998): 50-4.

___, *Couple, filiation et parenté aujourd'hui. Le droit face aux mutations de la famille et de la vie privée* (Paris: Odile Jacob, 1998).

___, 'L'avenir à reculons', *Esprit*, 240 (1999): 72-85.

___, 'PaCS, sexualité et différence des sexes', *Esprit*, 257 (1999): 139-81.

___, 'L'autre en soi; l'intolérance à la mixité', *Revue des deux mondes*, décembre (1999): 143-52.

___, 'La côte d'Adam. Retour sur le pardaoxe démocratique', *Esprit*, 3-4 (2001): 10-22.

Tin, L.-G., *Dictionnaire de l'homophobie* (Paris: Presses Universitaires de France, 2002).

Tisseron, S., 'Le rapt des origines', *Libération*, 12 août 2004, p. 27.

Tort, Michel, 'Homophobies psychanalytiques', *Le Monde*, 15 octobre 1999, p. 18.

___, 'Quelques conséquences de la différence "psychanalytique" des sexes', *Les Temps modernes*, 609 (2000): 170-215.

Verdier, P., *L'Adoption aujourd'hui* (Paris: Editions Bayard, 1999).

Vigarello, G., 'Les paradigmes d'une histoire de l'enfance', *Le Débat*, 121 (2002): 154-57.

Vincent, T., *L'Indifférence des sexes: critique psychanalytique de Bourdieu et l'idée de domination masculine* (Strasbourg: Editions Arcanes, 2002).

240 *The Gay Republic*

Wallach Scott, Joan, *Gender and the Politics of History* (New York: Columbia University Press, 1998).

___, *La Citoyenne paradoxale. Les féministes françaises et les droits de l'homme.* (Paris: Albin Michel, 1998).

___, 'Feminist Family Politics', *French Politics, Culture and Society*, 17 (1999): 12-23.

Warner, M., *Fear of a Queer Planet. Queer Theory and Social Theory* (University of Minnesota Press, 1993).

Weston, K., *Families We Choose* (New York: Columbia University Press, 1997).

Winter, J.-P., 'Du phantasme à la loi: la question de l'homoparentalité', *Revue des deux mondes*, mai (2001): 93-102.

Weeks, Jeffrey, *Sex, Politics and Society: The Regulation of Society since 1800* (London: Longman, 1981).

___, *Sexuality and its Discontents: Myths, Meanings and Modern Sexualities* (London: Routledge and Kegan Paul, 1985).

___, *Invented Moralities: Sexual Values in an Age of Uncertainty* (Cambridge: Polity Press, 1995).

___, 'The Sexual Citizen', *Theory, Culture and Society*, 15 (1998): 35-52.

Wittig, M., *La Pensée straight* (Paris: Baland, 2001).

Yonnet, P., 'PaCS: un mariage républicain', *Le Débat*, 12 (2000): 105-8.

Youf, D., 'Construire un droit de l'enfance', *Le Débat*, 121 (2002): 158-66.

Zucker-Rouvillois, E., 'L'expertise familiale ou la perte du doute scientifique', in E. Fassin and D. Borrillo (eds), *Au-delà du PaCS* (Paris: Presses Universitaires de France, 1999).

Index

'accouchement sous X' 156, 156n50
ACT-Up New York 120
ACT-Up Paris 111, 120–130, 132,
   171, 182n35, 198–9, 201
   communitarianism of 120
   community of 120
   counter-productive policies of
      182
   and the militant homosexual
      couple 181–2
   'outing' policy 182, 216, 217,
      218–20, 221–2, 228–9
   and positive discrimination 127–
      9, 228
Adam 46
adoption/filiation 63, 137–9, 141–2
   adoption case studies 142–50
   amongst African tribes 163–4
   and the child's rights of origin
      150–157, 153n41, 162, 164
   constructing filiation 155
   'désaffiliation' 157–64
   historical context of filiation 155
   horizontal filiation 161–2
   and the law 138, 142–9, 152–3,
      156, 162–5
   and the maternal/paternal axis
      150–157
   open adoptions 142, 164, 165
   opposition to gay adoption 58,
      142–50
   origins of adoption 142
   'pluriparentalité' 157–64,
      185n44
   undisclosed adoptions 142–3,
      162, 164
   see also 'homoparentalité'
African tribes, filiation 163–4
Agacinski, Sylviane 33–4, 37, 53,
      53n29, 54, 70, 150n29, 182–

4, 185, 186, 188
agency 64, 87, 89
   as prerequisite to the social 226–
      7
   social as prerequisite to 90, 226
Aides group 111, 121–2, 126
AIDS
   and ACT-UP Paris 120–122,
      124, 129
   crisis 102, 107, 120–122, 228
   see also HIV
Anatrella, Tony 65–6, 67–8n73, 214
Annual Conference of Bishops, 1998
      181
anthropology
   dual nature of 55
   and 'la différence des sexes' 43–
      64
   relative norms of 60
   universalist tendencies of 59
anti-PaCS demonstrations 207, 216,
      219
APGL (L'Association des parents et
      futurs parents gays et
      lesbiens) 143–4, 161, 162–3,
      164
Arcat-Sida 126
argumentation 167, 214
artificial insemination 79, 161, 162
asceticism, gay 229
assimilationism 33
assisted reproductive techniques 79,
      79–80, 142, 149, 158, 161,
      162
*Association pour la fondation de
      service politique* (AFSP) 21
authenticity 229
autonomy, individual 81–2, 84–7,
      90, 93

242 *The Gay Republic*

Bachelot, Roselyne 22–3
Bakchine, Serge 150–151
Barraud, Cécile 48, 60n51, 64
Bech, Henning 132, 222
Bendle, Mervyn 109, 113–14n29, 116, 130–131
Bernstein, Mary 110, 111, 112, 116, 117, 129, 196
Bersani, Leo 10, 72–3, 74, 75, 97, 101, 103, 110–11n19, 131, 205, 205n25, 208, 228
Bertho, Alain 225–6, 227, 229
'Bien' 35, 36
Bill of Human Rights (UK) 209n29
Billé, Louis-Marie 21, 22, 23, 25
Bioethics 142–3
biological determinism 61, 62, 64
biological difference 126
    'la différence des sexes' as (essentialist position) 37–8, 45, 47–58, 57n43, 61, 63–4, 66, 69–73, 130, 155, 182, 185, 188, 213, 216
biological parents 146
birth act 158
birth rates
    falling 19–20, 20n10
    outside marriage 20, 20n11
bishops 22, 180, 181
Bloche, Patrick 211
Bodin, Jean 35
body
    death of the sexual 63
    and the 'personne juridique' (social use of) 83, 84, 92
    as puppet of nature and culture 62–3
    sexualisation of the 49, 50, 51, 63
    and the 'sujet du désir' (private use of) 83, 84
Bonnet, Marie-Jo 37–8, 121n50, 132, 171–2, 179, 195, 196–8, 199–203, 206, 207, 215, 222, 223
Borrillo, Daniel 94–6, 94n39, 139,

153–4, 215n40, 219
Bosset, Bernard 108, 123
Bourcier, Marie-Hélène 71
Bourdieu, Pierre 10, 88, 88n27, 101–8, 111, 112, 112n25, 117–18, 119, 120, 122, 123–5, 127, 128, 129, 130, 131, 132–3, 139, 141, 159, 170, 181, 193, 194, 195, 201, 221, 227
bourgeois 159
Boutin, Christine 21, 27, 207
Bové, José 78
Bozon, Michel 4–5, 9–10
Breton, Stéphane 82–8, 90, 91–3, 96, 97, 226
Britain
    Bill of Human Rights 209n29
    citizenship 3n5
    same-sex marriage 6
Butler, Judith 73, 114–15

Cadoret, Anne 63
Calvès, Gwénaële 128
Castells, Manuel 109, 116
Catholic church 19–26, 41, 75, 158
    and homosexuality 21–27, 23n21, 41–2
    and 'la différence des sexes' 52, 182
    and the PaCS 15, 20–23, 24
    and political economy 25
census 76
children
    and PaCS 26
    symbolism of 147, 151–2
    see also adoption/filiation
citizenship 1–4
    British 3n5
    and constitutions 76–7
    democratic 18, 29, 137, 140–141, 148
    equality of 5–6, 188
    and freedom 76–7
    homosexual 1, 3, 5–6, 137–40, 226, 228
    legal redefinition of 95

politicisation of 15, 18–19, 29
and sexual orientation 3, 4
shifting definitions of 3
and social space 9
see also French republican
citizenship; sexual citizenship
civil society *see laïque* society
closet 196, 220–222
CNRS 212
Code du travail, Article 122-45, 210
cohabitation
legal issues 6–7
rising trend of 20, 20n12
Cohen, Ed 116, 118–19, 118n44,
131, 132–3
Cohen-Tanugi, Laurent 78
Collin, Françoise 54, 225–6, 227,
229
Collin, Thibauld 21
'coming out' 107, 108, 133, 220–
222, 229
'rhetoric' 113–15, 114n30, 118,
131
'commun' 225–6
communitarianism 17, 19, 127, 180–
183, 185, 188, 193, 198, 222,
228
and concubinage 177–8
and homosexual identity 103,
105, 121–3
and republicanism 171–2
community, lesbian/gay 102, 120–
124
concubinage/*union libre* 6, 20n12,
30, 33, 169–81, 190, 194
contracts for 174
definitions of 173–5, 179
demise of 175, 176
heterosexual 177, 179
and the law 169–70, 173–8, 179–
81
legal rights of 169–70
and material assets 174
and PaCS 179–81
constitutions
and citizenship 76–7

freedom of 76–7
French 1, 2
written 1
constructionism
construction of filiation 155
construction of gender 70–71
construction of identity 70
construction of 'la différence des
sexes' 47, 47n4, 48, 50–52,
57, 63–4, 70–73, 182, 188
construction of lesbian and gay
identity 74, 101, 112–13, 115,
130–131
construction of sexuality 10
essentialism within 109, 113,
116, 131
see also deconstructionism
Corcuff, Philippe 80, 80n14
couples, gay 167–94
concubinage/*union libre* 169–70,
173–81, 194
marriage 189–94, 189n56,
192n72
private/public dialectic 181–8
creation mythology 46–7
CUS 169–70, 175–7, 179, 191

De Certeau 113
De l'Esprit des lois (Montesquieu)
75–6, 78
death, rationalising of 51n23
Debray, Régis 16, 17, 18, 19, 30, 31
deconstructionism 118–19, 118n45
decriminalisation of homosexuality
94
defamation 208–9, 216, 217
dehumanisation of homosexuality 95
Dekeuwer-Défossez, Françoise 173
Delaisi de Parseval, Geneviève 79,
149
democracy 2, 9, 36, 156–7
and the church 23–4
and citizen/constitution
inequality 76
and control of the social sphere
11

and homosexual identity 103
and 'la différence des sexes' 58
and the public face of
homosexuality 25
and sociology 60–61
democracy/republicanism binary 41–
2, 77, 81–2, 138, 156, 159,
167
and the gay community 122
tensions of 108
democracy/universalism binary 171–
2
democratic citizenship 18, 29, 140–
141
definition 140
and gay adoption/filiation 137,
148
responsible 140, 141
democratic egalitarianism 17
'democratic republic' 149
'democratic woman' 92
democratisation 32, 42, 156–7, 159
of the family 159, 160
immunity of universalism to 195
location within the social 30
of the private life 12, 139–40,
149
of the republic 15, 17, 28, 29,
139, 149, 187–8
and sexual difference 38
Denmark 6
Derrida, Jacques 34, 113
'désaffiliation' 157–64
desire
heterosexuals as subjects of 183,
184
homosexuals as objects of 183,
184
legislation of 181
difference 11
as claim to inclusion 140
constraint of 78
and equality 76
strategies of 108–13, 116–19,
118n44, 120, 129, 131
and universalism 33–8, 34n45,

227
see also diversity; 'la différence
des sexes'; sexual difference
differentialism 78–9, 82, 93
discrimination 204
against gay filiation 143–5, 154,
161
against homosexual unions 170
anti-discriminatory legislation
208–12, 209n29, 222–3
in the workplace 203, 209, 210,
222–3
see also homophobia; positive
discrimination
disembodiment 63
displacement 204
dissolution of homosexuality 202
diversity 8, 12, 18
see also difference
divorce 160, 161
rates of 20, 20n13
dominant order
subversion of 10–11
see also heteronormative order;
masculine heterosexual
domination
double bind, of homosexuality 24
Douste-Blazy 27
Dubreuil, Eric 150, 153, 161–2
Dumont, Louis 46, 47
Duvert, Cyrille 58n45

egalitarianism, democratic 17
'égalité de droit' 127
'égalité de fait' 127
Eire 3n5
Eliacheff, Caroline 64–5
Elovich, Richard 121
embodiment 119
see also disembodiment
Emmanuelle B (case study) 143–4,
145, 149
enlightenment, and sexual difference
49, 50–52, 63
Epstein, Steven 117, 118, 118n44
equality 75–6, 139–41, 154

of citizenship 5–6, 188
and difference 76
for homosexuals 11–12, 22–3,
30, 168, 171
of laws 3
and the post-PaCS debate 139
of rights 4, 5, 7–8, 11–12, 15
sexual 11–12, 22–3, 30, 37, 42,
53n29, 168, 171, 199, 200,
201, 203
universal 18, 31, 33–42, 128,
140–141, 171, 176, 180–181,
187
women's 37, 198
see also inequality
Eribon, Didier 10, 101, 102, 104,
116n36, 118, 131, 132–3,
194, 220, 221, 228, 229
Erikson, E. 113–14n29
'esprit de loi' 83
Esprit (journal) 53, 82, 154, 157
essentialism
and gay identity 74, 109, 113,
130–131
and 'la différence des sexes' 47,
48–58, 61, 63–4, 66, 69–73,
130, 155, 182, 188, 213, 216
within constructionism 109, 113,
116, 131
ethnic model 117, 117n39
Etudes (journal) 24
euphemisms, and homosexuality 94–
5, 94n39
European Court of Human Rights
144, 191
European law 78, 98
European parliament 209
Eve 46
exclusion 30, 38, 53
of women 35, 36
experts 78–9, 98

'fait social' 11, 89–93, 96, 101, 102,
227
family 156–9
breakdown 160

as category 159
decline of the 141–2n10, 156–61
deinstitutionalisation 159
democratisation 159, 160
destabilisation 32
far-right views on 25, 41
heterosexual model of the 154,
159
homosexuality as threat to 65–6
individualisation of the 159
mythical ideal of the 32
and the PaCS 20–21, 32
size 19
and the state 157–8, 159
traditional 19, 32–3, 41
and 'une politique familiale' 19
see also step-families
Fassin, Eric 7–8, 53, 54–5, 56, 57–
61, 69, 75, 139, 140, 150,
151, 153–4, 157, 168, 170,
178, 188, 189, 191, 192, 193,
194, 196
father, infantile identification
with/desire for 204–5
feminism 197–201
and 'la Différence' 48–9
and 'la différence des sexes' 54
and the PaCS 54
politicised 37
and psychoanalysis 64–5
FHAR (Front Homosexuel pour
Action Révolutionnaire) 197–
9, 202
fidelity 190
filiation see adoption/filiation
Fine, Agnès 142, 161, 163–4, 171
Finkielkraut, Alain 156, 157, 159,
160
Folléa, Laurence 219
Foucault, Michel 52, 131, 227, 229
Fourest, Caroline 207
freedom 76–7
of expression 3
of the individual 86–7
Freedom of the Press law 1881,
amendment 2004 138, 208–9,

211
French republican citizenship 1, 2–4, 8, 11–12, 168
  adoption/filiation 137
  contemporary 15–16
  and difference 227
  formulation of 15
  ideal 11
  and the public/private binary 31
  rapprochement with gay citizenship 137
  relocation 226
  and sexual difference 45
  subversion of 12
French Revolution 49
Fretté, Philippe 144–5, 146, 148, 149
Freud, Sigmund 65, 66, 67, 68, 204
Freudian theory 69, 70, 204–5
frugality 76
Furet, François 77

Garlick, Steve 51n20, 51n23
Garréta, Anne F. 37, 42, 61–2, 63, 143n14, 186n48
Gauchet, Marcel 10, 89–91, 93, 95, 96, 97–8, 101, 137, 171, 195, 227
gay identity *see* lesbian and gay identity
Gay Men's Health Crisis (GMHC) 121
Gay Pride 103, 107, 108, 109, 120–121, 123, 129
  see also Lesbian and Gay Pride march
gender, social construction of 70–71
gender identity 71, 72
general, theory of the (Rousseau) 76
Gernsheim, Elisabeth-Beck 164
Giddens, Anthony 109
globalisation 16
Gloss 71
God 51–2
Godelier, Maurice 62–3
Golias (Catholic journal) 21
good, common 149

see also 'Bien'
Gross, Martine 153n41, 162
guilt 227

habitudes 88–9, 97
habitus 88–9, 88n27, 97, 221
hajib (headscarf), banning of the 3n5, 106
Handman, Marie-Elisabeth 64, 71
Hauser, Jean 169
Heinach, Natalie 34n45
Héritier, Françoise 58, 59, 59n46, 60, 150n31
heteronormative order 53–4, 61, 70, 73, 201, 228
  and the closet 220–221
  domination of homosexuality 193
  and filiation 146
  and homosexual mimesis 195, 197
  privileging of the 214–15
heterosexism 40, 41, 53
heterosexual model of the family 154, 159
heterosexuality 199
  gay sex as threat to 205–6
  symbolic order of 60
  see also heteronormative order; masculine heterosexual domination
historicism 56, 61
historicity 56, 57
HIV 124, 171
  see also AIDS
Hobbes, Thomas 35
Hocquenghem, Guy 73, 110–11n19, 131, 228
holistic societies 49–50
'homoparentalité' 58n45, 147
  opposition to 58, 59n46, 65
  see also adoption/filiation
homophobia 9, 155, 195–223
  and the AIDS crisis 107
  anti-discriminatory legislation against 208–12, 209n29, 222–

3
contextualisation 206
definition 204
generic 217–18
inevitable nature of 207
linguistic 217–18
and mimesis 201–2
and 'outing' 204, 211, 216–22
of psychoanalysis 67
psychological theory of 204–5, 206
of the right 27
silent/verbal dialectic 206–9, 210, 215
sociological theory of 205–6
as threat to new ideologies 212–16
violence of 196, 202
and workplace discrimination 203, 209, 210, 222–3
homoprejudice 204
Homosexualité et socialisme 210–11

Iacub, Marcela 52, 63, 78n11, 79–80n13, 139, 153–4, 153n41, 158, 162, 212
idealism, republican 16–17, 31
identification
with otherness 118
paternal 204–5
sexual 118
identity
construction 70
gender 71, 72
national 18
universal 70
see also lesbian and gay identity; sexual identity
identity categories 115
identity politics 115–19, 122, 132–3
immigration
contemporary issues 3, 3n5
as danger to the republic 16
gay partners' rights 125
and universal equality 33, 34
in vitro fertilisation 158

incest 151
individual(s) 11
autonomy of 81–2, 84–7, 90, 93
dependence on society 87, 88–91, 96
freedom of 86–7
legal definition of 82
legal recognition of 97–8
as 'personne juridique' 82–4, 86, 90–93, 95–7
rights of 25
role in society 80–81
and the social 10, 87–93, 96, 98, 99
socialisation of 81, 88–90
state participation and representation 29
submission to the whole 77
as 'sujet du désir' 82–7, 90–92, 96–7
individualisation 4, 88–91
culture of 156–7
of the family 159
individualism 12, 180
as danger to society 80n14
extreme 9, 80, 99
and 'la différence des sexes' 65–6
and the law 80–81
move towards 20, 32–3
über 99
inequality
of citizen/constitution 76
homosexual and the law 176
marriage and 188–93
women and 35, 172, 203
inheritance rights 125
'insémination artificielle avec donneur' (IAD) 79
institutionalisation 202
institutions 105
integrationism 110–11, 122, 123, 140, 171, 181–4, 193, 201, 222, 226, 228
integrationism/communitarianism, *rapprochement* 171

248 *The Gay Republic*

invisibility
 of homophobia 207–8, 210, 215
 of homosexuality 104, 107, 207–8, 215, 221

'je', tyranny of the 80
Jésu, Frédéric 151
John Paul II, Pope 21
Jospin, Lionel 26, 172, 191, 207
Journal du sida 122
Journal of Homosexuality 196
judges 78–9, 98
juridic culture
 arbitrational 78–81, 98
 assimilatory 78, 80–81, 98
'Juste' 35, 36

Kandel, Liliane 49, 54, 57
Kaufmann, Jean-Claude 88–9, 90, 97
Kriegel, Blandine 16, 18–19, 31

La Déclaration des droits de l'homme 1, 2, 89
 contemporary relevance 2
'la Différence' 48–9
'la différence des sexes' 8, 34, 37–41, 45–74, 102–3, 178, 178n27, 181–8, 182n35, 192, 225, 228
 anthropological perspective on 54–64
 as biological difference (essentialist position) 37–8, 45, 47, 48–58, 57n43, 61, 63–4, 66, 69–73, 130, 155, 182, 185, 188, 213, 216
 and democracy 58
 holistic approach to 49–50, 61
 and homophobia 213–14, 216
 and homosexual filiation 151–2, 154–5, 164
 normalisation of 37–8, 37n52, 40, 45, 48, 63
 politicisation of 53
 and psychoanalysis 64–9, 70
 queer theory of 48, 70–74

replacement with individualism 65–6
 and social agency 64
 social construction of ('sexe social') 47, 47n4, 48, 50–52, 57, 63–4, 70–73, 182, 188
 symbolic order of 52, 53, 54, 61–2, 63–4, 186–7
 used as argument against 'homoparentalité' 147
 used as weapon against gay equality 154, 164
'la différence entre les sexes' 47
La Domination masculine (Bourdieu) 101, 102, 108, 112, 112n25, 120, 122, 130, 139
'la loi Mattéi' 143
La Revue des deux mondes (journal) 212
'la vie privée' 8, 18, 24–5, 29, 33–34, 38–9, 75, 180, 194, 218
 see also private life/space
Labrusse-Riou, Catherine 155–6, 158–9, 160, 164
Lacan, Jacques 67, 68
Lacanian theory 66–7, 69, 70
laïque society 22, 25, 28
language
 and the law 84–5, 86–7
 of negotiation 163
Languerrand, Emeric 122
latent homosexuality 192
Lauretis, Teresa de 104n3, 109
law 11, 93–9, 196
 and adoption/filiation 138, 142–9, 152–3, 156, 162–5
 anti-discrimination 208–12, 209n29, 222–3
 and arbitrational juridic culture 78–81, 98
 as artificial 85
 and assimilatory juridic culture 78, 80–81, 98
 and concubinage/*union libre* 169–70, 173–8, 179–81

crisis of 75–99, 101, 227
decentralisation 80
equality of 3
European 78, 98
and the 'fait social' 11, 89–93, 96, 101
and homosexual inequality 176
and judges and experts 78–9, 98
and language 84–5, 86–7
legitimacy of 81, 89–93, 96, 97, 98, 99, 101, 226–7
and the Madison model 78
mythology of 86
and norms 85–6, 90
and PaCS 93–6, 97
and the 'personne juridique' 82–4, 86, 90–93, 95–7
and the private lives of individuals 79–80, 148–9
and the promotion of inequality 78n11
'règle' 11
and social reality 90
and social space 75, 79
submission to 77
and the 'sujet du désir' 82–7, 90–92, 96–7
and universalism 82, 99
see also legal recognition of homosexuals
Le Débat (journal) 80n14, 88
Le Monde (newspaper) 28, 123, 124, 126, 144, 150, 151, 153–4, 157, 173
Le Pacte d'intérêt commun (PIC) 169
Le Pourhiet, Anne-Marie 34n45, 36n50
Le Zoo 71
leaseholds 174
Lefort, Claude 10, 29–30, 31, 75, 171
left, political and intellectual 28–33
and the PaCS 28–9, 30, 31–2
and social change 30–31
legal recognition of homosexuals 32, 180, 194
homophobic response to 207–8, 215
illusory 200, 202
and PaCS 29, 32, 39, 42, 97, 111, 138, 165, 168, 180, 200, 202
right's opposition to 26–7
and same-sex marriage 6, 168
struggle for 94
as threat to integrationism 183
Legendre, Pierre 58, 84, 150n31
legitimacy 29–30, 98
in the 'fait social' 89–93
of the law 81, 89–93, 96, 97, 98, 99, 101, 226–7
principle of 11, 12
Lellouche, Pierre 206
Lenoir, Remi 157–8
lepensisme 22
les droits de l'homme 10, 15, 19, 42, 101
and the autonomy of the subject 90
contemporary relevance of 29, 32
guise of 40
and the left 29
politicisation 32, 33
'les droits de rapport' 29
Les Temps modernes 53
lesbian betrayal, by the lesbian and gay movement 196–202
lesbian and gay identity 10, 72–4
and ACT-Up Paris 111, 120–130, 132
and biological essentialism 74, 109, 113, 130–131
bodily approach to 119
and 'coming out rhetoric' 113–15, 114n30, 118, 131
and concubinage 176
construction of 74, 101, 112–13, 115, 130–131
core 109, 113–14, 116, 118, 130–131, 133
'degaying' of 72–3
as fluidity 116–17, 116n36

identity for critique 110
identity for education 110
and masculine heterosexual
domination 102–6, 111–12,
132
politicisation of 130
and positive discrimination 127–
30
queer theory of 104n3, 112–20,
131–2
and realism 105–6
splintered 109–10
and strategies of difference 108–
13, 116–19, 118n44, 120,
129, 131
and strategies of sameness 108–
13, 110–11n19, 116–17, 118–
19, 120, 129, 131
and subversive politics 9, 74,
101–33
'uniform/collective' 102, 108
unique essence of 74
Lesbian and Gay Pride march 120,
121n50
1998 124
1999 203
2001 138
Lesbian and Gay studies 107, 214
Lévi-Strauss, Claude 60
liberation, sexual 9
Liberté politique (Catholic journal)
21
'l'intérêt général' 8, 191–2, 194
Locke, John 77
Loraux, Nicole 212
Lourdes conference 1998 22

Maastricht Treaty 78
Madison, James 78, 98
Mamère, Noël 138
Mangeot, Philippe 123, 124
Maniglier, Patrice 56–7, 60, 69
marginalisation 10–11, 22, 227
marriage 19–20, 41, 158–9, 164,
168–70
breakdown 160

concubinage and 175, 176, 177–8
decline of 19–20, 19–20n9, 175,
180
and filiation 155
heterosexual institutionalisation
of 172–3
and PaCS 22, 32
privileges of 189
and procreation 19
promotion of inequality by 188–
93
same sex 138, 189–94, 189n56,
192n72, 196
legal recognition of 6, 168
as threat to heterosexuality
191, 192
symbolism of 190–191
uniqueness 191
Martel, Frédéric 73, 73–4n91, 122,
132, 139, 171–2, 193
masculine heterosexual domination
40, 46, 102–6, 111–12, 200
and the challenge of lesbianism
197
and homosexual identity 102–6,
111–12, 132
homosexuality as threat to 102
and the erosion of homosexual
identity 102, 103, 132
subversion of 103, 105, 112
*see also La Domination
masculine* (Bourdieu)
material assets 174
maternity, proof of 158
medically assisted procreation 79,
79–80, 142, 149, 158, 161,
162
Meeks, Chet 221
Mégret, Bruno 25
Mendès-Leite, Rommel 7
Meunier, Alexis 123
Meylan, Michel 206
Michel, Jean-Pierre 211
militancy 34n45, 181–2, 204, 219
mimesis 195, 196–202
egalitarian 199–202

and the encouragement of
homophobia 202
and protection from homophobia
201–2
Ministrie de l'Emploi et de la
Solidarité 174
minorities 227
protection of 77
submission to the majority 77, 78
misogyny, gay male 197–8, 200, 201
'mixité' 185–6, 185n44, 192, 212–
13, 214, 228
MLF (Mouvement de la Libération
des Femmes) 197–9, 202
modernity 108–13, 116, 130
and sexual difference 49–52,
51n20
as transient phase 18
and universalism 35, 40
monogamy 190
Montesquieu, baron de 75–8, 98
Montouh, Hugues 93–4, 94n39,
127n62
multiculturalism 17
Muñoz, Véronique Darde 175n19
Muray, Philippe 114n30
Muselier, Renaud 143, 144
Myard, Jacques 206

Naïr, Sami 2–3
narcissism 80, 99
National Assembly 27, 168, 206,
217
National Front 25
national identity 18
Nationality, Immigration and
Asylum Act 2002 3n5
Nature/Spirit axis 51
negotiation, language of 163
normalisation
of homosexuality/gayness 72–3,
73–4n91, 129, 131–2, 193,
222
of 'la différence des sexes' 37–8,
37n52, 40, 45, 48, 63
Normand, Jean 120, 121

norms
incompatibility of psychoanalysis
with 68–9
and the law 85–6, 90
naturalisation/legitimisation of
70
sexual 75
transformation in social space
45–6, 74, 75
see also heteronormative order

object-choice, homosexual 204–5
objects, sexual 183, 184
omnipotence 80
'outing' 182, 196, 204, 211, 216–22,
228–9
logic of 217–19, 222
and the private/public debate
216, 218, 219
and the problematic of naming
216, 217–18
pros and cons of 216–17, 218–19

PaCS (Pacte civil de solidarité) 4, 6–
10, 15–16, 33, 59, 59n46, 81,
103, 106, 112, 169, 175–6,
184, 187–8, 194, 195–6, 198–
202
and ACT-Up Paris 124–6
and adoption/filiation 137–65,
138, 154, 165
and the Catholic church 20–23,
24
as challenge to the republic 42–3
and concubinage 179–81
and the CUS 170
definition of 179
effects of 129
and equality 38–42
feminist response to 54
functions of 9
and homophobia 203, 206–7,
211, 215–16
influences 8–9, 11
and 'la différence des sexes' 45,
47–8, 55, 63, 71

and the law 93–6, 97
and the left 28–9, 30, 31–2
and the legal recognition of
  homosexual union 111, 138,
  165, 168, 180
limitations of 34–5, 138, 171,
  172–3, 179
  failure to provide full equality
  38
  illusory legal recognition 200,
  202
  intolerant tolerance of 215–16
and marriage 189, 190, 191
moral impact of 21, 22
normalising nature 132
and the political right 20, 25–8,
  30
psychoanalytic contributions to
  67
and the recognition of difference
  34–5, 38
and the republic 19, 42–3, 180–
  181
and the republican/democratic
  binary 41
and sexual difference 37
traditionalist criticisms of 65–6
and the uniqueness of the gay
  couple 177
and universalism 38–41
as victory for male mimesis 202
see also anti-PaCS
  demonstrations; post-PaCS
  debate
paedophilia 214
  association with homosexuality
  211
  fears of 151
parents
  biological 146
  see also adoption/filiation;
  'homoparentalité'
parity debate/*paritaires* 37, 39, 106,
  112, 126, 126–30, 128–30,
  172, 187, 195, 198, 198–200,
  201, 203, 228

and 'la différence des sexes' 47,
  54–5, 57, 57n43, 70, 71
particularism 106–7, 128, 130
  of the gay couple 176, 177–8
  and the republic 180
Patton, Cindy 108, 112–14, 116,
  118, 119, 131, 132–3
personal, as political 119, 133
'personne juridique' 11, 82–4, 86,
  90–93, 95–7
  and the body 83, 84, 92
  and sexuality 83, 84
  and the social 83, 84
phallocentrism 65, 205–6, 208
Pisier, Evelyne 10, 34–6, 38, 39, 40,
  41, 42, 53, 70, 145–6, 148,
  151, 152–3, 155, 164, 172,
  181, 196, 201, 212, 214–16
'pluriparentalité' 157–64, 185n44
positive discrimination 127–30,
  128–9n66, 198, 228
post-PaCS debate 165, 201
  politicisation 139, 141
postmodernity 108–14, 130–133
Poulantzas, Ariane 79
Pouliquen, Jan-Paul 28, 180, 181
Pratt, Murray 10, 72, 73, 74, 75, 101,
  104, 194, 228
pre-Oedipal situation 204–5
pregnancy 79–80, 79–80n13
Présent (journal) 211
private life/space 2–3, 18, 106
  democratisation of 12, 139–40,
  149
  desexualisation of 11–12
  judicial control of 79–80, 148–9
  state control of 146
  see also 'la vie privée'
private/public binary 4–5, 12, 31, 42,
  181–8
  and homosexuality 24–5, 42
  and 'outing' 216, 218, 219
  rapprochement between 139,
  147, 148, 149–50
procreation 19
  see also adoption/filiation;

Index

assisted reproductive techniques 'procréation médicale assistée' (PMA) 79–80, 149, 161
'projet de loi de modernisation sociale' 209n29, 210
Prokhoris, Sabine 32, 66–7, 67n70
psychoanalysis 184
  and feminism 64–5
  and gay filiation 145, 145n20, 146–8, 151–3
  and homophobia 67, 204–5, 206
  and homosexuality 64–5, 67–9
  and 'la différence des sexes' 64–9, 70
  and latent homosexuality 192
  and norms 68–9
public opinion 77
public space 2–3, 106
  and democratic representation 29
  and the state 29–30
  see also private/public binary

Queer Factory 71
queer politics 115
queer theory 48, 70–74
  of homosexual identity 104n3, 112–20, 131–2
Quinqueton, Denis 28, 180, 181

realism 105–6
Redman, Peter 204–6, 208
Reeser, Todd 102
rehabilitation of homosexuality 7
Renaissance 49, 63
repression 197–8, 205, 208
republic 15–43, 27, 167, 225
  and concubinage 177
  contemporary relevance of 31
  and the couple 180, 183–4
  crisis of 15, 16
  defence of 16–17, 19, 31, 40–41
  definition 16–19
  democratic 149
  democratisation of 15, 17, 28, 29, 139, 149, 187–8

gay 3
  and gay adoption/filiation 144–5, 155–6
  homosexual community within 122
  and homosexual identity 103, 105
  and homosexuality in the private sphere 24–5
  homosexuality as serving and subverting the 8
  idealism of 16–17, 31
  immunity to change/evolution 17–18
  and marriage 180, 189, 191
  mystical nature of 17
  need for modification 31–2
  and the PaCS 19, 42–3, 180–181
  and sexual difference 168
  sexual homogeneity of 178
  subject-state link 16
  and subversion 195, 227–8
  and tolerance 196
  transcendent qualities 16, 30, 31
  see also French republican citizenship
'republican man', contemporary 91–3
republican state
  decreased power of 29–30
  and public space 29–30
republicanism 2, 9, 140–142, 167–8
  assets of 225
  and the collapse of the 'end of French exceptionalism' 77
  and the 'commun' 225–6
  'compassionate' 186
  and concubinage 175, 176, 177, 179
  and control of the social sphere 11
  and equality 109
  and family and marriage 142
  and gay filiation 147–8, 155–6
  as outdated 225, 226
  and PaCS 180–181

and the post-PaCS debate 139
pressure to reform 187
and sexual difference 181
sham of tolerance 215–16
see also French republican
citizenship
republicanism/democracy binary *see*
democracy/republicanism
binary
right, political 19–28, 30–31, 41, 75
and homosexuality 26–8, 41–2
identity crisis of 27–8
and the PaCS 20, 25–8, 30
and the status quo 30–31
rights
equality of 4, 5, 7–8, 11–12, 15
lesbian and gay 5, 125–6
and the 'personne juridique'/
'sujet du désir' 90
of succession 174
*see also La Déclaration des
droits de l'homme; les droits
de l'homme*
Rosenczveig, Jean-Pierre 151
Roudinesco, Elisabeth 37, 37n52,
70, 152
Rousseau, Jean Jacques 35, 75, 76,
77
RPR 26, 143, 144

same duty, notion of 34
sameness, strategies of 108–13, 110–
11n19, 116–17, 118–19, 120,
129, 131, 195, 196, 198–9,
228–9
Sarkozy, Nicolas 26
Scandinavia 6
Schor, Naomi 33, 34, 38, 53
science 55–6, 57–8
abuse of 59–60
as 'expertise' 10, 59–60, 147
role in political discourse 59–60,
61, 64
Sedgwick, Eve 221
Seidman, Steven 72, 72n85, 73–4,
75, 101, 116n35, 117n39,

118n45, 119, 131–2, 221, 222
Seifert, Lewis 102
self 119
separatism 228
sex, gay, as threat to heterosexuality
205–6
sex roles 213
'sexe', and 'sexualité' 199–200, 202,
203
sexes, complementarity of 49
sexual citizenship 5, 10–12, 75, 137–
40
and the church 21
components of homosexual 140
privatisation of 30
and sexual difference 46
and the social 75
sexual difference 5, 36–41, 37n52
and the church 24–5
and the left 31
normalisation of 37–8, 37n52, 40
in the public domain 24–5
recognition 139
and the republic 168, 181
and the right 27
and sexual citizenship 46
see also 'la différence des sexes'
sexual diversity 8, 18
sexual equality 11–12, 22–3, 30, 37,
42, 53n29, 168, 171, 199,
200, 201, 203
sexual identity 52, 183
and the law 81
queer theory of 70, 71–4
sociological perspectives of 61
see also lesbian and gay identity
sexual liberation 9
sexualisation, of the body 49, 50, 51,
63
'sexualité', and 'sexe' 199–200, 202,
203
Sexualities (journal) 204
sexuality 212–14, 226
Bozon on 4–5, 9–10
homosexuality 'as a-normative'
24

Index

organic model of 213
and the 'personne juridique' 83, 84
queer theory of 71
as social construction 10
and the 'sujet du désir' 83, 84
and universalism 140
'sexué'/'sexuel' 184–5, 186–7, 213–14, 216
Silverman, Kaja 204
Simmel, Georg 190
Simon, Patrick 227–8
Singly, François de 20, 32, 139, 175, 175n19, 191
Slama, Alain-Gérard 77–9, 80, 81, 91, 96, 98
social change 30–31
social facts 89–90
social judgement 4, 5
social responsibility 10
social space 9–12, 167, 226–8
abstraction of 9, 10
agency/autonomy as prerequisite for 87, 93, 96, 98, 226–7
concept of 9
cultural replacement of 17
as defining space of citizenship 9
fight for the control of 75, 84, 87
and the individual 10, 87–93, 96, 98, 99
and the law 75, 79
and the 'personne juridique' 83, 84
as prerequisite to agency 87, 226
revalidation as democratic space 137–8
and science 60
and the subversion of dominant orders 10
and the 'sujet du désir' 83, 84
and the transformation of social norms 45–6, 74, 75
socialisation 81, 88–90
society
as external imposition on the individual 87

individual's dependence on 87, 88–91, 96
sociology 57–8, 60–61, 64
SOS-Homophobie 206, 209
specificity 195
state
and concubinage 175
and the family 157–8, 159
and marriage 168–9
modern/postmodern 108–13
see also republican state
status quo 30–31, 226
Steinberg, Sylvie 49–50, 51
step-families 163, 164–5
stigma 10–11, 125
strategic practicality 228
subject
autonomy of 81, 84, 85, 86, 87, 90, 93
heterosexuals as 183, 184
subjugation, of homosexuality 40
subversion 8–12, 139, 194, 196, 227–9
embedding 106–7
and lesbian and gay identity 9, 74, 101–33
and the republic 195, 227–8
succession, rights of 174
'sujet du désir' 11, 82, 82–7, 90–92, 96–7
and the body 83, 84
and sexuality 83, 84
Sullivan, Andrew 23n21, 189n56
surrogacy 142
symbolic
alteration of the 58n45
as natural 67
as norm 62–3
and the recognition of homosexuality 200
and socio-political structures 56–7, 60
unsubstantiated authority of 66–7
symbolic order 184
a priori 69
of 'la différence des sexes' 52,

53, 54, 61–2, 63–4, 186–7
Symbolic Order (psychoanalytic) 67
    death of 69, 70
symbolic subversion 104–7, 112,
    119, 124
symbolics, rise of 69, 70
symbolism 103–5, 195, 223
    children's 147, 151–2
    of 'la différence des sexes' 186
    marital 190–191
*Syndicat national des enterprises
    gaies* (SNEG) 123

Taguieff, Pierre-André 2, 16–18, 19,
    31, 39
Théry, Irène 10, 34–5, 37, 38, 42,
    46–7, 49–50, 53, 54, 58, 139,
    150n30, 154–5, 156–7, 159–
    61, 163, 164–5, 168, 170,
    172, 174–9, 175, 182–3, 184–
    7, 185n44, 188, 189, 191,
    192, 201, 212–14, 213n37,
    216
Théry, Irène n17
Thévenot, Père Xavier 24–5
Thomas, Yan 82–3, 84, 85–6, 86, 87,
    90, 91, 92, 93, 95, 226
tolerance 42, 183–6, 196, 207–8, 218
    by the church 24
    controlled 226
    of differences 17
    'intolerant' 215–16
Tort, Michel 67–9, 67n70, 67–8n73,
    70, 152, 153, 162
traditionalists 15, 41
    opposition to homosexuality 65–
    6
    and sex roles 213
Traschen, Frances 221
Trigano, Shmuel 39–40, 41, 42

UDF 27
union libre see concubinage/*union
    libre*
United States 6, 107, 108, 109–10,
    116, 131, 132

universal equality 18, 31, 33–42,
    171, 176, 180–181, 187
    and positive discrimination 128
universal will 92
universalisation 106
universalism 2–6, 11, 15–43, 139,
    167–8, 188, 193–4
    abstract 38, 39
    and ACT-Up Paris 120
    and anthropology 59
    as assimilationism 33
    as betrayal 36
    challenges to 12
    and communitarianism 17
    and concubinage 176, 178
    criticisms of 35–6, 36n50, 42
    definition 33
    democratic credibility of 36
    and difference 33–8, 34n45, 227
    flexible 39–40
    and gay community 122
    and gay filiation 147–8
    gay male 198, 199
    heteronormative 201
    and homosexual identity 101,
        103, 105–6, 108, 111, 129–30
    and homosexuality in the private
        sphere 24–5, 29
    immunity to democratic change
        195
    integrative 17–18, 24–5, 29, 75
    and 'la différence des sexes' 45
    and the law 82, 99
    as male sexual order 46, 47, 200,
        202, 203, 215
    and modernity 35
    need for reform 31–32
    and PaCS 181
    and parity 37, 39
    and particularism 106–7
    and positive discrimination 128–
        9
    pre-conditions to 227
    radical 38, 215–16
    redefinition 39–41
    responsibility for its own

destruction 227
and sexual equality 126–7
and sexuality 140
and strategies of sameness 111
subversion of 8, 101, 129–30
and tolerance 196, 215–16
transcendence of 225–6, 227–9
universalism/democracy binary 171–2

Vannson, François 206
Vauglin, François 210–11
vengeance
  gay male 197
  of 'outing' 219
Verboux, Mathieu 124
Vial, Père de 21
Villiers, Philippe de 206
visibility of homosexuality 207, 215

Wallach Scott, Joan 56, 154–5, 178
Watney, Simon 205
Weeks, Jeffrey 140–141, 149

will
  general/common 77, 78
  universal 92
Winter, Jean-Pierre 146–8, 151
Wittgenstein, Ludwig 84–5
women
  'democratic woman' 92
  equality for 37, 198
  exclusion of 35, 36
  inequality of 35, 172, 203
  and sexual difference 36–7
  symbolic inequality of 172
  violence against 203
  see also lesbian betrayal; lesbian
    and gay identity
workplace, discrimination in the
  203, 209, 210, 222–3

Yonnet, Paul 10, 40–41, 42–3, 101,
  103, 127, 139, 168, 170–171,
  178, 180, 181, 193, 194, 228

Zappi, Sylvia 227, 228
Zeldin, Theodore 1